STATUTORY INTERPRETATION

Statutory interpretation involves the reconstruction of the meaning of a legal statement when it cannot be considered as accepted or granted. This phenomenon needs to be considered not only from the legal and linguistic perspective, but also from the argumentative one - which focuses on the strategies for defending a controversial or doubtful viewpoint. This book draws upon linguistics, legal theory, computing, and dialectics to present an argumentation-based approach to statutory interpretation. By translating and summarizing the existing legal interpretative canons into eleven patterns of natural arguments - called argumentation schemes - the authors offer a system of argumentation strategies for developing, defending, assessing, and attacking an interpretation. Illustrated through major cases from both common and civil law, this methodology is summarized in diagrams and maps for application to computer sciences. These visuals help make the structures, strategies, and vulnerabilities of legal reasoning accessible to both legal professionals and laypeople.

Douglas Walton is a world-renowned scholar in the field of argumentation. Over his career, he authored or co-authored over fifty books and over 400 refereed journal articles. His work is interdisciplinary in style and is regarded by scholars and professionals as seminal in the field.

Fabrizio Macagno is Assistant Professor of Philosophy and Communication at the Universidade Nova de Lisboa (FCSH, NOVA). He has published several papers and books on definition, emotive language, presupposition, argumentation schemes, and dialogue theory, including *Argumentation Schemes* (Cambridge, 2008). He has also worked as a consultant in forensic linguistics at the international law firm, Martinez and Novebaci.

Giovanni Sartor is Professor in Legal Informatics at the University of Bologna and Professor in Legal Informatics and Legal Theory at the European University Institute, Florence. He holds an ERC-advanced grant (2018) for the project Compulaw, and has published widely in legal philosophy, computational logic, legislation technique, and computer law.

Statutory Interpretation

PRAGMATICS AND ARGUMENTATION

DOUGLAS WALTON
University of Windsor

FABRIZIO MACAGNO
Universidade Nova de Lisboa

GIOVANNI SARTOR
University of Bologna

CAMBRIDGE
UNIVERSITY PRESS

CAMBRIDGE
UNIVERSITY PRESS

University Printing House, Cambridge CB2 8BS, United Kingdom

One Liberty Plaza, 20th Floor, New York, NY 10006, USA

477 Williamstown Road, Port Melbourne, VIC 3207, Australia

314-321, 3rd Floor, Plot 3, Splendor Forum, Jasola District Centre, New Delhi - 110025, India

103 Penang Road, #05-06/07, Visioncrest Commercial, Singapore 238467

Cambridge University Press is part of the University of Cambridge.

It furthers the University's mission by disseminating knowledge in the pursuit of
education, learning and research at the highest international levels of excellence.

www.cambridge.org
Information on this title: www.cambridge.org/9781108454070
DOI: 10.1017/9781108554572

First published 2021
First paperback edition 2022

A catalogue record for this publication is available from the British Library

Library of Congress Cataloging in Publication data
NAMES: Walton, Douglas N. author. | Macagno, Fabrizio, author. | Sartor, Giovanni, author.
TITLE: Statutory interpretation : pragmatics and argumentation / Douglas Walton, University
of Windsor; Fabrizio Macagno, Universidade Nova de Lisboa; Giovanni Sartor, University
of Bologna.
DESCRIPTION: Cambridge, United Kingdom ; New York, NY : Cambridge University Press,
2021. | Includes bibliographical references.
IDENTIFIERS: LCCN 2020019566 | ISBN 9781108429344 (hardback) | ISBN 9781108554572 (ebook)
SUBJECTS: LCSH: Law – Interpretation and construction. | Law – Language. | Semantics (Law)
CLASSIFICATION: LCC K290 .W35 2021 | DDC 340/.1–dc23
LC record available at https://lccn.loc.gov/2020019566

ISBN 978-1-108-42934-4 Hardback
ISBN 978-1-108-45407-0 Paperback

For Karen with love – Doug
For Chrysa with love – Fabrizio
For Lia with love – Giovanni

Contents

Figures

Tables

Acknowledgments

The authors would like to thank the University of Windsor, the Faculdade de Ciências Sociais e Humanas of the Universidade Nova de Lisboa, the European University Institute of Florence and the University of Bologna for their support. They would also like to thank Christy Goldfinch for proofreading this book; while for the possible typos and mistakes the authors acknowledge their own full responsibility, she is responsible for the hundreds for mistakes that this volume does *not* contain.

This work was supported by the Fundação para a Ciência e a Tecnologia (research grant no. PTDC/FER-FIL/28278/2017), and the ERC-Advanced project Compulaw, Grant Agreement-833647.

Introduction

Statutory interpretation is of crucial importance for legal practice and theory, political discussions, ethical issues, and public information. For instance, a substantial majority of the US Supreme Court's case load involves statutory interprertation, nearly two-thirds of its docket by one recent estimate, and in the years ahead, US courts will be asked to interpret the meaning of thousands of sections of legislation. As Katzmann (2014, 3–10) emphasized, the interpretation of legal texts affects not only daily rulings in the courts at all levels, but even political issues vital to the legal system such as televised confirmation hearings for US Supreme Court nominees. Statutes affect all aspects of our daily lives, including the most pressing public policy issues at a given time. However, although ideally the language of the statute should be clear, the texts passed by legislative bodies, such as the US Congress, can be vague, ambiguous, structurally complex in expression, or even apparently logically inconsistent. Fundamental values of our societies, emerging in the controversies on the issues of freedom of speech, abortion, marriage, or self-defense, are primarily debated as matters of interpretation. Interpretation in itself is problematic, even though it is the fundamental basis of the relationship between legal theory and legal practice. Law journals are filled with articles on how statute should be interpreted (Katzmann, 2014, 3–5); but, unlike chemists who pore over professional journals, judges normally do not have the time to read the law reviews, as their workload is often overwhelming (Easterbrook, 1990, 782; Baum, 2009, 12–14; Epstein, Landes, and Posner, 2013, 39–42). Dozens of canons of legal interpretation have been developed over the years (see for instance, Scalia and Garner, 2012), but their role, nature, and use are controversial (Sinclair, 2005; Llewellyn, 1949). Raging controversies have focused on the very nature of interpretation, namely on whether the courts should look only to the text, the wording of the statutes, or also to contextual matters. But such controversies have led to even deeper doubts and disagreements, such as what counts as a context (Easterbrook, 2017, 83–84).

In this territory of conflicting theories, two interrelated questions led us to developing the ideas that are presented in this book: What instruments can we offer to the practitioners who have very little time to decide on individual cases, and justify their decisions? What insights can these instruments yield to laypeople who wish to comprehend the logic and the legal nature of these decisions, which can influence their lives and their choices,? The answer that we have arrived at and that we will try to defend through analyzing many legal cases, discussing and evaluating many theories, and addressing many theoretical challenges, comes down to one central point: the skill of using evidence-based arguments to both critically question and defend conclusions in an orderly way. These arguments are verbal means of using reasoning grounded on the facts of a case and the normative rules (norms) that define our lives as rational and social beings with respect for law (Walton, 1990). The use of arguments and the related skills of addressing, assessing, and integrating opposing viewpoints characterize not only our cognitive development but our use of reasoning skills to guide our way through our lives as social beings (Kuhn, Cheney, and Weinstock, 2000). We all need use arguments on a daily basis, as we all have doubts and different views that we need to justify.

An argumentative approach to statutory interpretation does not always result in an outcome showing how and why one side wins over the other side in the contest of argumentation. It is not meant to replace a judge or a human jury. But it can tell us a lot about how to interpret, identify, analyze, and evaluate the arguments on both sides, in some cases showing why one argument can be weighed against another and evaluated as stronger or weaker. In particular, in this book we use these argumentation tools to address the problem of interpretation. The question addressed is how to compare two or more competing interpretations and decide which one is better, based on the arguments and evidence in the given case. We see this kind of evaluation and explanation of interpretative argumentation as a practical task.

Easterbrook underscored that what is missing in the theories of interpretation is a simple instrument. "Rules of interpretation," he observed, "must reflect the resources available to the task," which implies "a relatively simple and mechanical approach to interpretation" (Easterbrook, 2017, 96). Our challenge in this book is to show how interpretation is an argumentative activity, one that aims at producing arguments that can be developed, understood, and assessed using simple tools that have been examined and classified during the whole history of dialectical argumentation since Aristotle's *Topics*. This implies regarding statutory interpretation under a different perspective and discovering a new order in the temple of legal theories and legal canons. Our goal is to "interpret" interpretation as resting on a limited number of types of arguments that anyone can find and recognize immediately in his or her own experience or discourse.

This aim, however, also implies justifying the presuppositions on which this argumentation approach is grounded, as applied to legal argumentation. This is why we needed to combine insights from different disciplines: legal theory, linguistics, argumentation, and artificial intelligence. Thus, we explain legal disputes as a type of argumentative activity, in order to address them using argumentative tools. We show that statutory interpretation is essentially pragmatic, as pragmatic is the nature of arguments. We argue that interpretation is essentially a matter of arguments, and that arguments stem from a limited number of logic-semantic patterns (Hitchcock, 2017), which we call argumentation schemes (Walton, Reed, and Macagno, 2008). We show how these patterns can be assessed based on critical questions, and classified in dichotomies that allow choosing them for both production and analytical purposes (Macagno and Walton, 2015; Walton and Macagno, 2015). This is obviously an ambitious undertaking, but it was made possible by joining current resources of argumentation theory to the types of arguments recognized by MacCormack and Summers (1981) as those most prominently used to support or attack competing interpretations of statutes in legal practice.

The method built in this book combines theory and application. Chapter 1 summarizes the existing literature on legal interpretation, including commentaries on the canons of interpretation and other analytical tools used by lawyers to put forward arguments supporting and attacking controversial interpretations of legal documents, as well as the theories of interpretation put forward and widely discussed in law and philosophy of law. In Chapter 2, we introduce the relationship between statutory interpretation and argumentation theory, showing how the former can be conceived as a dialectical decision-making process. In Chapter 3, we use linguistic methods and approaches, especially those that have been developed in the field of pragmatics, to address central problems such as semantic and syntactic ambiguity. Chapter 4 addresses specific interpretative issues not widely taken into account in the traditional literature, such as those pertaining to definitions and implicit content, by building on leading theories from pragmatics and argumentation and using them to analyze legal cases. In Chapter 5, we develop and apply methods drawn from the literature in ancient dialectics and its modern developments in the field of argumentation for analyzing, evaluating, and finding arguments, including argumentation schemes and argument graphs, sometimes called argument maps or argument diagrams (originally deriving from Wigmore's evidential charts). These tools allow bringing to light the implicit components of interpretative arguments, and detecting possible weaknesses through the use of lists of critical questions. In Chapter 6, we rely heavily on recent work in artificial intelligence, especially formal and computational models of argumentation that have recently been developed, from whose applications to the domain of legal argumentation (within the field of AI and law) we draw extensively.

The purpose of this book is to provide a set of defeasible argumentation schemes that are applicable to the argumentation in legal cases where there are reasonable differences of opinion on the issue of how a statute should properly be interpreted. These schemes are intended to help computational systems of legal argumentation move forward in their quest to devise technologies that can be applied to the very common and fundamentally important legal problem of statutory interpretation.

Our approach to statutory interpretation combines five different disciplines, each providing a different perspective on legal argumentation: the contemporary field of argumentation theory, legal theory, pragmatics, dialectics and its modern developments, and AI & law.

0.1 AN ARGUMENTATIVE APPROACH TO INTERPRETATION

It is up to the politicians to make the rules of law by formulating and passing statutes and regulations. Judges and lawyers have the job of applying these statutes to cases that pose issues that need to be resolved in courtrooms or other legal settings. One might think that this task could be carried out by computational systems that are capable of logically reasoning from the facts of a case along with the applicable legal rules to automatically generate a conclusion on how to rule in that case. Just input the facts, let the program identify the relevant rules, let the system apply the relevant rules and determine whether the conditions of each rule are satisfied, and then explain the chain of reasoning to the user (Ashley, 2017, 1). This sort of approach is often called mechanical jurisprudence.

However, for several reasons, this approach turned out to be of limited use. One is that since statutes are expressed in natural language, the terms and sentences in them are typically vague and ambiguous. Moreover, the meanings of such natural language terms change over time as new situations, such as advances in science, extend and twist the meanings that can be attached to those terms. And as everyone knows, statutes and regulations are often written in technical legal language that is a formidable obstacle for the ordinary citizen to understand. Typically, as we well know, there are arguments in trials on both sides that turn on the issue of what some term, phrase, or sentence should properly or legally be taken to mean.

Another reason concerns the limitations of the traditional approaches to logic as applied to arguments in a courtroom setting, where there can be reasonable arguments on both sides even where there is agreement on the facts and the rules. Still another reason is that legal rules and regulations are typically open to exceptions. This means that legal reasoning, certainly in the common law system, is typically case-based reasoning of the kind requiring that exceptions to a rule be taken into account (Ashley, 2017, 1).

Traditional logic has not had much success in dealing with case-based reasoning of this kind. Deductive logic is based on universally quantified generalizations of the form "for all x"; it does not allow for exceptions to exclude the applicability of the rule, causing the argument based on this rule to be defeated.

Moreover, deductive logic does not enable us to cope with inconsistency very well. In deductive logic, if the premises are inconsistent with each other, any proposition at all is allowed to follow logically. Inductive reasoning (of the kind based on numerical probability values) is sometimes useful in law, such as in cases of expert testimony (e.g., in genetics). However, assigning precise numbers to facts and rules in order to enable a numerical calculation to determine whether the conclusion follows or not by inductive reasoning (e.g., in non-expert witness testimony) has not generally been found useful for typical instances of legal rulings based on statutory interpretation of the kind we are interested in here. And applying inductive reasoning of this sort generally assumes that the evidential databases making up the premises are consistent. In typical cases of arguments about statutory interpretation, inconsistency is the norm, because in such cases there are reasonable arguments on both sides, so conflict within the body of evidence accepted as relevant is always present.

Most importantly, logic-based formalisms break down when applied to cases where much of the relevant evidence supporting the pro and con arguments on each side is based on conflicting rules and precedents (Berman and Hafner, 1988). To move forward in these sorts of cases the argumentation approach is needed, since it enables us to cope with conflicts of opinion. These conflicts are indeed the typical phenomena characterizing those cases in which statutory interpretation is the key problem.

Until recently, however, deductive logic had a decisive advantage over accounts of reasoning based on argumentation, namely, it could provide a precise, mathematical account of inferences and their validity. Only in recent years has argumentation been able to catch up, thanks to the development of formal models of computational argumentation, building upon the results of research in nonmonotonic reasoning (for an account relating to the law, see Prakken and Sartor, 2015). Such systems are designed to solve problems that arise from applying rules that are subject to exceptions, so-called defeasible rules, to real cases that exhibit conflicts exposed by reasonable arguments on both sides. They are designed to work with forms of argument called defeasible argumentation schemes that enable reasoning from a set of premises to tentatively lead to a conclusion subject to the posing of critical questions that can shift the burden of proof back onto the proponent of the argument to provide further evidence.

This book fully endorses the argumentation approach, and indeed it expands, tests, and modifies the argumentation model of statutory interpretation developed in our prior work (Walton, Sartor, and Macagno, 2016; Macagno, Walton, and Sartor, 2018; Macagno and Walton, 2017; Walton, Sartor, and Macagno, 2018). This theoretical proposal can be considered as a normative dialectical model of interpretation. It is a model in the sense that it provides an abstract structure of interpretative arguments, focusing on the argumentation schemes being given in favor and against an attribution of meaning. It is normative in the sense that it aims to determine (and predict) how an argument can be defeated, countered, or weakened, and a tacit premise or conclusion can be retrieved and argued for or against. Finally, it is dialectical as it is designed to take contextual factors into account as part of the evidence to support or attack an interpretation, such as the purpose of the document, or the problem the authors or signers of the document were trying to solve.

The model proposed is abstract, in the sense that it is supposed to apply to the interpretative reasoning used in different legal systems. For this reason, the challenge of this book lies in bringing to light the common "logical" skeleton that underlies different legal traditions and procedures, each characterized by its specific interpretative canons and rules. While most of the cases analyzed are common law cases of the kind that would be familiar to American legal practitioners (more specifically decisions of the Supreme Court of the United States in leading civil and criminal cases), we also provide some examples drawn from decisions passed by courts of different countries – such as the European Court of Justice, the Supreme Court of the United Kingdom, and the Court of Cassation of Italy. The legal reasoning behind statutory interpretation is thus regarded as transcending the narrower jurisdictional issues. This broader application of the theoretical framework makes the book applicable and readable on a worldwide basis.

The justification of our interpretations is based on patterns of reasoning that we use in everyday discussions. Interpretation is thus a matter of arguments, or rather argumenta-tion, as it is concerned with how reasons supporting a hypothesis about the meaning of a statement are assessed and compared. This approach highlights a root common to pragmatics and legal theory, reducing the systems of canons and maxims peculiar to the two disciplines to the most generic patterns that describe the structure of arguments. This identification of a common mechanism has several advantages. First, it provides a systematic approach to the assessment of interpretative arguments. Critical questions can guide the evaluation of the reasons by pointing to the potential defeasibility aspects. Second, the representation of arguments as schemes characterized by specific semantic relations allows the reconstruction of unstated assumptions (Macagno, 2015; Macagno and Damele, 2013; van Eemeren and Grootendorst, 1992, Chapter 13; Walton, 2008). The explicit part of interpretative arguments is the tip of an iceberg; only by unveiling what the speakers take for granted in their reasoning is it possible to be aware of the sources of disagreement. Third, this argumentation-based approach makes it possible to reduce complex argumentative structures, characterized by many different interpretative canons, to simplified and schematic representations of conflicting arguments. This simplification reduces complex and long discus-sions and judgments to graphic summaries that can be more easily handled and understood. This argumentative model can in a certain sense be used for translating the complexity of the law into a language that can be understood by laypeople and for placing multiple reasons into a basic structure that can be better analyzed by practitioners.

0.2 THE LEGAL THEORY PERSPECTIVE

Our approach can be considered as the continuation of an ancient idea. If we go back to Cicero's *Topica*, we notice that this Latin lawyer was using what we now call argumentation to explain the reasoning used in legal cases. Cicero was indeed one of the first scholars to translate legal reasoning into instruments that can be taught and understood by laypeople. The argumentative view of legal interpretation has characterized different theoretical accounts of legal discourse, from Perelman and Tarello (Perelman, 1979; Tarello, 1980) to many modern and contemporary works (MacCormick and Summers, 1991; Alexy, 1989; Dascal and Wróblewski, 1988; Scalia and Garner, 2012; Guastini, 2011). The basic idea behind these writings is that the first step toward building an evidence-based model of argumentation – namely, a way of weighing the evidential worth of one interpretation against another – is to identify certain characteristic forms of interpretative argument. The expectation is that this first step will lead to finding a general framework for approaching legal disputes that arise from a conflict of opinions on how a particular statement or proposal should properly be interpreted. Once an interpretative dispute is set in this framework, the way is paved to seeing how the argumentation technique of analyzing the arguments on both sides of an issue can be applied. Chapter 2 explains how in this procedure it is helpful to distinguish the different kinds of arguments typically involved in such disagreements of interpretation.

While legal interpretation is one of the most debated and investigated topics in legal theory, and the consideration of its pragmatic dimension has characterized some fundamental approaches to legal reasoning (see for instance Tarello, 1980), the advances in pragmatics are seldom taken into consideration by legal philosophers and practitioners. While legal practice is essentially argumentative, legal argumentation, despite its classical tradition is not comparable in influence with the other currents of legal philosophy. Moreover, while interpretation is essentially argumentative, and arguments are essentially instances of language use, argumentation and pragmatics are two separate and very little related fields. Even though there are notable exceptions and the interdisciplinary studies across these areas are growing, they remain isolated works or projects, and remain confined to the analysis of the relations between either pragmatics and law, or argumentation and law, or argumentation and pragmatics. The five-pronged interdisciplinary approach with which the problems of statutory interpretation are studied in this book using methods from argumentation theory, linguistics, and artificial intelligence has not been previously attempted or even envisaged.

0.3 THE PRAGMATICS PERSPECTIVE

First and primarily, when we speak of legal interpretation, we refer to the linguistic activity of reconstructing the intended meaning of a text or a portion thereof, namely sequences (or utterances) expressed in a specific co-text and context. Statutory interpretation, as referring to a specific type of text and human activity, falls essentially in the pragmatic domain. In contrast with semantics, in which meaning is defined only as a property of expressions in abstraction from particular situations, speakers, or hearers (Leech, 1983, 6), pragmatics is the study of meaning in relation to speech situations (or the use of language) (Huang, 2014, 2; Jaszczolt, 2018, 134). It addresses the ways in which the linguistic context determines the proposition expressed by a given sentence in that context (Stalnaker, 1970, 287). As Kecskes put it (Kecskes, 2013, 21):

> Pragmatics is about meaning; it is about language use and the users. It is about how the language system is employed in social encounters by human beings. In this process, which is one of the most creative human enterprises, communicators (who are speaker-producers and hearer-interpreters at the same time) manipulate language to shape and infer meaning in a socio-cultural context. The main research questions for pragmatists are as follows: why do we choose to say what we say? (production), and why do we understand things the way we do? (comprehension).

Interpretation is not mere decoding; it is aimed at retrieving the meaning expressed by a specific statement in a specific context for a specific purpose, considering specific rules, presumptions, conditions, and roles. More specifically, statutory interpretation is about the interpretation of legal texts, which have unique institutional and linguistic characteristics.

For this reason, the second and essential dimension of our object of study is the analysis of the features that define this type of text and activity. While pragmatics commonly concerns how and why we comprehend or produce specific utterances in an ordinary – noninstitutional – setting, our object of study requires considering constraints that are not ordinary, such as the notion of legal system, the powers of the judicial activity, the purpose and the effects of legal statements, the procedures and the boundaries of legal disputes concerning the meaning of a text.

Resources from linguistics are used to address the interrelation between a contextualist approach to interpretation (Charnock, 2007) and the pragmatic (more specifically Gricean and neo-Gricean) accounts of meaning. Pragmatics addresses the relationship between the linguistic code (the linguistic means used in the interaction), the producers-interpreters of the code, and the context of the interaction (Kecskes, 2013). In the most general definition, pragmatics focuses "on how meaning is shaped and inferred during social interaction." In linguistic-philosophical pragmatics, the core of communication is the speaker's intention (meaning), as it is recognized and reconstructed through pragmatic inferences that are the focus of linguistic investigation (Kecskes, 2013; Capone, 2016). The discrepancy between sentential (semantic and syntactic) meaning and utterance meaning is bridged by pragmatic processes that involve enrichment (Butler, 2016; Carston, 2002).

In the law, the concept of "canon of interpretation" is often used for referring to specific justifications advanced to account for an interpretative decision. However, canons for legal interpretation are often used as labels to characterize empirically certain patterns of legal reasoning, without the support of an underlying analytical and linguistic theory. We offer such a theory, which builds on argumentation and a neo-Gricean approach to implicitness. Chapter 4 proposes a functional model of legal interpretation, in which the focus of the analysis is placed on the actual or potential reasons (explicit or tacit) supporting or critically questioning an interpretation. This model investigates the implicit dimension of communication in terms of arguments, building on the idea of reasoning from the best interpretation. This account develops the canons of interpretation into precise technical instruments for representing the interpretative process. In this model, legal interpretation is conceived as a pragmatic process, aimed at establishing the meaning of statements in legal sources by taking into account what was specifically stated and what is implied by the context of use. The book provides an argumentation-based linguistic approach to legal interpretation that aims at explaining how interpretative choices can be justified, defended, and evaluated.

0.4 THE DIALECTICAL PERSPECTIVE

The dialectical dimension addresses what defines interpretation vis-à-vis comprehension, namely a disagreement concerning the meaning of a natural language text. Interpretation is not concerned with how we understand or produce texts, but with how we establish the acceptability of a specific reading thereof. Since our object of study addresses a disagreement and the verbal ways to solve it, it falls in the domain of argumentation. Arguments are a social and verbal means for contending with a difference – such as an unsolved problem or an unproven hypothesis – between two or more parties (Walton, 1990, 411). They are reasons advanced for leading the interlocutor to accept a position, or to overcome a doubt concerning a position. These reasons are not purely and only logical constructs, as they are based primarily on natural inferences that are used in patterns of defeasible reasoning. Argumentation – or more precisely dialectics in the medieval sense of the word – has been traditionally devoted to the analysis of the structure, nature, and classification of the *loci* or *maximae propositiones* on which we ground our arguments.

Dialectics is by definition a multifaceted discipline, the crossroad between logic, linguistics, and pragmatics that is necessary for analyzing our complex object. How can we provide a complete picture of statutory interpretation by selecting one or at maximum two of its essential, defining dimensions? How can we talk of interpretation while disregarding its argumentative nature, or of statutory interpretation while dismissing the fact that it is an inherently pragmatic phenomenon? The multidimensional analysis that this book endeavors to provide can offer a new perspective not only on the interpretation of specific legal texts, but on interpretation of texts in general. Our proposal is to conceive argumentation as the core of the process of establishing the best reading of a document. In this sense, the pragmatic and linguistic regularities, rules, and presumptions, and the legal norms, procedures, and assumptions developed in legal theory become parts and contents of an argumentative structure in which the crucial role is played by the methods used for assessing the strength of the arguments and the roots of the disagreements. Interpreting a text is thus matter of argumentation, namely reconstructing the reasoning, the presuppositions, and the evidence provided in support of or against the reconstruction of the meaning of a statement to establish the less defeasible hypothesis.

This argumentative process is pragmatic. Meaning is regarded as the expression of a communicative intention, where "communicative" includes different types of human action, including the imposition of duties, prohibitions, and obligations. This intention can be retrieved primarily by the evidence provided, namely the language in a specific context. However, argumentation – or at least the approach to argumentation endorsed in this book – does not primarily address the problem of how utterances are comprehended, and why, but rather how their meaning is *reconstructed* for establishing whether a hypothesis about what they mean is acceptable. Argumentation starts from doubts and leads to defeasible conclusions through the assessment of reasons and evidence. The doubt in interpretation concerns the meaning of a statement or a part of text, and the goal is to reconstruct this meaning based on the elements available to the hearers or readers. Reconstruction is not the same as attribution of meaning or understanding. In interpretation, we justify why we reach a hypothesis; we make explicit the reasons that lead us to believe that an interpretative hypothesis is tentatively acceptable. These reasons may or may not mirror our psychological comprehension mechanisms; they are, however, unquestionable evidence of how we justify why we comprehend an utterance in a certain way.

The choice of a legal context, and more specifically the area of interpretation of statutes, has a specific purpose. Legal discourse and legal discussions about legal texts have some fundamental differences relative to other types of contexts and uses of language. First, in the law we have access to evidence concerning the reasons brought for or against a specific reconstruction of meaning. In this sense, legal discussions about statutory interpretation represent the clearest and most accessible corpus of interpretative disputes and arguments. Second, these discussions have a result that is justified considering the merits and the weaknesses of the contrary arguments. For this reason, judgments represent evidence of how the interpretative arguments are evaluated and ordered. Third, despite the legal reluctance to be involved in linguistic and pragmatic matters, these texts provide thorough reflections about how meaning is reconstructed, considering its context and its purpose. The study of statutory interpretation and legal interpretative discussions is not only a strategy for showing how an approach works; rather, it is a source for understanding how the broader phenomenon of interpretation can be conceived. Legal interpretation in a sense contributes to linguistic and pragmatic theories through its very practice.

0.5 THE AI AND LAW PERSPECTIVE

Computational models of legal argumentation have several advantages over previous models based on classical logic. First, the current computational models have the nonmonotonic property of allowing the inferences in a chain of argumentation to be modified once new evidence comes in. Second, these computational models, like real legal argumentation in a trial, allow the conclusion of a defeasible argument to be acceptable based on premises that are accepted. In other words, the absolute truth or falsity of the propositions in an argument are not at issue. Rather, a standard of proof is set in place and for the argumentation of one side to be successful, it is only necessary for it to reach the required standard of proof. This means that arguments supporting or attacking a proposition can contradict or even defeat each other, but that is not the end of the game, as long as the mass of evidence-based argumentation on the one side meets its burden of proof, as defined by the standard of proof set at the opening stage of the procedure, and is therefore sufficient to defeat the mass of evidence-based argumentation on the other side. So, what capabilities does a computational model need to have to apply in a useful way to problems of statutory interpretation?

As Ashley (2017, 54) pointed out, to fit with the program of argumentation for statutory interpretation of MacCormack and Summers (1991), an interpretative system must be able to model case-based reasoning using rules, cases, underlying social values, and legislative purposes. There are several formal and computational systems that are capable of modeling acceptable defeasible argumentation. There are abstract argumentation models in which the concept of an argument is primitive and the basic notion used to evaluate argumentats is a graph structure in which some arguments attack and defeat other arguments. What seems to be a better fit, however, is a structured argumentation model in which the premises and conclusions of arguments are represented as nodes in a graph, configured in such a way that one argument can attack the premises of another argument, or its conclusion, or the argument itself.

As Ashley (2017, 129) showed in his survey of argumentation systems applicable to solving problems of statutory interpretation, there are a number of structured argumentation models that are suitable for evaluating legal argumentation. These models also have other interesting capabilities, such as the capability to find new arguments to support a claim by finding premises in an evidential database in a legal case. The step that needs to be taken, and that is already implicit in the account of interpretative argumentation of MacCormack and Summers (1991), is to see the traditional legal canons of interpretation as having the potential to represent different kinds of arguments pro and con a disputed interpretation. The next step required is to build this argumentation-based approach into a formal and computational model of structured argumentation. Ashley (2017, 129) considers the Carneades Argumentation System (Gordon, Prakken, and Walton, 2007) as a formal and implemented computational model that can be used to illustrate the useful features of computational models generally, because it can be presented in legally intuitive terms and it contains concepts useful for modeling legal argumentation such as proof standards and argumentation schemes. In this system, a proposition is acceptable if, given the pro and con arguments up to that stage and a given case, the conclusion can be determined to be acceptable given the arguments modeled by the system up to that stage, along with some assumptions that can be provisionally determined by the user.

A brief word of clarification here may be helpful to the general reader on the question of how to interpret the argument diagrams representing the argumentation in the cases analyzed throughout the book. We want to make it clear from the beginning that we are doing our best to explain how the models and tools described and applied in the book can be applied specifically to the problem of how statutes drafted by politicians rather than by professionals in the legal system, such as lawyers and judges, have to be interpreted, analyzed, and evaluated as part of the process of evaluating evidence in the courts.

We have proceeded in this fashion in order to make things as simple as possible for readers who have a law background, or other disciplinary background, but who at this point have no acquaintance with any of the formal models or computational tools that are currently being used in artificial intelligence and law, a somewhat specialized area of research. We have used what we hope to be a simple and easily understandable generic system of drawing argument diagrams that does not require the user to be familiar with any specific computational model or diagramming tool. The reader should feel quite free to use her or his favorite editor to create these diagrams and explain them to his or her students or colleagues. We hope these diagrams will help explain to the readers the potential of the argumentation methodology that can help with problems of statutory interpretation.

The core of our method is to visualize the argumentation that can be used by both sides to support or attack any interpretation proposed of a problematically written statute (such as one containing a semantic or syntactic ambiguity) by means of drawing an argument diagram, or argument map as it is usually called in computing, for any legal case where statutory interpretation is a problem. We are well aware that in using the structured and formalistic argumentation approach there is the danger of confusing readers more than explaining to them how the courts can do a better job of grappling with the hard (so-called wicked) problems of statutory interpretation. The methods that we advocate include the application of argumentation schemes, argument diagrams, and other such tools to model the reasons pro and con a particular interpretation of a statute, or indeed of any other legal document where interpretation of natural language text is required. Don't worry if you are a legal practitioner, a judge, or anyone at all, who is not familiar with the state-of-the-art argumentation tools currently being used in artificial intelligence. We try our best to explain everything from the ground up.

Though we drew our diagrams using yEd, a graph editor, many of the examples in the book have been visually represented after the fashion of the Carneades Argumentation System, a computational tool, with the ultimate conclusion of the chain of argumentation shown at the left and the various premises and conclusions in that chain indicated as propositions flowing from the evidence in the case to the ultimate conclusion. (We followed the conventions of Carneades version 2; a more advanced version, version 4, has argumentation schemes hardwired into the system.) This way of visually representing these argument diagrams is a little different from the way some readers may be familiar with, a way that presents the ultimate conclusion at the top of the diagram and all the evidence represented as a chain of argumentation flowing upward and culminating in that final conclusion. Don't worry about this. The graph can be presented either way, and one style of graph can automatically be drawn the other way using yEd or any of the many other software tools available for drawing, analyzing, and evaluating argumentation by building an argument diagram of this sort.

Many of the diagrams used in the book have different purposes. For example, some of them are used to draw graphs classifying the different types of arguments used for statutory interpretation. The purpose of this book is to model argumentation schemes representing the different kinds of arguments that can be used pro or con a particular interpretation that is being proposed. In other words, to put it very simply, the purpose of the book is to recast the traditional canons of interpretation as to forms of distinctive and identifiable forms of argument that can be defined clearly and precisely. This is another instance where the use of a graph structure presented visually as a diagram is extremely helpful for summarizing and explaining the results we arrived at by analyzing the many different examples of problematic statutory interpretation scattered throughout the book.

0.6 THE WAY FORWARD

An argumentative approach to statutory interpretation is a risk. Analyzing a phenomenon by combining two perspectives is already a challenge, as it necessarily implies a distortion of two ways of looking at a state of affairs. The pragmatics used in legal theories about interpretation is an adaptation of pragmatic theories, applied to legal theory through an argumentation viewpoint. The advantage that this multidimensional and multidisciplinary approach offers is that by furnishing practical tools to aid with the procedure of reasonable interpretation of a text purporting to represent a justifiable interpretation of the statute, the argumentation on both sides can be made explicit and represented visually in a graph structure, an argument map, that displays the whole network of argumentation in a case. To take the first steps toward accomplishing the objective of producing this argument technology, we are going first to adapt the theories of legal interpretation to fit a pragmatic perspective, and then use pragmatic theories to extend our argumentation-based approach. This effort, however, does not replace what already exists. Instead, its goal is to show how the complexity of legal canons and legal theories can be regarded and read using the instruments that we already use in everyday conversation, namely our arguments. The awareness of the reasons that we use when we interpret our language is the same awareness of the patterns that courts and legal practitioners use in supporting an interpretative hypothesis or establishing its acceptability.

We hope that the theory we have put forward in this book is groundbreaking, at least for its effort to outline a truly interdisciplinary view of our research object. Given the scale and the depth of the problem as indicated by the remarks of Katzmann (2014) cited above, we realize that we can hardly claim to have resolved the many conflicts about statutory interpretation. However, we can reasonably claim to have set out a tentative but promising direction that applies these new tools and resources from allied fields to address our questions with some promising measure of success. We are hoping, at any rate, that our efforts will suggest a new path of research that others can take as a useful step, a way forward amidst the ongoing legal problems and controversies posed by statutory interpretation.

REFERENCES

Alexy, Robert. 1989. A *Theory of Legal Argumentation: The Theory of Rational Discourse as Theory of Legal Justification.* Edited by Neil McCormick and Ruth Adler. Oxford, UK: Clarendon Press.

Aristotle. 1991. "Topics." In *The Complete Works of Aristotle, Vol. I,* edited by Jonathan Barnes. Princeton, NJ: Princeton University Press.

Ashley, Kevin. 2017. *Artificial Intelligence and Legal Analytics.* New York, NY: Cambridge University Press.

Baum, Lawrence. 2009. *Judges and Their Audiences: A Perspective on Judicial Behavior.* Princeton, NJ: Princeton University Press.

Berman, Donald, and Carole Hafner. 1988. "Obstacles to the development of logic-based models of legal reasoning." In *Computer Power and Legal Language,* edited by Charles Walter, 185–214. Westport, CT: Greenwood Press.

Butler, Brian. 2016. "Law and the primacy of pragmatics." In *Pragmatics and Law: Philosophical Perspectives,* edited by Alessandro Capone and Francesca Poggi, 1–13. Cham, Switzerland: Springer.

Capone, Alessandro. 2016. "The role of pragmatics in (re)constructing the rational law-maker." In *Pragmatics & Cognition,* edited by Alessandro Capone and Francesca Poggi, 21:141–157. Cham, Switzerland: Springer.

Carston, Robyn. 2002. *Thoughts and Utterances: The Pragmatics of Explicit Communication.* Oxford, UK: Blackwell Publishing Ltd.

Charnock, Ross. 2007. "Lexical indeterminacy: Contextualism and rule-following in Common Law adjudication." In *Interpretation, Law and the Construction of Meaning: Collected Papers on Legal Interpretation in Theory, Adjudication and Political Practice,* edited by Anne Wagner, Wouter Werner, and Deborah Cao, 21–47. Amsterdam, Netherlands: Springer.

Cicero, Marcus Tullius. 2003. *Topica.* Edited by Tobias Reinhardt. Oxford, UK: Oxford University Press.

Dascal, Marcelo, and Jerzy Wróblewski. 1988. "Transparency and doubt: Understanding and interpretation in pragmatics and in law." *Law and Philosophy* 7(2): 203–224. https://doi.org/10.1007/BF00144156.

Easterbrook, Frank. 1990. "What's so special about judges?" *University of Colorado Law Review* 61: 773–782.

Easterbrook, Frank. 2017. "The absence of method in statutory interpretation." *University of Chicago Law Review* 84(1): 81–97.

Eemeren, Frans van, and Rob Grootendorst. 1992. *Argumentation, Communication, and Fallacies: A Pragma-Dialectical Perspective*. Hillsdale, NJ: Lawrence Erlbaum Associates.

Epstein, Lee, William Landes, and Richard Posner. 2013. *The Behavior of Federal Judges: A Theoretical and Empirical Study of Rational Choice*. Cambridge, MA: Harvard University Press.

Gordon, Thomas, Henry Prakken, and Douglas Walton. 2007. "The Carneades model of argument and burden of proof." *Artificial Intelligence* 171(10–15): 875–896. https://doi.org/10.1016/j.artint.2007.04.010.

Guastini, Riccardo. 2011. *Interpretare e Argomentare*. Milano, Italy: Giuffrè.

Hitchcock, David. 2017. *On Reasoning and Argument: Essays in Informal Logic and on Critical Thinking*. Cham, Switzerland: Springer.

Huang, Yan. 2014. *Pragmatics*. Oxford, UK: Oxford University Press.

Jaszczolt, Kasia. 2018. "Pragmatics and philosophy: In search of a paradigm." *Intercultural Pragmatics* 15(2): 131–159. https://doi.org/10.1515/ip-2018-0002.

Katzmann, Robert. 2014. *Judging Statutes*. New York, NY: Oxford University Press.

Kecskes, Istvan. 2013. *Intercultural Pragmatics*. Oxford, UK: Oxford University Press.

Kuhn, Deanna, Richard Cheney, and Michael Weinstock. 2000. "The development of epistemological understanding." *Cognitive Development* 15(3): 309–328. https://doi.org/10.1016/S0885-2014(00)00030-7

Leech, Geoffrey. 1983. *Principles of Pragmatics*. London, UK: Longman.

Llewellyn, Karl. 1949. "Remarks on the theory of appellate decision and the rules or Canons about how statutes are to be construed." *Vanderbilt Law Review* 3: 395–406.

Macagno, Fabrizio. 2015. "Presupposition as argumentative reasoning." In *Interdisciplinary Studies in Pragmatics, Culture and Society*, edited by Alessandro Capone and Jacob Mey, 465–487. Cham, Switzerland: Springer.

Macagno, Fabrizio, and Giovanni Damele. 2013. "The dialogical force of implicit premises. Presumptions in enthymemes." *Informal Logic* 33(3): 361. https://doi.org/10.22329/il.v33i3.3679.

Macagno, Fabrizio, and Douglas Walton. 2015. "Classifying the patterns of natural arguments." *Philosophy and Rhetoric* 48(1): 26–53. https://doi.org/10.1353/par.2015.0005.

Macagno, Fabrizio, and Douglas Walton. 2017. "Arguments of statutory interpretation and argumentation schemes." *International Journal of Legal Discourse* 2(1): 47–83. https://doi.org/10.1515/ijld-2017-0002.

Macagno, Fabrizio, Douglas Walton, and Giovanni Sartor. 2018. "Pragmatic maxims and presumptions in legal interpretation." *Law and Philosophy* 37(1): 69–115. https://doi.org/10.1007/s10982-017-9306-4.

MacCormick, Neil, and Robert Summers, eds. 1991. *Interpreting Statutes: A Comparative Study*. Aldershot, UK: Dartmouth.

Perelman, Chaïm. 1979. *Logique Juridique. Nouvelle Réthorique*. Paris, France: Dalloz.

Scalia, Antonin, and Bryan Garner. 2012. *Reading Law: The Interpretation of Legal Texts*. Eagan, MN: Thomson West.

Sinclair, Michael. 2005. "Only a sith thinks like that: Llewellyn's dueling canons, one to seven." *New York Law School Law Review* 50: 919–992.

Stalnaker, Robert. 1970. "Pragmatics." *Synthese* 22(1–2): 272–289. https://doi.org/10.1007/BF00413603.

Tarello, Giovanni. 1980. *L'interpretazione della Legge*. Milano, Italy: Giuffrè.

Walton, Douglas. 1990. "What is reasoning? What is an argument?" *Journal of Philosophy* 87: 399–419. https://doi.org/10.2307/2026735.

Walton, Douglas. 2008. "The three bases for the enthymeme: A dialogical theory." *Journal of Applied Logic* 6(3): 361–79. https://doi.org/10.1016/j.jal.2007.06.002

Walton, Douglas, and Fabrizio Macagno. 2015. "A classification system for argumentation schemes." *Argument and Computation* 6(3): 219–245. https://doi.org/10.1080/19462166.2015.1123772.

Walton, Douglas, Christopher Reed, and Fabrizio Macagno. 2008. *Argumentation Schemes*. New York; NY: Cambridge University Press.

Walton, Douglas, Giovanni Sartor, and Fabrizio Macagno. 2016. "An argumentation framework for contested cases of statutory interpretation." *Artificial Intelligence and Law* 24(1): 51–91. https://doi.org/10.1007/s10506-016-9179-0.

Walton, Douglas, Giovanni Sartor, and Fabrizio Macagno. 2018. "Statutory interpretation as argumentation." In *Handbook of Legal Reasoning and Argumentation*, edited by Giorgio Bongiovanni, Gerald Postema, Antonino Rotolo, Chiara Valentini, Giovanni Sartor, and Douglas Walton, 519–560. Dordrecht, Netherlands: Springer.

1

Interpretation and Statutory Interpretation

1.1 THE IDEA OF INTERPRETATION

The English word "interpretation" comes from Latin *interpretatio*, from *interpres*, originally meaning an intermediary, broker, or agent, and then also an explainer or translator (De Vaan, 2008, 307). In its turn *interpres* seems to have resulted from the fusion of *inter* (between) and *praes*, a word that possibly shares the same root with the Latin *pretium* (price), thus being linked to the idea of an economic exchange (lending, buying, or selling). The semantic area of "interpretation" is also covered by terms of Greek origin, such as "exegesis" and "hermeneutics," often used in religious contexts. In Latin, *intepretatio* was used normally as a synonym for translation (McElduff, 2009), which included both transposing a text into a different language and explaining the meaning of a text to one who does not understand it (Cicero *De Legibus*, 1.14.9). However, *interpretatio* was also used in a broader sense, for referring to the activity of interpreting "laws, dreams and omens as well as languages, though the notion of transferring information of one sort or another from person to person or from god to person is always key to its usage" (McElduff, 2009, 136).

In the medieval dialectical tradition, and in particular in Abelard, *interpretatio* was a technical term. It was used for the activity of explaining the meaning of a word completely unknown, such as (normally) a foreign word (Abaelardus, *Dialectica*, 583–584), in particular, by reference to word's etymology, or to the analysis of its component morphemes (Abaelardus, *Dialectica*, 340).

The strict relationship between *interpretatio* and translation is also maintained in the following centuries (Rener, 1989, 273–280), reserving the specification of "*interpretatio paraphrastica*" to the explanation of the language of an original, elucidating obscure words and passages.

The term "interpretation" is used today in a very broad range of domains: whenever Y is an account, endorsed by actor A, of object X, we may say that an actor A interprets X as Y, or that Y is an interpretation of X by A. Omitting the actor (the interpreter) we may just say X is interpreted as Y, or that Y is an interpretation of X. Let us consider, for instance, *Google-Spain* (Case C-131/12, decided on May 13, 2014), where the European Court of Justice (ECJ) affirmed that the "processing of personal data" in the 1995 European Data Protection Directive also includes the processing of web pages by search engines, regardless of the fact that such processing (harvesting, indexing, and searching all available content) concerns all kinds of data and does not distinguish personal data from any other piece of information. We may say that in this case the ECJ interpreted the expression "processing of personal data" as also covering the operation of search engines, or that the ECJ's interpretation of "processing of personal data" also covers the operation of search engines. As this example shows, and as we will discuss later, an interpretation of a text or an expression (i.e. the use of a linguistic item) does not need to be a full account of its meaning; it may also address a partial aspect of what would be a full account of such a text or expression. In particular, the interpretation of a linguistic expression may just affirm that the expression includes or excludes a certain class of entities.

The term "interpretation," and the verb "to interpret," may be used to refer to a cognitive process, namely, the activity that delivers a certain account of an object, as well as to the outcome of that process, namely to the account being delivered (see Tarello, 1980 39ff.). Thus, in our example, in the locution "interpretation of 'processing of personal data' by the ECJ", the term "interpretation" may on the one hand refer to a sociocognitive activity, the process of reasoning and discussing by the judges through which they determined the meaning of the expression "processing of personal data." The same locution may, on the other hand, also refer to the outcome of that activity – the conclusion endorsed by the ECJ on the basis of that activity, namely the specification that "processing of personal data" also includes the activity of search engines. In this regard, the term "interpretation" behaves no differently than other terms that are used to refer both to individual or collective cognitive processes and to their outcome, such as the terms "understanding" or "perception."

1.2 INTERPRETATIONS OUTSIDE OF THE LAW

Our focus is only statutory interpretations, namely, those accounts of (fragments of) legislative texts that are meant to reconstruct the meaning and legal effect of such texts. However, as we shall see in the following sections, the term "interpretation" is also used in many other contexts.

1.2.1 *Interpretation in Science*

We may say that a scientific theory interprets a set of natural phenomena, meaning that the theory provides an account of those phenomena, usually in terms of causal explanations and corresponding forecasts. For instance, Francis Bacon in his "New Organon" (Bacon, *Novum Organum*) provided researchers with "Directions for the Interpretation of Nature." In a similar spirit, Galileo Galilei in the "Assayer" connected the interpretation of texts and the construction of causal mathematical models by claiming that "the book of nature is written in the language of mathematics" (Galilei, *Il Saggiatore*).

However, in current scientific discourse the idea of interpretation is rarely applied directly to theories of natural phenomena, except with regard to competing high-level visions, among which the empirical data do not support a definitive choice (e.g., the different "interpretations" of quantum mechanics). The term "interpretation" is more often applied to the analysis of empirical data. In empirical sciences interpreting a set of data means providing an account of such data, though not necessarily a fully developed scientific theory. In statistics, or data science, for instance, "interpreting" a set of data involves (a) identifying particular dependencies and correlations between these data (the variables) – for example, between smoking habits and lung cancer, or between vaccination and various illnesses; (b) making hypotheses on this basis (see Abbott, 2016, 9); and possibly (c) moving from the identification of correlation to the construction of causal models (see Pearl, 2000).

The notion of interpretation as "making sense of empirical data" is also used in the context of legal evidence, to emphasize the fact that different accounts of the same data may be possible, as happens in legal cases involving complex evidence, in particular, scientific evidence. Such interpretations can be supported by arguments pointing to the grounds for preferring one causal account over another, based on the extent to which that account is supported by the data, and corresponds to accepted scientific theories.

1.2.2 *Interpretations of Intentional Systems*

The notion of an interpretation assumes a peculiar characterization when it is applied to human behavior, or more generally to intentional systems, namely systems having a goal-directed behavior. Such systems tend to select and implement the actions that are appropriate to achieve their goals. They may also form intentions, namely, determinations to perform the selected actions, which persist until the intended action is accomplished or the intention withdrawn. In such cases the system's behavior can be accounted for (interpreted/explained) by adopting the "intentional stance" (Dennett, 1997), that is, by assuming that the system implements the actions that it has selected, according to its beliefs in order to achieve its goals.

When human action is at stake, intentional interpretation also includes taking account of other aspects of human psychology, such as emotions and norms. This kind of interpretation may be required in criminal cases. For instance, to prove that an accused has committed a crime, in the absence of direct evidence, the prosecution may need to show that the accused had sufficient motives for engaging in the criminal action, based on the contextual interpretation of his or her antecedent or subsequent behavior. Similarly, to establish that the accused had the required *mens rea* (e.g., the intention to kill the victim), an interpretation of his or her behavior may be needed. In such cases, opposed arguments are often developed, supporting one or other interpretations of the behavior of the accused (he intended to kill the victim versus he did not want that unfortunate outcome).

The idea that an understanding of human action requires interpretation is at the center of Dilthey's (1989) account of historical cognition, according to which human action can be accounted for by the psychology of the human actors, to be understood historically, namely in the context of the culture of their time. This idea has been further developed in the context of the so-called hermeneutical studies, according to which the interpretation of a cultural object results from the dialectical tension, interrogation, and merging between two historically conditioned cultural horizons or traditions: the contemporary environment of the interpreter and the past environment of the object being interpreted (Gadamer, 1989). The idea that the study of human action requires an interpretation (of the psychological determinants of the individual action), according to an intentional perspective, is also at the basis of the social theory by Max Weber, who argues that sociology is "a science which attempts the interpretative understanding of social action in order thereby to arrive at a causal explanation of its course and effects" (Weber, 1978, 4).

Still different issues pertain to the interpretation of human attitudes, thoughts, or dreams within psychology and psychoanalysis, which focus on conscious and unconscious psychic determinants and effects. For instance, in his famous "Interpretation of Dreams," Sigmund Freud affirms that dreams are "psychical phenomena of complete validity-fulfilments of wishes; they can be inserted into the chain of intelligible waking mental acts" (Freud, 1965, 200).

1.2.3 *Interpretation in Communication*

Let us now move from intentional actions in general to intentional communicative actions, namely, actions through which a communicator intentionally transmits some information to a receiver, which is supposed to know that the sender has this intent in performing that action. In such cases, according to Paul Grice (1969), the meaning (to be detected through the interpretation) of the communicator's action consists in a multilayered intention of the communicator: (1) his intention i_1 that his action engenders a certain response in the receiver; (2) his intention i_2 that the receiver recognizes intention i_1; (3) his intention i_3 that the receiver's recognition of i_1 provides the latter with a reason for her response. For instance, the meaning of the action of a police officer raising his traffic paddle to order a driver to stop consists in (1) his intention i_1 to make the driver stop, through this action; (2) his intention i_2 that the driver should recognize i_1 (i.e., that the paddle raising was meant to make her stop); (3) his intention that the driver's recognition of i_1 motivates her to stop. According to Searle (2007), this account should be refined by distinguishing the speaker's intention to perform a certain speech act (e.g., the intention to order the driver to stop), having certain success conditions (that its content is realized, namely that the driver stops), from the speaker's intention to communicate this speech act to the hearer, by having the hearer recognize this very communicative intention.

Interpretation takes a further turn when it concerns a linguistic expression, namely, a symbolic sequence endowed with a conventional meaning. In communication using a conventional language, a distinction emerges between the semantics of the message (what the message says according to semantic rules of the language) and the speaker's meaning (what the speaker intends to communicate), by using an expression that has certain conventional semantic meaning. To capture the speaker's meaning, presuppositions and implicatures of communicative behavior have to be taken into account (Grice, 1975), according to pragmatics, namely the study of how the context of use of linguistic expressions (which have a semantic meaning according to linguistic conventions) affects their meaning. In this connection we may want to distinguish what the speaker meant, what he should reasonably have meant, what the hearer understood, or how she should have understood, given the pragmatic clues and the linguistic conventions that were accessible to her in the context of the speech act.

1.2.4 *Interpretation in Art*

The idea that the meaning of a linguistic expression is determined by the speaker's intention – though quite plausible with regard to individual communication – becomes questionable when the expression is put in writing or in any way recorded on a permanent medium, being destined to open audiences. With regard to works of art, various approaches to interpretation can be distinguished, on whose merit critics themselves are divided: 1) actual intentionalism, according to which determining the meaning of a text consists in retrieving the intention of its authors; 2) anti-intentionalism or conventionalism, according to which meaning is only determined by linguistic conventions and general background knowledge, the identity of the author being irrelevant; 3) hypothetical intentionalism, according to which meaning is determined by the best hypotheses that an ideally careful and informed audience would form about the actual author's intentions; 4) reader-response theory, according to which meaning is determined by the understanding of individual readers or of their communities; 5) value-maximization theories, which assume that meaning is determined by the interpretations "that make the work out to be artistically more meritorious as literature are to be preferred" (Davies, 2007, 185).

When a text continues to be relevant through time, as is the case for some literary works (e.g., the creations of Homer, Dante, or Shakespeare), and some legal document with persistent validity (e.g., the US Constitution, the UN Declaration of Human Rights, the Italian Civil Code), a further issue emerges, namely, whether the meaning of a text is fixed by the circumstances existing at the time when it was produced, or whether the text may acquire a new meaning in the present context. Is the meaning of the text fixed by the intention of its author and the understanding of its contemporary audience, or is it rather determined by the understanding "interpretative community" that is presently accessing it (Fish, 1989)?

1.3 LEGAL INTERPRETATION

After this short and sketchy overview of various kinds of interpretation and corresponding issues, let us specifically address legal interpretation.

1.3.1 *The Object of Legal Interpretation*

Multiple sources contribute to the law: statutes (enactments by legislative bodies), constitutions and constitutional revisions, administrative regulations, international treaties, judicial decisions, administrative decisions, soft laws (such as guidelines and recommendations), private acts (such as wills and contracts), legal customs, and other normative social practices. All such sources have to be interpreted to determine their content, and consequently, their contribution to the law.

However, here we focus only on legislation broadly understood, namely, on explicit authoritative statements meant to change the legal system, by establishing new norms, and possibly modifying and removing preexisting norms. Such statements are enacted by legal authorities – usually collective bodies – and are directed to multiple addressees, namely citizens, administrative agencies, and law enforcers.

A typical instance of these statements is represented by statutory documents produced by legislative bodies, such as parliaments and other legislative assemblies. Statutory documents are the result of procedures that culminate in the approval of such documents. They become binding from the moment of their approval, or rather, as is often the case, after their publication and, possibly, after a time lapse meant to enable citizens to know of the new norms and adapt to them (this time lapse is called *vacatio legis* in civil law jurisdictions).

As statutes convey legal norms, they provide guidance to all those who have a disposition to be guided by the law. A statute is primarily directed to the addressees of the norms it introduces, that is, to the holders of normative positions – rights, powers, entitlements, duties and responsibilities – directly or indirectly conferred by the statute. However, the statute is also directed to the adjudicators of cases involving the application of these norms, and particularly to judges.

The interpretations by addressees and adjudicators mutually interact, and as a consequence, they usually tend to converge. On the one hand, the interpretation by the addressees is guided by the expected interpretation of the adjudicators, since the addressees, to be successful in future litigations, have to comply with or at least use the norms as interpreted by the adjudicators. On the other hand, the interpretation of adjudicators is guided by the interpretations of the norm addressees, to the extent that adjudicators do not want to frustrate the expectations of well-meaning addressees (the interaction of these expectation was described in Fuller, 1981).

1.3.2 *The Practical Significance of Legislative Interpretation*

To exemplify the practical significance of legal interpretation we consider some recent cases involving Facebook. Facebook not only tracks the behavior of its users – in particular for the purpose of sending them targeted advertising and messages – it also combines the data obtained through different services it controls, such as the communication services WhatsApp and Messenger. The contract (terms of service) that users accept in order access the Facebook social network includes a clause according to which Facebook has the option of merging users' personal data obtained within Facebook with the personal data obtained within other services controlled by Facebook. This practice has been challenged by some Facebook users, who have addressed data protection authorities and competition authorities, claiming that this practice violates EU data protection law (the General Data Protection Regulation – GDPR), since users' consent to the combination of their data under such conditions is invalid.

According to EU law (Article 6 of the GDPR), the processing of personal data is only permissible when it has a legal basis, and consent is the only legal basis that can apply to the merging of users' data by Facebook: if users have not given a valid consent to the combination of their data collected through different services, the combination of these data will have no legal basis. Consequently such a combination will be unlawful, and will be subject to civil and administrative sanctions for unlawful processing of personal data. Thus, the issue to be addressed to determine the legality of Facebook's practice is whether users' agreement to the combination of data collected from different services may count as a valid *consent* to it. For this purpose we have to take into account the way in which "consent" is defined in the GDPR, which at Article 4(11) states that "'consent' of the data subject means any freely given, specific, informed and unambiguous indication of the data subject's wishes by which he or she, by a statement or by a clear affirmative action, signifies agreement to the processing of personal data relating to him or her." There is no doubt that Facebook users affirmatively agree to the processing consisting in the merging of data obtained through different services. However, we may wonder whether the agreement is free, since Facebook requires its users to agree to this processing in order to use the Facebook social networking service, a service which is provided under conditions of market dominance, and for the delivery of which the data from other services are not needed.

Thus the interpretative issue to be considered to determine the legality of Facebook's behavior is whether the concept of "freely given indication of the data subject's wishes" is to be interpreted in such a way as to include the data subjects' agreement to a processing of their personal data, when, as in the Facebook case, the provision of a service, under condition of market dominance, is made conditional on the users' agreement to the processing and the processing is not necessary for the provision of the service.

The answer to this question has great practical implications. Let us assume that the concept "freely given indication of the data subject's wishes" is interpreted in such a way that it includes an agreement given under the conditions just described. Then the users' agreement to the Facebook clause would be lawful, Facebook could legally combine the data collected through different services, and users should be content with the freedom to choose between not using the Facebook social network at all or using it and letting Facebook combine the data.

Let us assume, on the contrary, that the expression "freely given indication of the data subject's wishes" is interpreted in the sense that an agreement given under the indicated conditions is not covered by it. Then Facebook, if it wants to comply with the law, should stop all processing based on such an agreement, and should give its users the opportunity to use the Facebook social service without agreeing to the combination of the data collected within different services. Data protection authorities (or judicial authorities), following this interpretation, should enjoin Facebook to terminate all processing based on the invalid agreement, and subject it to sanctions – up to millions of euros – for unlawful processing.

The latter interpretation was recently adopted by the German Competition Authority (*Bundeskartellamt*), whose president, Andreas Mundt, made the following statement: "Voluntary [freely given] consent means that the use of Facebook's services must not be subject to the users' consent to their data being collected and combined in this way. If users do not consent, Facebook may not exclude them from its services and must refrain from collecting and merging data from different sources."

For another simple example of the practical implication of legal interpretation, consider the issue of whether the expression "cruel and unusual punishment" – which describes the punishments that are prohibited by the Eighth Amendment to the US Constitution – also includes the death penalty. If that expression is interpreted in this way, then the infliction of the death penalty is constitutionally prohibited in the United States, laws imposing that penalty are invalid, judges are forbidden from imposing the death penalty, and criminals have the right not to be subject to it. If on the contrary this expression is understood as not including the death penalty, then the infliction of the death penalty is constitutionally permitted, the laws imposing it are valid, judges have an obligation to impose the death penalty when required by criminal statutes, and criminals under appropriate conditions are liable to it. The legal interpretation of "cruel and unusual punishment" can make the difference between life and death.

1.3.3 *Legal Interpretation and Legal Decision*

These examples show the peculiar practical significance of legal interpretation, namely, the way in which it may affect individual and social interests. This practical significance is determined by the fact that legal norms play a role in decisional process of citizen and officers (Conte and Castelfranchi, 2006). On the one hand, both citizens and officers have the propensity to view legal norms as reasons for thoughts and actions: when they are convinced that a legal norm exists, they tend to act accordingly (Pattaro, 2005). On the other hand, they have the propensity to view valid legal texts (legal sources) as generators of legal norms, namely, the norms resulting from the appropriate interpretation of such texts. This means that a law-compliant addressee/adjudicator will have the propensity to respect the norms that she considers to be the (correct) interpretation of valid legal texts.

A well-meaning complier will in fact adopt a reasoning scheme having the following structure:

1. General premise 1: If a norm X is the right interpretation of provision Y in a valid legal document Z, then X is a valid legal norm.

2. General premise 2: If X is a valid legal norm, then I will adopt X as a standard for my behavior and comply with it or apply it as required.

Assume that a norm addressee or adjudicator endorses both premises 1 and 2 and that she also believes that a particular norm is the right interpretation of a certain provision in a certain valid legal document. The addressee or adjudicator will consequently adopt that norm and behave accordingly (e.g., issuing a fine against Facebook).

For instance, assume that an employer adopting general premises 1 and 2 faces a case in which one of his employees, a woman in a same-sex relationship, whose partner gave birth to a child, asks for fifteen days' paid leave, based on a legislative provision stating that "the father is entitled to fifteen days of paid leave at the birth of his child."

Assume that the employer believes the expression "father" in that provision has to be interpreted liberally, in such a way that it may also includes a woman being the same-sex partner of the mother of the child. Consequently, he will conclude that the provision establishes a norm to that effect, that is, that "the father (interpreted as including the same-sex partner of the mother) is entitled to fifteen days of paid leave at the birth of his (or her) child." By applying that norm, the law-compliant employer will provide the leave.

Assume now that the employer, on the contrary, believes that the interpretation of the expression "father" in that provision includes only the male person who is the biological father. In this case, the law-compliant employer, by applying this latter interpretation of the same provision would refuse the leave. Assume that the woman being refused the leave sues her employer. Then the judge, depending on the way in which she interprets the provision at issue, will order the employer to grant or not to grant the leave.

The practical significance of legal interpretation explains why legal interpretation is so important and controversial: debates on legal interpretation are not merely theoretical exchanges (as is the case for other kinds of interpretation); different legal interpretations lead to different decisions being made and then enforced using public force. The practical relevance of legal interpretation concerns not only the actors that comply with or apply and enforce the norms they believe to be expressed in legal document. It also concerns the actors that recommend certain interpretations, or the rejection of certain interpretations, and in particular doctrinal jurists.

1.3.4 *Descriptive and Evaluative Interpretative Assertions*

We have to distinguish two kinds of interpretative claims. The first includes descriptive assertions to the effect that, as a matter of fact, a certain expression has been, or is likely to be, interpreted in a certain way (by certain individuals or bodies). For instance, we may truthfully state that in *Google-Spain* the ECJ interpreted the term "controller" in the 1995 Data Protection Directive as including also search engines, while other judges had previously interpreted this term as not including search engines. Similarly, we may state that until the 1980s the Italian judiciary interpreted the term "damage" in the civil code as only including pecuniary losses, and that since then the interpretation has evolved, so that now this term also includes health damage not involving a reduction in earning capacity, and further kinds of non-monetary prejudice.

The second kind of interpretative claim includes the evaluative assertions to the effect that it is better, preferable, or most correct to interpret a certain provision or expression in a certain way. For instance, before *Google-Spain*, various authors argued that the word "controller" in the EU Data Protection Directive should not be interpreted as including search engines, since search engines index all data present on the open web and have no control over what data is uploaded on the web by third parties. This argument was also endorsed by the EU Advocate General in his opinion preceding the decision of the ECJ in *Google-Spain*. Other authors argued that, on the contrary, "controller" should be interpreted as including also search engines, since search engines choose to process all data present on the open web, and therefore they also choose to process whatever personal data happens to be there.

Descriptive and evaluative interpretative assertions have independent assertability conditions. We may consistently affirm that a certain expression is interpreted in a certain way (by certain actors) and claim at the same time that this same expression should preferably be interpreted in a different way. For instance, we may consistently say that the ECJ, in *Google-Spain*, interpreted the notion of controller in such a way as to include search engines, but that it should not have interpreted the notion of "controller" in that way. After the decision of the ECJ, the situation has changed, with regard to the justification of the legal interpretation of that expression. Now there is an additional, and stronger argument, for interpreting "controller" as the court did, namely, the very decision of the court, in combination with the view that precedents of the ECJ have some binding or persuasive force. Thus, one may consistently affirm that before the decision of the court "controller" should have been interpreted as not including search engines, but that now it should be interpreted as including them.

When speaking of interpretative claims and interpretative arguments supporting them, we shall focus on evaluative claims affirming the legal preferability of one interpretation over specified or unspecified alternatives. The distinction between descriptive and evaluative interpretative claims is relatively clear when we oppose assertions on what interpretations have been adopted or are likely to be adopted by certain interpreters, or on what interpretations should preferably be adopted in a new case. The distinction between descriptive and evaluative interpretative claims is less clear concerning the claims concerning the justification of certain interpretations based on certain goals, values, attitudes, or preferences. In this case, interpretative claims tend to transform into technical prescriptions on what interpretation would better achieve certain outcomes. For instance, it may be claimed that we should interpret the term "controller" as excluding search engines, if we want to prevent search engines from engaging in online censorship (as their controllership entails a responsibility to block access to personal data unlawfully published by third parties), or on the opposite, that we should interpret this term as including search engines, if we want to provide a stronger protection of online privacy.

Assertions to the effect that that a certain interpretation "may" or "might" be adopted by a certain legal interpreter or in a certain legal system also can be ambiguous. Consider for instance the assertion that the ECJ might as well have interpreted the notion of controller as not including search engines. This assertion could be used to convey an evaluation, namely, the view that this interpretation too would have been legally acceptable, remaining within the space of discretion legitimately enjoyed by the ECJ. The same assertion could also be used to convey a less selective and evaluative message, merely to point to the fact that resources existed in the EU legal system that would allow the construction of arguments supporting this assertion (even though such arguments would have little chance of success and little merit). Or the same assertion could also be used in more empirical tone, just to point to the uncertainty preceding the decision of the ECJ on that matter.

In Chapter 6, we shall provide a logical characterization of the assertions establishing that a certain proposition may or must be adopted as a possible or a necessary interpretation within a certain legal context (characterized by a set of accepted interpretative canons).

1.4 THE SCOPE OF LEGAL INTERPRETATION

The concept of legal interpretation, broadly understood, covers every attempt at determining the meaning of a statutory provision, and every outcome of such attempts. However, more restricted uses of the term "interpretation" have also been proposed, as well as attempts to segment the semantic field covered by the term "interpretation," distinguishing different kinds of interpretations.

1.4.1 *Interpretation and Understanding*

The scope (the extension) of the term "interpretation" can be restricted in two opposite directions: on the one end, easy and immediate determinations can be viewed as instances of mere "understanding" rather than interpretations; on the other end, complex and reasoned/evaluative determinations can be viewed as "constructions" rather than mere interpretations (Figure 1.1).

Understanding	Interpretation strictly understood	Construction
Interpretation broadly understood		

FIGURE 1.1 Understanding, interpretation, and construction

 The distinction between understanding and interpretation concerns whether the transition from a linguistic expression in a legal document to the meaning of that expression is "automatic" and unreflected or rather involves a stage of doubt, after which one of the available options is consciously selected. The idea that automatic understanding has to be distinguished from doubt-solving interpretations stems from the observation that competent language users normally comprehend the meaning of most sentences effortlessly, without consciously questioning their content. In this regard, sentence comprehension is not different from other cognitive mechanisms for recognition and classification, such as the perceptual identification of objects or human faces: quick responses are delivered by automatic and unconscious mechanisms, and reasoned reflection is only called upon when such mechanism fail to deliver definite outcomes, or when reasons emerge to doubt their outcomes.

 Even for syntactically ambiguous sentences (e.g., "time flies like an arrow"), the most plausible meaning is usually selected automatically, by default, through our psycholinguistic mechanisms for sentence comprehension. Such unconscious mechanisms perform, in a fraction of a second, complex combinations of partially parallel analyses involving phonological, syntactical, and semantic aspects of the sentences being read, and deliver outputs that are not consciously questioned by the reader, unless reasons to do so emerge (Newman, Forbes, and Connolly, 2012). This also applies to the comprehension of legislative statements: the prima facie meaning of such statements, as delivered by "automatic" mechanisms for sentence comprehension, is only challenged when we become aware of reasons to doubt the prima facie output.

Thus, the separation between understanding and interpretation requires us to distinguish situations of clarity and situations of doubt, an idea that is expressed by the traditional saying *in claris non fit interpretatio* (in clear matters interpretation does not take place). One perspective would consist in assuming that a legal text is clear when semantic rules unequivocally determine its meaning, and it is unclear when pragmatics – the reference to the context – is needed to solve indeterminacies. However, this perspective does not fit the distinction between automatic and reflected determination of meaning (nor the complex relationship between semantics and pragmatics). On the one hand, the determination of the meaning of an expression may be automatic also when pragmatic aspects are involved, these aspects being processed by our unconscious sentence comprehension mechanisms; on the other hand, reflection may be needed also when the semantics of the linguistic expressions seems to determine univocally its meaning, but this meaning appears to be incompatible with pragmatic aspects with which the reader is familiar. For instance, in the example of the paid paternity leave, the semantics of the English language would exclude the application of the term "father" to the lesbian partner, but a reader aware of pragmatic-teleological legal considerations (pertaining to equality with regard to same-sex partnerships, or to the needs of the child of the couple) may immediately question that meaning ascription.

Dascal and Wróblewski indeed argue that the distinction between understanding and interpretation in a strict sense (doubts-solving interpretation) should not be mapped onto the distinction between semantics and pragmatics. They consider that interpretation in a strict sense is needed for "an ascription of meaning to a linguistic sign" when the meaning of that sign "is doubtful in a communicative situation, i.e., in the case its 'direct understanding' is not sufficient for the communicative purpose at hand" (Dascal and Wróblewski, 1988, 204). Thus, the determination of whether there is clarity ultimately pertains to pragmatics, since it requires determining whether a contextually adequate inquiry on the meaning of a text would raise reasonable doubts. The fact that the prima facie, "automated" understanding delivers an ascription of meaning does not exclude that doubts can be raised at a later time, based on contextual clues (e.g., in case the prima facie meaning leads to unwanted consequences, or is in conflict with the intention of the legislator as resulting from the parliamentary debates, etc.). For instance, the notion of a "natural family based on marriage," contained in the Italian Constitution, was understood for decades as univocally pointing to the union between a man and a woman, but recently the debate on gay marriage has challenged this notion, introducing doubts. This example shows how the prima facie understanding of a legal provision may be challenged by new information, so that what appeared to be clear may fall under doubt, and the determination of the meaning may consequently require interpretation in a strict sense.

In conclusion, the distinction between understanding and interpretation in a strict sense points to different ways of coming to a determination of a meaning: on the one hand the direct, automatic, and unreflected understanding, and on the other hand the reasoned, mediated, doubt-resolving interpretation in a strict sense. This distinction does not provide us with a noncontextual way of determining when one or the other way of ascribing meaning is needed.

Let us consider, for instance, how we would apply the distinction between understanding and interpretation to the famous example of a provision stating that "vehicles are not allowed in the park" (Hart, 1958, 607). Mere understanding – involving no conscious doubt resolution – would lead us to assume that a car is a vehicle for the purpose of this provision, and that a wheelchair or the kick scooter of a child are not. This unreflected meaning determination results not only from the semantics of the word "vehicle" – which on the contrary may, according to some dictionary definitions, also include wheelchairs and kick scooters – but rather from our familiarity with the fact that private cars are usually excluded from public parks, while wheelchairs or kick scooters are usually allowed in. This meaning ascription is confirmed by the fact that no negative emotional reaction is aroused by the presence of these transportation means in the park, given that no nuisance is caused by them. On the other hand, a bicycle is likely to raise doubts (does "vehicle" only include motor-powered carriers, or also some human-powered ones?), given its size, the way in which it may affect pedestrians, and the fact that in some public parks bicycles are indeed forbidden.

1.4.2 *Interpretation and Construction*

The concept of interpretation in a strict sense has also been opposed to the idea of construction, the latter involving an outcome that goes beyond interpretation in a strict sense (see our Chapter 3 for a further discussion on this topic).

According to Solum (2009), the distinction between construction and interpretation concerns the opposition between the determination of linguistic meaning (including semantics and pragmatic conventions) of a provision and the determination of its legal effect. As an example of interpretation, Solum mentions the conclusions by Justice Scalia in *District of Columbia* v. *Heller*, 554 U.S. 570 (2008), that the "right to keep and bear arms," in the text of the Second Amendment to the US Constitution, means "the individual right to possess and carry weapons in case of confrontation." According to Solum, this determination was an instance of mere interpretation, rather than construction, since it was obtained by focusing on how this expression would be understood at the time of its utterance, according to facts pertaining to the language and culture of the time. Legal construction, on the other hand, "gives legal effect to the semantic content of a legal text." As examples of legal constructions, Solum lists, with regard to the First Amendment:

(1) the prior restraint doctrine, (2) the rules that define the freedom of speech doctrine governing expression via billboards, and (3) the distinction between content-based regulations and content-neutral time, place, and manner restrictions.

Arguably, such theories, developed by the US legal doctrine and judiciary, went much beyond whatever can be understood as the semantic meaning of the first amendment, that just reads "Congress shall make no law . . . abridging the freedom of speech."

As another example of judicial construction, consider the principle of mutual recognition under EU law. This principle was affirmed in the case *Rewe-Zentral v. Bundesmonopolverwaltung für Branntwein* (1979), known as *Cassis de Dijon*, concerning the sale in Germany of a liqueur (Cassis de Dijon) having a lower level of alcohol than required by German law on fruit liqueurs. The European judges ruled that goods that "have been lawfully produced and marketed in one of the member states" can in principle be "introduced into any other member state," even if they fail to meet the requirements established for goods produced in the latter state. This principle was presented by the judges as resulting from Article 34 of the Treaty stating that "Quantitative restrictions on imports and all measures having equivalent effect shall be prohibited between Member States." In this case too, arguably, the ruling of the judges went much beyond whatever could be seen as the semantic meaning of the Article 34, at the time in which it was enacted.

The distinction between interpretation and construction can also be mapped into the distinction proposed by Soames (2013) between identifying what legal content lawmakers asserted in adopting a certain linguistic expression, and rectifying that legal content. The first (identification) consists in determining "what the lawmakers meant and what any reasonable person who understood the linguistic meanings of their words, the publically available facts, the recent history in the lawmaking context, and the background of existing law into which the new provision is expected to fit, would take them to have meant" (Soames, 2013, 598). The second (rectification) consists in changing the law, namely, in introducing new law by modifying the legislatively asserted content. According to the deferentialist approach normatively supported by Soames, this should only happen when there is the need to precisify the legislative content or harmonize its content with the content of other laws or with the purpose for which the law was adopted. This deferentialist approach was not adopted, according to Soames, in important cases, such as those in which the US Supreme Court recognized new constitutional rights, nonenumerated in the US Constitution.

The distinction between interpretation and construction tends to separate the domain of evaluative choices from the domain of factual inquiry meant to determine what the prescribers might have intended to state and what their addressees might have reasonably comprehended. This distinction, however, cannot easily be mapped into the distinction between empirical and evaluative analyses of meaning. The difficulty is particularly relevant with regard to teleological interpretation. In some cases, an interpretation favoring the purposes of the prescriber fits into the idea of enriching the content of a prescription with pragmatic inferences. Consider for instance a municipal regulation requiring restaurants to have "clean and well-kept indoor restrooms." Such a prescription would certainly implicate that such restrooms should not only be clean and well-kept but also open and accessible to the restaurants' patrons (Marmor, 2008, 441). However, the usual idea of pragmatic inference does not seem to apply to those cases in which the prescriber's goal and the ways to achieve it are not part of the apparent communicative intention of the prescriber, even though they can be determined without resorting to moral evaluations, relying on mere counterfactual reasoning – what would the prescriber have stated, had he considered certain features of the case at stake? A classic example is *Church of the Holy Trinity* v. *United States*, 143 U.S. 457 (1892), which concerned whether the prohibition to facilitate the importation of "labor or service of any kind" also included the transportation of a foreign clergyman to be employed by the Holy Trinity Church. The US Supreme Court interpreted this provision as only concerning manual work, and in any case as not concerning religious ministers. This interpretation was supported by teleological considerations pertaining on the one hand to the economic purpose of the regulation (preventing the competition of cheap labor) and on the other hand to the need to preserve and support religious practice. Such considerations, while clearly pertaining to goals pursued by the legislator of the time, were not included in the linguistic meaning of its message, as intended by the legislator (who did not focus on the case of clergy when enacting this provision) and understood by its addressees (see Marmor, 2008, 427–429).

1.4.3 *Legal Construction and Creation of New Law*

The distinction between interpretation and construction is often mapped into the distinction between finding the existing law and creating new law. However, whether construction involves the creation of new law depends not only on the gap between the linguistic meaning of the input documents and the output of the construction, but also on views on the connection between law and political morality (i.e., ideas on justice, on the function of the State, on the relation between the State and its citizens).

In fact, constructions are often based on normative considerations pertaining to political morality, which are in principle irrelevant to the determination of linguistic meaning. However, whether such constructions may be considered as new laws also depends on assumptions concerning the nature of the law and its relationship with morality. If we assume that the law already contains (includes) moral-political reasons, then we may also assume that it already includes (implies) the constructions that are justified by such reasons, even before such constructions are adopted by the competent authorities, or become part of the shared legal culture. If we assume, on the contrary, that the law is based only on social sources, we should conclude that the law does not include any constructions that – while fitting good moral principles – have not yet been adopted by decision makers or by the community of legal experts.

Consider for instance the *Roe* v. *Wade* (1973) decision of the US Supreme Court, which ruled that the US Constitution implies a right to privacy, including a woman's liberty to have an abortion. This judgment was arguably based on a "political" view of the US Constitution that emphasized individual autonomy, the limitation of state power, and judicial activism. If we assume that these ideas pertain to the political morality (the view on how a State should be organized and what its relations to the citizens should be) that was most appropriate to the United States at that time, we can conclude that indeed *Roe* v. *Wade* was well decided. If we further assume that the law includes aspects of political morality, we may say that the ruling of this case was somehow, even before the decision, a part of the US law, being supported by the "best construction" of that law, according to valid principles of political morality. Note that this perspective assumes to some extent metaethical cognitivism, namely, the view that is possible to know what political morality requires (that political morality is not just a matter of preferences).

Thus, the view that the law includes principles and moral values leads us to the conclusion that correct constructions do not create new law, but are rather findings of what the law already is. This idea was developed in particular by Ronald Dworkin (1985), according to whom the purpose of legal reasoning in hard cases is to discover the best construction of the law, by balancing considerations of fit (adherence to history and social sources) and justification (political morality). A similar view was also developed by Robert Alexy (2002), according to whom there is a necessary connection between law and morality, so that the most morally justified interpretations of legal sources are part of the law, when the law is approached from the perspective of a participant in the legal system.

If we assume, on the contrary, that moral principles are not included in the law – regardless of their substantive merits – we must conclude that the *Roe* v. *Wade* decision was not implied by the preexisting US law; it rather consisted in a change in that law. Some may think that this change was welcome, given the urgency of the issue and the inertia of legislators; others that the same change should not have been made, either for its substantive wrongness, or since it violated principles of judicial deference. In both cases, however, the legal theorist refusing to merge law with political morality would conclude that the ruling of *Roe* v. *Wade* was not part of the preexisting law.

Thus, the view that legal construction creates new law is generally endorsed by those authors that adopt an exclusivist positivistic perspective, according to which the law only is determined by social facts, and in particular, by authoritative legal sources (see Marmor, 2002). Such social facts may also include legally relevant values and principles shared by the members of community or by legal scholars and decision makers, but such shared values and principles, given also the diversity of political preferences that usually coexist in a legal community, rarely support a single legal construction, to the exclusion of all alternatives.

1.4.4 *Conclusion on Understanding, Interpretation, and Construction*

The tripartition of the semantic field of legal interpretation into the three areas just presented – understanding, interpretation strictly understood, and construction – emphasizes important differences in the ways in which the legal significance of authoritative texts may be determined.

The notion of understanding points to the fact that the determination of the meaning of a linguistic expression – in legal reasoning as also in commonsense reasoning – is often the outcome of unreflected automatic cognitive processes. Only when doubts emerge, are the cognitive mechanisms for unconscious sentence comprehension supplemented by the conscious and reasoned analysis of alternative interpretations, and hopefully with the choice of one of them. Under this perspective, the opposition between understanding and interpretation may be descriptively relevant to distinguish different meaning-determinative processes. However, this opposition does not provide us with a criterion to determine in advance whether unreflected understanding or conscious interpretation is needed relatively to a certain text, since the need to switch from understanding to interpretation hangs on whether doubts emerge relatively to the meaning of the text, which does not depend only on the semantics of that text, but rather also on its context and on the information that is made available to the reader.

The notion of construction points to the fact that the determination of the legal effect of authoritative documents in some cases requires inputs that go beyond the linguistic resources available to the originators and the addressees of such documents at the time in which the documents were produced. In particular, such inputs may include considerations pertaining to political morality broadly understood. The distinction between interpretation strictly understood and construction is descriptively relevant, since it points to different aspects of meaning ascription process, which involve different premises and inferences. However, this distinction also fails to provide us with a clear criterion to determine in advance what approach is needed, since even when linguistic analysis gives a clear outcome, further considerations may indicate a different conclusion, and the choice of whether to give preference to linguistic or to other considerations may depend on evaluative assessments.

In conclusion, while the distinction among understanding, interpretation in a strict sense, and construction provides us with useful perspectives to look at meaning ascriptions in the legal domain, it is difficult to clearly demarcate the scope of these concepts. Therefore, we shall use the term "interpretation" to cover all meaning ascriptions to normative documents, including automatic ones (understanding) as well as those based on nonlinguistic clues (construction). We shall, however, occasionally use the terms "understanding" and "construction" respectively to point to instances of interpretation in which automatic determination of meaning or nonlinguistic elements are at stake.

1.4.5 *Interpretation and Semantics*

The distinctions just presented – understanding versus interpretation strictly understood versus construction – are based on the types and uses of the grounds used in interpretative reasoning: no ground is consciously considered in the automatic understanding; only linguistic-pragmatic grounds are taken into in interpretation in a strict sense; and extralinguistic grounds are used in construction.

A different classification, often used in civil law systems, focuses on the outcome of interpretation, more precisely on the relation between this outcome and the semantics of the text being interpreted, as resulting from linguistic rules. Three kinds of meaning ascriptions are correspondingly distinguished: (1) declarative interpretation, which assigns to the interpreted expression the meaning that is most immediate and plausible according to semantic rules and generally shared presuppositions; (2) extensive or restricted interpretation, which deviates from declarative meaning but is still consistent with linguistic conventions; and (3) analogy or reduction (exception), which provides for extensions or restrictions of the scope of a legal norm that do not fit usual linguistic conventions (see Figure 1.2). The distinction between extensive interpretation and analogy is particularly relevant in criminal law, in legal systems where the use of analogy is forbidden in that specific body of law.

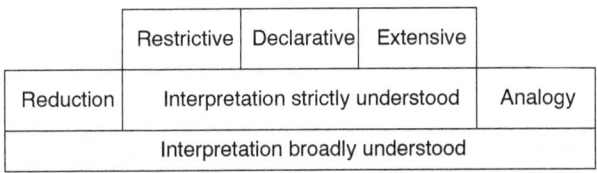

FIGURE 1.2 The scope of interpretations

Using the example of the rule "no vehicles in the park," we may say that an interpretation that views this rule as applying to all motor-powered vehicles capable of carrying an adult person may possibly be viewed as declarative. An interpretation that includes bicycles in the prohibition could be viewed as extensive, while an interpretation that excludes electric scooters could be viewed as restrictive. Finally, an interpretation that includes wheelbarrows could be viewed as analogical, while an interpretation that excludes golf carts could be viewed as a reduction.

As an example of the difference between extensive interpretation and analogy, consider the issue of unauthorized reproduction of software, as it was to be addressed in Italy before a new law was enacted (in 1983). The Italian judges approached the issue by referring to the provisions establishing civil damages and criminal sanctions for the unauthorized reproduction of literary works. They applied civil damages to the unauthorized reproduction of software, assimilating it through an analogy to the unauthorized reproduction of literary works. However, they did not apply criminal sanctions, considering that the expression "literary work" could not be interpreted as including software, even under the most extensive interpretation.

The difficulty in demarcating extensive interpretation from analogy is shown by another Italian case, which concerned a radio station (Vatican Radio) that emitted strong electromagnetic waves, allegedly causing nuisance and harm to people living nearby. The judges issued a (mild) criminal sanction against the managers of the radio, by applying extensively (though without the need of an analogy, according to their assessment) a criminal prohibition against causing harm and nuisance by "throwing things": they assumed that radio waves could be viewed as a kind of "thing," and that emitting radio waves could be viewed a way of "throwing" such "things." Whether this was really an extensive interpretation or rather a masqueraded analogy is an issue that cannot be addressed here (and for which probably no uncontroversial answer can be found).

As an example of reduction of the scope of a legal provision that goes beyond what appears to be its most restrictive linguistic interpretation, consider again the *Holy Trinity* case, where teleological interpretation led the US Supreme Court to exclude from the scope of the expression "labor or service of any kind" the service of a clergyman, which appears to be undoubtedly included in the semantic meaning of that phrase.

1.4.6 *Cognitive and Decisional Interpretation*

The distinction between interpretation in a strict sense and construction is connected, but not identical, to the distinction between scientific interpretation and political interpretation proposed by Hans Kelsen (1967, Ch. 8), and to the similar distinction between cognitive and decisional interpretation advanced by Guastini (2015). Such distinctions are based on the opposition between the identification of the different possible interpretative options that are offered by the legislative language, and the choice of one among such options (see also Pino, 2013), in the context of legal practice.

For Kelsen, scientific interpretation understood as the "cognitive ascertainment of the meaning of the object that is to be interpreted" can only determine "the frame which the law that is to be interpreted represents, and thereby the cognition of several possibilities within the frame" (Kelsen, 1967, 351). On the contrary, the selection of one of these meanings, for the purpose of legal decision, is not an act of cognition, but rather an act of will, which is inspired by political preferences. Thus, following Kelsen's analysis, the scientific determination of the meaning of the term "vehicle" in the example above would consist in distinguishing multiple alternative notions of a vehicle, as covering, for instance, all devices capable of transporting humans, or only motor-powered devices, and so on. The choice of one of those meanings would consist in a political determination, broadly understood, inspired by the fact that the interpreter attributes a prominence to the certain evaluative considerations. Such considerations may lead the interpreter, for instance, to include also bicycles in the scope of "vehicle," and consequently to make them forbidden in the park.

It seems that Kelsen's approach to scientific interpretation can be understood in two ways. According to a first perspective, the alternative meanings to be identified through scientific interpretation consist in the opportunities that are offered by the linguistic syntax and semantics of the provision being interpreted. In a second perspective, the meanings to be determined though scientific interpretation consist in the interpretative conclusions that are offered by all kinds of legal arguments in use. These interpretative conclusions may fail to include some grammatically possible meanings, but they may also go beyond what appears to be grammatically acceptable (as would happen when an analogy or a reduction is involved). The second approach is advocated by Guastini, for whom the cognitive interpretation aims to "identify, of a normative document, the different possible meanings (taking into account linguistic rules, different interpretative techniques being used, the dogmatic opinions widespread among jurists, etc.) without selecting any one of them" (Guastini, 2011, 27–28, authors' translation). Decisional interpretation, on the contrary, consists in selecting and arguing for one of these meanings.

Kelsen's analysis of interpretation provides for a descriptive approach to interpretation, which consists in mapping what appears to be admissible in the context of a certain language or legal culture. This analysis may however be the basis of a prescriptive approach to interpretation, which encourages the decision maker to refer to its individual conscience or moral/political preferences in making fundamental interpretative decisions, given that the law leaves a broad set of alternatives open for individual choice. This view is developed by Bobbitt (1991), who argues that when conflicting interpretations are possible, according to the available arguments, the choice should be a matter for the conscience of the decision maker.

The idea that linguistic meanings offer a range of possibilities to legal interpretation can also be linked to the famous distinction proposed by Hart (1958, 607) between the "core" meaning of general terms, which covers standard or prototypical cases of their application, and the surrounding penumbra. The penumbra includes "debatable cases" to which the application of the term is neither obvious nor obviously ruled out. These cases will "each have some features in common with the standard cases to which the concept is certainly applicable; they will lack other features or be accompanied by features not present in the standard case." Following this perspective, we might say that the range of possible linguistic interpretations of a general term is obtained by including or rather excluding from the meaning of the term any classes that are located in the term's penumbra. For example, both the inclusion of bicycles in the extension of the term "vehicle" and their exclusion from it may be viewed as distinct, linguistically possible, interpretations. The presence in a penumbral case of features that are in common with the standard cases for the application of the term may support arguments for the inclusion of the penumbral case in the term's meaning (extension), while the presence of different features may support arguments for its exclusion (see Section 3.1 below). Fuller (1957, 630) contrasted Hart's position, arguing for a prominent role for purpose and pragmatics in legal interpretation. Consequently, he observed that legal interpretations cannot be confined within the borders of the ordinary language meaning of the terms used by legislator.

1.5 REASONS IN INTERPRETATION: FROM TEXTS TO PURPOSES AND VALUES

The interpretation of legal or other normative texts has been the object of theoretical reflection from ancient times. For instance, in Roman law we can find the famous recommendation by Celsus that interpreters should not focus only on the literal meaning of the text to be interpreted, but rather address its purpose: "To know the laws doesn't mean to know the text of the law, but understanding its force and power," and that by Paulus, who pointed out that the "letter" should not be slavishly followed when it contradicts the "spirit."

In this section, we will not provide a full account of interpretative argumentation – as this will be developed in the following chapter – but rather briefly consider what main reasons can be advanced to support an interpretation.

1.5.1 *Reasons and Motives for Interpretation*

We may oppose on the one hand the *motives* of interpretation, namely, the psychological factors that may lead an interpreter to select one or another interpretation, and on the other hand the *reasons* for the interpretation, namely, those aspects that, within a certain legal culture, support a certain interpretation, that is, provide appropriate grounds for it. The motives of an interpretation may consist in any kind of psychological determinants: they may include whatever factors may induce a party to adopt one interpretation rather than another, they may pertain to individual interests as well as to social values, and they may be illicit as well as licit.

For instance, in 2001 the Court of Appeal of Palermo condemned an Italian judge in the Supreme Court of Cassation for collaborating with the Mafia. According to the Palermo Court, this judge had ordered the release of forty-two individuals accused of participating in organized crime (some of whom were well-known Mafia bosses), based on a peculiar interpretation of a statutory provision, which the judge had adopted in order to favor such individuals. This provision addressed the way of computing the detention time before conviction, for the purpose of establishing whether the maximum pre-conviction detention term had been reached, after which the accused should be released. It established that in the computation of the detention time before conviction, the time of trial sessions involving the accused individuals was not to be included. This provision had been created to address the fact that the defendants used various delaying tactics to prolong trials in order to reach the maximum pre-conviction detention time before the end of the proceedings, so that they could be released. The accused judge, however, had interpreted this provision in such a way that that the non-inclusion of the trial sessions would require a specific judicial order to that effect. Since no such order had been issued in the proceedings involving the forty-two accused, the time of their trial sessions was included in the calculation of their pre-conviction detention time. Consequently, it was determined that their detention had exceeded the maximum time, and they were released.

The Court of Palermo considered that the accused judge had adopted this interpretation precisely to favor the Mafia bosses, to whom he was connected, and convicted him for the crime of "external participation in mafia association" (in Italian, "*concorso esterno in associazione mafiosa*"). His conviction was then annulled by the Italian Supreme Court, who argued that there was no decisive evidence that the judge had adopted this interpretation for this unlawful purpose; he might as well have genuinely opined that this was the legally correct interpretation of the statutory provision at issue, an opinion supported by appropriate – through by no means univocal – legal clues.

For our purpose, it is sufficient to remark that the purpose of obtaining the release of the Mafia bosses could have been a (unlawful) motive for adopting the interpretation but could not have constituted a reason for it, in the context of Italian law at the time.

1.5.2 *Reasons for Interpretations*

Let us now focus on what may count as acceptable inputs for a legal interpretation, inputs that may not only motivate the interpreter to adopt that interpretation but may also be viewed as valid reasons justifying the adoption of the interpretation.

In continental Europe, the analysis of legal interpretation by Carl von Savigny (1840) has been particularly influential, and is often reproduced, sometimes with refinements and additions, in many accounts of legal interpretation. Savigny, after affirming that interpretation has the purpose to "reconstruct the thought dwelling in the law," distinguishes four "elements" of interpetation: the grammatical, the logical, the historical, and the systematic. The grammatical element concerns the semantic meaning of the words used by the legislator according to linguistic rules. The logical element consists in combining word meanings to determine the meaning of whole provisions. The historical element concerns the changes that the text was meant to produce in the historical context in which it was enacted. The systematic element addresses the relation between the text being interpreted and the entire system of law.

To these four elements, Savigny adds a fifth, the ground of the law (*ratio legis*), and distinguishes two aspect thereof: previous high-level laws, to be implemented through the law being interpreted, and the objectives pursued by the legislator. He argues that while the ground is no part of the content of the law strictly understood, it can be cautiously used to determine that content.

In the many years that have passed since Savigny's account, multiple approaches and ideas have been presented to develop or attack his analysis. In particular, various approaches to interpretation have focused on what Savigny called "the grounds of law," namely the objective or purpose of the text being interpreted. This idea has been prominent since the end of the nineteenth century in continental and common law legal cultures, which tended toward what is also called legal pragmatism, namely, the view that legal provisions are tools used by legislator to achieve certain ends, and should be interpreted accordingly (Jhering, 1913; Holmes, 1899).

Various trends in legal theory and judicial practice, both in the civil law and in the common law domain, have indeed emphasized the role of purpose in interpretation, and the possibility to override the prima facie meaning of legal texts in order to achieve certain social goals or to protect certain interests. Originally the idea of purpose was focused on the objective pursued by the legislator, or on how the legislator meant to adjudicate between competing interests (according to the so-called jurisprudence of interests, see Heck, 1914). Following World War II, the first aspect of the "ground of law" as indicated by Savigny, namely the reference to higher laws, has become prominent. In the context of international and regional human right charters and of national constitutions, the teleological analysis has been driven by the rights and social goals indicated in such documents. As interpretation aims at multiple purposes, involving competing rights and values, proportionality (Alexy, 1989) becomes a key aspect of it (Bongiovanni and Valentini, 2018; Sartor, 2018). Purposive interpretation has become so dominant that it tends to absorb all the other elements of interpretation (Barak, 2007).

1.5.3 *The Semantics of Words and their Combinations*

The first element of interpretation, according to Savigny's account, consists in the meaning of the single terms used in a legislative provision. Usually, it is not necessary to point at the semantic rules specifying such meanings, these rules being shared and undisputed presuppositions. However, a discussion on linguistic meanings is relevant in some controversial cases. For example, in *ACLU* v. *Clapper*, 785 F.3d 787 (2015), the American Civil Liberties Union argued that the mass collection of phone metadata by the US government was not authorized by Section 215 of the Patriot Act, which only authorized the collection of data "relevant to investigation." In agreeing with the ACLU, the judges cited the definition of "investigation" in the Oxford dictionary: "examine (a matter) systematically or in detail; to make an inquiry or examination into." They excluded that the mass collection of data to identify suspects to be inquired or to support future inquiries would qualify as an "investigation" according to this linguistic specification.

The second element to be considered, in Savigny's list, is the way in which words are combined into sentences. The "compositional" meaning resulting from the combination of word meanings into syntactic structures is usually noncontroversial, since only one such combination is syntactically correct, or at least only one stands out as being clearly more sensible than others. However, in some cases syntax comes to the fore; when the legislative provision allows for multiple equally plausible syntactic structures, the choice among them becomes legally relevant (for a further analysis, see our Section 3.2). For instance, in Case C-486/12 the European Court of Justice had to interpret Article 12 of the 1995 Data Protection Directive, which gives data subjects the right to obtain a copy of their data "without excessive delay or expense." The issue to be addressed was whether data controllers could require data subjects to pay a small fee in order to obtain the data. The answer to this issue depended on whether the locution "without excessive delay or expense" was to be read as "without excessive delay and without excessive expense" or rather as "without excessive delay and without any expense," namely, on whether the scope of "excessive" covers both "delay" and "expense," or whether it only concerns "delay." Following the first interpretation, the request of nonexcessive fees would be permissible; following the second it would be forbidden, that is, the data subject would have the right to obtain the data at no cost.

The court examined how this provision was expressed in other languages (in EU law, legal documents are delivered in all official languages, each version having the same legal value). In French, as in other languages in which adjectives are postponed to the word they qualify, the adopted formulation ("*sans délais ou frais excessifs*") indicated unambiguously that the term "excessive" also applied to expenses. Thus, the judges adopted the latter interpretation, as required by the interpretative principle, often used by the ECJ, that multilingual legislative documents should preferably be given meanings that are compatible with all linguistic versions.

1.5.4 *The Historical Context in Which the Legislative Text Was Adopted*

The extent to which legal interpretation depends on historical context is at the center of the debate between the so-called originalist and evolutionary (or living tree) doctrines. According to the originalist perspective, the correct interpretation of a legal text is permanently fixed by the legal-cultural-social context existing at the time when that text was enacted; according to the evolutionary perspective, interpretation may change through time, and reflect the evolution of law, politics, and culture. As an important example of a decision inspired by an originalist approach, we can mention *District of Columbia* v. *Heller*, by the US Supreme Court on

June 26, 2008. This decision, adopted with a 5–4 majority, struck down a District of Columbia statute prohibiting the possession of useable handguns in the home, on the ground that this prohibition violates the Second Amendment to the US Constitution, which reads "A well-regulated Militia, being necessary to the security of a free State, the right of the people to keep and bear Arms, shall not be infringed." According to Justice Scalia's majority opinion, this article also covers the right to possess weapons for the purpose of individual self-defense, a conclusion that is reached by considering the English law of the time, which, according to Justice Scalia, included a right to bear arms for self-defense (for a critical discussion see Solum, 2009).

   As is well known, the idea of originalism can be approached in multiple ways. A key distinction is that between "original intent," namely, the purpose pursued by the legislator, as it can be retrieved by parliamentary debates and preparatory materials, and "original meaning," namely, the understanding of the people at the time, given the culture and legal system of the day. An example of an interpretation inspired by original intent may possibly be found in the *Slaughter-House Cases*, decided by the US Supreme Court in 1873. These cases concerned a Louisiana statute that conferred to a single corporation a monopoly over the New Orleans slaughtering business. The law was considered to be consistent with the Fourteenth Amendment, granting all citizens "equal protection of the laws," since, according to the judges, the Fourteenth Amendment had only one "pervading purpose" at the time in which it was enacted, the protection of the newly emancipated slaves (it did not apply to commercial companies).

   A number of approaches exist on how to understand originalism, or how to combine it with the need to take into account the evolution of the law, culture, and social attitudes (see for instance Balkin, 2018). The reference to original intent may be substituted by a reference to hypothetical intent (what legislators would have intended to establish through the provision at stake had they been rational, or respectful of fundamental legal principles), or to the present legislators (what would today's legislators have intended to establish through such a provision). For instance, one may argue with regard to the prohibition of "cruel and unusual punishments" that had the US legislators of the time been aware as we are today of the sufferings caused by the implementation of a death penalty and of its current unusualness, they would have considered it to be both cruel and unusual.

1.5.5 *Coherence with Other Norms, and with the Purposes of the Norm and of the Systems*

Finally, the idea that norms have to be put in the context of the legal system as a whole, and be coherent with it, plays a key role in interpretative reasoning (on coherence, see Peczenik, 2005, Chapter 4). This traditional requirement has acquired a particular relevance in the context of fundamental rights and more generally of constitutional provisions, where it supports the choice of interpretations that best fit constitutional principles.

As a recent example, consider the judgment adopted by the European Court of Justice in *Scarlet v. Sabam* (2012), where the ECJ had to determine whether a Belgian judge could order an internet service provider (Scarlet) to filter all communications in order to identify unlawful downloads of copyrights materials. The ECJ had to interpret Article 15 of the 2000 eCommerce Directive, which prohibits member states from establishing "general obligation on providers ... to monitor the information which they transmit or store" or "to seek facts or circumstances indicating unlawful activity." The court – by considering this provision in the context of the EU directives on the protection of intellectual property and the fundaments right to privacy, economic initiative, and intellectual property – concluded that EU law precludes injunctions obliging providers to filter all communications in order to identify the transmissions of copyrighted content.

A very controversial example is a recent Italian legislative provision (Article 4 of legislative decree 113/2018), according to which a residence permit granted further to an asylum application "does not amount to a registration as a resident." The purpose of this provision, as explicitly stated by the leaders of the majority parties in parliamentary debates and in the media, was to prevent asylum applicants from being registered as residents (and obtaining the social benefits that are dependent upon residence). However, the Civil Court of Florence (order 361/2019) ordered a municipality to accept a request for registration presented by a person whose asylum application was still pending. The judge argued that the new provision – to be coherent with other Italian rules that conferred residence based on the ascertained determination to settle on a municipality, as well as with requirement of equality and nondiscrimination in the Italian Constitution – should not be interpreted as excluding asylum applicants from the registration of residence. According to the judge, the provision should rather be interpreted as affirming that the mere presentation of an asylum application was insufficient to this purpose; the application had to be combined with the applicant's determination to reside in the city in which he or she was applying for residence. By adopting an interpretation that contradicted the clear intention of the legislator enacting the interpreted provision, the judge in this case refused to act as an agent of that legislator, his refusal being based on consideration pertaining to coherence with other laws (enacted by previous legislators) and with constitutional norms, as interpreted by the judge.

The coherence between a specific provision and other provisions in the legal system was also at stake in *Dunnachie v. Kingston-upon-Hull City Council*, discussed by MacCormick (2005). This case concerns a claim for a compensation for non-pecuniary damages by an employee who had been unfairly dismissed, and as a result claimed to have suffered humiliation, injury to feelings, and distress. The key issues to be addressed in this case pertained to the interpretation of Section 123(1) of the UK Employment Rights Act 1996, which reads that "the amount of the compensatory award shall be such amount as the tribunal considers just and equitable in all the circumstances having regard to the loss sustained by the complainant in consequence of the dismissal." To determine whether the claimant should be compensated not only for his financial losses, but also for his psychological harm, the scope of the expression "loss" had to be determined. The employee argued that an interpretation of this provision in the context of, and in coherence with, all the relevant sections of the statute would grant him the recovery of *losses* other than financial losses narrowly construed. The employer argued that the relevant sections of the current UK legislation only allows for the recovery of *financial loss*, this interpretation corresponding to the ordinary meaning of the expression "loss."

1.6 ARGUMENT SCHEMES IN LEGAL INTERPRETATION

From the argumentation perspective, an interpretative statement – namely, the claim that a certain legislative expression should be interpreted in a certain way – is a claim that can be supported through arguments. These arguments can be attacked by other arguments, which, in their turn, may the object of further attacks. For instance, in Italian law there has been, through the years, a progressive extension of the kinds of damages that can be indemnified under civil law. The starting point of the debate was the established view that the notion of indemnifiable loss covers only pecuniary losses, since this is usually the meaning of "loss" in ordinary language and in legal tradition. A counterargument was built for the conclusion that non-pecuniary "losses" (e.g., permanent physical impairments, such as disability or disfigurement, that do not affect one's capability to earn through one's work) should also be compensated, based on the view that physical integrity and health are rights established in certain provisions of the Italian Constitution, directly enforceable in court. This counterargument was endorsed by the Italian judiciary, even though it was contested on the ground that recognizing compensation for non-pecuniary losses would lead to increased litigation, insurance cost, and so on. The latter counter-counterargument was in its turn attacked by arguing on the one hand that the realization of constitutional values should be a prevailing concern, and on the other hand that the inconveniences resulting from the compensation for non-pecuniary damages could be limited by defining precise standardized criteria for computing the amount of damages for non-pecuniary losses.

As this example shows, the process of the justification of an interpretation may consist in a dialectical process involving the construction or arguments and counter-arguments. The outcome of the process consists in an architecture of arguments and counterarguments that as a whole supports the interpretative claim (we shall provide a precise analysis in Chapter 6).

In the following we shall present three lists of types of argument (which we refer to as "argument schemes") provided by leading legal theorists – Giovanni Tarello, Neil MacCormick and Robert Summers, and Jack Balkin – at different points in time

(1980, 1991, and 2018), and with regard to different cultural contexts (Italy, worldwide comparison, and US constitutional law).

1.6.1 *Tarello's List of Interpretative Arguments*

The Italian legal philosopher Giovanni Tarello (1980, Chapter 8) lists fourteen types of interpretative arguments:

1. *Arguments a contrario* reject interpretations departing from literal meaning.
2. *Analogical arguments* support interpretations according to which the meaning of an expression in a legal provision is extended to apply a rule to a case not regulated by the given provision (a case which is included in neither the core nor the periphery of the application area of the provision), but presents a relevant similarity with the cases covered by it.
3. *Arguments a fortiori* support interpretations according to which a legal provision is applied to cases that are not covered by the terms of that provision, but deserve, to a higher degree, the same discipline as the cases covered by the provision.
4. *Arguments from completeness of the legal regulation* exclude interpretations that create legal gaps.
5. *Arguments from the coherence of the legal regulation* exclude interpretations of different legal statements that make them conflicting.
6. *Psychological arguments* support interpretations driven by the actual intent of the authors of the text.
7. *Historical arguments* support interpretations giving a legal statement the same meaning that was traditionally attributed to other statements governing the same matter.
8. *Apagogical arguments* exclude interpretations that generate absurdities.
9. *Teleological arguments* support interpretations contributing to a purpose pertaining to the goals or interests that the law is supposed to promote.
10. *Nonredundancy arguments* exclude interpretations that would make the interpreted expression superfluous under the assumption that the legislator does not make useless normative statements.
11. *Authoritative arguments* support interpretations already given by authoritative courts or scholars.
12. *Naturalistic arguments* support interpretations aligning a legal statement to human nature or the nature of the matter regulated by that statement.
13. *Arguments from equity* support (exclude) (un)fair or (un)just interpretations.
14. *Arguments from general principles* support (exclude) interpretations that are supported by (incompatible with) general principles of the legal system.

Tarello's list, while being based on Italian legal practice, has been referred to in Perelman (1979), who discusses it with examples from French and Belgian law.

1.6.2 *MacCormick and Summers*

MacCormick and Summers (1991), in synthesizing the outcome of a comparative inquiry into statutory interpretation, identify a list of eleven kinds of interpretative arguments.

1. *Arguments from ordinary meaning* require that a term should be interpreted according to the meaning that a native speaker would ascribe to it.
2. *Arguments from technical meaning* require that a term having a technical meaning and occurring in a technical context should be interpreted according to its technical meaning.
3. *Arguments from contextual harmonization* require that a term included in a statute or set of statutes should be interpreted in line with the whole statute or set.
4. *Arguments from precedent* require that a term should be interpreted in a way that fits previous judicial interpretations.
5. *Arguments from statutory analogy* require that a term should be interpreted in a way that preserves the similarity of meaning with similar provisions in other statutes.
6. *Arguments from a legal concept* require that a term should be interpreted in line with the way it has been previously recognized and doctrinally elaborated in law.
7. *Arguments from general principle* require that a term should be interpreted in a way that is most in conformity with general legal principles already established.
8. *Arguments from history* require that a term should be interpreted in line with the historically evolved understanding of it.
9. *Arguments from purpose* require that a term should be interpreted in a way that fits a purpose that can be ascribed to the statutory provision, or whole statute, in which the term occurs.
10. *Arguments from substantive reasons* require that a term should be interpreted in line with a goal that is fundamentally important to the legal order.
11. *Arguments from intention* require that a term should be interpreted in line with the intention of the legislative authority.

MacCormick (2005) proposes grouping interpretative arguments into three main supercategories, over the above categories of interpretative arguments.

1. *Linguistic arguments* appeal to the linguistic context of a provision to support its interpretation (they are definitional arguments, according to Macagno and Walton, 2015, 2017). Linguistic arguments may include the first three items in the above list by MacCormick and Summers (1991).

2. *Systemic arguments* take into account the special context of the authoritative text within the legal system. Such arguments merge the authority of the source with the reconstruction of definitions from the text. Systemic arguments may include items 4 through 8 in the above list.
3. *Teleological-evaluative arguments* make sense of a text in light of its aim or goal (they are classified as pragmatic arguments by Macagno and Walton, 2015). Teleological-evaluative arguments may include items from 9 to 11 in the above list.

1.6.3 Balkin's List of Interpretative Arguments

As a recent list of argument types we can mention the proposal by Balkin (2018, 181–183), which focuses on US constitutional law, and is to some extent based on the analysis proposed by Bobbitt (1982).

1. *Arguments from text*, including arguments about definitions of words and phrases in the text; arguments that compare and contrast different parts of the text; arguments that compare the text with other texts; and arguments that employ traditional canons of statutory interpretation.
2. *Arguments about constitutional structure* and the structural logic of the constitutional system.
3. *Arguments from purpose*, including arguments about the purposes, intentions, and expectations of the people who lived at the time of the adoption of the Constitution and its subsequent amendments, as well as purposes attributed to the Constitution over time.
4. *Arguments from consequences*, concerning the likely consequences of interpreting the Constitution in one way rather than another.
5. *Arguments from judicial precedent*, based on previous judicial decisions, about what is holding and what is *dicta*, about what is controlling authority and what is merely persuasive authority.
6. *Arguments from political convention*, concerning political conventions and settlements that arise within institutions or branches of government, or among institutions or branches of government.
7. *Arguments from the people's customs and lived experience*, considering the public's customs, expectations, and ways of life and whether a proposed interpretation of the Constitution will conform to, vindicate, assist, defy, or disrupt them.
8. *Arguments from natural law or natural rights*, concerning rights that governments exist to secure and protect (natural rights), as well as what kinds of laws are necessary to protect human flourishing (natural law).
9. *Arguments from national ethos*, appealing to the character of the nation and its institutions and to important, widely shared, and widely honored values of Americans and American culture.

10. *Arguments from political tradition*, appealing to cultural memory, to the meaning of key events in American political history, and to the lessons to be drawn from those events.
11. *Arguments from honored authority*, appealing to the values, beliefs, and examples of cultural heroes in American life.

1.6.4 *The Legislator's Intention*

An important role in interpretative reasoning is played by what MacCormick (2005) calls "appeal to the lawmaker's intention." This idea, however, is controversial and can be understood in different ways.

First of all, we need to distinguish between the private, or sometimes illegal, goals that contribute to the choices of individual members of a legislative body (e.g., obtaining financial contributions in exchange for measures that favor certain individuals or companies), and the social goals that such members aim to achieve through their choices. Only the second kind of goals may be viewed as intentions of the legislator as a public body.

Second, we need to distinguish between the goals that were pursued by the legislator and the means that that the legislator intended to prescribe in order to achieve such goals. It may happen that a provision would achieve the goals aimed at by the legislator only if it were given a meaning that is different from what was intended by the legislator. For instance, a provision introducing a new tax may be effective only if it were applied differently from how the legislator apparently intended, to counter ways of eluding the tax that the legislator had not considered.

Third, we need to distinguish between those social goals that are pursued as a matter of fact by the legislator, according to its political ideology and vision of the public good, and the goal that the legislator should pursue, according to legal principles, constitutional requirements, and shared standards of political morality.

The three issues just mentioned lead to the distinction between the empirical intention that the historical legislator had, in issuing a certain provision, and the intentions that could be attributed to an ideal or rational legislator, in issuing the same provision. The distinction between the real and the ideal legislator's intention is complicated by the fact that what can be attributed to an ideal legislator is also dependent on the interpreter's views (1) on the most efficient ways to achieve the legislator's goals, (2) on the goals that should or should not be pursued by the legislator according to constitutional requirements and political morality, and (3) on the extent to which political morality and constitutional requirements should override the legislator's preferences. This issue is manifest in cases like that the above-mentioned case concerning immigrants' right to obtain residence, in which the judge refused to act as an agent of the Italian legislator, according to his view on the applicable constitutional principles.

The arguments that support interpretations based on the intention of the legislator, as observed by MacCormick (2005), tend to have a transcategorial nature: they tend to range across all interpretative schemes, as linguistic, systemic, or teleological-evaluative considerations can support the attribution of intentions to legislators (see Chapter 6). For instance, let us assume that the legislator has competently used ordinary language to express its intention in framing a provision. In this case, the interpretation of that provision that fits ordinary language will also capture the intention of the legislator. Similarly, if we assume that the legislator competently framed its provision in awareness of how it would fit with other legal provisions and principles, then the interpretation that most coheres with such provisions and principles will best meet the legislator's intention.

1.6.5 *Criteria for Comparing Interpretative Arguments*

As Karl Llewellin (1949) famously observed, different canons for legal interpretation may apply to the same provision and lead to opposite outcomes. In such cases a choice may be required of one among the alternative interpretative outcomes. For instance, in the *Dunnachie* case mentioned above, a choice was required between the outcome of an ordinary language argument, according to which the expression "loss" would be interpreted as "pecuniary loss," and the outcome of a teleological argument, according to which that expression would be interpreted as including also categories of non-pecuniary harm.

When a conflict of interpretative argument arises, the issue to be decided is which of such arguments should take the lead. The law may provide some general criteria for dealing with certain conflicts of this sort, though often such criteria fail to provide decisive clues. Alexy and Dreier (1991, 95–98) cite criteria such as the following: (1) in criminal law, arguments from ordinary meaning have priority over arguments from technical meaning; (2) in criminal law, generic arguments based on the intention of the legislator have priority over arguments not based on authority, but do not have priority over linguistic arguments. Similarly, it could be argued that considerations pertaining to constitutional principles are most relevant where fundamental rights are at stake, while considerations pertaining to legislative intention, or to teleology, are most relevant where economic or social policies are at issue.

There may be two ways to approach conflicts between interpretative arguments, and solve the legal indeterminacies resulting from the lack of decisive indication on how to adjudicate such conflicts.

The first, more optimistic, approach may consist in assuming that all indeterminacies are caused by the fact that the strength of interpretative canons is context dependent, and indeed related to the extent to which the rationale of each canon applies to the situation being considered. For instance, we may agree that an argument based on ordinary language tends to be stronger the more the ordinary language is univocal in a legal text, and the more it is important that people's expectations are respected (e.g., in the definition of crimes). Thus, even if it is not possible to determine in the abstract which canon should prevail in all cases, it should be possible to build reasonable arguments on why one canon should prevail over the opposed canon in any given context.

The second, less optimistic, approach, more consonant to realistic traditions in legal theory, assumes that whenever the law fails to give a clear answer to a conflict of interpretation, there is no shared or rational way to approach the matter: it is up to judicial discretion or to judicial conscience to decide one way or the other, according to the ethical or political preferences.

1.6.6 *Rationales for Interpretative Canons*

Interpretative argument schemes have a double nature.

On the one hand, they may merely be viewed as conventions for legal reasoning, namely, positive components of a certain legal system (participating in legal tradition and culture) that determine what is generally considered as a relevant argument in that system. Under this perspective, interpretative argument schemes do not need justification; the justification of their use within a legal system consists in the mere fact that they are part of it, so that their use is indeed authorized by the conventions, or the "grammar," of that legal system (for this idea, see Patterson, 1996). Following this approach, no legally relevant criticism can be brought against the way in which such schemes are currently used in legal reasoning. Thus, if an originalist approach to interpretation is used within a certain jurisdiction, this would be part of the grammar or language game currently in use in that jurisdiction, and could not be critically addressed from a legal perspective.

On the other hand, interpretative schemes may be viewed as appropriate ways to achieve legal determinations, which can be assessed according to the outcomes that are obtained through their use, relatively to the legal and social values at stake. Under this second, critical, perspective, interpretative argument schemes and their relative importance may be supported by reasons and subject to criticisms, and such reasons and criticisms may be relevant to their legal use. Interpretative schemes may be supported by rationales pointing to the beneficial outcomes resulting from their application in favorable contexts or can be contested based on the negative outcomes resulting from their application in unfavorable contexts.

The latter approach is developed by Walton and Sartor (2013), who argue that for establishing whether an argument scheme should be used in a dialogue, a party to that dialogue may consider:

1. to what extent the use of the scheme by that party is likely to lead the party to appropriate epistemic or practical conclusions;
2. to what extent the use of the scheme by that party is likely to advance that party's goals in the dialogue; and

3. to what extent the use of the scheme by that party is likely to advance the goals (and values) underlying the dialogue itself and the practice in which it is embedded.

Argument schemes such as those listed above can indeed be provided with appropriate rationales that pertain to the legal process and the functioning of the legal systems. For instance, the ordinary language canon can be supported by considerations pertaining to legal certainty (citizens tend to form expectations concerning the application and enforcement of legal rules, based on the ordinary language meaning of legislative texts), the division of powers (respect for ordinary language may limit judicial discretion and abuses of judicial power), formal equality (the generality of ordinary language may prevent idiosyncratic interpretations), and so on (for some consideration on the importance of ordinary language, see Beccaria 1764, Chapter 4). Ordinary language arguments could also be supported by the rationale of respecting the legislative intention, to the extent that it can be assumed that the legislator was carefully using ordinary language to express its intentions.

Similarly, arguments from coherence can be supported by considering that the expectations based on different legal norms, as well as the acts through which such norms are complied with and applied (by citizens, administrators, and judges), should not interfere with one another, but rather operate in a synergetic way.

The reliance on some inference schemes is often criticized in legal reasoning. For instance, a debate on the merits and limits of different kinds of originalism persists in US law, while in Continental legal systems there is an ongoing debate on the extent to which precedents should be followed. In both such debates, reasons pertaining to legal certainty and limitation of judicial discretion are opposed to reasons in favor of innovation, experimentation, and adaptation to new context and values.

In considering the merit of using certain argument schemes, we should consider that legal arguments can be used correctly or incorrectly, and they can be suitable for a specific context while being inappropriate for other contexts. In particular, we need to take into account whether the reasoners who are supposed to use an argument scheme have the cognitive capacities to apply it correctly, considering their institutional role, competence, and resources. For instance, it may be argued that judges should not base their interpretations on controversial moral appreciations, or on complex economical assessments, since they have neither the resources nor the legitimation to engage in such assessments (see Sunstein and Vermeule, 2003).

The evaluation of shared argument schemes must take into account the fact that coordination in argumentation may be a value in itself: the mere fact that an argumentative convention is in place may provide a reason to stick to that convention, even when the convention is not optimal relative to other possible conventions. Thus, the mere fact that an argument scheme is generally adopted may support its persistent adoption, as long as having that additional argument scheme in the legal repertoire is better than not having it, and no smooth transition to a better alternative is available (see Walton and Sartor, 2013). This can explain why the use of argument schemes in legal reasoning shows both conventionality and path dependency. Once a certain reasoning scheme has become established, not only is it individually convenient to use it, but its general use contributes to shape interactions, support dialogues, and provide mutual acceptance and stability.

REFERENCES

Abaelardus, Petrus. 1970. *Dialectica*. Edited by Lambertus Marie de Rijk. Assen, Netherlands: Van Gorcum.

Abbott, Martin Lee. 2016. *Using Statistics in the Social and Health Sciences with SPSS and Excel*. Hoboken, NJ: John Wiley & Sons.

Alexy, Robert. 1989. *A Theory of Legal Argumentation: The Theory of Rational Discourse as Theory of Legal Justification*. Edited by Neil McCormick and Ruth Adler. Oxford, UK: Clarendon Press.

Alexy, Robert. 2002. *The Argument from Injustice. A Reply to Legal Positivism*. Oxford, UK: Oxford University Press.

Alexy, Robert, and Ralf Dreier. 1991. "Statutory interpretation in the Federal Republic of Germany." In *Interpreting Statutes. A Comparative Study*, edited by Neil MacCormick and Robert Summers, 73–121. Aldershot, UK: Dartmouth.

Bacon, Francis. 2000. *The New Organon [Novum Organum, 1627]*. Edited by Lisa Jardine and Michael Silverthorne. Cambridge, UK: Cambridge University Press.

Balkin, Jack M. 2018. "Arguing about the constitution: The topics in constitutional interpretation." *Constitutional Commentary* 33: 145–255.

Barak, Aharon. 2007. *Purposive Interpretation in Law*. Princeton, NJ: Princeton University Press.

Beccaria, Cesare. 1764. *Dei Delitti e delle Pene*. Livorno. Livorno, Italy: Coltellini.

Bobbitt, Philip. 1982. *Constitutional Fate: Theory of the Constitution*. Oxford, UK: Oxford University Press.

Bobbitt, Philip. 1991. *Constitutional Interpretation*. Oxford, UK: Blackwell Publishers Ltd.

Bongiovanni, Giorgio, and Chiara Valentini. 2018. "Balancing, proportionality and constitutional rights." In *Handbook of Legal Reasoning and Argumentation*, edited by Giorgio Bongiovanni, Gerald Postema, Antonino Rotolo, Giovanni Sartor, Chiara Valentini, and Douglas Walton, 581–612. Dordrecht, Netherlands: Springer.

Cicero, Marcus Tullius. 1999. *On the Commonwealth and on the Laws*. Edited by James Zetzel. Cambridge, UK: Cambridge University Press.

Conte, Rosaria, and Cristiano Castelfranchi. 2006. "The mental path of norms." *Ratio Juris* 19 (4): 501–517. https://doi.org/10.1111/j.1467–9337.2006.00342.x.

Dascal, Marcelo, and Jerzy Wróblewski. 1988. "Transparency and doubt: Understanding and interpretation in pragmatics and in law." *Law and Philosophy* 7(2): 203–224. https://doi.org /10.1007/BF00144156.

Davies, Stephen. 2007. *Philosophical Perspectives on Art*. Oxford, UK: Oxford University Press.

Dennett, Daniel. 1997. "True believers: The intentional stance and why it works." In *Mind Design II: Philosophy, Psychology, and Artificial Intelligence*, edited by John Haugeland, 57–79. Cambridge, MA: MIT Press.

Dilthey, Wilhelm. 1989. *Selected Works. Volume I: Introduction to the Human Sciences*. Edited by Rudolf Makkreel and Frithjof Rodi. Princeton, NJ: Princeton University Press.

Dworkin, Ronald. 1985. "Is there really no right answer in hard cases?" In *A Matter of Principle*, edited by Ronald Dworkin, 119–145. Cambridge, MA: Harvard University Press.

Fish, Stanley. 1989. *Doing What Comes Naturally: Change, Rhetoric, and the Practice of Theory in Literary and Legal Studies*. Oxford, UK: Clarendon Press.

Freud, Sigmund. 1965. *The Interpretation of Dreams [Die Traumdeutung, 1900]*. New York, NY: Avon Books.

Fuller, Lon. 1957. "Positivism and fidelity to law – A reply to Professor Hart." *Harvard Law Review* 71(4): 630–672.

Fuller, Lon. 1981. *The Principles of Social Order*. Edited by Kenneth Winston. Durham, NC: Duke University Press.

Gadamer, Hans-Georg. 1989. *Truth and Method*. Edited by Joel Weinsheimer and Donald Marshall. New York, NY: Continuum.

Galilei, Galileo. 1960. "The assayer [Il Saggiatore, 1623]." In *The Controversy on the Comets of 1618*, edited by Stillman Drake and Charles Donald O'Malley, 151–336. Philadelphia, PA: University of Pennsylvania Press.

Grice, Paul. 1975. "Logic and conversation." In *Syntax and Semantics 3: Speech Acts*, edited by Peter Cole and Jerry Morgan, 41–58. New York, NY: Academic Press.

Grice, Paul. 1969. "Utterer's meaning and intention." *The Philosophical Review* 78(2): pp. 147–177.

Guastini, Riccardo. 2011. *Interpretare e Argomentare*. Milano, Italy: Giuffrè.

Guastini, Riccardo. 2015. "A realistic view on law and legal cognition." *Revus. Journal for Constitutional Theory and Philosophy of Law/Revija Za Ustavno Teorijo in Filozofijo Prava*, 27: 45–54. https://doi.org/10.4000/revus.3304

Hart, Herbert Lionel Adolphus. 1958. "Positivism and the separation of law and morals." *Harvard Law Review* 71(4): 593–629.

Heck, Philipp. 1914. "Gesetzesauslegung und Interessenjurisprudenz." *Archiv Für Die Civilistische Praxis* 112(1): 1–318.

Holmes, Oliver Wendell. 1899. "The theory of legal interpretation." *Harvard Law Review* 12: 417–420. https://doi.org/10.2307/1321531.

Jhering, Rudolf von. 1913. *Law as a Means to an End*. Boston, MA: The Boston Book Company.

Kelsen, Hans. 1967. *Pure Theory of Law*. Berkeley, CA: University of California Press.

Llewellyn, Karl. 1949. "Remarks on the theory of appellate decision and the rules or canons about how statutes are to be construed." *Vanderbilt Law Review* 3: 395–406.

Macagno, Fabrizio, and Douglas Walton. 2015. "Classifying the patterns of natural arguments." *Philosophy and Rhetoric* 48(1): 26–53. https://doi.org/10.1353/par.2015.0005.

Macagno, Fabrizio, and Douglas Walton. 2017. "Arguments of statutory interpretation and argumentation schemes." *International Journal of Legal Discourse* 2(1): 47–83.

MacCormick, Neil. 2005. *Rhetoric and the Rule of Law*. Oxford, UK: Oxford University Press.

MacCormick, Neil, and Robert Summers, eds. 1991. *Interpreting Statutes: A Comparative Study*. Aldershot, UK: Dartmouth.

Marmor, Andrei. 2002. "Exclusive legal positivism." In *The Oxford Handbook of Jurisprudence and Philosophy of Law*, edited by Jules Coleman, Kenneth Einar Himma, and Scott Shapiro, 105–124. Oxford, UK: Oxford University Press.

Marmor, Andrei. 2008. "The pragmatics of legal language." *Ratio Juris* 21(4): 423–452. https://doi.org/10.1111/j.1467-9337.2008.00400.x.

McElduff, Siobhán. 2009. "Living at the level of the word: Cicero's rejection of the interpreter as translator." *Translation Studies* 2(2): 133–146.

Newman, Randy, Kelly Forbes, and John Connolly. 2012. "Event-related potentials and magnetic fields associated with spoken word." In *The Cambridge Handbook of*

Psycholinguistics, edited by Michael Spivey, Ken McRae, and Marc Joanisse, 127–156. Cambridge, UK: Cambridge University Press.

Pattaro, Enrico. 2005. *The Law and the Right*. Dordrecht, Netherlands: Springer.

Patterson, Dennis. 1996. *Law and Truth*. Oxford, UK: Oxford University Press.

Pearl, Judea. 2000. *Causality: Models, Reasoning and Inference*. Cambridge, MA: MIT Press.

Peczenik, Aleksander. 2005. *Scientia Juris: Legal Doctrine as Knowledge of Law and as a Source of Law*. Dordrecht, Netherlands: Springer.

Perelman, Chaïm. 1979. *Logique Juridique. Nouvelle Réthorique*. Paris, France: Dalloz.

Pino, Giorgio. 2013. "Interpretazione cognitiva, interpretazione decisoria, interpretazione creativa." *Rivista di Filosofia del Diritto* 2(1): 77–102.

Rener, Frederick. 1989. *Interpretatio: Language and Translation from Cicero to Tytler*. Leiden, Netherlands: Brill.

Sartor, Giovanni. 2018. "Defeasibility in law." In *Handbook of Legal Reasoning and Argumentation*, edited by Giorgio Bongiovanni, Gerald Postema, Antonino Rotolo, Giovanni Sartor, Chiara Valentini, and Douglas Walton, 315–364. Dordrecht, Netherlands: Springer.

Savigny, Friedrich Carl von. 1840. *System des Heutigen Römischen Rechts*. Berlin, Germany: Veit.

Searle, John. 2007. "Grice on meaning: 50 years later." *Teorema: Revista Internacional de Filosofía* 26(2): 9–18.

Soames, Scott. 2013. "Deferentialism: A post-originalist theory of legal interpretation." *Fordham Law Review* 82: 597–617.

Solum, Lawrence. 2009. "*District of Columbia v. Heller* and originalism." *Northwestern University Law Review* 103(2): 923–982.

Sunstein, Cass, and Adrian Vermeule. 2003. "Interpretation and institutions." *Michigan Law Review* 101(4): 885–951.

Tarello, Giovanni. 1980. *L'Interpretazione della Legge*. Milano, Italy: Giuffrè.

Vaan, Michiel De. 2008. *Etymological Dictionary of Latin and the Other Italic Languages*. Leiden, Netherlands, and Boston, MA: Brill.

Walton, Douglas, and Giovanni Sartor. 2013. "Teleological justification of argumentation schemes." *Argumentation* 27(2): 111–142. https://doi.org/10.1007/s10503-012-9262-y.

Weber, Max. 1978. *Economy and Society: An Outline of Interpretative Sociology*. Berkeley, CA: University of California Press.

CASES CITED

ACLU v. Clapper 2015 785 F.3d 787.

Church of the Holy Trinity v. United States 1892 143 U.S. 457.

District of Columbia v. Heller 2008. 554 U.S. 570.

Dunnachie v. Kingston-upon-Hull City Council 2004 UKHL 36.

Google Spain SL and Google Inc. v. Agencia Española de Protección de Datos (AEPD) and Mario Costeja González 2014 ECLI:EU:C:2014:317.

Rewe-Zentral v. Bundesmonopolverwaltung für Branntwein 1979 ECLI:EU:C:1979:42.

Roe v. Wade 1973. 410 U.S. 113.

Scarlet Extended SA v. Sabam 2012 ECLI:EU:C:2011:771.

X 2013, Case C-486/12, ECLI:EU:C:2013:836.

2

Statutory Interpretation as Problem Solving

2.1 INTRODUCTION

For many readers the paradigm of argumentation in a legal setting is that of the trial, an instance of the type of dialogue called the persuasion dialogue or critical discussion in the argumentation literature (van Eemeren and Grootendorst, 1992; Walton, 1999; Prakken, 2009). This setting is an adversarial one. For example, in a criminal case the prosecution's role is not only to support its claim that the defendant committed the crime by bringing forward evidence, but also to attack the arguments of the other side, defend its own arguments against these attacks, and prove its own claim to the standard required, that of beyond reasonable doubt. With this paradigm in mind, it is easy to jump to the generalization that legal argumentation is a kind of persuasion dialogue in which each side is trying to persuade the trier of fact to accept its view of the matter (Feteris, 1999, 171–174; Kloosterhuis, 2013). This approach, however, fails to describe the specific legal activity commonly referred to as "interpretation," consisting in "puzzling over, considering, arguing about and determining the meaning and scope of an object of interpretation" (Twining and Miers, 2010). In this activity, the use of arguments is crucial, but the goal is not to establish the acceptability of a viewpoint, but rather to make a decision on the meaning to attribute to a legal statement.

The argumentation in these cases is best classified as a species of problem-solving dialogue (Anderson, 2013; Chiassoni, 2016) – namely a kind of decision making (Walton and McKersie, 1966; Walton and Toniolo, 2016; Walton, Toniolo and Norman, 2016). The problems to be solved involve in part those affecting ordinary language interpretation, and include ambiguity (Martí and Ramírez-Ludeña, 2016), vagueness (Jaszczolt, 2017), antiquated language and situation (see for instance the US Constitution), framing definitions of unclear or contested concepts or terms, or definitions that may conflict with those in ordinary language (Jori, 2016, 43), defeasibility (generalizations) (Marmor, 2016a), inconsistency (with other documents; within the same document; with precedent cases), and implicit meaning (Morra, 2016; Macagno and Walton, 2017, 135–138; Sbisà, 2017).

In this chapter we will show how to use argumentation based on evidence and argumentation schemes to examine the pros and cons of the opposed arguments by both sides. We will show that in contrast with cases of persuasion dialogue, the solution to the problem is not provided by burden of proof. Instead, the type of problem-solving argumentation used in cases of statutory interpretation starts with an opening, where a problem of the kind often called the "mischief" in law is stated. Next is an argumentation stage where critical examination of the evidence and the pro–con argumentation lead to different recommendations for action, and different policies or proposals are put forward as ways to solve the problem. In this stage, these proposals are evaluated based on their possible or actual consequences, feasibility conditions, etc. The last stage is the closing one, where the policies or proposals are ordered in a kind of hierarchy and that which is considered to be the "best" is accepted. It is possible that at this stage no proposals are accepted (because they are in conflict with other considerations) and the overall process needs to go back to the formulation and analysis of the proposals. What the solution is depends on what the problem is in the given case at issue, and on how well the proposals to solve the problem are defended in the open forum of the argumentation stage.

The chapter shows how, in contrast to persuasion dialogue where burden of proof is the main instrument for argument evaluation over the three stages of the dialogue, in problem-solving dialogue the discussion is more collaborative and burden of proof is not so important. Hence the chapter will take an instrumentalist approach to statute interpretation that is based on defeasible reasoning (Sartor, 1995, 2018), and an argumentation framework in which defeasible argumentation schemes are vitally important. The argumentation model of problem-solving dialogue put forward in this chapter is an application and extension of the instrumentalist theory of statute interpretation constructed by Twining and Miers (2010).

Section 2.2 briefly introduces the reader to the general idea of the instrumentalist theory. In Section 2.3 the leading example of statutory interpretation given by Twining and Miers (2010) is presented and the arguments pro and con the instrumentalist interpretation of the example are identified and analyzed using argument diagrams. Section 2.4 shows how the simplified model of problem-solving behavior given by Twining and Miers relates to the kind of problem solving well known in artificial intelligence, where it is associated with distributive problem solving in multiagent systems in which problem solvers in a group can work together collaboratively to solve problems they are unable to solve individually (Wooldridge, 2009). Section 2.5 argues that problem solving of this kind is a species of deliberation dialogue, a formal dialogue model well known in the recent literature in artificial intelligence (McBurney, Hitchcock and Parsons, 2007; Kok et al., 2010). Section 2.6 presents a simple example of problem solving of the kind we are all familiar with in our daily activities, and briefly contrasts it with a famous example representing a much more complex type of problem solving familiar to engineers. Section 2.7 presents a general argumentation model that gives an algorithm showing how the sequence of problem-solving argumentation in these examples should proceed. The model shows how the sequence of steps in a case of problem solving can be fitted to a dialogue model that has three stages: an opening stage, an argumentation stage, and a closing stage. Section 2.8 applies the model to a legal case of statutory interpretation to illustrate how argumentation schemes are applied during the stages of a problem-solving dialogue. Section 2.9 summarizes the purpose of the law and relevance, and the last section presents four conclusions.

2.2 INTERPRETATION AS DECISION MAKING

Twining and Miers (2010, 115) contrast two ways of looking at rules as being especially pervasive, among the many ways one can look at rules in different disciplines. One is to see rules as things in themselves that have an existence independent of any purpose or reason that may have originally inspired the rule. In this view, the rule is there to be followed and the task of the interpreter of the rule is simply to find the objective meaning of the text and apply it without taking into account its purposes or consequences. This perspective can be broadly referred to as "textualism," considering this latter term as referring to the approach to interpretation "concerned primarily with the plain, or popular, meaning," of a provision, in the context of the legal document containing it and of other legal sources (Murrill, 2018, 5). According to the so-called "originalism," the focus is rather placed on the meaning that a provision had at the time of its drafting and ratification, assuming that its textual meaning is fixated ("fixation thesis") at that time (Solum, 2011).

The different view, which Twining and Miers (2010, 114) call instrumentalism, and which stems from Robert Summers' view of rules as techniques of social management (Summers, 1971), broadly speaking considers a rule as a means to an end in a problem situation (we can compare this approach to the current commonly labeled as "pragmatism," see Murrill, 2018, 12–13). In this view, rules are considered to be "instruments of policies aimed at solving problems" (Twining and Miers, 2010, 114). In this perspective, the interpreters of the rule need to see the framers of the rule as rational agents who were attempting to solve a particular problem; the solution they arrived at was expressed in the natural language text that they use to formulate it and was set in place as a legal rule (compare this principle with the notion of "living constitution," see Rehnquist, 1975). Often, the solution was indeed a procrastination of a decision. The solution of a specific problem was to leave the statement of law – or more precisely the linguistic item(s) that causes the interpretative dispute – intentionally vague in order to allow it to be specified according to the particular circumstances and needs. As Poscher put it (2016, 76–77):

> [E]ven if a decision on a borderline case is easy to take, premature precisifications might incur opportunity costs. Refraining from precisification allows us to postpone a decision on borderline cases to a later time, when information might have

improved ... The legislator must use vague terms to unload the burden of precisification first onto the courts, which will deal with it by means of legal construction on a case-by-case basis.

The delegation of precisification to courts leads to considering the interpretative process
by legal decision-makers (judges) as a decisional one. In this sense, the instrumentalist
view of law leads to an instrumentalist approach to legal interpretation. Legal interpretation can be defined as involving two distinct types of decisions (Schiffer, 2016, 41):

> The first interpretative act is to decide what is to count as the law promulgated by the
> text, and, once that is decided, the second interpretative act is to decide how that law
> applies to a particular case or cases, particularly to cases to be decided by the judge's
> court.

The first interpretative activity is aimed at reconstructing rules of law from statements of law. However, this process is not an end in itself. It has a very specific
practical goal, which is to decide on a problematic case. Legal interpretation is not
meant to describe meaning but rather to contribute to social purposes, a concept that
can also be found in the following statement (Dworkin, 1986, 58):

> Interpretation of works of art and social practices, I shall argue, is indeed essentially
> concerned with purpose not cause. But the purposes in play are not (fundamentally)
> those of some author but of the interpreter.

So, in the instrumentalist view here adopted statutory interpretation is a decision-
making process based on a twofold tension. On the one hand, the interpreters (judges)
need to solve a specific problem within a specific context; however, their means are the
statements of law, which are "suspended in a vacuum" (Poggi, 2012), namely not
instantiated in any specific context. On the other hand, the interpreters need to ground
their decision on the meaning of the law, but the meaning of the law, and more
importantly its specific purpose, can be reconstructed considering the needs in
a specific time and situation. The tension between the constraints of the context
conveyed by the whole legal text and the intention of the interpreters results in an
argumentative process, which takes place not only between the two parties, but also
between the "collective intention" (Poscher, 2016, 66) that can be reconstructed from
the legal text and its interpreters.

The notion of judicial interpretation as decision making has another crucial
ambiguity. It can refer to the reasoning process by the agents (the judges) or the
justifications they provide in support of their decision (which can be taken as a mere
"formality" independent of the actual interpretative reasons, see Tarello, 1980,
70–71). This distinction is also crucial for analyzing the relationships between the
linguistic and pragmatic approaches to interpretation and the interpretative theories
advanced in philosophy of law. The perspective defended in this book mirrors the
twofold nature of justification. On the one hand, it is a rhetorical activity (where
"rhetorical" is taken in its classical meaning as the art of supporting a viewpoint

through specific instruments – the topics) aimed at increasing the acceptability of an interpretative conclusion. On the other hand, the reasons provided have two characteristics: (1) they have been developed through an interpretative reasoning; and (2) they are the most persuasive for the audience, which includes not only society at large, but more importantly the community of legal interpreters (present and future). For this reason, the justification of judicial interpetations does not *necessarily* mirror the *actual* interpretative reasoning of the *individual* interpreters, but rather expresses the most effective (and, considering 2, the strongest) interpretative "inner" argumentation that the collective body in charge of such an interpretative decision intended to make public (based on 1) (Damele, 2011). In any case, the arguments are what allows the social control of the interpretative activity, and such arguments are found not in the interpretative reasoning conceived as a cognitive and mental activity, but in the explicit, and thus social, justification of the interpretation (van Eemeren and Grootendorst, 2004, 1). This justification is done through schemes of rhetorical argumentation (Tarello, 1980, 71; 85–86), whose preferential use depends on the culture (Damele, 2011, 2014).

The rhetorical view of interpretation is also coherent with some current accounts of "contextual interpretation," in which the interpretative activity *sensu stricto* is regarded as a decision-making process concerning dimensions of meaning construction that cannot be processed presumptively, that is, automatically. These dimensions or meanings involve more complex considerations of the context and lead to a justification that can be expressed through arguments. This view can be described through the following quote (Kompa, 2016, 219):

> [Contextual interpretation] is essentially concerned with purposes. Context sensitivity is resolved in context by appealing to salient purposes and a common understanding of what means (banning certain kinds of vehicles form the park) it would be proper to apply in order to achieve a particular end (less noise in the park). Making explicit how the context sensitivity has been resolved, i.e. how the ordinance ought to be interpreted in the case at hand, amounts to justifying that a particular entity ought or ought not to be included in the extension of the context-sensitive term "vehicle" as it was employed in the formulation of the ordinance. Interpretation and justification are two sides of the same coin.

Here, contextual interpretation – in which the concept of "context" is interpreted pragmatically as including both the co-text constituted by the whole legal text, the background assumptions, and the presumptions governing the interlocutors' behavior (Crowe, 2013, 411; Marmor, 2016b, 162) – is shown to be grounded on the notions of "common understanding" and "salient purposes." The textual evidence is combined with the goal that the law can be presumed to pursue.

One can easily see how this instrumentalist view of statutory interpretation needs the interpreter to describe the process of arriving at a reasonable interpretation by going through a sequence of steps. A clear example is provided by one of the United

Kingdom's most famous legal cases, *Heydon's Case* [1584] EWHC Exch J36, which led to the interpretative principle called the "Mischief Rule" (see Twining and Miers, 2010, 114). In this case, the Barons of the Exchequer outlined the sequence clearly by stating that there were four questions that need to be considered in a specific order when arriving at a decision on how to interpret a statute.

Q1: What was the common law before the making of the Act?

Q2: What was the mischief and defect for which the common law did not provide?

Q3: What remedy did the parliament devise to cure the disease?

Q4: What was the true reason for the remedy?

Based on this sequence, the advice given by the Barons was for the judges to always make a construction that will suppress the mischief, advance the remedy, and suppress clever evasions that might be used to get around the remedy. It is added that the outcome of following this procedure correctly is to come up with an interpretation of the rule that conforms to the true intent of the framers of the Act. This document is a very clear expression of the instrumentalist view that openly brings out the contrast with the textualistic rule-based view that takes no account of the intentions for purposes of the framers of the Act when interpreting a rule.

2.3 THE FIRE ENGINE EXAMPLE

The leading example that Twining and Miers (2010, 53–58) use to illustrate how the instrumentalist view works, and how it contrasts with the rule-based view, is the *Buckoke* case (*Buckoke* v. *Greater London Council* [1970] 2 All ER 193).

2.3.1 *The Arguments of the Fire Engine Example*

The controversy that started the procedure in this case was the question of whether it should be the duty of the driver of a fire engine to stop for a red light. The Fire Brigades Union argued that the driver must always follow the law by waiting until the light turns green. However, the chief officer of the London Fire Brigade argued that as long as the driver stops for a second to make sure that the road is clear, he can go through a red light to get to the fire as soon as possible. The controversy was discussed by several committees and government agencies, but they all declined to interfere by legislation. At that point the chief officer of the London Fire Brigade, supported by the Greater London Council, issued a directive. It said that fire engine drivers are obliged to follow the law just as other drivers must do, but if the fire engine driver, once he stops, carefully observes the traffic conditions around him, and rings his bell vigorously, he can proceed through a red light as long as he uses extreme caution. However, the Fire Brigades Union argued that this directive should be considered illegal because it would encourage fire engine drivers to break the law.

Based on this argument, the union brought an action against the Greater London Council and ordered their union members not to travel with drivers who refused to follow the law.

The statutory provisions that were drafted in order to address the problem concluded that even though the letter of the law requires that firefighters are not to shoot through a red light, just as all drivers are so required, public interest may demand that they should not be punished as long as there is no risk of a collision and the urgency of the case demands going through the red light. The conclusion acknowledged that calling this an offense without exception would open the way to endless discussions in fire stations. Recognizing an exception to the rule, which could be applied in circumstances where some particular requirements were met, resulted in a statute that was meant to solve this problem.

The actual wording of the instruction issued by the chief officer of the London Fire Brigade, given with the support of the Greater London Council, is quoted in Case 2.1 (Brigade Order 144/8, dated February 3, 1967, from Twining and Miers, 2010, 54):

CASE 2.1: THE FIRE ENGINE

Traffic light signals – Drivers of fire brigade vehicles are under the same obligation at law to obey traffic light signals as the drivers of other vehicles. If however, a Brigade driver responding to an emergency call decides to proceed against the red light, he is (unless signaled to proceed by a police constable in uniform) to stop his appliance, car, or other vehicle at the red light, observe carefully the traffic conditions around him, and to proceed only when he is reasonably sure that there is no risk of a collision; the bell is to be rung vigorously and/or the two-tone horn sounded and the blue flashing light(s) operated. Extreme caution is to be used and the driver is not to cross until it is clear that the drivers of other vehicles appear aware that he is proceeding. The onus of avoiding an accident in such circumstances rests entirely on the Brigade driver, who is to remember that a collision might well prevent his vehicle from reaching its destination and might also block the road for other essential services; no call is so urgent as to justify this risk.

This case is particularly interesting for the purposes of interpretation. As Twining and Miers point out, the controversy focused on one crucial dimension of legal interpretation, namely the nature of the normative generalization. The case concerned the following legal statement (*Traffic Signs Regulations and General Directions* 1964, regulation 34a):

> The red signal shall convey the prohibition that vehicular traffic shall not proceed beyond the stop line.

This statement was subject to two distinct interpretations – to two distinct pragmatic enrichments – namely representations of what is communicated that does not correspond to "the semantic content of the sentence uttered," but to "something richer, to which meaning and obvious background assumptions have both contributed" (Soames, 2009, 411). This process resulted in two distinct specific semantic representations (Recanati, 1987, 224; Jaszczolt, 1999, 2; Carston, 2002, 2004; Atlas, 2005, 38; Kissine, 2012). The two sides of the dispute were represented by the Fire Brigades Union (FBU), which argued in favor of admitting no exceptions to the prohibition, and the chief officer of the London Fire Brigade (CO), who maintained that the rule should be defeasible, namely admit exceptions when it is necessary or reasonable. The generalization explicitly stated by the legal statement is thus pragmatically enriched in two distinct ways (we signal such enrichments using angle brackets):

1. No-exception rule (FBU): The red signal shall convey the prohibition that <in every possible case> vehicular traffic shall not proceed beyond the stop line.

2. Defeasible rule (CO): The red signal shall convey the prohibition that <in normal circumstances> vehicular traffic shall not proceed beyond the stop line <unless exceptions apply>.

In both cases, the semantic representation – and in particular the scope of the prohibition – is subject to a pragmatic enrichment (Depraetere, 2014), which specifies the kind of generalization expressed. The two interpretations result in two distinct types of argument (Walton, 2006, 49–53), namely a deductive and a plausible one. The argument of the Fire Brigades Union proceeds by deductive reasoning, concluding that fire engine drivers can never go through a red light, even in an emergency situation. In contrast, the argument of the chief officer of the London Fire Brigade relies on interpretation 2, taking the generalization as holding provisionally subject to exceptions that can be argued for.

2.3.2 *Mapping the Fire Engine Example*

The argumentative structure of the legal dispute can be represented through the argument diagram of Figure 2.1, which shows the crucial argument that is grounded on the distinct interpretations of the legal statement (a1)[1] together with the arguments a2 and a3, provided by the chief officer. These latter arguments can be modeled as undercutters (Pollock, 1995; Walton, Reed, and Macagno, 2008, Chapter 7) of argument a1, namely as arguments attacking the inferential link between the premises and the conclusion – in our case, the interpreted generalization. The argument diagram drawn in Figure 2.1 adopts the style of the Carneades Argumentation System (Gordon, 2010) (discussed further in Chapter 6), where the rectangular nodes contain propositions that act as premises or conclusions in the

---

[1] We label the specific arguments with a lower-case letter "a."

arguments and the round nodes indicate inferential passages from a set of premises to a conclusion. This way of representing arguments visually as a diagram that takes the form of a graph is descended from the older graphical method of charting legal evidence used by Wigmore (1931). Little attention was paid to Wigmore's charting method at the time, but it was recently rediscovered by argumentation theorists, practitioners of informal logic, and Anglo-American "new evidence" scholars such as Anderson and Twining (1991), Schum and Tillers (1991), and Schum (1994), and widely put to good use.

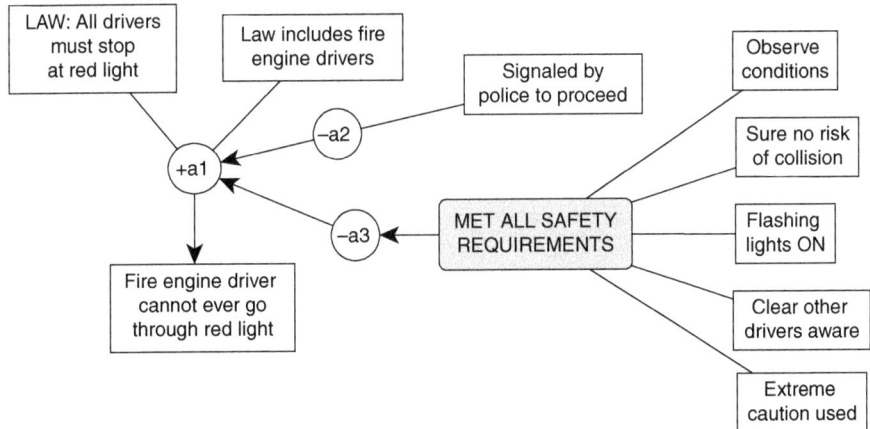

FIGURE 2.1 Mapping the arguments of the fire engine example

The argument on the union side (the FBU) is shown as argument +a1. The "+" means it is a pro argument. It is a deductively valid form of argument. One premise says that by law all drivers must stop at a red light. The other premise says that this law includes fire engine drivers. However, the inference of the conclusion from the premises is subject to a twofold attack (con arguments a2 and a3), signaled by the minus sign in the argument node. Con argument a2 cites an exception to the rule that all drivers must stop at a red light. The exception is an instance where the driver is signaled by a police officer to safely proceed through the red light for the purpose of giving aid in an emergency. Argument a3 can be modeled in the same way as a counter argument attacking the argument a1 by citing a list of safety requirements, the argument being the contention that if all these safety requirements are met, the argument a1 should be defeated in this particular instance by the exception. The safety requirements are that the fire engine driver should be aware of the particular conditions in the circumstances of the case, should be sure there is no risk of collision if he proceeds through the red light, should operate his flashing lights and other warning mechanisms, should use his knowledge of the circumstances to be clear that other drivers are aware that he is proceeding through the red light, and finally that he uses extreme caution when going through the red light. The basic argument is that if all these safety requirements are met in a given case, then this finding should be regarded as sufficient to defeat the original argument a1.

The legal dispute concerns the effects of the con arguments a2 and a3 on the inferential link of a1. According to the interpretation of the normative statement as a universal generalization (FBU), the inferential link is not subject to any exception. This means that either one of the premises can be attacked or the conclusion can be challenged by bringing con arguments against it, but the argument link between the premises and conclusion cannot be attacked. The CO interpretation, in contrast, takes the normative generalization to be of a kind that is potentially subject to exceptions, and that can be defeated if a legitimate exception is found in properly argued for (Anderson and Twining, 1991; Anderson, 1999). In this instance we see that there are two exceptions expressed in the form of counter arguments a2 and a3.

This general mapping shows the difference in the burden of persuasion between the two parties. For the FBU, it is sufficient to support the no-exception interpretation, while the CO has to defend the presumptive interpretation of the normative statement and the acceptability of the exceptions allowing the norm not to apply to the specific case. For this reason, the CO argumentation is more complex, as the chief officer of the London Fire Brigade needs to reject the no-exception interpretation and the reasonableness of the exception considering the purpose of the norm. Figure 2.2 shows how the argumentation put forward in the instruction issued by the chief officer of the London Fire Brigade can be represented as a pro and con argument configuration.

Figure 2.2 shows how the CO interpretation (an "instrumentalist" interpretation) of the argumentation in the fire engine example instantiates two distinct argumentative principles, called *habitudines* in the ancient dialectical tradition (Abaelardus, *Dialectica*, 263–264), guaranteeing the passage from the premises to the conclusion. The first, represented by the node +PR ("practical reasoning"), consists of a desired goal that can be pursued through the best possible means. The second, represented in the argument –NC, considers the negative consequences of an action and links them to the acceptability of the action itself. In argumentation theory, these arguments can be expressed using the argumentation scheme for practical reasoning and the scheme for argument from negative consequences (Macagno and Walton, 2018).

The argument from practical reasoning takes us from what is called Goal, the goal of saving lives, along with the other premise that the means to save lives in this instance is to allow fire engines to go through a red light under the right conditions, as explained in Figure 2.1. This latter premise is in turn supported by an argument from cause to effect (+C_1): the predictable effect of going through is to arrive earlier and arriving earlier can cause the saving of lives.

The next part of the argumentation shown in Figure 2.2 is the counterargument – NC, based on the two premises that going through leads to risking lives, and that risking lives is bad (should be avoided). The former premise is in turn backed by three arguments from cause to effect (+C_2, +C_3, and +C_4). The argument +C_2 links

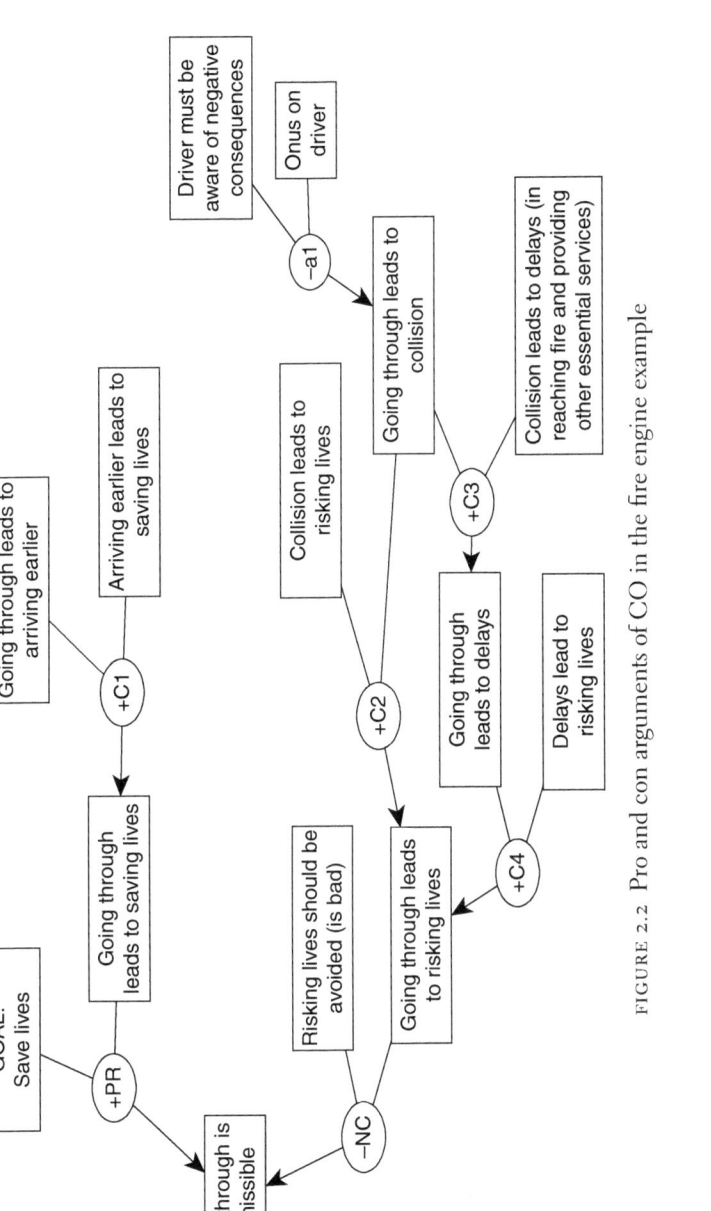

FIGURE 2.2 Pro and con arguments of CO in the fire engine example

going through to risking lives: as a predictable effect of going through is to collide, and a possible effect of collision is putting someone's life at risk, going through can cause risking lives. The causal arguments +C3 and +C4 link the risk of collision with the risk of life, as collision predictably causes delays not only of the fire engine, but also of other life-saving services such as an ambulance, and delays can cause the risking of lives.

The last argument that we can find in this map, labeled −a1, is a counterargument. It is an attack on the basic premise on which the argument from negative consequences is based (going through leads to collision) and states that such a collision might not happen as long as the driver is aware of these negative consequences and takes care to avoid them.

Looking over Figure 2.2 as a whole, it is possible to see that there are two main lines of argument. The first is that a fire engine should be allowed to go through a red light because this action might save lives. The rest of the argumentation is a sequence of arguments starting with +C2 and +C3, based on the premise that a collision is possible and that such a collision might cost lives. These two arguments result in an argument from negative consequences (−NC) that acts as a counterattack against the original practical reasoning argument. But then there are also two other arguments to take into account, both arguments against the crucial premise that such a collision might cost lives.

2.4 PROBLEM SOLVING

An argumentative approach to the issue of analyzing statutory interpretation is inherently grounded on the notion of problem solving. This view, commonly shared in legal theory, is often confused in argumentation theory with the concept of persuasion or critical discussion (see Feteris, 1999).

2.4.1 *The Notion of Problem Solving*

Twining and Miers (2010, 72) worked out what they call a simplified model of problem-solving behavior as going through seven distinct stages, which can be summarized as follows:

1. clarification of the agent's objectives and general position;
2. perception by the agent of facts comprising a particular situation;
3. evaluation of one or more elements in this situation as being mischievous, undesirable, or as presenting an obstacle to the attainment of a goal;
4. identification of possible courses of action that might be taken in order to solve the problem;
5. predictions of likely obstacles and costs for each of the possible courses of action;

6. announcement of general policies that might be means of dealing with the problem;
7. implementation of the action selected out by evaluating the alternatives.

Twining and Miers (2010, 71) think of this procedure as one of collective decision making by a group of agents who are attempting to solve a problem that affects all of them. The main thesis of their theory of statutory interpretation is that they see it as an instance of problem solving. This puts them in opposition to what they call the traditional approach of interpreting cases and statutes in which the rules of statutory interpretation and the doctrine of precedent provide the tools for interpreting a case or statute. They see their instrumental approach to interpretation as an alternative to the traditional approach, because their approach pays more attention to the context by looking at the nature of the problems confronted in a given case and by seeing the use of rules as responses to such problems (Twining and Miers, 2010). In general, they see their instrumental approach as comparable to the kind of problem solving that takes place in everyday living, for example in learning to operate an unfamiliar machine by coping with the difficulties and obstacles perhaps through trial and error.

Problem solving has been recognized as a distinctive form of practical reasoning in many fields, even though there are differences in formulating the stages of the procedure. Most agree with the procedure outlined by Twining and Miers in certain respects. Bransford and Stein (1993) have set out what they called the problem-solving cycle involving several distinct stages: recognize the problem, define the problem, try to find a strategy to fix it, figure out what can be done with the resources at hand, monitor progress, and evaluate the proposed solution that has been arrived at. They also added another stage to the procedure – using a solution based on a prior solution to an analogous problem. This technique applies very well to problem solving in the common law system, which is heavily based on precedents. Arguments from precedent are based on the principle that "like cases should be treated alike" – namely, when there is no material difference between two cases, the legal treatment thereof should not be materially different (Endicott, 2000, 58). The determination of what counts as "material difference" between two cases is based on a pattern of argument called argument from analogy (Macagno and Walton, 2009; Macagno, 2017; for a discussion of the distinctions at a psychological/communicative level between precedent and analogy, see Schauer, 2013). The properties of a case that are relevant to the application of a legal provision are abstracted and then applied to the distinct case (Macagno and Walton, 2009; Macagno, Walton, and Tindale, 2014).

Like Twining and Miers, Bransford and Stein (1993) have a stage where proposed solutions are elicited. They also depict problem solving in the middle stages as moving forward toward a solution through a sequence of actions where means are connected to goals (practical reasoning). Finally, they see this procedure as culminating in a closing stage where proposed solutions are tested by some criteria to try to determine which is the best one for achieving the goal that been identified.

In the field of engineering, the starting point for some particular instance of problem solving may be the failure of some process or product so that a correction to prevent future failures is needed. In the field of psychology, problem solving is treated as a cognitive process that has been widely examined experimentally in both human and animal studies. In artificial intelligence, problem solving is treated as a computerized procedure for searching to find a means to solve a problem. Goal-directed practical reasoning is clearly central to computer science. But all fields have the idea that there is a procedure of problem finding prior to the procedure of solving the problem. In general, it is distinctive of problem solving that there is a goal to be reached, though not necessarily a goal that pertains to decision making.

2.4.2 *Problem Solving in Computer Science*

Problem solving has been recognized as especially important in computer science, most notably in artificial intelligence. In their influential textbook, Russell and Norvig (1995, 53) argue that a "problem" is defined by a goal and a set of means for achieving the goal (practical reasoning). An intelligent agent, whether an auto-mated or a human one, using search procedures has to try to find out which path in a connected sequence of actions and events moves toward the goal state earlier identified. By their account, problem solving is carried out by an intelligent agent searching through alternative paths in a graph representing a sequence of states, actions, and events representing several alternative paths that lead to the goal (Russell and Norvig, 1995, 55). The problem is taken to be solved when the agent decides what to do by finding the best sequence of actions – where "best" is defined by criteria such as cost, time, or other values – among the alternative paths.

Poole and Mackworth (2010, 71) define "problem solving" in a comparable fash-ion as a search procedure that an intelligent agent uses to achieve its goals by finding a path that is essentially a sequence of actions that will achieve its goal. Problem solving generally in computing is modeled as a graph structure. The problem is to be solved by using search tools to find a path from the start node to a goal node in a directed graph. As they put it (Poole and Mackworth, 2010, 72), the agent is searching among these paths to find one or more sequences that will lead to the goal it has formulated. A simple example is shown in Figure 2.3.

The directed graph represents three available courses of actions, each modelled as a path emanating from the original state, the leftmost node. The rational agent has four choices. It can take the top path, the middle path, the bottom path, or the path indicated by the grey nodes. Only the top three paths lead to the goal, marked by the capital G contained in the rightmost node, so the bottom path is ignored. If the agent takes the top path there is a sequence of eight nodes leading from the original goal node.

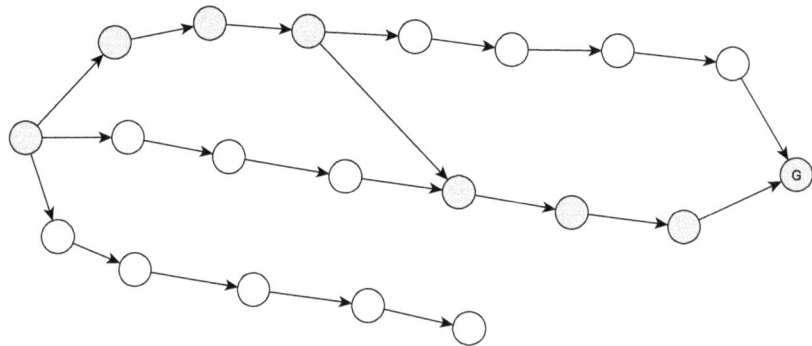

FIGURE 2.3 A problem-solving graph with four paths

However, if the agent takes the middle path or the path illustrated by the grey nodes, there are only seven nodes. The middle path is the best solution to the problem, at least according to the criterion that the shorter path to the goal, other things being equal, is better.

2.4.3 *Cooperative Problem Solving*

The kind of problem solving we have in mind in this chapter is called cooperative distributed problem solving in multiagent systems (Wooldridge, 2009, 190). It applies to cases in which a group of problem solvers can work together to solve problems that they cannot deal with individually. Although each agent in the group can work independently, the problem they confront cannot be solved without cooperation. The agents in such a system must agree from the beginning to share a common goal, even though individually they will have their own goals, interests, and opinions. There is a benevolence assumption; that is, it is assumed that the individual goals of each agent must give way to the initial goal agreed upon by the group if they are in conflict with the latter goal. This means that problem solving is a considerably less adversarial type of dialogue than a critical discussion or persuasion type of dialogue in which each party is trying to prove that its opinion is right and to show, by attacking the opinion of the other side, that its opinion is open to critical doubt.

From a point of view of argumentation theory, problem solving can be seen as a species of deliberation dialogue having a dialogue structure with three stages. In this view, the goal of dialogue is to arrive at a decision on what to do in a particular set of circumstances where a group of rational agents needs to do something, because even doing nothing represents an action that has consequences. First there is an opening stage where the problem is formulated as a real problem to be solved and not something that just looks like a problem. Then there is an intermediate stage where a goal is stated and where one or more means for achieving the goal are elicited and individually evaluated. Finally, there is a closing stage where the means are comparatively evaluated to decide which proposed solution is arguably the best one to choose. This final stage is often identified with what is called decision making, but how decision making should work as a form of rational cognition has been widely studied and applied in many other fields, such as in particular decision theory. Therefore one should expect that drawing a clear distinction between decision making and problem solving is a hotly contested issue. It may turn out that problem solving, modeled as a species of deliberation dialogue, is an argumentation-based theory of decision that can complement decision-theory.

2.5 DELIBERATION DIALOGUE

There is a growing literature in artificial intelligence stemming from the original formal argumentation model of deliberation dialogue originally presented by McBurney, Hitchcock, and Parsons (2007), called the MHP model. In this model, deliberation is represented as a procedure that starts from a situation where a group of agents confront a choice on what course of action to take in a set of circumstances requiring a decision to be made in order for them to move forward with their plan of action meant to achieve some common goal. Deliberation is modeled as a formal procedure that starts with an opening stage where a question is raised about what should be done, passes through six intervening stages, and ends in a closing stage where a decision on the action is taken by the group. The eight stages can be briefly outlined as follows.

1. *The opening stage.* The group is presented a single question, called the governing question, and asks what should be done next.
2. *The inform stage.* During this stage the group discusses how the given circumstances pose constraints on moving ahead with the goal and the actions that need to be taken to move toward it.
3. *The propose stage.* Proposals for taking action are put forward.
4. *The consider stage.* Arguments for and against the proposals that have been made so far are considered.
5. *The revise stage.* Proposals can be revised or withdrawn, in light of the factual information about the circumstances that has been collected.
6. *The recommend stage.* Each agent has an opportunity to accept, reject, or recommend any proposal that has been put forward.
7. *The confirm stage.* For the dialogue to reach closure, each agent must confirm acceptance of one of the proposals.

8. *The closing stage.* At this stage, the group concludes which course of action to adopt, based on the argumentation advanced and evaluated in the previous stages.

In the formal MHP dialogue model, the so-called protocol refers to the set of procedural rules governing each of the moves that can be made by each of the agents at each stage of the dialogue. A move is defined as a speech act of one kind or another that each of the participants can take turn putting forward in response to the previous moves. For example, there is a speech act of making a proposal, one for making an assertion, one for requesting that the other party justify an assertion, one for claiming whether a proposal should be accepted or rejected, one for retracting a claim made in a previous move, and one for withdrawing from the dialogue.

The eight stages of the dialogue can be divided into three subparts: an opening stage, an argumentation stage, and a closing stage (Walton, Toniolo, and Norman, 2016, 158). At the opening stage, the issue is formulated describing a choice to be made. During the argumentation stage, proposals are put forward, considered, and revised in light of arguments that are put forward for and against any particular proposal being considered. The proposals are evaluated by weighing these pro and con arguments against each other to determine which side has the stronger argument. However, it is an important part of this procedure that information about the particular circumstances of the case that is relevant to the arguments may need to be collected during an information-seeking interval. In such cases there is often a shift from the pure deliberation dialogue to an information-seeking type of dialogue. As facts about the situation are collected, this information will affect how the premises of the arguments should be accepted or rejected, based on the incoming evidence. The third stage is the closing stage, where these arguments are used to determine which proposal has best survived the counterattacks against it, based on the arguments supporting it.

To take this shifting back and forth from deliberation to information-seeking dialogue into account, Walton, Toniolo, and Norman (2016, 161) proposed a revised model featuring an open knowledge base. In this model, a knowledge base is set in place at the opening stage and can be updated during information-seeking intervals in the deliberation dialogue. An especially important feature is that the knowledge base can be continually updated as new information about the circumstances of the particular case comes to be known. These changes coming into the knowledge base give the deliberation the flexibility it needs to update and modify proposals. To extend the model to allow for such possibilities, the model of Walton, Toniolo, and Norman (2016, 162) introduced a speech act called *disclose*, which enables one agent to bring in a new piece of information not previously known at earlier stages of the dialogue so that other agents can be informed about it and use it to provide and to revise premises of the arguments used during the argumentation stage. In this model during the argumentation stage there is a continual cycle of proposing, considering, and revising as the new information comes in from the open knowledge base. The deliberation dialogue is closed when enough information has been collected, given time and cost constraints, and the agents have discussed the matter by supporting and criticizing all the proposals thoroughly enough to determine the best course of action to take.

2.6 A SIMPLE EXAMPLE OF PROBLEM SOLVING

Problem solving is an activity that all of us engage in all the time in our daily lives, even though we may not have the occasion to try to describe how it works at an abstract level. It can be carried out by individuals or by groups of agents acting together, in which cases it can be more complex and more woven in with other cognitive processes. The following case has been frequently used as an example of problem solving (Walton, 2015, 149–153; Walton and Toniolo, 2016, sec. 3.1; Walton, Toniolo, and Norman, 2016). A simplified version can be used to explain how problem solving works as a species of rational thinking. Let's call it the scanner example here (previous versions of it were called the printer example).

EXAMPLE 2.1 THE SCANNER EXAMPLE

Brian had a scanner attached to his printer, and whenever he scanned a document, an ugly black line appeared down the middle of the scanned page. His first thought was to return the printer to the store where he bought it, or to the manufacturer, but this would likely involve a trip to the store, or other efforts that would temporarily deprive him of the use of the scanner, which he needed right away. To try to solve the problem, he put the name of his printer along with the model maker in a brief description of the problem into Google. The search turned up the manufacturer's manual, which contained a troubleshooting guide with a series of instructions on how to solve the problem. The list of instructions explained that the paper passes over a small strip of glass at one side of the larger piece of glass that you see when you open the top. The instructions told him to carefully clean this glass with a soft, dry, lint-free cloth. He did that but when he tried scanning another document the black line was still there. Below that instruction there was another one that said that on some models this strip of glass is covered by a piece of plastic and that what should be done is to remove that piece of plastic and clean the glass underneath. Examining the small strip of glass described in the instructions he saw that there was a thin plastic film covering it. After several attempts to pull at the edges from the piece of glass he found there was a small black mark in the middle of it at the bottom. He tried cleaning the plastic using some optical cleaner fluid. But that didn't work. The black mark was very hard to remove, and when he put the plastic part back in place the scanner still produced a black line down the middle of any paper printed. Next he wondered whether there might be some other way to remove the black mark, and he showed it to his wife Anna to ask for advice. She used some detergent and a soft cleaning pad and removed the black mark. Brian then took the plastic part back to the printer and inserted it very carefully into its original place. Finally, as a test, he scanned a piece of paper and found that there was no longer a black line down the middle of the page. This showed that the problem had been solved.

A model of the problem-solving procedure from start to end is shown in Figure 2.4. The start point for the sequence of actions is the light grey circular node at the center left. The first step is the formulation of the problem that Brian is confronted with. The next step is his goal of removing the black line. The first solution Brian considered was to send the printer back to the manufacturer, but as indicated in the example he realized that this action would have negative consequences. Hence this sequence of actions ends at the round darker node at the top right, meaning "stop." The next action is for Brian to conduct a search on Google to try to get some information from the manufacturer or other users of this printer. Solution 2, which Brian found on the manufacturer's website, was to clean the strip of glass, but that sequence of actions failed to solve the problem, as indicated by the middle dark circular node. Finally, Brian moved to solution 3, which turned out to be successful, as indicated by the lighter node at the bottom right.

A more famous and complex example of problem solving is the NASA Hubble Space Telescope launch in 1990. The blurry images the scientists and engineers

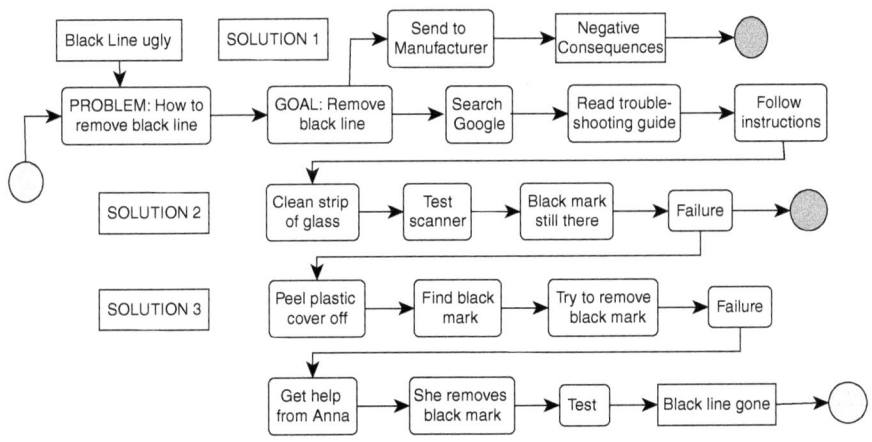

FIGURE 2.4 Problem solving in the scanner example

received on Earth showed that the main mirror was ineffective for viewing the distant stars and galaxies they wanted to study. The project was judged to be a failure, due to a "spherical aberration," meaning that the primary mirror and the secondary mirror were not focusing on the same location in order to produce a clear image. This problem was thus proposed as the opening stage. There were further lengthy discussions, and finally the team came up with a proposal that they thought might succeed. At the next stage, a team of engineers built a device called COSTAR (Corrective Optics Space Telescope Axial Replacement), and a team of five astronauts were sent to Hubble to change the configuration of the mirrors and insert the new device into Hubble. As everyone knows, it was a big success. The problem was solved.

2.7 AN ARGUMENTATION MODEL OF PROBLEM SOLVING

As mentioned above, problem solving configured as an argumentation model is a species of deliberation dialogue that has three stages: an opening stage, an argumentation stage, and a closing stage. There are three requirements of the opening stage. First, there needs to be a group of agents working together to try to achieve or at least work toward a common goal in the circumstances they confront. Second, there has to be a set of factual circumstances that the agents are aware of that pose a problem. A problem is something that prevents them from achieving this goal, as things stand. Third, the group has to be able to state what the problem is, in language they can all understand. This third requirement is needed to rule out the possibility that what they think is a problem is really not a problem at all, perhaps because there is some more or less straightforward way already in place for moving past the supposed obstacle. If this is the case, no problem-solving dialogue is necessary.

During the argumentation stage, to begin with, proposals or policies for action need to be elicited from the participants that might solve the problem. A proposal puts forward a path – a sequence of actions – that can go around the obstacle that poses the initial problem, and move the action plan toward the goal formulated at the opening stage. An important function of the argumentation stage is to identify possible courses of action that have some real potential to get past the obstacles and lead to the goal. Once these courses of action are mapped out, inevitably there will be more specific problems found in each of them, which can be fixed and solved.

During the closing stage, the aim is to arrive at a conclusion on how to solve the problem. This conclusion is to be arrived at by comparatively evaluating the lines of action that were considered during the argumentation stage. The best is the one that has best survived critical examination, given the circumstances of the initial situation and the new information that has come in. For these reasons it can be accepted as the best way forward to achieve the ultimate goal of the dialogue. It should only be accepted if it has been shown to be the most workable solution to the original problem

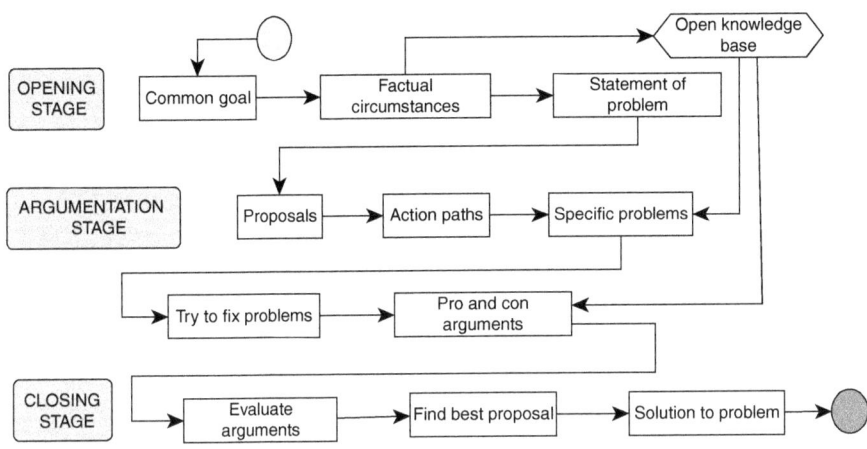

FIGURE 2.5 The three stages of problem-solving dialogue

formulated at the opening stage, although the problem itself can be (and may need to be) reformulated as new information about the circumstances comes in.

This model of problem solving clearly fits the scanner example very well, but further research could also apply it to much more complex examples of the kind illustrated by the COSTAR example. As shown generally in Figure 2.5, the way to solve the problem confronted at the opening stage is to use pro and con arguments to support or attack the proposals that are put forward. These arguments characteristically make use of schemes of argument (which we will explain in more detail in Chapter 5 under the label of "argumentation schemes") of the kinds explained in Chapter 1, such as argument from purpose and so forth. The schemes are then used as tools to evaluate the arguments at the closing stage.

2.8 APPLYING THE MODEL TO A LEGAL CASE

The account of legal controversies as decision-making processes in which arguments are presented pro and con a specific decision can be used to analyze the structure of legal judgments, in which a decision is justified by the court in writing by representing the dialectical opposition of the parties' arguments in favor of different proposals. The computational tools designed in the areas of computational argumentation and artificial intelligence and law can be used to visualize the reasons and the conclusions defended by each party, allowing the identification of the crucial issues underlying a legal controversy. This approach, however, involves dimensions of legal interpretation that can be analyzed through the combination of instruments of argumentation and pragmatics. To illustrate how this account can be used, we consider once again the case *Google Spain SL, Google Inc.* v. *Agencia Española de Protección de Datos (AEPD), Costeja Gonzalez* (2014, ECLI:EU:

C:2014:317), decided before the Court of Justice of the European Union on May 13 2014. This case shows not only the process of decision making, but also the argumentative structure of the analysis of the pro and con arguments concerning each proposal made, and the strategy used by the court to decide the case.

2.8.1 *The Decision-Making Process*

The *Google Spain* case concerned protection of the private data of individuals with regard to web searches, in light of the Charter of Fundamental Rights of the European Union. The dispute can be summarized as follows (*Google Spain* v. *Costeja Gonzalez*, at 14–17):

CASE 2.2: THE DATA PROTECTION CASE

The complaint was based on the fact that, when an internet user entered Mr. Costeja González's name in the search engine of the Google group ("Google Search"), he would obtain links to two pages of the *La Vanguardia* newspaper, of January 19 and March 9 1998 respectively, on which an announcement mentioning Mr. Costeja González's name appeared for a real-estate auction connected with attachment proceedings for the recovery of social security debts. Mr. Costeja González requested, first, that *La Vanguardia* be required either to remove or alter those pages so that the personal data relating to him no longer appeared or to use certain tools made available by search engines in order to protect the data. Second, he requested that Google Spain or Google Inc. be required to remove or conceal the personal data relating to him so that they ceased to be included in the search results and no longer appeared in the links to *La Vanguardia*.

The AEPD (the Spanish Data Protection Authority) upheld the complaint in so far as it was directed against Google Spain and Google Inc. The AEPD considered in this regard that operators of search engines are subject to data protection legislation given that they carry out data processing for which they are responsible and act as intermediaries in the information society. The AEPD took the view that it has the power to require the withdrawal of data and the prohibition of access to certain data by the operators of search engines when it considers that the locating and dissemination of the data are liable to compromise the fundamental right to data protection and the dignity of persons in the broad sense, and this would also encompass the mere wish of the person concerned that such data not be known to third parties. The AEPD considered that that obligation may be owed directly by operators of search engines, without it being necessary to erase the data or information from the website where they appear, including when retention of the information on that site is justified by a statutory provision.

The decision of the AEPD was appealed to a Spanish court, which had to consider crucial issue: whether an internet search engine (Google, in this case) must consider requests from data subjects to erase information concerning them. The case concerned in particular two articles of Directive 95/46, namely Articles 12(b) and 14(a):

- *Right of access (to erasure)*. Member States shall guarantee every data subject the right to obtain from the controller [...] as appropriate the rectification, erasure or blocking of data the processing of which does not comply with the provisions of this Directive, in particular because of the incomplete or inaccurate nature of the data;
- *Right to object*. Member States shall grant the data subject the right: at least in the cases referred to in Article 7(e) and (f), to object at any time on compelling legitimate grounds relating to his particular situation to the processing of data relating to him, save where otherwise provided by national legislation. Where there is a justified objection, the processing instigated by the controller may no longer involve those data[.]

The Spanish judges referred the relevant interpretative issues to the Court of Justice of the European Union, which was presented with a series of questions relative to the interpretation of Directive 95/46, namely a series of interpretative issues leading to distinct and interrelated decision-making processes, focused on the problems summarized and simplified in the following list:

A. The interpretation of the concept of "**processing**": Should a search engine be considered as "processing" personal data within the search function?
B. The interpretation of the concept of "**data controller**": Should Google Inc. or Google Spain be considered as data controllers of the personal data contained in the web pages that it indexes?
C. The interpretation of "**right to erasure**": Should Google Search be required to withdraw from its indexes an item of information *published by third parties*, without simultaneously notifying the owner of the web page on which that information is located?
D. The interpretation of "**right to object**" (or "right to oblivion" or "right to be forgotten"): Should the rights to erasure and blocking of data be extended to enabling data subjects to address search engines directly in order to prevent indexing of the information relating to them personally, published on third parties' web pages?

This general structure of the questions that the court had to decide upon were given opposite answers by the two parties to the legal controversy, namely Google Spain (GS) and Mr. Costeja González and the AEPD. The structure of the decision-making process can be represented in Figure 2.6.

Google Spain used a strategy addressing the multiple classifications, which are at the basis of the application of the obligations set out in the directive. By rejecting the

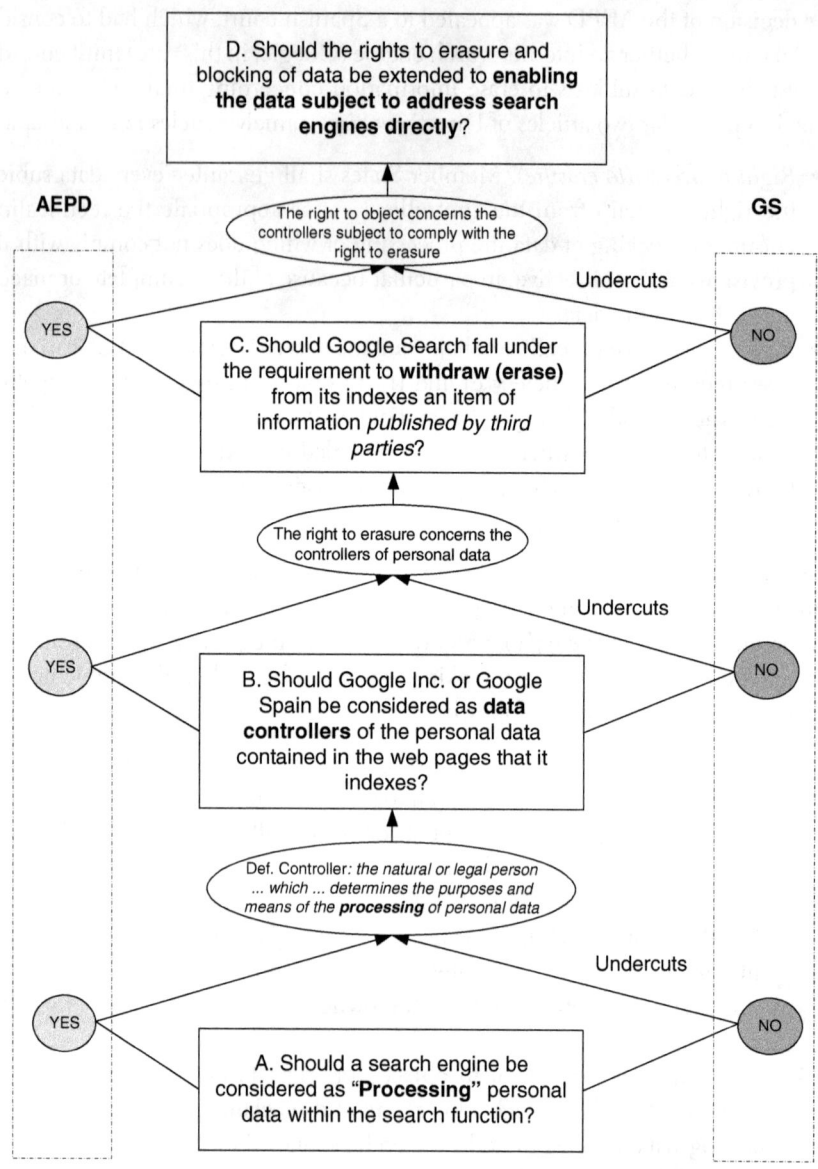

FIGURE 2.6 The decision-making process in the data protection case

classification of the activities of a search engine as "processing," it undercuts the
possibility of classifying it as a "data controller"; by objecting to its classification as
a data controller, the obligations resulting from the right to erasure cannot be applied
to the search engine, and *a fortiori* the obligations concerning the right to object. The
court had to make decisions concerning the arguments put forward by each side.

2.8.2 *The Decision-Making Arguments*

The argumentative structure of the decision-making process consists in a series of arguments and rebuttals. The court took into account the arguments of both parties and provided its own opinion on the interpretation of the directive, leading to an argumentation structure that can be represented in Figure 2.7.

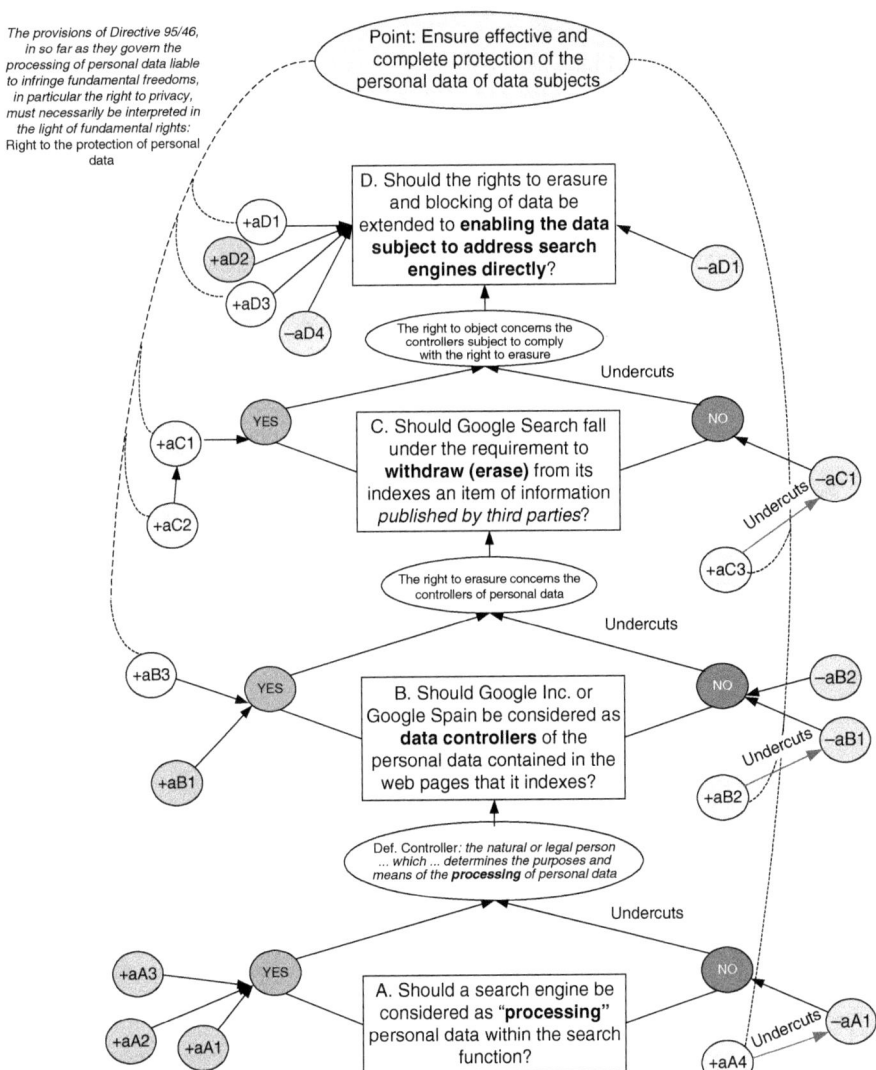

FIGURE 2.7 The arguments of the decision-making process in the data protection case

The arguments represented in Figure 2.7 are summarized as follows, indicating the argumentation scheme(s) that capture the inferential links and the corresponding interpretative canon(s):

Question A: Interpretation and application of the concept of "processing."

–aA1. Classification from definition of "processing." Those data have already been published on the Internet and are not *altered* by the search engine (argument from classification – argument from ordinary meaning).

+aA1. Classification from the legal definition of "processing." Any operation or set of operations that is performed upon personal data, whether or not by automatic means, such as collection, recording, organization, storage, adaptation or alteration, retrieval, consultation, use, disclosure by transmission, dissemination or otherwise making available, alignment or combination, blocking, erasure or destruction. An operator of a search engine "collects" such data, which it subsequently "retrieves," "records," and "organizes" within the framework of its indexing programs, "stores" on its servers and, as the case may be, "discloses" and "makes available" to its users in the form of lists of search results (argument from classification – systematic argument, namely, a legal provision setting out the legal definition).

+aA2. Greek, Spanish, Italian, Austrian and Polish governments and the European Commission consider that that activity quite clearly involves "data processing" (argument from example).

+aA3. Previous decisions of the court concerning a similar case. The court has already had occasion to state that the operation of loading personal data on an internet page must be considered to be such "processing" within the meaning of Article 2(b) of Directive 95/46 (see Case C-101/01 *Lindqvist* EU:C:2003:596, paragraph 25) (argument from analogy – argument from *analogia legis*).

+aA4. Purpose of the law. A general derogation from the application of Directive 95/46 in such a case would largely deprive the directive of its effect – see previous decisions (argument from consequences – absurdity argument supported by argument from analogy – argument from precedent).

Question B: Interpretation and application of the concept of "data controller."

–aB1. A search engine does not exercise control over the personal data published on the web pages of third parties.

–aB2. Greek government does not consider search engines as "controllers" (argument from example)

+aB1. Legal definition. To exclude the operator of a search engine from the definition of "controller" would be contrary to the clear wording of Article 2(d) (argument from classification – systematic argument, namely, a legal provision setting out the legal definition).

+aB2. Purpose of the law. The notion of a "controller" was broadly defined in the Data Protection Directive to ensure protection (purpose of Article 2(d)); to exclude the operator of a search engine from that definition would be contrary to the purpose of the directive (argument from consequences – absurdity argument).

+aB3. The activity of a search engine is liable to affect significantly and additionally, compared with that of the publishers of websites, the fundamental rights to privacy and to data protection; the operator of the search engine is the person determining the purposes and means of that activity; therefore, it must ensure protection of data subjects (argument from consequences – teleological argument).

Question C: Interpretation and application of the "right to erasure."

–aC1. Appeal to the principle of proportionality. Any request seeking the removal of information must be addressed to the publisher of the website concerned because it is he who takes the responsibility for making the information public, who is in a position to appraise the lawfulness of that publication, and who has available to him the most effective and least restrictive means of making the information inaccessible (argument from practical reasoning – teleological argument based on the goal of the provision).

+aC1. Duties of data controller. The operator of the search engine as the controller in respect of that processing must ensure, within the framework of its responsibilities, powers, and capabilities, that that processing meets the requirements of Directive 95/46, in order that the guarantees laid down by the directive may have full effect (argument from classification – systematic argument).

+aC2. Pursuance of the goal of the directive (purpose of the law). The inclusion in the list of results is liable to constitute a more significant interference with the data subject's fundamental right to privacy than the publication on the web page. The effective and complete protection of data users could not be achieved if a search engine operator had to obtain first or in parallel the erasure of the information relating to them from the publishers of websites (argument from practical reasoning – teleological argument based on the goals of the directive).

+aC3. Application of the principle of proportionality. In certain circumstances the data subject is capable of exercising the rights referred to in Article 12(b) and subparagraph (a) of the first paragraph of Article 14 of Directive 95/46 against that operator but not against the publisher of the web page (argument from the classification of a requirement as "necessary").

Question D: Interpretation and application of the "right to object."

–aD1. Previous opinions on the "right to oblivion" (similar to "right to be forgotten," which was the original implicit classification of the case). The Greek, Austrian, and Polish governments and the Commission consider that this question should be answered in the negative. Rights should be conferred upon data subjects only if the processing in question is incompatible with the directive or on compelling legitimate grounds relating to their particular situation, and *not merely because they consider that that processing may be prejudicial to them or they wish* that the data being processed sink into *oblivion* (argument from classification – systematic argument – of "request of deleting links" as "right to oblivion".

+aD1; +aD2. Previous opinions on the right to data protection. According to the Spanish and Italian governments, the data subject may *oppose* the indexing by a search engine of personal data relating to him where their dissemination through the search engine is prejudicial to him and his fundamental rights to the protection of those data and to privacy – which encompass the "right to be forgotten" – override the legitimate interests of the operator of the search engine and the general interest in freedom of information (argument from classification – systematic argument – of "request of deleting links" as "right to object," supported by an argument from classification – systematic argument – of "right to be forgotten" as an instance of "right to object," supported by a practical reasoning argument – teleological argument based on the goals of the directive).

+aD3. Purpose of the law. If the inclusion in the list of results displayed following a search made on the basis of his name of the links to web pages published lawfully by third parties and containing true information relating to him personally is inadequate, irrelevant, or no longer relevant, or excessive in relation to the purposes of the processing at issue carried out by the operator of the search engine, the information and links concerned in the list of results must be *erased* upon the data subject's request in the light of his fundamental rights under Articles 7 and 8 (argument from practical reasoning – teleological argument based on the goal of the directive).

–aD4. Purpose of the law. The right to request that the information in question no longer be made available to the general public should override the interest of the general public in finding that information, unless there is a preponderant interest of the general public in having, on account of inclusion in the list of results, access to the information in question.

The argumentative structure of the controversy can be also represented as a dialectical process in which the pro and con arguments are assessed.

2.8.3 *The Argumentative Structure of the Dialectical Decision-Making Process*

The dialectical assessment of the questions to be decided upon by the court can be represented through charts that indicate the function of the different arguments advanced. This type of representation can be useful for determining not only the strategies of each party and the court, but more importantly for weighing the strength of the pro and con arguments. This process can be framed through Carneades, which allows including the types of argument used and their function.

The first problem (A) can be represented as a network of arguments (nodes) supported by premises and presumptions (indicated in elliptical circles). The arguments can be directed to the conclusion (either supporting it, in case of "+" arguments, or rejecting it, in case of "–" arguments) or against another argument. In this latter case, the argument plays the function of undercutter (indicated by an "undercut" label on the arrow). Figure 2.8 (and the other ones representing the argumentation structures of the other problems) has been drawn based on the general framework of the Carneades software.

Figure 2.8 represents how the different arguments are related to each other. In particular, the court relies on a twofold argumentative strategy. The first strategy is a positive one, in the sense that the interpretation of "processing" to include search engines is supported by two kinds of interpretative argument – the analogical (in a very broad sense) arguments based on previous opinions and decisions (the two lower arguments +aA3 and +aA2) and the classificatory argument based on the statutory definition of the term (+aA1). In terms of assessment, this latter argument can be considered as effective because it relies on a hierarchy of the presumptions underlying interpretative argument that is established, in this case, by the ordinary-meaning rule (Farber, 1992, 548), according to which the ordinary meaning shall be used unless there is a clear indication of a contrary one – in this case a statutory

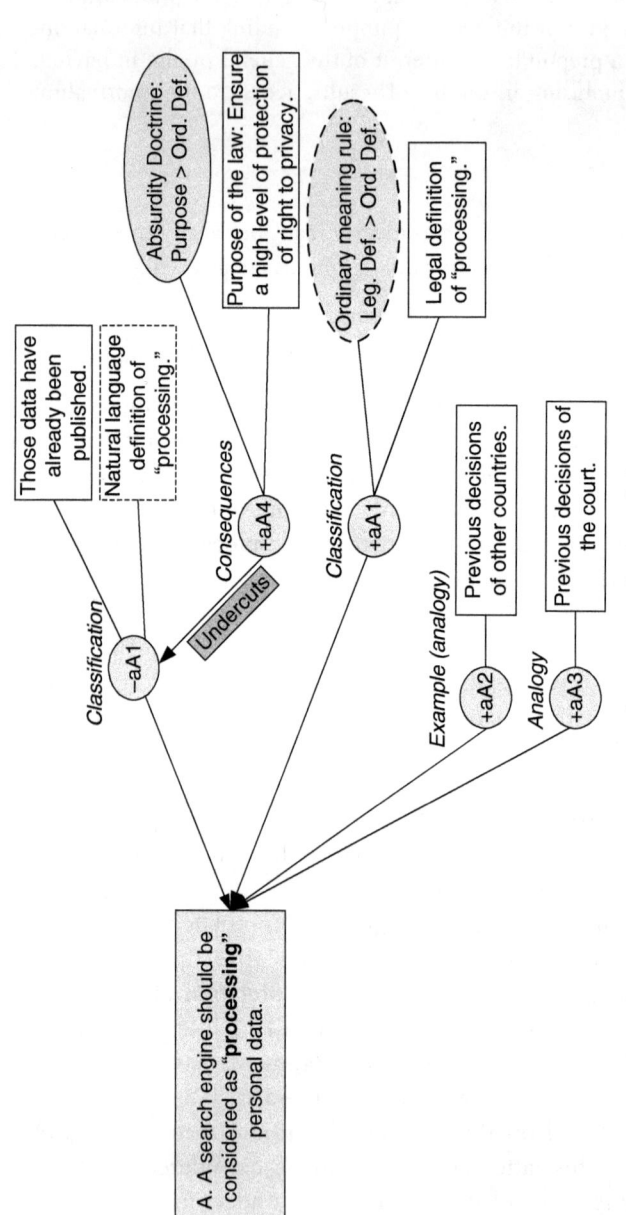

FIGURE 2.8 Processing of personal data

definition. This presumption, however, is not appealed to by the court, and is included in the diagram only as an additional note (dotted circle) for the purpose of assessment.

The second strategy (+aA4) is a negative one, namely an undercut. GS's argument against the classification of the activities of a search engine as "data processing" is attacked by an argument aimed at undermining the criteria for using the ordinary language definition. The court points out that a derogation (in this case, the failure to apply the legal norm to a search engine) would prevent the directive from pursuing its goals. This argument does not simply consist in advancing a stronger argument in favor of a contrary conclusion, such as was the case with +aA1. Rather, it is only directed at the reasonableness of the classification: relying on the absurdity doctrine (stating that judges may deviate from even the clearest statutory text when a given application would otherwise produce absurd results, Manning, 2003, 2388), the court objects to the very decision of using a definition leading to an outcome that is detrimental to the very purpose of the directive. In this case, the notion of purpose of the law and the absurdity of the results is directly appealed to by the court (the presumption is indicated then as an additional premise).

The discussion of the second question (B) can be also represented by distinguishing this twofold strategy, namely the level of arguments and counter-arguments and the level of undercutters. The structure is represented in Figure 2.9.

The two argumentation structures analyzed in Figures 2.8 and 2.9 concern the interpretation of specific terms, whose definitions are used by the parties to the controversy to classify the search engine's activities and the search engine itself in opposite ways. The other two questions that the court addressed concerned the application of two provisions establishing the data controller's obligations toward two crucial data subject rights – the right to erasure and the right to oblivion.

Concerning the right to erasure (Question C), two crucial practical arguments were advanced. GS appealed to the principle of proportionality, according to which the freedom of actions should not be limited beyond what is required for pursuing the purposes of public interest – in this case, the protection of the data subject's right (Długosz, 2017, 286). The argument is a practical one, in which the ordering of the possible means to achieve the protection of a fundamental right is established by the extent to which they enable the satisfaction of the right. Since the right to erasure can be protected most effectively by the publisher of the website, it is not necessary that the web engine should be subject to the obligation of fulfilling the data subject's request – and thus this obligation should not be imposed on GS. The court addressed this argument pursuing a positive and negative strategy. On the

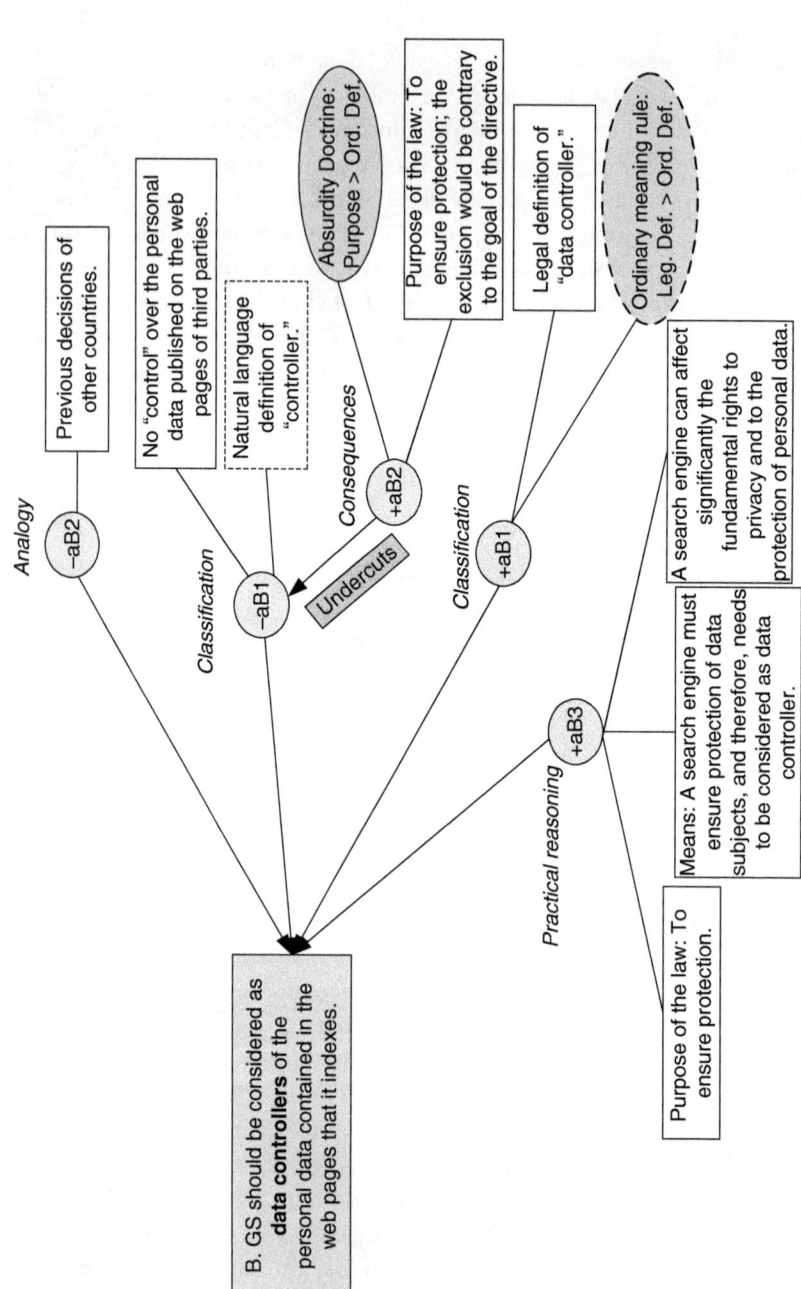

FIGURE 2.9 Data controller

negative side, an undercutter (an attack to the relation between premise and conclusion) is used, attacking the application of the principle of proportionality, namely the premise that the goal of the directive (protection of the right to erasure) is *always and under all circumstances* pursued most effectively by the publisher. The positive strategy consists in an opposite argument from practical reasoning. According to this argument, the duties imposed on the data controller to protect the data subject's rights can be pursued either by imposing the obligation only on the publisher, or also on the search engine. However, such rights are more strongly affected through searches on web engines, and effective protection of data users could not be achieved if the data must only be erased by publishers of websites (which would also involve a violation of the publishers' freedom of expression). Thus, the first solution would not optimally satisfy fundamental right and the goals of the directive (an implicit argument from consequences – absurdity argument, which is part of the practical reasoning). For this reason, the second solution needs to be chosen. The structure of the argumentation of this phase of the decision-making process is represented in Figure 2.10.

The last decision-making issue concerns the data subject's right to request the deletion of links to web pages published lawfully by third parties and containing true information relating to him (Question D). GS argued that previous decisions of other countries refused to acknowledge this request, as the right to be forgotten needs to be based on specific reasons and not merely on the data subject's desire (–aD1). The court decided to make an opposite decision, based on a complex strategy. First, the implicit classification of the case under the "right to be forgotten" was reclassified under the "right to object," claiming that the latter included the former (+aD2). This move allowed the court to use other precedents, and more importantly to frame the case under the provisions protecting the fundamental rights (recital no. 25; Art. 14 of the Directive) (+aD1). The other arguments proceeded from this classification and from a practical reasoning based on the purpose of protecting the "fundamental rights" of data subjects in case of irrelevant information (+aD3), and in case of information that is not conflicting with another right, namely the right to information (anticipating and defusing a possible attack – aD4). The structure of this argument is represented in Figure 2.11 ("data subject" is abbreviated to "DS").

In all four of these decision-making processes, focused on distinct interpretative problems that needed to be resolved, we can notice a common thread, namely the preponderant use by the court of the argument based on the "purpose of the law." This dimension needs to be analyzed in detail, as it represents a dimension in which the fields of pragmatics and legal interpretation intersect, and where the specific features of the legal context become crucial.

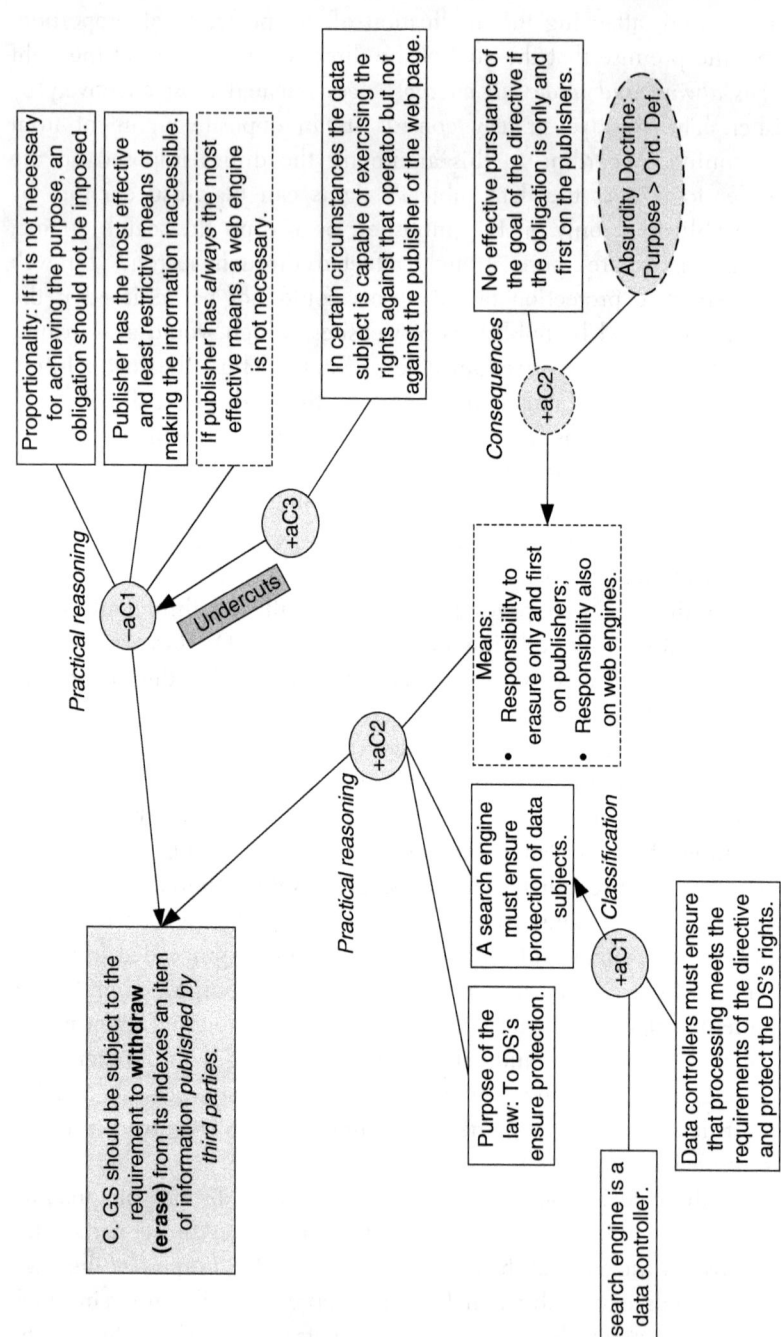

FIGURE 2.10 Right to erasure

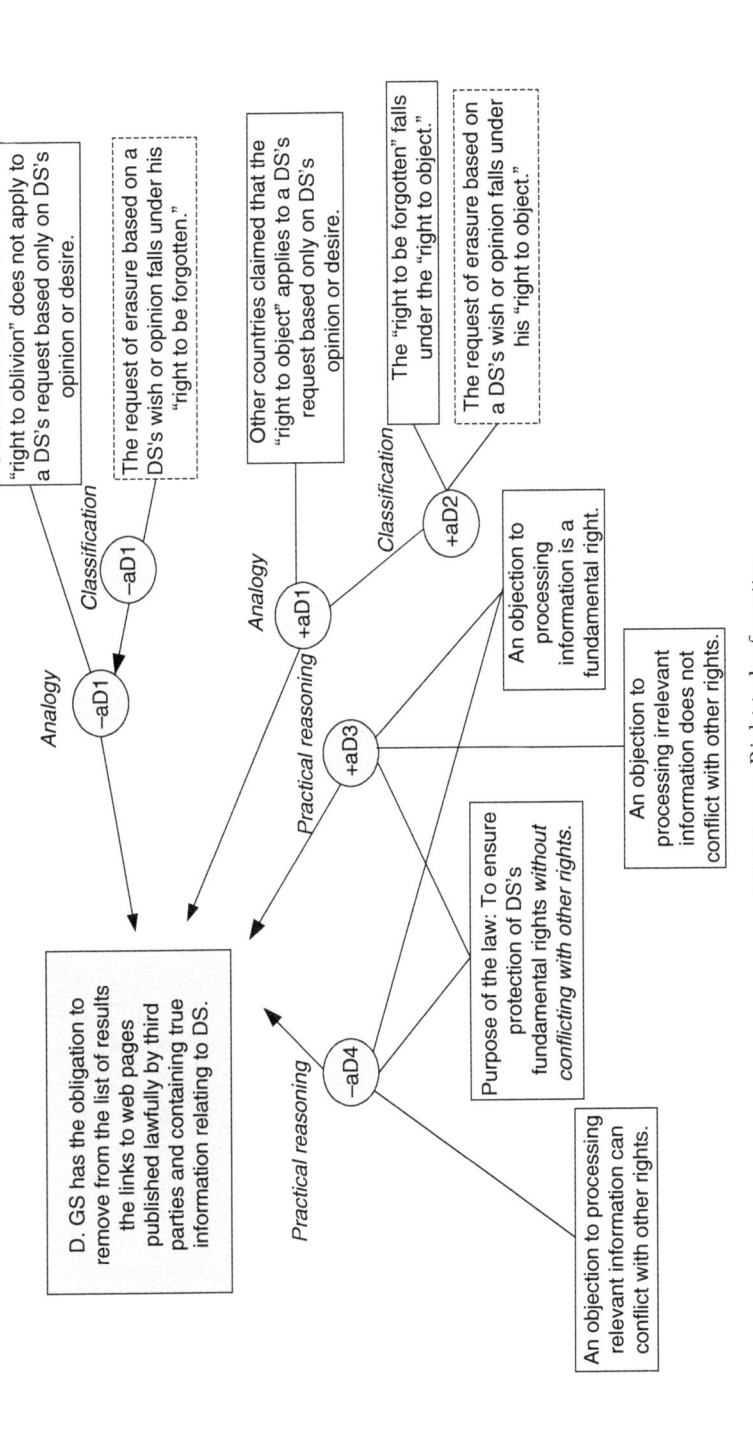

FIGURE 2.11 Right to be forgotten

2.9 THE PURPOSE OF THE LAW AND RELEVANCE

The questions represented in Figure 2.6 were discussed and evaluated by the court starting from a crucial interpretative issue, namely the fundamental purpose of the directive. The court, from the beginning, pointed out that the purpose of Directive 95/46/EC was "to ensure a high level of protection of the fundamental rights and freedoms of natural persons, in particular their right to privacy, with respect to the processing of personal data." As shown in Figure 2.7, the "purpose of the law" characterized several arguments (+aA4, +aB2, +aB3, +aC2, +aC3, and +aD3) that were crucial for determining the outcome of the decision making.

The appeal to and the reconstruction of the "purpose of the law" plays a crucial role in any approach that regards judicial interpretation in terms of decision making, or rather, as the justification of a decision. Regardless of the overall philosophical attitude toward interpretation – whether contextualist, textualist, or intentionalist – the appeal to the intention underlying a legal statement is a crucial argument. As we will discuss in Chapter 5, the inferential reasoning that is triggered can be represented according to two distinct "practical" types of argument, namely (a) the argument from practical reasoning, connecting the goal (intention) with the best means (specific interpretation leading to the pursuance of the goal), or (b) the argument from consequences (conflict with the obvious purpose). This inference is, however, based on the notion of "intention" and more importantly the arguments that are used to establish the "purpose of the law."

The concepts of "purpose of the law" and "intention of the legislator" can be analyzed in pragmatics under the key notion of "speaker's (or communicative) meaning," which was defined by Grice as the effect (response) that an utterance is intended to produce in an audience, by means of the audience's recognition of that intention (Grice, 1957, 385, 1968, 230). Meaning is thus regarded as presupposing an intention (Poscher, 2016, 67), and more specifically the intention to produce some effects on the audience (the prohibition of a specific behavior, for example). The recognition of this intention can be retrieved through the "cues" that the speaker provides, which need to be maximized, namely those clues have to be given that have the highest probability of being successful, considering the common knowledge shared by the interlocutor (Nunberg, 1979, 169). The most important cue is clearly semantic meaning, namely the level of interpretation drawn from a set of conventions governing the subset of the "normal uses" (Nunberg, 1979, 153) and from which the other uses can be pragmatically derived. This level needs to be considered together with other cues (Poscher, 2016, 68–69):

> [S]emantic meaning is usually the steppingstone for our inferences about a speaker's intentions, because we infer that she connected the intentions standardly connected with an utterance type with her utterance token. But speakers are not tied to the semantic meaning of signs when they make use of them, as long as they can be confident that there are enough contextual clues to infer the intentions they connect with their use of a term.

The cognitive mechanisms underlying this principle were set out in the relevance theory and its principle of relevance: "Every act of ostensive communication communicates a presumption of its own optimal relevance" (Sperber and Wilson, 1995, 158). Equating relevance with *information that is worth the hearer's attention* (Wilson, 1998, 64; Wilson and Sperber, 2012, 177), the cognitive processing of an utterance follows a principle of economy (Zipf, 1949), stated as follows: "an assumption with greater contextual effects is more relevant; and, other things being equal, an assumption requiring a smaller processing effort is more relevant" (Sperber and Wilson, 1995, 125). The relevance of an assumption is thus a scalar notion, it consists in the "yield" between the contextual effects of an assumption in a given context and effort required to process it in the given context (Sperber and Wilson, 1995, 123–125).

This pragmatic perspective is crucial for analyzing the nature and the force of the arguments underlying the justification of the reconstruction of the "purpose of the law." In our *Google Spain* case, the reconstruction of the "speaker's intention" was justified as follows:

> It is to be noted in this context that it is clear in particular from recitals 18 to 20 in the preamble to Directive 95/46 and Article 4 thereof that the European Union legislature sought to prevent individuals from being deprived of the protection guaranteed by the directive and that protection from being circumvented, by prescribing a particularly broad territorial scope. (*Google Spain* at 54)

> [T]he effective and complete protection of the fundamental rights and freedoms of natural persons which the directive seeks to ensure . . ., in particular their right to privacy, with respect to the processing of personal data, a right to which the directive accords special importance as is confirmed in particular by Article 1(1) thereof and recitals 2 and 10 in its preamble (see, to this effect, Joined Cases C-465/00, C-138/01 and C-139/01 *Österreichischer Rundfunk and Others* EU:C:2003:294, paragraph 70; Case C-553/07 *Rijkeboer* EU:C:2009:293, paragraph 47; and Case C-473/12 *IPI* EU:C:2013:715, paragraph 28 and the case-law cited). (*Google Spain* at 58)

These justifications can be reconstructed as based on two types of interpretative arguments:

1. Systemic arguments, which consist in abductive arguments aimed at drawing the purpose of the directive from the meaning retrieved less problematically from other statements of the same directive, and in particular:
   a. the provisions of Article 1(1) of the Directive; and
   b. the recitals 2, 10, 18 to 20 and 25 in the preamble of the Directive.
2. Authoritative arguments, namely arguments based on the authority of previous decisions or opinions that expressed interpretations of the purpose of the directive, which correspond to an argument from expert opinion (the opinion of previous judges or authorities cannot be ignored) and from analogy (if X was interpreted as meaning M in a previous or similar circumstance, X needs to be interpreted as meaning M now).

In this view, the court established on contextual and precedential grounds the purpose of the law, which was then used as the principle for interpreting the concepts and the rights that were controversial.

2.10 CONCLUSIONS

The first conclusion is that the argumentation model of the problem-solving dialogue presented in this chapter can represent interpretative argumentation. Combining problem solving as used in artificial intelligence with how it is employed in law according to the Twining-Miers theory has led to an argumentation model that was applied to some real examples of problem solving in statute interpretation. The second conclusion is that what has been shown by building this argumentation model both supports and extends the instrumentalist theory of Twining and Miers (2010). The third conclusion is that argumentation tools, such as argument diagrams and argumentation schemes, can be used to show how the capability of the new model to analyze and evaluate argumentation in relatively simple cases of statutory interpretation is potentially applicable to a broader range of more complex cases. The fourth conclusion is that approaches to problem solving in computer science and in law can be combined within an argumentation theory, to show promise of models that are generalizable to both fields. This fourth conclusion especially brings out the interdisciplinary nature of the research in this chapter.

REFERENCES

Abaelardus, Petrus. 1970. *Dialectica*. Edited by Lambertus. Marie de Rijk. Assen, Netherlands: Van Gorcum.

Anderson, Bruce. 2013. "Weighing and balancing in the light of deliberation and expression." In *Legal Argumentation Theory: Cross-Disciplinary Perspectives*, edited by Christian Dahlman and Eveline Feteris, 113–123. Amsterdam, Netherlands: Springer.

Anderson, Terence. 1999. "On generalizations I: A preliminary exploration." *South Texas Law Review* 40: 455–481.

Anderson, Terence, and William Twining. 1991. *Analysis of Evidence: How to Do Things with Facts, Based on Wigmore's Science of Judicial Proof*. Boston, MA: Little, Brown and Company.

Atlas, Jay David. 2005. *Logic, Meaning, and Conversation*. Oxford, UK: Oxford University Press.

Bransford, John, and Barry Stein. 1993. *The Ideal Problem Solver: A Guide to Improving Thinking, Learning, and Creativity*. New York, NY: Worth Publishers.

Carston, Robyn. 2002. *Thoughts and Utterances: The Pragmatics of Explicit Communication*. Oxford, UK: Blackwell Publishing Ltd.

Carston, Robyn. 2004. "Explicature and semantics." In *Semantics: A Reader*, edited by Steven Davis and Brendan Gillon, 817–845. Oxford, UK: Oxford University Press.

Chiassoni, Pierluigi. 2016. "Legal interpretation without truth." *Revus: Journal for Constitutional Theory and Philosophy of Law* 29: 93–118.

Crowe, Jonathan. 2013. "The Role of Contextual Meaning in Judicial Interpretation." *Federal Law Review* 41(3): 417–442. https://doi.org/10.22145/flr.41.3.2.

Damele, Giovanni. 2011. "Rhetoric and persuasive strategies in High Courts' decisions: Some remarks on the recent decisions of the Portuguese Tribunal Constitutional and the Italian Corte Costituzionale on same-sex marriage." In *Argumentation*, edited by Michał Araszkiewicz, Matej Myška, Terezie Smejkalová, Jaromír Šavelka, and Martin Škop, 81–93. Brno, Czech Republic: Masarykova UP.

Damele, Giovanni. 2014. "*Analogia Legis* and *Analogia Iuris*: An overview from a rhetorical perspective." In *Systematic Approaches to Argument by Analogy*, edited by Henrique Ribeiro, 243–256. Amsterdam, Netherlands: Springer.

Depraetere, Ilse. 2014. "Modals and lexically-regulated saturation." *Journal of Pragmatics* 71: 160–177. https://doi.org/10.1016/j.pragma.2014.08.003.

Długosz, Joanna. 2017. "The principle of proportionality in European Union Law as a prerequisite for penalization." *Przegląd Prawniczy Uniwersytetu Im. Adama Mickiewicza* 7(1): 283–300.

Dworkin, Ronald. 1986. *Law's Empire*. Cambridge, MA: Harvard University Press.

Eemeren, Frans van, and Rob Grootendorst. 2004. *A Systematic Theory of Argumentation: The Pragma-Dialectical Approach*. Cambridge, MA: Cambridge University Press.

Eemeren, Frans van, and Rob Grootendorst. 1992. *Argumentation, Communication and Fallacies*. Hillsdale, NJ: Erlbaum.

Endicott, Timothy. 2000. *Vagueness in Law*. Oxford, UK: Oxford University Press.

Farber, Daniel. 1992. "The inevitability of practical reason: Statutes, formalism, and the rule of law." *Vanderbilt Law Review* 45: 533–560.

Feteris, Eveline. 1999. *Fundamentals of Legal Argumentation*. Amsterdam, Netherlands: Springer.

Gordon, Thomas. 2010. "An overview of the Carneades Argumentation Support system." In *Dialectics, Dialogue and Argumentation. An Examination of Douglas Walton's Theories of Reasoning and Argument*, edited by Christopher Reed and Christopher Tindale, 145–156. London, UK: College Publications.

Grice, Paul. 1957. "Meaning." *The Philosophical Review* 66(3): 377–388. https://doi.org/10.2307/2182440.

Grice, Paul. 1968. "Utterer's meaning, sentence meaning and word-meaning." *Foundations of Language* 4: 225–242. https://doi.org/10.1007/978-94-009-2727-8_2.

Jaszczolt, Kasia. 1999. *Discourse, Beliefs and Intentions*. Oxford, UK: Elsevier.

Jaszczolt, Kasia. 2017. "Slippery meaning and accountability." In *Pragmatics and Law*, edited by Francesca Poggi and Alessandro Capone, 3–22. Cham, Switzerland: Springer.

Jori, Mario. 2016. "Legal pragmatics." In *Pragmatics and Law*, edited by Alessandro Capone and Francesca Poggi, 33–60. Cham, Switzerland: Springer.

Kissine, Mikhail. 2012. "Sentences, utterances, and speech acts." In *Cambridge Handbook of Pragmatics*, edited by Keith Allan and Kasia Jaszczolt, 169–190. New York, NY: Cambridge University Press.

Kloosterhuis, Harm. 2013. "The rule of law and the ideal of a critical discussion." In *Legal Argumentation Theory: Cross-Disciplinary Perspectives*, edited by Christian Dahlman and Eveline Feteris, 71–83. Amsterdam, Netherlands: Springer.

Kok, Eric M, John-Jules Meyer, Henry Prakken, and Gerard Vreeswijk. 2010. "A formal argumentation framework for deliberation dialogues." In *Argumentation in Multi-Agent Systems. ArgMAS 2010. Lecture Notes in Computer Science, Vol 6614*, edited by Peter McBurney, Iyad Rahwan, and Simon Parsons, 31–48. Berlin, Heidelberg, Germany: Springer.

Kompa, Nikola. 2016. "The role of vagueness and context sensitivity in legal interpretation." In *Vagueness and Law: Philosophical and Legal Perspectives*, edited by Geert Keil and Ralf Poscher, 205–227. Oxford, UK: Oxford University Press.

Macagno, Fabrizio. 2017. "The logical and pragmatic structure of arguments from analogy." *Logique et Analyse* 60(240): 465–490. https://doi.org/10.2143/LEA.240.0.3254093.

Macagno, Fabrizio, and Douglas Walton. 2009. "Argument from analogy in law, the classical tradition, and recent theories." *Philosophy and Rhetoric* 42(2): 154–182. https://doi.org/10.1353/par.0.0034.

Macagno, Fabrizio, and Douglas Walton. 2017. *Interpreting Straw Man Argumentation. The Pragmatics of Quotation and Reporting*. Amsterdam, Netherlands: Springer.

Macagno, Fabrizio, and Douglas Walton. 2018. "Practical reasoning arguments: A modular approach." *Argumentation* 32(4): 519–547. https://doi.org/10.1007/s10503-018-9450-5.

Macagno, Fabrizio, Douglas Walton, and Christopher Tindale. 2014. "Analogical reasoning and semantic rules of inference." *Revue Internationale de Philosophie* 270(4): 419–432.

Manning, John. 2003. "The absurdity doctrine." *Harvard Law Review* 116(8): 2387–2486. https://doi.org/10.2307/1342768.

Marmor, Andrei. 2016a. "Defeasibility and pragmatic indeterminacy in law." In *Pragmatics and Law: Philosophical Perspectives*, edited by Alessandro Capone and Francesca Poggi, 15–32. Cham, Switzerland: Springer.

Marmor, Andrei. 2016b. "Pragmatic vagueness in statutory law." In *Vagueness and Law*, edited by Geert Keil and Ralf Poscher, 161–176. Oxford, UK: Oxford University Press.

Martí, Genoveva, and Lorena Ramírez-Ludeña. 2016. "Legal disagreements and theories of reference." In *Pragmatics and Law: Philosophical Perspectives*, edited by Alessandro Capone and Francesca Poggi, 121–139. Cham, Switzerland: Springer.

McBurney, Peter, David Hitchcock, and Simon Parsons. 2007. "The eightfold way of deliberation dialogue." *International Journal of Intelligent Systems* 22(1): 95–132. https://doi.org/10.1002/int.v22:1.

Morra, Lucia. 2016. "Conversational implicatures in normative texts." In *Interdisciplinary Studies in Pragmatics, Culture and Society*, edited by Alessandro Capone and Jacob Mey, 537–562. Cham, Switzerland: Springer.

Murrill, Brandon. 2018. "Modes of constitutional interpretation." Washington, DC. www.crs.gov.

Nunberg, Geoffrey. 1979. "The non-uniqueness of semantic solutions: Polysemy." *Linguistics and Philosophy* 3(2): 143–184. https://doi.org/10.1007/BF00126509.

Poggi, Francesca. 2012. "Contextualism, but not enough. A brief note on Villa's theory of legal interpretation." *Revus. Journal for Constitutional Theory and Philosophy of Law/Revija Za Ustavno Teorijo in Filozofijo Prava*, no. 17: 55–65.

Pollock, John. 1995. *Cognitive Carpentry*. Cambridge, MA: MIT Press.

Poole, David, and Alan Mackworth. 2010. *Artificial Intelligence: Foundations of Computational Agents*. Cambridge, MA: Cambridge University Press.

Poscher, Ralf. 2016. "An intentionalist account of vagueness: A legal perspective." In *Vagueness and Law: Philosophical and Legal Perspectives*, edited by Geert Keil and Ralf Poscher, 65–93. Oxford, UK: Oxford University Press.

Prakken, Henry. 2009. "Models of persuasion dialogue." In *Argumentation in Artificial Intelligence*, edited by Guillermo Simari and Iyad Rahwan, 281–300. Boston, MA: Springer.

Recanati, François. 1987. *Meaning and Force: The Pragmatics of Performative Utterances*. New York, NY: Cambridge University Press.

Rehnquist, William. 1975. "The notion of a living constitution." *Texas Law Review* 54: 693–706.

Russell, Stuart, and Peter Norvig. 1995. *Artificial Intelligence: A Modern Approach*. Upper Saddle River, NJ: Prentice Hall.

Sartor, Giovanni. 1995. "Defeasibility in legal reasoning." In *Informatics and the Foundations of Legal Reasoning*, edited by Zenon Bankowsk, Ian White, and Ulrike Hahn, 119–157. Dordrecht, Netherlands: Springer.

Sartor, Giovanni. 2018. "Defeasibility in law." In *Handbook of Legal Reasoning and Argumentation*, edited by Giorgio Bongiovanni, Gerald Postema, Antonino Rotolo, Giovanni Sartor, Chiara Valentini, and Douglas Walton, 315–364. Dordrecht, Netherlands: Springer.

Sbisà, Marina. 2017. "Implicitness in normative texts." In *Pragmatics and Law: Practical and Theoretical Perspectives*, edited by Francesca Poggi and Alessandro Capone, 23–42. Cham, Switzerland: Springer.

Schauer, Frederick. 2013. "Why precedent in law (and elsewhere) is not totally (or even substantially) about analogy." In *Legal Argumentation Theory: Cross-Disciplinary Perspectives*, edited by Christian Dahlman and Eveline Feteris, 45–56. Dordrecht, Netherlands: Springer.

Schiffer, Stephen. 2016. "Philosophical and jurisprudential issues of vagueness." In *Vagueness and Law: Philosophical and Legal Perspectives*, edited by Geert Keil and Ralf Poscher, 23–48. Oxford, UK: Oxford University Press.

Schum, David. 1994. *The Evidential Foundations of Probabilistic Reasoning*. Evanston, IL: Northwestern University Press.

Schum, David, and Peter Tillers. 1991. "Marshalling evidence for adversary litigation." *Cardozo Law Review* 13(1): 657–704.

Soames, Scott. 2009. "Interpreting legal texts: What is, and what is not, special about the law." In *Philosophical Essays*, 1:403–424. Princeton, NJ: Princeton University Press.

Solum, Lawrence. 2011. "What is originalism? The evolution of contemporary originalist theory." In *The Challenge of Originalism: Essays in Constitutional Theory*, edited by Grant Huscroft and Bradley Miller, 12–41. Cambridge, UK: Cambridge University Press.

Sperber, Dan, and Deirdre Wilson. 1995. *Relevance: Communication and Cognition*. Oxford, UK: Blackwell Publishing Ltd.

Summers, Robert. 1971. "The technique element in law." *California Law Review* 59(3): 733–751. https://doi.org/10.15779/Z38KX9V.

Tarello, Giovanni. 1980. *L'Interpretazione della Legge*. Milano, Italy: Giuffrè.

Twining, William, and David Miers. 2010. *How to Do Things with Rules: A Primer of Interpretation*. Cambridge, UK: Cambridge University Press.

Walton, Douglas. 1999. "Dialectical relevance in persuasion dialogue." *Informal Logic* 19: 119–143. https://doi.org/10.22329/il.v19i2.2323.

Walton, Douglas. 2006. *Fundamentals of Critical Argumentation*. New York, NY: Cambridge University Press.

Walton, Douglas. 2015. *Goal-Based Reasoning for Argumentation*. Cambridge, MA: Cambridge University Press.

Walton, Douglas, Christopher Reed, and Fabrizio Macagno. 2008. *Argumentation Schemes*. New York, NY: Cambridge University Press.

Walton, Douglas, and Alice Toniolo. 2016. "Deliberation, practical reasoning and problem-solving." In *Argumentation, Objectivity, and Bias: Proceedings of the 11th International Conference of the Ontario Society for the Study of Argumentation (OSSA), May 18–21, 2016*, edited by Pat Bondy and Laura Benacquista, 1–19. Windsor, ON: OSSA.

Walton, Douglas, Alice Toniolo, and Timothy Norman. 2016. "Towards a richer model of deliberation dialogue: Closure problem and change of circumstances." *Argument & Computation* 7(2–3): 155–173. https://doi.org/10.3233/AAC-160009.

Walton, Richard, and Robert McKersie. 1966. "Behavioral dilemmas in mixed-motive decision making." *Behavioral Science* 11(5): 370–384. https://doi.org/10.1002/bs.3830110506.

Wigmore, John Henry. 1931. *The Principles of Judicial Proof*, 2nd Ed. Boston, MA: Little, Brown & Company.

Wilson, Deirdre. 1998. "Discourse, coherence and relevance: A reply to Rachel Giora." *Journal of Pragmatics* 29(1): 57–74. https://doi.org/10.1016/S0378-2166(97)00012-X.

Wilson, Deirdre, and Dan Sperber. 2012. *Meaning and Relevance*. Cambridge, UK: Cambridge University Press.

Wooldridge, Michael. 2009. *An Introduction to Multiagent Systems*. Chichester, UK: John Wiley & Sons.

Zipf, George Kingsley. 1949. *Human Behavior and the Principle of Least Effort: An Introduction to Human Ecology*. Cambridge, UK: Addison-Wesley.

CASES CITED

Heydon's Case. 1984 EWHC Exch J36.

Buckoke v. *Greater London Council* [1970] 2 All ER 193.

Google Spain SL and Google Inc. v. *Agencia Española de Protección de Datos (AEPD) and Mario Costeja González* 2014 ECLI:EU:C:2014:317.

Bodil Lindqvist v Åklagarkammaren i Jönköping 2003 ECLI:EU:C:2003:596

3

Interpretation and Pragmatics – Legal Ambiguity

3.1 INTRODUCTION. AMBIGUITY AND INTERPRETATION

Ambiguity in law is essentially connected with interpretation. The concept of ambiguity commonly used in the legal context can be summarized in the following definition (Solan, 2004, 862):

> Courts sometimes define ambiguity this way: "A statute is ambiguous if it is susceptible of more than one reasonable interpretation." The same description is used to describe contractual ambiguity: "In attempting to interpret such plans, our first task is to determine if the contract at issue is ambiguous or unambiguous. Contract language is ambiguous if it is susceptible to more than one reasonable interpretation."

This definition is only apparently clear and simple. In fact, in order to understand what it means it is necessary to analyze first the concept of [§1.1] interpretation and then the related concepts of [§1.2] ambiguity, [§1.3] ordinary meaning, and [§1.4] vagueness.

3.1.1 Interpretation

The understanding of the legal concept of ambiguity rests on the definition of "interpretation." To analyze the relationship between pragmatics, philosophy of language, and legal theory, it is necessary to bring to light the different theoretical approaches to this crucial notion.

In philosophy of language, "interpretation" is commonly analyzed by distinguishing the interpretative sentences, characterized by the established synonymity between two expressions, and the speech act of uttering them (Naess, 2005a, 50): "If P says '«a» means «b»,' or uses any other of the skeletal forms of interpretative sentences, we shall say that he 'performs a verbalized act of «interpretation»'; he 'explicitly interprets «a» to mean b.'"

Thus, interpretation within philosophy of language is a hypothesis about language usage (Naess, 2005a, 51). In law, the concept of interpretation focuses on two distinct dimensions, the processing and justification level, i.e., the type of "interpretative" act and the grounds provided for it.

In most legal theories, understanding the meaning of the law is regarded as corresponding to interpretation (Endicott, 2000, 11; Patterson, 1993), conflating and often confusing two things (Endicott, 2000, 13): the reconstruction of the communicative meaning of a text and the justification thereof in case it is doubtful or controversial (Macagno, 2017; Macagno and Capone, 2016). Legal theories have focused on the distinction between interpretation and construction. According to Solum, interpretation concerns the determination of the "communicative content" – also referred to as "linguistic meaning" or "semantic content." Construction is a further activity – essentially related and interconnected with interpretation – but conceived as a further cognitive act (Schiffer, 2016, 41), consisting in drawing inferences from such an interpretation, namely applying rules to cases and establishing the relationship between legal doctrines and decisions and the linguistic meaning of the text (Solum, 2009, 973, 2013, 455–457). Construction is commonly associated with the activity of establishing the "cutoff point" of vague predicates (Marmor, 2014, 100), namely their precization (Naess, 2005c), which needs to be established considering the specific context (Marmor, 2014, 101).

This distinction between interpetation and construction draws a line between on the one hand two types of interpretation, the "semantic" one and the "interpretative" one (Barnett, 2011, 65), where "interpretative interpretation" refers to the identification of the semantic meaning in context, and on the other hand construction as the activity of applying the interpreted meaning to specific factual circumstances (Barnett, 2011, 66). In this sense, the determination of the ambiguity of a statute precedes the problem of applying it to the specific case (Farnsworth, Guzior, and Malani, 2010, 258):

> Courts often treat ambiguity as a kind of gateway consideration when they interpret a statute. If the statute is ambiguous, the judge might then become interested in sources of guidance, such as legislative history, that wouldn't otherwise be considered. Or ambiguity might cause a judge to defer to an agency's view of the statute, as under the *Chevron* doctrine. Or ambiguity might cause a judge to resort to a canon of construction such as the rule of lenity, or the doctrine that courts should prefer interpretations of ambiguous statutes that avoid difficult constitutional issues, or the rule that ambiguous statutes will be interpreted to avoid conflict with foreign law, or many others.

Ambiguity thus concerns the possibility that a statute can bear different meanings for an ordinary reader. Construction, in contrast, is an activity that presupposes a specific property of the text, namely its "underdeterminacy," defined as the property affecting a legal text with respect to a given case when "the set of results in the case that can be squared with the legal materials is a nonidentical subset of the set of all imaginable results" (Solum, 1987, 473). Thus, underdeterminacy is constrained by the legal text and other considerations, and concerns the borderline cases.

The difference between the two concepts can be drawn also at a pragmatic (dialogical) level. Judicial construction is not an activity aimed at establishing how a legal statement is understood by the ordinary reader but rather is a decisional activity. The underdeterminacy of a legal text delegates some decisions of application to judges (Strauss, 1996, 1571), constraining them not to contradict the meaning of the legal text (at least in most cases, see Slocum, 2017, 35) (Barnett, 2011, 70; Slocum, 2017, 30; Tiersma, 1995). Judicial construction is a decision-making process resulting in a performative (declarative) act of giving an authoritative meaning to a text, while interpretation is a type of inquiry consisting in assertions through which the hearer expresses his or her inference of the communicative intentions of the speaker or writer (which may mirror his or her own mental processes) (Naess, 2005b). As Tiersma put it (Tiersma, 1995, 1099):

> [I]t should be evident that when judges engage in statutory construction, they are not merely interpreting, but are declaring meaning. Statutory construction occurs only inside a formalized institutional structure. Within that judicial institution, it is judges who are authorized to construe statutes. Lawyers, linguists, and laypersons can all interpret statutes on the basis of ordinary language principles, and they are free to assert and argue their interpretations. Yet no one but judges can construe a statute. And once a judge does so – thus giving it an authoritative meaning – other institutional actors are bound by it. Of course, a lower court can still assert its own interpretation of a statute in the text of its opinion, and lawyers can openly disagree with the higher court's construction. But in carrying out their institutional role of adjudicating cases, lower courts must follow the higher court's construction.

The pragmatic distinction concerns also the ordering of these two dialogical activities. Courts first engage in the activity of interpretation, applying the general principles of statutory construction to the language of the statute, to determine whether the language is ambiguous. This determination is the starting point for the process of construction, whether it is aimed at rejecting the ordinary meaning, narrowing it to exclude its application to a case that would result in an outcome contrary to the legislator's intent (Slocum, 2017), or deciding on its underdeterminacy (Slocum, 2016b, 4).

This distinction, however, should not hide the correspondence and interconnection between the two concepts. Constitutional construction is constrained by the linguistic meaning of the text (Solum, 2009, 939), and is complementary to interpretation, as a judge engages in construction when the disambiguation of a legal statement does not solve the legal dispute or when the interpretation (or even unambiguous understanding) of the text would lead to results unacceptable or undesirable from a legal perspective (Tiersma, 1995, 1099–1101). At the level of the reasoning underlying these two dialogical activities, we notice that they are both interpretative activities in a broad sense, and they are both based on the use of different types of evidence and presumptions. The similarities between the two concepts can be brought to light by taking into account the notions of ambiguity and vagueness that underlie this distinction, revealing their common pragmatic nature.

3.1.2 *The Meanings of Ambiguity*

The legal concepts of interpretation and construction highlight the distinction and relationship between ambiguity and vagueness (Schiffer, 2016, 47). To address these distinctions, it is useful to rely on the literature in philosophy of language and pragmatics, starting from the definition of ambiguity. Naess provided the following description of this concept (Naess, 2005a, 31): « . . . is ambiguous» =D. «There is at least one pair of instances of « . . . » such that the first member of the pair expresses a different meaning from the second.»

This definition is general, as it includes both its pragmatic sense, concerning the use of an expression in a specific context (namely the expression token), and its semantic one, which takes into account a "grammatical" unit, namely a component of the linguistic system abstracted from its use (Gullvåg and Naess, 1996). In this perspective, the "potential" ambiguity that affects the lexical items and the syntactic construction of the semantic representation becomes actual when it results in an ambiguity that concerns the use of the expression. The distinction between these two levels of ambiguity is shown in Table 3.1 (Macagno and Bigi, 2018; Walton, 1996, 262).

TABLE 3.1 *Levels of ambiguity*

Potential ambiguity (grammatical ambiguity)		
Lexical	Syntactic	Intonational
Homographs Different definitions	Different syntactic construction	Different deep structures manifested by different intonations
Pragmatic ambiguity	
Actual	Imaginary
Semantic ambiguity: Different enriched semantic representations	Incompatible inferences that can be drawn from the utterance

The distinction between homonymy and polysemy is drawn based on linguistic conventions. While homonymy is linguistically defined as two separate linguistic conventions governing the use of a word (such as "bank," meaning both the riverside and the building), polysemy is intuitively defined as the association of different normal and related uses for the same word, namely in terms of synchronic processes that derive one use from the other (Nunberg, 1979, 145). These two phenomena are usually distinguished in linguistics through syntactic tests: while anaphoric rules may ignore the difference between two polysemic uses ("The window was broken so many times that it had to be boarded up," referring to both the opening and the glass), the condition of linguistic identity is required in cases of ambiguity ("Bill gave Harry a file, and received one from Jane" cannot be used to mean that Bill gave Harry a tool, and received a dossier) (Nunberg, 1979, 150).

The crucial distinction that Table 3.1 points out is between potential and pragmatic ambiguity, the latter in turn distinguished between actual and imaginary. Actual ambiguity concerns the pragmatic level of what is said (Bezuidenhout, 1997; Carston, 2002, 2013; Soames, 2009), namely the enrichment of the semantic representation resulting from compositional semantics. Without considering the processing cognitive level at which these operations occur (Gibbs, 1992; Jaszczolt, 2006), at a theoretical level we can distinguish the inferences that are drawn to decode, specify, and enrich the semantic representation (and thus solving actual ambiguity) from those that are aimed at drawing what is meant, namely further inferences having as a conclusion what the speaker intends to communicate (addressing imaginary ambiguity).

At the level of the semantic representation, we can distinguish several types of ambiguity. The first two are the result of the two types of grammatical ambiguity, as they concern the decoding of the message, which, when affected by lexical and syntactic ambiguities (also called grammatical ambiguities), can result in different semantic representations. However, the disambiguation processes can involve inferences that are contextual in nature. We consider the following examples of disambiguation (Levinson, 2000, 174):

1. Lexical ambiguity (Lyons, 1977, 550) (includes homonymic words and homographs)
   a. The view could be improved by the addition of a *plant* out there (shrubbery).
   b. The view would be destroyed by the addition of a *plant* out there (factory).
2. Syntactic ambiguity (prepositional-phrase attachment)
   a. Mary left [the book] [on the bus].
   b. Mary left [the book on the atom].
   c. He looked at the kids [in the park] with a telescope.
   d. He looked at the kids [in the park with a statue].

In both cases, the sentences are disambiguated by considering the common ground, which would make some interpretations unreasonable. In both cases, pragmatic principles are used to decide the meaning of the lexical item or of the phrase attachment that can be consistent with the context (Sperber and Wilson, 1995, 186), based on the Gricean principle of relevance (Grice, 1975, 47): "I expect a partner's contribution to be appropriate to the immediate needs at each stage of the transaction. If I am mixing ingredients for a cake, I do not expect to be handed a good book or even an oven cloth (though this might be an appropriate contribution at a later stage)."

As mentioned before, one of the crucial features distinguishing between interpretation and construction pertains to addressing pragmatic ambiguity. However, pragmatic disambiguation is not the only type of ambiguity resolution, as the general semantic representation needs to be processed pragmatically in order to derive from it a truth-conditionally evaluable proposition (Jaszczolt, 1999, 2). Usually, in pragmatics such ambiguities are called "semantic ambiguities" and include interpretative phenomena distinguished from lexical or syntactic "disambiguation" (Atlas, 2005, Chapter 1; Levinson, 2000, 174–186), such as indexical resolution, reference identification, ellipsis unpacking, and generality narrowing. Such phenomena are related to the *pragmatic* notion of "underdetermination" of the semantic representation of a sentence (or "what is said") (Atlas, 2005, 40), and govern the passage from a semantic nonspecific structure to a proposition that can carry a truth-value (or be enforceable, as in case of orders). We summarize the most important types of semantic ambiguity (as defined by Jaszczolt above) as follows:

3. Indexical resolution
    a. Suppose A is in Los Angeles and B is in New York and the following exchange takes place:
       A: "Where's the conference being held?"
       B: "It's being held here" ("here" does not refer to the exact location of the speaker in that very moment, but rather to the university in New York where the conference takes place).
4. Reference identification
    a. The only vote for Felix was his ("his" can refer to either Felix himself, or the candidate that does not correspond to Felix).
    b. The king is powerful ("the king" can refer to the person who is the king at the time of the utterance or to the role of the king) (Bezuidenhout, 1997; Capone, 2011; Jaszczolt, 1999).
5. Ellipsis unpacking
    a. A says "Who came?" and B replies "John" ("John" is elliptical and the whole sentence needs to be reconstructed, resulting in "John came").
6. Generality narrowing
    a. Fixing this car will take some time ("some time" means "longer than expected," otherwise it would be a tautology).
    b. I've eaten breakfast ("I have eaten" means "I have just eaten" or "I have eaten breakfast this morning," and does not refer to the fact that the speaker is a breakfast eater).

These different types of sources of ambiguity need to be solved to reconstruct "what is said" through pragmatic (contextual) inferences (Carston, 2002; Kissine, 2012, 17; Recanati, 1987, 224), which are in turn based on presumptions of different kinds, including those referring to the goal and the topic of the conversation (Atlas, 2005, 38).

This account of pragmatic ambiguity can shed light on the concept of legal ambiguity. The distinction between interpretation and construction captures different types of ambiguity, all of which are pragmatic in nature. Legal ambiguity refers to the attribution of meaning to specific tokens, namely statutes, texts uttered (stated) in a "minimal" but actual context (the legislature), with a specific (even if general) goal, regulating the behavior of the people based on basic principles such as fairness and equality. For this reason, the first specification that can be introduced in the aforementioned definition is that we are dealing with a pragmatic notion of ambiguity – we are analyzing not (only) grammatical ambiguity, but pragmatic ambiguity, as contextual (pragmatic) considerations are frequently necessary for retrieving and justifying the "meaning" of the text (Asgeirsson, 2012). Moreover, even if minimal, the context plays a crucial role in interpretation, even if only for the purpose of establishing the weight of the specific evidence used to support an interpretation. Considering the atemporal effects of a legal text, and the impossibility of determining the specific speaker's intention underlying a collective act, the inferences drawn in legal interpretation are usually based on the type of evidence that is considered stronger in this specific context, namely the co-textual one (Slocum, 2017; Tiersma, 2001).

3.1.3 *Interpretation and the Blurred Notion of Ordinary Meaning*

The difference between construction and interpretation brings to light the crucial role that the attribution of the *linguistic* meaning to a legal text plays in interpretative disputes (intended in a broader sense). Ambiguity is essentially related to the "plain meaning" or "ordinary meaning" rule (Strauss, 1996), which is considered the most important rule of interpretation (Scalia and Garner, 2012, 6). It establishes that "in determining the scope of a statute, we look first to its language, giving the words used their ordinary meaning" (*Moskal v. United States*, 498 U.S. 103, 108 (1990)). The plain meaning rule sets the criteria for determining whether a statute is ambiguous, or at least the presumption in favor of its unambiguous or ambiguous nature (*United States v. Missouri Pacific R.R. Co.*, 278 U.S. 269, 278 (1929)): "[W]here the language of an enactment is clear and construction according to its terms does not lead to absurd or impracticable consequences, the words employed are to be taken as the final expression of the meaning intended."

This rule sets the procedure for the process of statutory interpretation. The principles of statutory interpretation can apply only if the "language" is ambiguous – or leads to absurd or impracticable results. Otherwise, the text is normally given its ordinary meaning (Slocum, 2016b, 5), which is presumed to be the stronger indicator of the legislator's communicative intent (Strauss, 1996, 1570). Thus, while other types of evidence, such as legislative history or external evidence about the "purpose" and the "intention" of the legislator, are not excluded, they are commonly considered as weaker than the plain meaning (Slocum, 2017, 33–34), and, therefore, such types of evidence need to be backed by arguments.

The concepts of ambiguity and "plain meaning" raise two crucial issues, namely the meaning of "ordinary meaning" and the boundaries of the "language" of the law, or rather the role of the context and the definition of context itself (Solan, 2004, 867–868). First, the ordinary meaning of the words in a legal text is defeasibly linked to the meaning of the same words as used in everyday conversation. Legal texts are not constituted only of words having ordinary, linguistic meaning, but in lack of evidence of deviations, they need to be interpreted in light of accepted and typical standards of communication, and according to the meaning that their words have in ordinary (nonlegal) communication (Slocum, 2016b, 2). This principle sets a presumption: the linguistic (ordinary) meaning is presumed but it can be overcome by arguments that the court finds persuasive. This presumption sets a corresponding burden on the parties to the dispute, since "the amount of evidence necessary to confirm the linguistic meaning of a provision as its legal meaning is less than that necessary to reject the linguistic meaning in favor of a nonliteral meaning" (Slocum, 2017, 26).

The second issue, the role of context, concerns the relationship between the "plain meaning" and the types of pragmatic ambiguity that is different from disambiguation. The concept of plain meaning or language of the law is at the center of heated discussions, as it is used to refer to both "stereotypical (or apparently a-contextual) meaning" (Kecskes, 2013, 136), and the "clear" or obvious meaning, which, however, can be established based on contextual considerations (Baude and Doerfler, 2017, 545):

> Courts and scholars sometimes use the phrase "plain meaning" to denote something like ordinary meaning – i.e., the normal meaning, or the meaning one would normally attribute to those words given little information about their context . . . Again, the "plain meaning rule" uses this latter sense of "plain" – the meaning that is clear or obvious . . . [T]he Court has also said that the "meaning – or ambiguity – of certain words or phrases may only become evident when placed in context," and context is sometimes conceived quite expansively.

Ambiguity is defined by the notion of plain meaning; however, plain meaning is determined based on contextual considerations, and through the resolution of types of ambiguity that do not correspond solely to disambiguation. As Solum pointed out, "literal meaning" cannot be equated solely with semantic (and underspecified) content. Context contributes to the interpretation of a text through different aspects of "pragmatic enrichment" (Marmor, 2014, Chapter 1; Solum, 2013, 465–466). The problem of ambiguity and "plain meaning" thus leads to analyzing the dichotomy between the "language" and the "extraneous" information used to determine the unequivocal or correct interpretation (Baude and Doerfler, 2017).

A clear case that can illustrate the problem of context and pragmatic ambiguity in relation to interpretation is *Smith* v. *United States*, 508 U.S. 223 (1993). The case concerned the following article of the federal code, which mandates certain penalties if the defendant "uses a firearm" during and in relation to any crime of violence or drug trafficking (18 U.S.C. § 924(c)(1)):

> Except to the extent that a greater minimum sentence is otherwise provided by this subsection or by any other provision of law, any person who, during and in relation to any crime of violence or drug trafficking crime (including a crime of violence or drug trafficking crime that provides for an enhanced punishment if committed by the use of a deadly or dangerous weapon or device) for which the person may be prosecuted in a court of the United States, uses or carries a firearm, or who, in furtherance of any such crime, possesses a firearm, shall, in addition to the punishment provided for such crime of violence or drug trafficking crime[, be sentenced to additional imprisonment.]

The problem posed before the Supreme Court was whether trading an automatic weapon to an undercover officer for cocaine was an instance of "using a firearm during and in relation to a drug trafficking crime." When the plain meaning of a criminal statute is ambiguous, the lenity rule establishes that doubts are resolved in favor of the defendant (*Smith*, 508 U.S. at 246). Thus, the crucial interpretative problem was to establish whether the language was indeed ambiguous, and thus whether this case was matter of interpretation or construction. The Court found – contrary to the defendant's argument – that the law was not ambiguous, as "the dictionary definitions and experience make clear, one can use a firearm in a number of ways" (*Smith*, 508 U.S. at 230). Moreover, according to the Court, the context disambiguates this notion, as in the other statutory provisions the phrase "to use a firearm" or its synonyms are used with a meaning that is not limited to "the use of a firearm as a weapon."

This case, however, raises the problem of determining the boundaries of ambiguity in law. In pragmatics, the interpretation of this statute would be considered as a typical case of pragmatic enrichment, a pragmatic process distinct from pragmatic disambiguation and aimed at broadening or narrowing the meaning. "To use a firearm" can be given a broad meaning ("use for any purpose"), or a narrow meaning ("use as a weapon") (*Smith*, 508 U.S. at 246). However, in both cases the interpreter engages in an activity aimed at solving a semantic ambiguity through inferences. The verb "to use something" is underspecified, as a meaning constituent (the logical argument/variable corresponding to the goal of its use) is not expressed and thus needs to be contextually provided (Recanati, 2012) through the process of pragmatic enrichment called "saturation" (Schiffer, 2016, 43). The sentence is enriched in the sense that it is supplemented with contextually recoverable extra materials: the speaker omitted some implicit qualifications of what he or she said, which need to be provided by the hearer through contextual inferences (Bach, 2000, 263). However, such tacit constituents are necessary: "[U]nless such a constituent is provided, the utterance fails to express a definite proposition" (Recanati, 2002, 308). Thus, the determination of the purpose, whether it is interpreted extensively as "for any purpose" or narrowly as "to shoot," is a matter of pragmatic enrichment rather than of pragmatic disambiguation (Asgeirsson, 2012).

The problem of "ordinary meaning" seems to be related not so much to the problem of determining the "dictionary meaning" of expressions, but rather to the reconstruction of the specific, enriched semantic representation of the legal statement. This analysis of the notions of ordinary meaning and interpretation explains how presumptions of different types can contribute to this pragmatic process, and more importantly how they can be ordered. On the one hand, the "ordinary meaning" can be retrieved by enriching the general semantic representation through defaults (Heine, Narrog, and Jaszczolt, 2015; Jaszczolt, 2005b), or through defeasible inferences to the first unchallenged alternative: "[W]e reason by default, unless we have evidence that we should not." In this view, a default is regarded as an automatic, effortless conclusion drawn in lack of contrary evidence and until contrary evidence is provided (Jaszczolt, 2005a, 46), based on different types of information including word meaning and socio-cultural information (Jaszczolt, 2007, 50–52, 2011, 13). On the other hand, interpretation is performed by solving the pragmatic ambiguity of a legal text by taking into account the contextual evidence provided by the legal text, which defeats the defaults commonly used in ordinary enrichment. In this sense, the ordinary meaning that is retrieved through the interpretation process differs at a pragmatic/dialogical level from the outcome of judicial construction only when the judges depart from enriched semantic representation of the text). In order to analyze the nature of the interpretative decision and the interpretation/construction distinction, it is necessary to describe in detail the object of construction, vagueness, and see how it is related to semantic ambiguity.

3.1.4 *Ambiguity and Vagueness*

The opposition between construction and interpretation is crucially based on the difference between the concepts of vagueness and ambiguity, and more importantly on their causes. Vagueness can be analyzed starting from the concept of precization and its theoretical distinction from interpretation. As Naess put it (Naess, 2005c, 50): "That expression U is a precization of expression T means that all reasonable interpretations of U are reasonable interpretations of T and that there is at least one reasonable interpretation of T that is *not* a reasonable interpretation of U. This definition can be expanded to include terms as well."

Precization is thus a specific type of interpretation, which is nonreflexive (as U cannot be a precization of itself), asymmetrical, and transitive (Naess, 2005c). Vagueness is solved by making our object more precise. However, we need is to determine what can be vague.

Vagueness, like ambiguity, is a pragmatic notion, as it concerns the meaning that an expression token has in a specific context; most importantly, it involves a decision that needs to be made on the specific meaning of an expression. While ambiguity becomes a legal problem when it comes to determining whether a legal provision can be given two distinct meanings, vagueness is legally relevant when it is involved in the application of a rule to a case (Barnett, 2011, 68–69): "Although most words are potentially vague, we do not face a problem of vagueness until a word needs to be applied to an object that may or may not fall within its penumbra. When this happens we must engage in construction."

Vagueness is the actual occurrence of an unlegislated case (Williamson, 2002, 91) that results from the *possibility* of vagueness (Endicott, 2000, 38; Waismann, 1951), namely words (terms, predicates) or sentences characterized by "a region of definite application, a region of definite non-application and a penumbra in which it neither definitely applies nor definitely fails to apply" (Williamson, 2002). Since both a vague statement and its negation do not exclude its borderline cases, they are both possibly true in such cases (Williamson, 2002). For example, "bald" is a vague predicate, as it is hard to determine when a person ceases to be not bald and becomes bald.

Vague predicates, terms, or sentences are characterized by two features, called by Schiffer "penumbral profile" and "penumbral shift" (Schiffer, 2016, 31–32). Penumbral profile concerns the conditions of truth, falsity, or indeterminacy, or reference, of predicate, sentence, or singular term tokens (i.e., the instantiations of expression types in a specific context by virtue of the speaker's intention in producing them). Thus, for example, two predicate tokens have the same penumbral profile if either token is true/false or indeterminate whether it is true or false of something, so is the other. The other characteristic, penumbral shift, concerns the relationship between the expression tokens and their context: two distinct tokens (instantiations or uses) of the same vague expression (type) can have different penumbral profiles in different contexts (namely different conditions for determining their truth/falsity/ indeterminacy or reference). For example, the expression "Bob is the bald one" referring to a person who shaves his head (or has little hair) can be true in a context in which the interlocutors want to identify Bob (among other people with hair), but false if uttered to describe serious cases of alopecia. These problems become relevant when the penumbral profile of an utterance is not known (penumbral ignorance), and the utterance is reported (such as "X said that Bob is bald"), but a decision needs to be made, such as in the legal context.

Vagueness raises a crucial legal problem that has fundamental implications for pragmatics and argumentation theory, namely the fact, mentioned above, that vagueness is a property of expression *tokens*, which are the product of the author's intentions in producing them (Schiffer, 2016, 32; see also Endicott, 2000, 53). For this reason, the determination of the vagueness of an expression relative to a specific case involves the context of interpretation, namely the context in which a decision needs to be made about the content of an utterance made in another context (Schiffer, 2016, 39). In this sense, the famous case of the legal rule that forbids one to take a vehicle into the public park ("All vehicles are prohibited from Lincoln Park") (Hart, 1958, 607) becomes vague not only when it needs to be applied to bicycles or roller skates, but also in "clear cases" of "vehicles," such as ambulances, namely cases to which the property "to be a vehicle" conventionally applies (based on genus-species inferences). However, the conventional meanings of the "types" – and thus the semantic representation resulting from compositional grammar – need to be distinguished from the meaning of the "tokens." As mentioned above, the a-contextual meaning resulting from composition needs to be pragmatically processed to be verifiable, namely to result in a proposition (Horn, 1995, 1145). Thus, the "literal meaning" of the prohibition ("All <motorized; or possibly conceivable; or . . . > vehicles are prohibited from Lincoln Park") is in fact the result of a pragmatic enrichment, based on a context imagined to be the stereotypical one (Kecskes, 2013, 141). The source of vagueness is thus the use of a legal statement in a context in which it is not possible to rely on the previous or stereotyped pragmatic inferences (conceived in the broad sense). In the case of the vehicles in the park, the specific context (Endicott, 2000, 53) leads to pragmatically specifying the semantic representation by considering more carefully other co-textual and contextual information (Horn, 1995, 1147): "It is not the feature [-+*ambulance*] that is relevant here, but whether the potential violation is excused by an implicit qualifier, *viz.* 'All *unauthorized* vehicles are prohibited from Lincoln Park,' with the understanding that the context (of law or of common sense) will determine how the implicit material is to be interpreted."

The precization of vague tokens is thus the result of a pragmatic processing aimed at providing implicit qualifications thereto. The source of vagueness is the use of a legal text (a type) in the specific context of making a decision on a specific case, and to determine the specific semantic representation of such a text we cannot automatically rely on the default enrichments that can be provided in a prototypical context. The pragmatic nature of the problem of vagueness and the pragmatic criteria used to enrich the semantic representation of a legal statement emerge clearly when the "defaults" used to reconstruct meaning conflict with other presumptions. One of the most famous cases of vagueness is *Church of the Holy Trinity v. United States*, 143 U.S. 457 (1892), which can be summarized as follows:

The Alien Contract Labor Law prohibits "the importation and migration of foreigners and aliens under contract or agreement to perform labor or service of any kind in the United States, its territories, and the District of Columbia." The Church of the Holy Trinity made a contract with an alien residing in England, the Reverend Walpole Warren, by which he was to remove to the City of New York and enter into its service as rector and pastor. The circuit court held that the contract was within the prohibition of the statute.

This case was decided first by specifying the meaning of the law presumptively. According to this view, the pastor was an "alien" migrating to the United States to perform "<professional and unprofessional, qualified and unqualified> labor <by the alien, compensated by the corporation> or service of any kind" in the United States. The lower court enriched the general semantic representation by relying on the presumption that the sufficiency of informative content was guaranteed ("Say as much as you can") (Horn, 1984, 1995, 1151): since the law did not specify that the labor was manual, the lower court excluded this precization. However, this stereo-typically contextual enrichment was objected to, as it allegedly conflicted with the presumable intention of the legislators (*Holy Trinity*, 143 U.S. at 459). For this reason, the Supreme Court pointed out a case of vagueness of the law, which was resolved by enriching it considering the "contextual evidence outside of that associated with the linguistic meaning of the textual language" (Slocum, 2017, 33–34). In this specific case, the enrichment was provided based on the co-textual evidence of the title of the act ("An act to prohibit the importation and migration of foreigners and aliens under contract or agreement to perform *labor* in the United States . . .") and the presumptive meaning of "labor," commonly narrowed to "<manual or unskilled> labor" (*Holy Trinity*, 143 U.S. at 463). This led to the enrichment "the importation and migration of foreigners and aliens under contract or agreement to perform <manual or unskilled> labor or <manual or unskilled> service of any kind." This pragmatic inference can be justified by the pragmatic R-principle (also called the "I-principle"), a correlate of the principle of least effort (Zipf, 1949), summarized as "Make your contribution Necessary. Say no more than you must" (Horn, 1984, 13) (see Chapter 4.8).

The problem of vagueness has thus a crucial pragmatic dimension, in which the linguistic considerations are not between an "ordinary" or "plain" meaning as opposed to the "intent" of the legislator, but between two distinct strategies and conflicting presumptions for reconstructing a controversial enriched semantic repre-sentation. In both cases, the presumptions used concern language used in context. The difference lies in the determination of the context, and the type of textual evidence used to support a hypothesis. In this view, legal disputes on ambiguity and vagueness become argumentative decision-making processes characterized by arguments provided in support of conflicting interpretative (in the broad sense) proposals. The analysis of the pragmatic dimension of legal interpretative disputes thus becomes intertwined with the analysis of the legal arguments and presumptions used, and the types and hierarchies of evidence on which they are grounded. To illustrate this argumentative dimension of this issue commonly confined to the realm of linguistic or legal considerations, it is useful to take into account three distinct types of legal disputes concerning different interpretative problems: syntactic ambiguity, syntactic and semantic ambiguity, and semantic ambiguity.

3.2 SYNTACTIC AMBIGUITY

Syntactic ambiguity clearly involves the problem of interpretation, as it concerns strictly the determination of the "meaning" of the legal statement. As pointed out above, disambiguation – and thus interpretation – is essentially related to pragmatic considerations. In this sense, the reconstruction of the "ordinary meaning" depends on the analysis not only of the grammatical rules, but also the contextual evidence that includes co-textual information, presumptions, and the hierarchy thereof. In this section, we will look at a case of statutory interpretation involving an ambiguity resulting from the application of syntactical conventions, to illustrate their relative importance in the argumentative determination of the meaning of the law.

3.2.1 *Pragmatics and the Rules of Grammar*

In pragmatics, the phenomena of syntactic ambiguity and disambiguation are commonly analyzed as strictly related to the rules of grammar, and not directly concerned by pragmatic operations *sensu stricto*, namely the reconstruction of the intended contextual inferences known as "implicatures." As Levinson put it in his criticism to the standard view (Levinson, 2000, 172):

> Here, there is a logical ordering of operations, so that the syntax provides strings with structural analyses, selected between by a disambiguation device of some sort (usually not directly addressed in linguistic theory). The disambiguated structure can then be associated with a semantic representation or logical form, which in turn can then be associated with a model-theoretic interpretation, but only after the "fixing" of indexicals with the aid of a highly restricted kind of pragmatic input – namely, the values of the pragmatic indices obtaining in the speech situation. The interpretation is then taken to provide a proposition expressed by the utterance on an occasion of use. The output of the semantics is then the input to the pragmatics, where Gricean mechanisms provide augmented (and occasionally, as in "flouts," altered) interpretations.

Contrary to this "grammatical" approach, Disambiguation is to be considered as an operation that, under the pragmatic approach called "relevance theory," falls under the operation called "explicature," a pragmatic processing aimed at developing and specifying the logical form that is the result of decoding "a combination of linguistically encoded and contextually inferred conceptual features" (Sperber and Wilson, 1995, 181; Wilson and Sperber, 2004, 260). For example, let us consider the following (Carston, 2004, 830):

1. Paracetamol is better. [than what?]
2. It's the same. [as what?]
3. He is too young. [for what?]
4. It's hot enough. [for what?]
5. The winners each get £1,000. [winners of what?]
6. I like Sally's shoes. [shoes in what relation to Sally?]

In these examples, a verifiable proposition is the result of pragmatic operations that fix the reference (such as in (3)) and more importantly make explicit the "linguistically present but imperceptible constituent" (in square brackets). Pragmatic processing intervenes not only to fix the reference of indexicals and "saturate" the expressions having unarticulated constituents, namely to ensure the "minimal propositionality" that can be verified, but also to contribute and enrich the semantic representation expressed (Carston, 2004, 831): "[I]n a great many contexts it is the enriched propositional form that is communicated and is taken by addressees to be the content of what is asserted – that is, the basis on which the speaker is judged to have or have not spoken truly."

In the case of legal texts, the problem of pragmatic enrichment more commonly arises not because the propositional meaning of the legal text cannot be determined, but rather when it is uncertain how the propositional content of the law should apply (the enriched semantic representation). These cases can be illustrated using some ordinary examples (Carston, 2004, 830–831):

1. Jack and Jill went up the hill [*together? alone?*].
2. Sue got a Ph.D. and [*then? at the same time?*] became a lecturer.
3. Mary left Paul, and [*as a consequence? then?*] he became clinically depressed.
4. She took out her gun, went into the garden, and killed her father [*with the gun, in the garden? without the gun? in the street?*].
5. I'll give you £10 if [*and only if? preferentially if?*] you mow the lawn.
6. John has [*exactly? more than?*] four children.
7. Louise has always been a great lecturer [*since she's been a lecturer? since she was able to talk?*].
8. There were [*approximately? exactly?*] fifty people in the queue.

All these examples can be enriched in different ways, resulting in specific semantic representations that have different truth values. The crucial aspect that can be fundamental for the theories of legal interpretation is that enrichment is a pragmatic mechanism that combines with but is distinct from the rules of grammar (the codified conventions of use). Each alternative interpretation in the examples above is the result of a pragmatic processing. In this sense, it is not possible to claim that one of the two possible interpretations corresponds to the "plain meaning" and the other the "pragmatic" or "intentionalistic" reading.

Levinson presented (Figure 3.1) the commonly accepted view in which the pragmatic operation of enrichment is distinguished from the grammatical one, and is different from the further inferences that are drawn after the semantic interpretation is provided (representing "what is meant") (Levinson, 2000, 173).

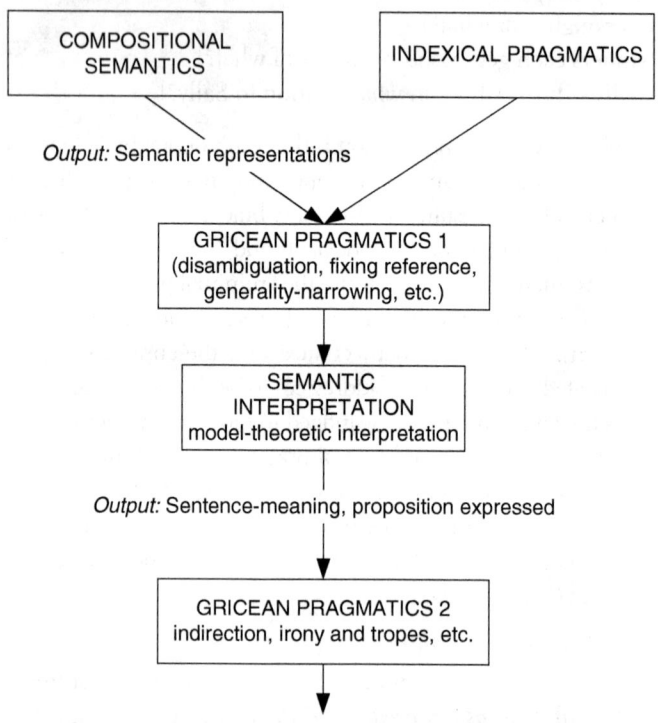

FIGURE 3.1 Decoding, disambiguating, and pragmatic operations

Even though this "received" view is extremely controversial in pragmatics, the distinction between the operations involved can be a criterion for distinguishing the "language" of an enactment from the inferences that can be drawn from it. In this sense, the "language" could correspond to "what is said," namely the specific semantic representation of an utterance, to be identified with the contribution of pragmatics, which can become the input for further pragmatic processing, aimed at retrieving what the speaker meant (implicitly) based on contextual information and "assumption schemas" (or scripts) (Sperber and Wilson, 1995, 181–182).

The problem of legal interpretation is comparable to the semantic interpretation of ordinary language. However, the theoretical problem underlying the description of this process is different, as the purpose of a theory of legal interpretation is not the processing of an utterance (or rather a legal provision) but the justification of its proposed meaning and the decision-making process used to determine it (Tarello, 1980, 85). In other words, in legal interpretation the focus is not on the cognitive processes involved in determining what is said or the speaker meant, but on how to solve interpretative conflicts (Alexy and Dreier, 1991; Guastini, 2011; Macagno and Capone, 2016; MacCormick, 1995, 2005; Tarello, 1980). More specifically, when an utterance (text) is subject to different readings (Dascal and Wróblewski, 1988; Patterson, 2004), the reasonableness and the plausibility (acceptability) of the conflicting interpretations need to be assessed based on their justifications, expressed as defeasible arguments (Bench-Capon and Prakken, 2010; Walton, 2002; Walton, Reed, and Macagno, 2008; Weinstock, Goodenough, and Klein, 2013; Wyner and Bench-Capon, 2007). In this sense, the problem of drawing the boundaries of the "language" of the law and determining what is "plain" needs to take into account the types of pragmatic processes involved, which need to be expressed as arguments.

3.2.2 *Syntactic Ambiguity and Interpretative Disputes*

The problem of analyzing the "language" of the law in determining and solving ambiguity can be illustrated through an example. In this case (called "the housing example"), Congress passed a statute called the Anti-Drug Abuse Act in 1988. A key part of the act reads as follows:

> **CASE 3.2: SYNTACTIC AMBIGUITY – THE HOUSING EXAMPLE**
>
> [Each] public housing agency shall utilize leases which ... provide that any criminal activity that threatens the health, safety, or right to peaceful enjoyment of the premises by other tenants or any drug-related criminal activity on or off such premises, engaged in by a public housing tenant, any member of the tenant's household, or any guest or other person under the tenant's control, shall be cause for termination of tenancy.[1]

When the US Department of Housing and Urban Development (HUD) implemented this regulation, it required public housing authorities (PHAs) to impose the following lease obligation on tenants:[2]

---

[1] 42 U.S.C. § 1437(d)(1)(6) (Supp. V 1994).
[2] *Department of Housing and Urban Development v. Rucker*, 535 U.S. 125, 129 n.2 (2002).

To assure that the tenant, any member of the household, a guest, or another person under the tenant's control, shall not engage in: (1) Any criminal activity that threatens the health, safety, or right to peaceful enjoyment of the PHA's public housing premises or by other residents or employees of the PHA, or (2) any drug-related criminal activity on or near such premises, any criminal activity in violation of the preceding sentence shall be cause for termination of tenancy, and for eviction from the unit.

This regulation became the object of an interpretative dispute in *Department of Housing & Urban Development* v. *Rucker*, 535 U.S. 125 (2002). Four public housing tenants were evicted under this rule, but later the legality of the rule was challenged on the basis of syntactic ambiguity. The challenge arose from the disputed question of whether the prepositional phrase (PP) "under a tenant's control" should attach low (namely only to the directly preceding noun phrase (NP), based on the so-called "right recursion" – called "alternating interpretation"), or high (modifying the entire NP, based on the so-called "left recursion" – called "stacking interpretation") (Langendoen, McDaniel, and Langsam, 1989). According to the alternating interpretation, the PP modifies only "another person," while according to the stacking interpretation it modifies also "a guest" and "any member of the household" (Bosanac, 2009, 137). A circuit panel ruled that it should refer to all three terms, but the Supreme Court subsequently reversed this decision.[3] The Supreme Court ruled that the Anti-Drug Abuse Act should be interpreted as permitting eviction of household members and guests whether the tenant was aware of drug activity or not.

The syntactic ambiguity between the two interpretations in this case can be represented as follows ("verb phrase" is indicated by "VP").

1a. Alternating interpretation: [NP the tenant], [NP any member of the household], [NP a guest], or [[NP another person [PP under a tenant's control]], [[VP shall not engage [PP in these acts]].

1b. Stacking interpretation: [NP the tenant], [[NP any member of the household], [NP a guest], or [NP another person] [PP under [NP a tenant's control]], [[VP shall not engage [PP in these acts]].

The ambiguity is based on the scope of the prepositional phrase, which can be either the nominal phrase (NP or simply N) directly adjacent thereto (1a) or the preceding conjunct or disjunct nominal phrases (1b). The two possibilities can be represented in the phrase structure trees shown in Figures 3.2 and 3.3 (Cowper, 2009, 35).

---

[3]   Ibid. at 130–131.

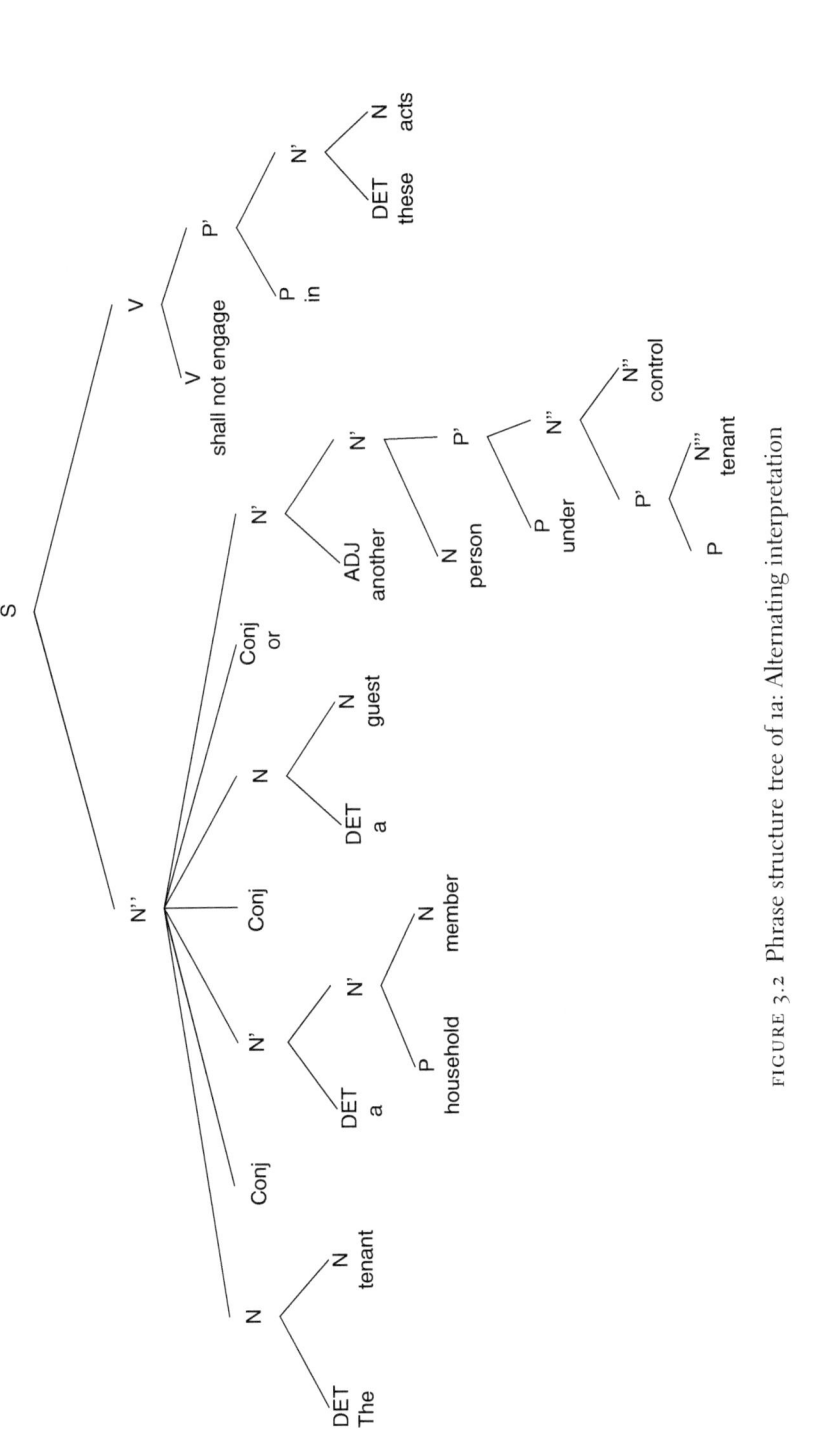

FIGURE 3.2 Phrase structure tree of 1a: Alternating interpretation

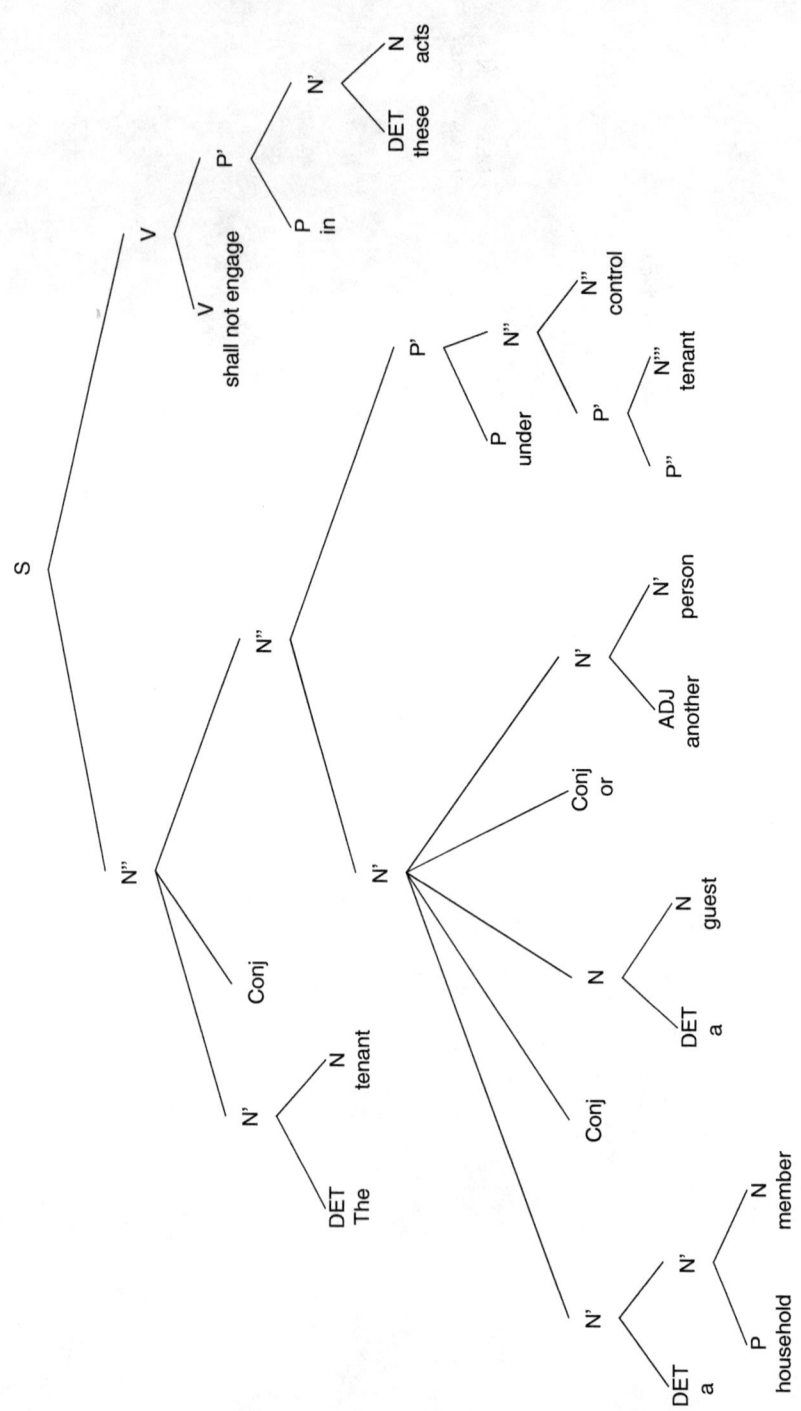

FIGURE 3.3 Phrase structure tree of 1b: Stacking interpretation

The syntactic ambiguity of the sentence led to several arguments by both parties, which are summarized in the opinion of the Supreme Court. The first crucial issue was establishing the plain meaning of the sentence based on grammatical rules. The argument is the following (*HUD* v. *Rucker*, at 131):

> The en banc Court of Appeals also thought it possible that "under the tenant's control" modifies not just "other person," but also "member of the tenant's household" and "guest." 237 F. 3d, at 1120. The court ultimately adopted this reading, concluding that the statute prohibits eviction where the tenant "for a lack of knowledge or other reason, could not realistically exercise control over the conduct of a household member or guest." Id., at 1126. But this interpretation runs counter to basic rules of grammar. The disjunctive "or" means that the qualification applies only to "other person." Indeed, the view that "under the tenant's control" modifies everything coming before it in the sentence would result in the nonsensical reading that the statute applies to "a public housing tenant ... under the tenant's control." HUD offers a convincing explanation for the grammatical imperative that "under the tenant's control" modifies only "other person": "by 'control,' the statute means control in the sense that the tenant has permitted access to the premises." 66 Fed. Reg. 28781 (2001).

The interpretation of the plain meaning of a sentence on pure "grammatical" grounds, however, can be highly problematic. Contrary to the opinion of the Supreme Court, according to the Stanford Automated Parser (Klein and Manning, 2003) the phrase structure would also support reading 1b, namely the structure in which the scope of the prepositional phrase includes all the preceding conjuncts (Figure 3.4).

In this notated structure, the prepositional phrase (PP) "under the tenant's control" refers to the whole set of nominal phrases (constituted of the four conjunct NPs). In this purely grammatical (syntactic) reading, the PP attaches not only to "other person," "member of the tenant's household," and "guest," but also "the tenant." The syntactic ambiguity of the sentence cannot be resolved based solely on the rules of grammar (sentence structure and word meaning). Also in computational linguistics, the problem of attachment is calculated based on contextual considerations, and in particular on the "contextual similar words" that the lexicon and the corpus considered can associate with the PP and the NP concerned (Pantel and Lin, 2000). However, these operations are purely statistical, and are thus only one of the possible arguments that can be brought in favor of an interpretation. In order to assess the strength of an interpretation, it is necessary to resort to other levels, or sources, of interpretation, belonging to the domain of pragmatics (Jaszczolt, 2007, 50–52, 2011, 13; Kaplan and Green, 1995). The problem is to analyze and describe these pragmatic operations, whose mechanisms are not usually analyzed in pragmatic theory (Levinson, 2000, 172).

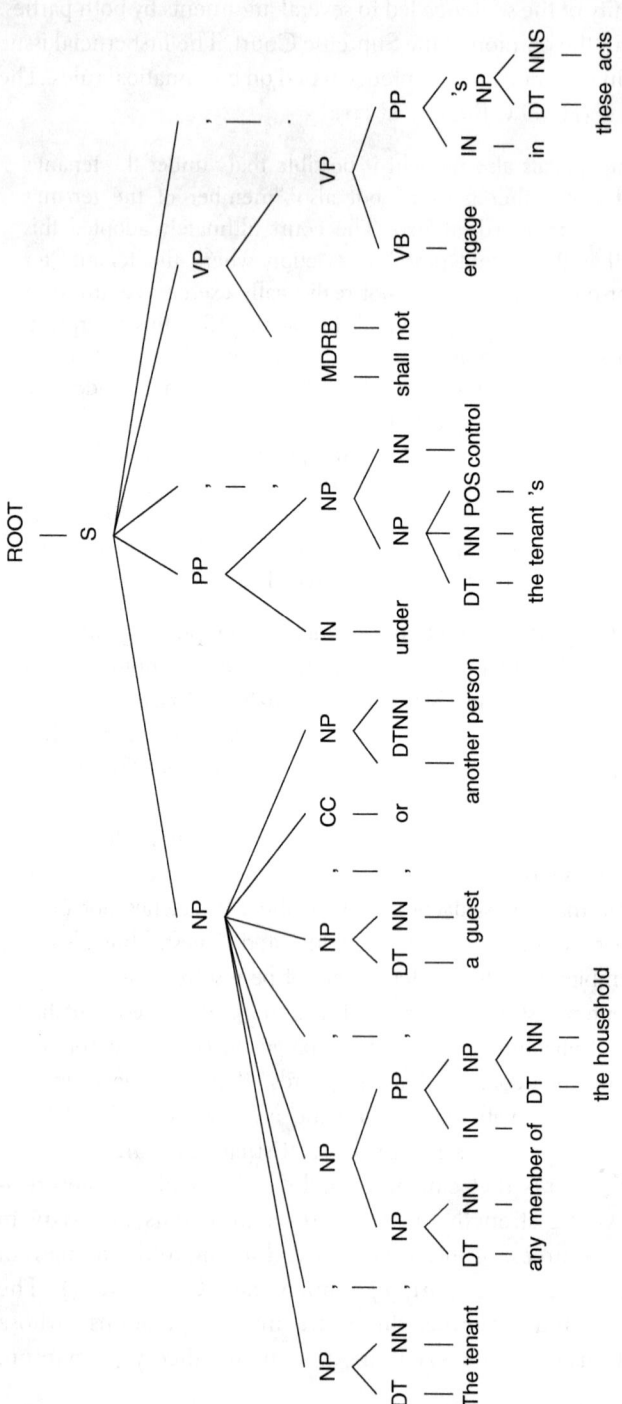

FIGURE 3.4 Phrase structure tree: Automated parsing

3.2.3 *Inferences and Syntactic Ambiguity*

In our introduction to the problem of ambiguity, we presented the pragmatic approach to the different dimensions of ambiguity, in which the pragmatic considerations involve not only the inferences drawn from "what is said" based on contextual information and the rules of discourse (particularized conversational implicatures), but more importantly the reconstruction of the implicit information needed for specifying and otherwise enriching the semantic representation of an utterance. In particular, we will rely partly on the lexicon of the neo-Gricean approach, as it is not intertwined with the cognitive dimension – which instead characterizes other fundamental pragmatic theories such as the Relevance Theory (Sperber and Wilson, 1995). As mentioned in the introduction, pragmatic inferences are needed for determining "what is said," as the grammatical conventions alone can be insufficient for disambiguating a sentence (Carston, 2004). These pragmatic operations intervene also at the level of syntactic disambiguation.

On the neo-Gricean perspective, three levels of interpretation need to be distinguished at a theoretical level. The two extreme levels of interpretation are the sentence-meaning and the speaker-meaning. The sentence-meaning is the output of the application of the rules of grammar, and it is commonly referred to as "decoding." The speaker-meaning is the result of the actual nonce or once-off inferences made in actual contexts by actual recipients with all of their rich particularities (conversational implicatures) (Levinson, 2000, 22). Between these two levels lies the utterance type (Atlas, 1989), resulting from the application of default rules associated with specific lexical items or syntactic constructions (e.g., "any" has an expansive meaning, that is, "one or some indiscriminately of whatever kind," *HUD v. Rucker, at* 131). This type of inferential mechanism is defaultive, as an utterance U "implicates i unless there are unusual specific contextual assumptions that defeat it" (Levinson, 2000, 16). The default rules used in this type of interpretation (x is normally interpreted as X_i) encode general expectations about how language is normally used (Levinson, 2000, 22), but such expectations involve social considerations (what speakers *take* as stereotypical or conventional behavior) (Atlas and Levinson, 1981, 49). This level corresponds to the so-called "semantic interpretation" in which from a general, nonspecific semantic representation (sentence-meaning), a truth-conditionally evaluable proposition (namely a specific, enriched semantic representation) is derived by means of pragmatic rules (see Jaszczolt, 1999).

At both the level of the sentence-meaning and utterance-meaning, pragmatic processes commonly referred to as (generalized) conversational implicatures are involved. In case of syntactic ambiguity, the so-called disambiguation process (Atlas, 2005, Chapter 1; Levinson, 2000, 174–177) relies on world knowledge and inferential principles represented by Grice in his maxims. For example, we consider the following examples (Levinson, 2000, 175):

1. He's an indiscriminate dog-lover; he likes some cats and dogs.

2. She heard some of the firecrackers in the kitchen.

Both sentences are ambiguous. In (1), "some" can have a broader (cats and dogs) or narrower (cats) scope. Both semantic representations lead to inferences based on Grice's maxim of quantity (Grice, 1975), or the neo-Gricean Q-principle "*Say as much as you (truthfully and relevantly) can*" (Horn, 1984, 1995; Levinson, 2000) (see Chapter 4.2 and Chapter 4.8). The former reading supports the conclusion that "he likes some, but not all, cats and dogs," while the latter, narrower reading leads to the inference that "he likes some but not all cats, and all dogs." However, only the second interpretation supports a conclusion compatible with the first clause ("he is an *indiscriminate* dog-lover"), and for this reason it is preferable over the former. The syntactic ambiguity of (2) is similar to the one detected in our Case 2, as the PP "in the kitchen" can be referred to the VP ("she heard") or to the NP ("some of the firecrackers"). However, the implicature that can be drawn from the second interpretation ("she heard some, but not all, the firecrackers that went off in the kitchen") can be hardly justified in normal circumstances.

The choice of one interpretation over another, for this reason, needs to be established based on pragmatic considerations, namely the contextual inferences and the presumptions commonly associated with the situation in which the sentence is used. As Levinson put it (Levinson, 2000, 175): "[T]he structural analysis that has a semantic interpretation that induces an implicature consistent with the context will be preferred over another analysis that induces an inconsistent implicature. Note that, on the assumption that [a given] interpretation is only implicated, the semantic content alone cannot account for the favored readings."

In both (1) and (2) above, the "inconsistency" of the implicature that can be drawn from the interpretation of the sentence is assessed based on world assumptions, in addition to semantic information. For example, in (1) the implicature that results in an inconsistency with the reading "he likes some, but not all, cats and dogs" is drawn from the following usually accepted premises:

a. "Indiscriminate" usually means "without careful judgment";
b. Who acts without careful judgment usually does not make distinctions;
c. Who loves without distinctions usually loves everyone.

These propositions have different levels of acceptability, and different natures. The first is a definition commonly accepted, and thus belongs to the "grammar" of a language. However, the second and third premises belong to encyclopedic information, and are only presumptive, acceptable in the absence of contrary evidence. Similarly, in (2) the choice between the two possible interpretations is based on the inconsistency between "she heard some, but not all, the firecrackers that went off in the kitchen" and the common knowledge assumption that "usually firecrackers are not ignited in the kitchen," and "usually people hear all the very loud noises close to them."

The role of inferences and common knowledge in disambiguation is thus of fundamental importance. As pointed out in the discussion above, in the neo-

Gricean approach some of the inferences involved in determining the "correct" interpretation can be reconstructed using Gricean maxims, or a modified version thereof. However, this approach does not account for all the inferences leading to possible contradictions, nor for the types of contextual information involved. To analyze the reasons that are, or can be, provided for an interpretation, to justify its reasonableness or acceptability, a more complex mechanism needs to be designed. The starting point is the examination of the arguments involved in the reconstruction of the "plain meaning" of a legal enactment, and more precisely of the syntactic structure thereof.

3.2.4 *Disambiguation in the Housing Example*

Pragmatic considerations and common knowledge assumptions play a crucial role in determining the best interpretation of a sentence in law. This is illustrated in the disambiguation of the syntactic ambiguity of Case 3.2, the housing example. The court rejected the interpretation based on the broad scope of the PP ("under the tenant's control") based on reasons drawn from different sources, including commonly accepted lexical meaning, presuppositions, and encyclopedic knowledge. As the court put it (*HUD* v. *Rucker*, at 130, numbering added):

> The court ultimately adopted this reading, concluding that the statute prohibits eviction where the tenant, "for a lack of knowledge or other reason, could not realistically exercise control over the conduct of a household member or guest." Id., at 1126 ...
> [1] Indeed, the view that "under the tenant's control" modifies everything coming before it in the sentence would result in the nonsensical reading that the statute applies to "a public housing tenant ... under the tenant's control." HUD offers a convincing explanation for the grammatical imperative that "under the tenant's control" modifies only "other person": [def] "by 'control,' the statute means control in the sense that the tenant has permitted access to the premises." 66 Fed. Reg. 28781 (2001). [2] Implicit in the terms "household member" or "guest" is that access to the premises has been granted by the tenant. Thus, the plain language of §1437d(*l*)(6) requires leases that grant public housing authorities the discretion to terminate tenancy without regard to the tenant's knowledge of the drug-related criminal activity.

The court advanced two arguments in support of its decision of upholding the alternating interpretation (1a), both grounded on the statutory definition ("def") of "control," namely "the tenant has permitted access to the premises." Based on this definition, the court classified as "nonsensical" the broader scope of the modifier (PP), based on the redundancy (Horn, 1991; Sadock, 1978) between what is said and what is entailed or presupposed:

1. The PP would modify an NP ("a public housing tenant ... under the tenant's control") resulting in a redundancy between what is said (under the tenant's control, i.e., the tenant has permitted access to the premises) and what is entailed by the NP (a tenant is one who has the occupation or temporary possession of tenements of another). The redundant information would be "the person who has permission to occupy the house of the landlord, who has permitted access to the premises to himself."

2. The PP would modify two NPs ("household member" and "guest" "under the tenant's control") resulting in a redundancy between what is said (under the tenant's control) and what is "implicit," namely:

   a. A presupposition. By definition, a guest is a person entertained in one's house. In order to be entertained in one's house, a person needs to be granted access thereto.

   b. A plausible and hardly rebuttable inference. A household member is a dependent for tax purposes. Therefore, members of a household usually live in the same dwelling, and in order to live in the same dwelling tenant's authorization needs to be granted.

The choice for a low-attached NP is based on considerations that are not purely syntactical, first of all the concept of redundancy, which is conversationally (and not grammatically) anomalous (Horn, 1991, 320). In argument (1), the court can rely on semantic information, and exclude an interpretation that is redundant and thus unreasonable. However, in (2) the redundancy is only the result of a defeasible inference, as in (2a), a guest can be entertained in tenant's house also without *his* authorization (he can be invited by someone else), while in (2b), a household member can be living elsewhere.

To address the problem of determining the "language of the law" and the "plain meaning" of a statute, it is necessary to analyze the set of presumptions that can be relied on in reaching the interpretation that is considered as "unambiguous."

3.2.5 *Mapping Presumptions and Arguments in the Housing Example*

The argumentation used by the court in establishing the interpretation of the disputed sentence consisted in two steps. First, the court distinguished two levels of arguments, namely the arguments used to claim that the statute is in fact syntactically ambiguous, and those that can be used after an ambiguity has been established. Only after the existence of an ambiguity has been proved is it possible to resort to the other arguments (rule of lenity, intention of the legislator, etc.). The arguments provided for and against the ambiguity of the disputed sentence can be summarized as follows (for the specific types of arguments, see our Chapter 1.6 and Chapter 5).

CONTRA AMBIGUITY (Low attachment)

The view that "under the tenant's control" modifies everything coming before it in the sentence would result in the nonsensical reading that the statute applies to "a public housing tenant . . . under the tenant's control."

Arguments:

1. Structural presumption (a presumption related to the "structure" of a legal text or system) (Economic argument): Legal texts normally have no redundant expressions.
2. Linguistic, specific presumption (Systematic argument): "By 'control,' the statute means control in the sense that the tenant has permitted access to the premises."
3. Linguistic, generic presumption (Natural meaning argument): Implicit in the terms "household member" or "guest" is that access to the premises has been granted by the tenant.
4. Structural presumption (Historical argument): In *Memphis Housing Authority* v. *Thompson*, the Tennessee Supreme Court noted that the statute, and the lease provisions that were derived from the statute, refer to four separate categories of people: (1) the resident; (2) household members; and (3) guests or (4) other persons under the resident's control.
5. Pragmatic presumption (psychological argument): In an effort to end what Congress termed the "reign of terror" imposed by drug dealers on public housing tenants, 42 U.S.C. 11901 (1994 & Supp. IV 1998), Congress enacted Section 1437d (l)(6) in 1988 and strengthened it in 1990 and 1996. A different interpretation deprives public housing authorities of an important tool to achieve safe and livable public housing, and to deprive public housing tenants of protection that Congress found to be of central importance for their security and well-being.

PRO AMBIGUITY (High attachment)

If a tenant has taken reasonable steps to prevent criminal drug activity from occurring, but, for a lack of knowledge or other reason, could not realistically exercise control over the conduct of a household member or guest, §1437d(l)(6) does not authorize the eviction of such a tenant.

Arguments:

6. Linguistic presumption (Natural meaning): "other" means "like the foregoing" (Swanson and Pilon, 2002).
7. Linguistic presumption (Natural meaning – pragmatic specification): "to be under control" usually means "to have one's behavior under control" (Swanson and Pilon, 2002).

8. Pragmatic presumption (*Analogia juris*): It conflicts with another legal provision (21 U.S.C. § 881(a)(7)) concerning forfeiture in which the property of "innocent" owners, having no knowledge of the illegal actions, may not be forfeited.
   Defeaters:
   - a. 42 U.S.C. § 1437(d)(1)(6), with which we deal here, is a quite different measure.
   - b. Pragmatic presumption (psychological argument): It is entirely reasonable to think that the government, when seeking to transfer private property to itself in a forfeiture proceeding, should be subject to an "innocent owner defense," while it should not be when acting as a landlord in a public housing project.
   - c. Structural presumption (*a contrario*): The forfeiture provision shows that Congress knew exactly how to provide an "innocent owner" defense. It did not provide one in §1437d(l)(6).
9. General pragmatic presumption (Absurdity argument): Construing the statute to permit eviction of tenants who are not shown to have known of the drug-related activity would be irrational and thus would require PHAs to include an unreasonable term in their leases.
   Defeaters:
   - d. Structural presumption (coherence of the law): The statute does not require the eviction of any tenant who violated the lease provision. Instead, it entrusts that decision to the local public housing authorities. It is not "absurd" that a local housing authority may sometimes evict a tenant who had no knowledge of the drug-related activity. Such "no-fault" eviction is a common "incident of tenant responsibility under normal landlord-tenant law and practice." 56 Fed. Reg., at 51567.
   - e. Pragmatic presumption (psychological argument): Regardless of knowledge, a tenant who "cannot control drug crime, or other criminal activities by a household member which threaten health or safety of other residents, is a threat to other residents and the project." 56 Fed. Reg., at 51567. It was reasonable for Congress to permit no-fault evictions in order to "provide public and other federally assisted low-income housing that is decent, safe, and free from illegal drugs."

The arguments leading to the best interpretation are represented in Figure 3.5.

This outline of the arguments used brings to light some differences in the arguments used. The first distinction is between argument 4 (in dotted line) and the other arguments. As the court pointed out, the argument from previous interpretations (4) is subordinated to the existence of an ambiguity in the text (535 U.S. 125, 132 (2002)); thus it can be considered only after the assessment of the other arguments. Therefore, the

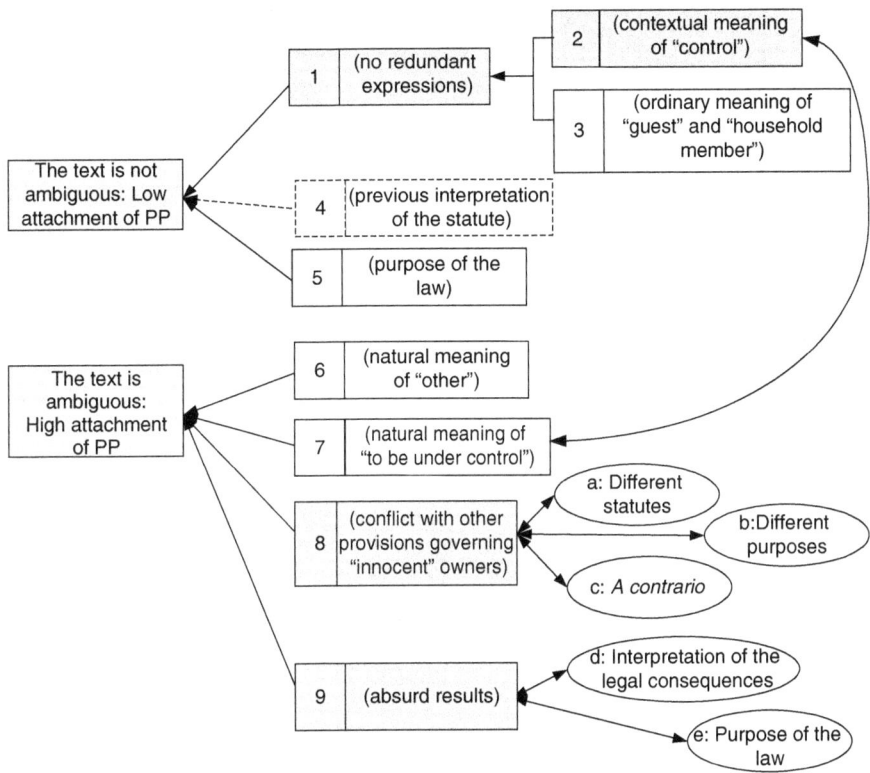

FIGURE 3.5 Arguments and counterarguments

problem of ambiguity needs to be determined based on the remaining eight arguments, aimed at establishing the interpretation of the "communicative content"
(Solum, 2015) of the disputed statement. A second distinction can be drawn, placing
these arguments in two categories, namely the arguments considering only the legal
effects of the legal provision (construction), namely arguments 5 and 9, and the
interpretative arguments (arguments 1, 2, 3, 6, and 7). These latter arguments are
different in their structure: while argument 1 is supported by the linked arguments 2
and 3 (the acceptability of 1 depends on the acceptability of both arguments),
arguments 6 and 7 are convergent, namely provide independent support to the
conclusion (Walton, 2002, 112, 2006, 141–148).

Considering the interpretative arguments, we notice, following Solum, that interpretation needs to take into account knowledge going beyond the rules of grammar.
For example, the "no redundancy" argument (1) is a conversational principle, which
in law can be established based on the presumptions governing the structure of the
legal statements. Similarly, the incoherence with other legal provisions (8) is
a contextual consideration that involves the structural presumption that the legal

system is coherent. The remaining arguments, 2, 3, 6, and 7, concern the interpretation of the terms of the potentially ambiguous statement and in particular "control." "Control" is defined by the court according to its legal definition, namely "permitting access to the premises." In contrast, the respondents resorted to a "pragmatic enrichment" of "to be under one's control" (Recanati, 2012; Solum, 2015), resulting in the interpretation of the expression as "controlling the behavior." According to this interpretation, no possible redundancy can be detected in the use of the phrase "under the tenant's control" and the implicit content vehiculated by "guest" and "household member." Their acceptability, however, is established based on the hierarchy of presumptions, namely the higher or lower defeasibility of the natural meaning presumption vis-à-vis the definition provided by a related legal statement. In this case, the court supported the latter statement, as potentially backed by other contextual presumptions (systematic argument).

3.3 SYNTACTIC AND SEMANTIC AMBIGUITY IN *HELLER*

The case *District of Columbia* v. *Heller*, 554 U.S. 570 (2008), is one of the most debated cases in philosophy of law, and one of the most controversial for its justification and the implications that resulted from it. In particular, the opinions delivered represent the most extensive contemporary debate on the role and notion of "original meaning" in interpretation (Solum, 2009, 924). The analysis of the sources of the ambiguity involved and the arguments advanced for solving it, in addition to the linguistic concerns related to the "literal meaning" of the Second Amendment of the US Constitution, illustrate the complex relation between argumentation, pragmatics, and ambiguity.

The case concerned the constitutionality of a local law of the District of Columbia, namely the Firearms Control Regulations Act of 1975, which banned residents from owning handguns, automatic firearms, or high-capacity semiautomatic firearms, and prohibited possession of unregistered firearms. A lawsuit was brought by six residents, claiming that the law infringed the individual right "to keep and bear arms" protected by the Second Amendment. The case went to the Supreme Court, which held, by a majority of 5–4, that banning handguns (arms commonly used for protection purposes) and prohibiting firearms from being kept in the home violates the Second Amendment.

3.3.1 *The Sources of the Dispute*

The interpretative dispute concerned the syntactic and semantic ambiguity of the text of the Second Amendment, which reads:

A well regulated Militia, being necessary to the security of a free State, the right of the people to keep and bear Arms, shall not be infringed.

This text led to two distinct interpretations, provided by Justice Scalia (majority opinion) and Justice Stevens (dissenting). The most important and debated source of ambiguity was the syntactic relation between the "prefatory clause" (or, more technically, the adjunct) and the "operative clause" (the main modal clause). Under Justice Scalia's interpretation, the "ordinary meaning" fixed by linguistic facts at the time of origin (when the provision was ratified) (Solum, 2009, 944) is determined by considering the adjunct ("A well regulated Militia, being necessary to the security of a free State") as announcing the purpose, but not limiting or expanding the scope, of the "operative clause." Pursuant to this first interpretation, the Second Amendment secures to the people a right to use and possess arms *in conjunction with* service in a well-regulated militia (*Heller* at 651); the adjunct was thus interpreted as indicating the purpose of preventing elimination of the militia (id. at 599). In contrast, the dissenting opinions (delivered by Justice Breyer and Justice Stevens) maintained that the Amendment protects "the right of the people of each of the several States to maintain a well-regulated militia" (id. at 637), rejecting the interpretation of the relationship between the two clauses of the Amendment as a general "logical connection" and instead delimiting the scope of the obligation (id. at 643–644).

This syntactic ambiguity led to another problem of semantic ambiguity, namely the precization of "the right *of the people.*" According to Stevens, the Amendment protects the right of the individuals specified the Amendment's preamble, namely, the individuals having a duty to serve in the militia. This specification conflicts with the alternative specification of the majority opinion, in which the underspecified notion of "the people" is determined as "all members of the political community" (and more precisely the set of "law-abiding, responsible citizens," *Heller* at 644–645) and specified for the purpose of "self-defence" (id. at 642).

The last source of disagreement resulting in a semantic ambiguity is the disambiguation and the enrichment of the clause "to keep and bear Arms." The first problem concerns the disambiguation of the conjunction. According to the majority opinion, the conjunction connects two independent phrases ("keep arms" and "bear arms") (id. at 582), thus resulting in a compound sentence, "the right to keep Arms and the right to bear Arms." In contrast, the dissenting opinion read the sentence as characterized by a compound verb, expressing a unitary right ("the right to keep and bear Arms"). In both cases, the issue lies in determining the attachment of the second conjunct (whether high or low). The second problem concerns the interpretation of the two verb phrases. According to the majority opinion, the first verb phrase ("to keep arms") cannot be considered as idiomatic – and thus needs to be interpreted as "to possess weapons" (id. at 582) – while the verb of the second conjunct was acknowledged to have – at the time in which the statute was drafted – the meaning of "carrying for a particular purpose – confrontation" but not in relation to an organized militia (id. at 584). In contrast, the dissenting opinion read the phrase "to bear arms" as idiomatic, having the meaning of "to serve as a soldier, do military service, fight." This meaning is reinforced by the preceding verb phrase "to keep arms," which at the time of the Second Amendment's drafting "describe the requirement that militia members store their arms at their homes, ready to be used for service when necessary" (id. at 646–650). In this sense, according to the dissenting view, the Amendment expressed the unitary right to possess and use firearms in connection with service in a state-organized militia.

3.3.2 *The Pragmatic Dimension of the "Ordinary Meaning" of the Second Amendment*

The *Heller* case is frequently cited in terms of conflict between two philosophical positions, the "textualist" one (Scalia's), defending the idea that the law shall be interpreted according to its "original meaning," and the "intentionalist" one (Stevens's), according to which the interpretation shall be aimed at reconstructing the purpose of the law (or the intention of the legislator). This conflict is commonly associated with two incompatible strategies for retrieving the meaning of a legal provision (Solum, 2009, 957):

> This disagreement between Justices Scalia and Stevens about the relationship between the prefatory and operative clauses points to a larger disagreement. While Justice Scalia inquired into the semantic content of the operative clause, Justice Stevens focused on the purpose or teleological meaning of the Second Amendment. In a rough way, this disagreement corresponds to the difference between original intentions originalism and original meaning originalism.

Regardless of whether this description mirrors the parties' actual interpretative strategies, the dichotomy between "original meaning" and "original intentions" fails to capture the linguistic processes that can lead to the interpretation of a statute. On the one hand, it is unclear the role that the extratextual appeal to the intentions of the legislator should have in interpretation. As pointed out in Section 2.1 above, the reconstruction of "what is said" (sentence-meaning) is distinct from and presupposed by the retrieval of "what is meant" (speaker-meaning). The interpretative dispute in *Heller* concerned the enrichment of the propositional form of the Second Amendment; it did not concern further implicatures that can be drawn from it. Moreover, the extratextual evidence provided was only an additional argument to the textual ones. On the other hand, the notion of "original meaning" is in itself linguistic nonsense if it refers to the propositional form resulting from the application of the linguistic rules and codified conventions. As argued above, this output could not be verified – namely, applied to specific circumstances – nor could its potential ambiguity be solved. As Schiffer pointed out (Schiffer, 2016, 42): "So, if textualism is to have any chance of being correct, 'the meaning the text had when it was created' must refer to the propositional content expressed by the sentence tokens produced by the authors of the text ..., and that is a content that is constrained but never determined by the meanings of the tokened sentences."

The problem underlying the textualism is that it does not reflect what is actually done in the interpretative practice. The role of context is in fact emphasized by Scalia, who claims that "neither written words nor the sounds that the written words represent have any inherent meaning. Nothing but conventions and contexts cause a symbol or sound to convey a particular idea" (Scalia and Garner, 2012, xxvii). The crucial point is that pragmatic processes are involved in determining what the law says, namely the propositional content of a legal provision. When the determination of the enriched semantic representation is disputed, what matters is the justification and the presumptions underlying them, which depend on different considerations, including normative and moral ones (Schiffer, 2016, 47–48).

The interpretation of a text (a legal one in this case) needs to be thought of as resulting from pragmatic operations, which can be compared, assessed, and argued for and against. In this sense, its meaning(s) is in part a function of the context (Solum, 2017, 141); the crucial point is to determine what context matters – whether the one in which the law is used or the one in which it was stipulated – and what presumptions prevail in case the presumptive arguments based thereon are not defeated. In *Heller*, both the dissenting and the majority opinion agreed on a fundamental point, namely that the context was the "original" one, the one in which the law was written. The crucial point is to see how the two positions diverged in developing their arguments.

3.3.3 *The Interpretative Arguments in* Heller

The arguments provided in *Heller* can be organized according to the conclusions defended and their nature. As pointed out above, both parties to this dispute intended to perform the same type of operation, namely enriching the propositional form of the Amendment. The first and most important set of conflicting conclusions concern the enrichment of the adjunct (prefatory clause). The enrichments and the supporting arguments are summarized as follows:

First issue

+A: "<*Whereas*> a well regulated Militia is necessary to the security of a free State, the right of the people to keep and bear Arms <*for military as well as nonmilitary purposes*> shall not be infringed" (*Heller* at 577).

−A: "<*In view of the fact that; within the limits of the need that*> a well regulated Militia, being necessary to the security of a free State, the right of the people to keep and bear Arms, shall not be infringed."

Majority opinion

+aA1: Rule of grammar (authority). The prefatory clause does not limit the operative one grammatically, but rather announces a purpose. The two clauses need to be logically connected, so that the prefatory clause can resolve an ambiguity in the operative clause; however, the former does not limit or expand the scope of the operative clause (Id. at 577–578).

+aA2: Authority of experts in support of +aA1. Nineteenth-century books on statutory interpretation point out the need to find a consistency between the two clauses.

+aA3 (implicit): A *contrario* argument. If the law fails to foreclose the interpretation that the right includes <*nonmilitary purposes*>, it means that it did not intend it.

Dissenting opinion

−aA1: A *contrario* argument. If the law omitted to specify that the "right of the people to keep and bear Arms" was *for civilian uses*, it means that it did not intend it (Id. at 642–643).

−aA2: (argument from) Sign from other state declarations (Pennsylvania and Vermont), in which the right to use weapons for civilian purposes was expressly protected (Id. at 642).

−aA3: Economic argument. The legislator cannot issue a useless statement of law. If the preamble fails to inform the meaning of the remainder of the text, it is a mere surplusage (Id. at 643).

The structure of this argumentation can be represented in Figure 3.6.

The arguments provided for and against show how the parties resort to similar arguments as a main strategy, namely *a contrario* arguments based on the authorities of experts or the analogy with similar provisions. However, the dissenting opinion advances an argument that both supports its point and undercuts the majority's argument, namely the economic argument. This issue is related to the second and third one, concerning the relationship between the right protected and the service in the "well regulated militia." The second issue concerns the specification of "the people."

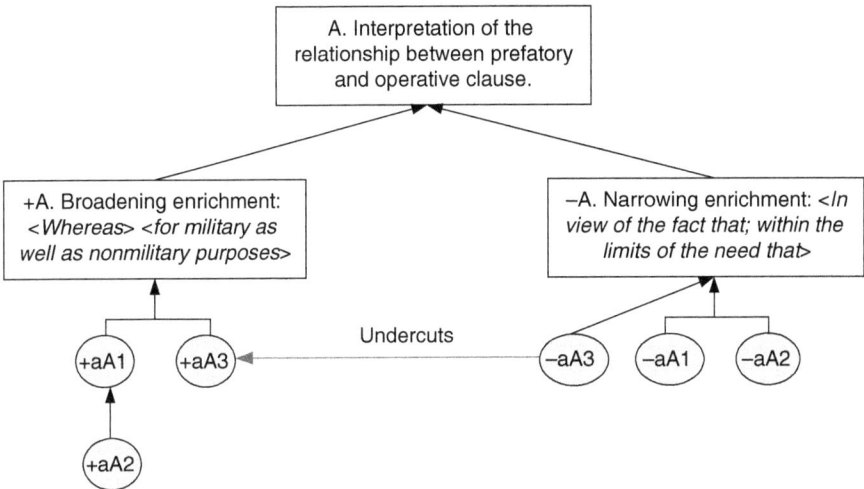

FIGURE 3.6 Arguments and counterarguments in the first issue of *Heller*

Second issue

+B: "A well regulated Militia, being necessary to the security of a free State, the <*individual*> right of <*all members of the political community (law-abiding, responsible citizens)*> to keep and bear Arms, shall not be infringed" (Id. at 580).

–B: "A well regulated Militia, being necessary to the security of a free State, the right of the people <*in the context of service in a well-regulated militia*> to keep and bear Arms, shall not be infringed" (Id. at 646).

Majority opinion

+aB1: Systematic argument. In all six other provisions of the Constitution that mention "the people," the term unambiguously refers to all members of the political community (Id. at 580).

+aB2: Absurdity argument. A group of people is not all members of the political community. Reading the Second Amendment as protecting the right to "keep and bear Arms" only in an organized militia therefore fits poorly with the operative clause's description of the holder of that right as "the people" (Id. at 580–581) (the law would be self-contradictory).

Dissenting opinion

–aB1: Systematic argument. In all six other provisions of the Constitution that mention "the people," it refers to members of a group performing an activity (Id. at 645).

–aB2: Analogy. Similarly, the words "the people" in the Second Amendment refer back to the object announced in the Amendment's preamble (Id. at 645).

–aA3 (implicit): Economic argument. The legislator cannot issue a useless statement of law. If the preamble fails to inform the meaning of the remainder of the text, it is a mere surplusage.

Underminer

–aB3: Negative systematic argument. The Court itself reads the Second Amendment to protect a "subset" significantly narrower than the class of persons protected by the First and Fourth Amendments; when it finally drills down on the substantive meaning of the Second Amendment, the Court limits the protected class to "law-abiding, responsible citizens." But the class of persons protected by the First and Fourth Amendments is not so limited; for even felons (and presumably irresponsible citizens as well) may invoke the protections of those constitutional provisions. The Court offers no way to harmonize its conflicting pronouncements.

Also in this case, the structure of the dispute can be represented in Figure 3.7.

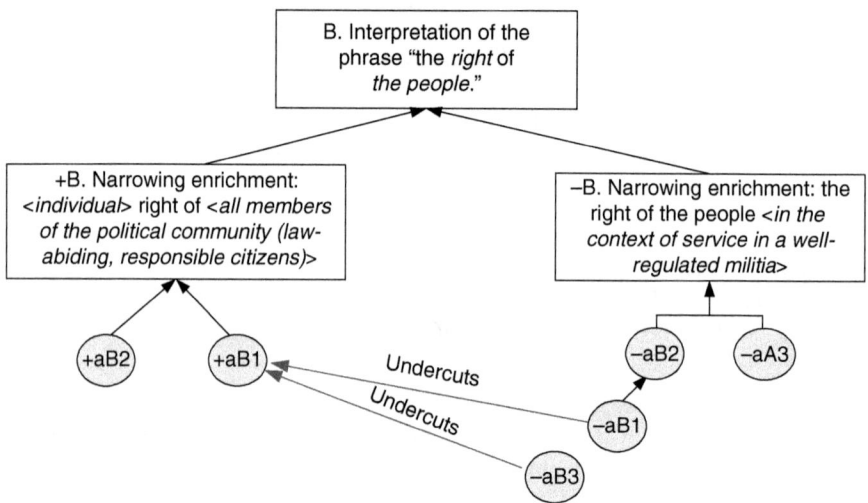

FIGURE 3.7 Arguments and counterarguments in the second issue of *Heller*

The structure of this argument points out how both the majority and the dissenting opinion build their arguments on the same presumption (the law is a systematic whole, and the terms used should bear the same meaning). In both cases, this argument can be compared to the pragmatic R-principle (make your contribution necessary – say no more than you must) (Horn, 1984), which combines the second pragmatic maxim of quantity, "Do not make your contribution more informative than is required" (Grice, 1975, 45), with the maxim of relation ("Be relevant"). In both cases, the analogy with the uses of the same phrase in other provisions is used to draw an inference about the meaning intended in the Second Amendment. However, while the whole argument of the majority opinion rests on such an analogy, the dissenting opinion combines the systematic argument (supporting a different type of narrowing) with the already emphasized economic argument (an argument grounded on the principle of relevance and corresponding to a dimension thereof).

The third and last issue is the focus of most of the two parties' arguments, and concerns the interpretation of "to keep and bear arms."

Third issue

+C: "A well regulated Militia, being necessary to the security of a free State, the right of the people to keep <*as a possession*> <*arms*> <*for militia and civil purposes*> and bear Arms <*for the purpose of offensive or defensive action*>, shall not be infringed" (Id. at 582).

–C: "A well regulated Militia, being necessary to the security of a free State, the right of the people to keep and bear Arms <*in connection with service in a state-organized militia*>, shall not be infringed" (Id. at 646).

Majority opinion

+aC1: Ordinary meaning (authority of dictionaries). "Keep Arms" means "have weapons" based on the dictionaries (Id. at 582).

+aC2: Analogy. In the written documents of the founding period there are examples that favor viewing the right to "keep Arms" as an individual right unconnected with militia service (Id. at 582).

+aC3: Ordinary meaning (authority of dictionaries). At the time of the founding, as now, to "bear" meant to "carry" (Id. at 584).

+aC4: Ordinary meaning (no backing). When used with "arms," the term has a meaning that refers to carrying for a particular purpose – confrontation (Id. at 584).

+aC5: Analogy. This natural meaning was also the meaning that "bear arms" had in the eighteenth century: nine state constitutional provisions written in the eighteenth century or the first two decades of the nineteenth, which enshrined a right of citizens to "bear arms in defense of themselves and the state" or "bear arms in defense of himself and the state" (Id. at 584).

+aC6: Authority of the preceding interpreters (authoritative argument). Three important founding-era legal scholars interpreted the Second Amendment in published writings. All three understood it to protect an individual right unconnected with militia service (Id. at 605).

+aC7: Authority of the preceding interpreters (historical argument). The nineteenth-century cases that interpreted the Second Amendment universally support an individual right unconnected to militia service.

Underminers

+aC8: Analogy used as an underminer. The opponents conclude from the fact that militia laws at the time required militia members to "keep" arms in connection with militia service that the phrase "keep Arms" has a militia-related connotation. This reasoning is similar to the claim that since there are many statutes that authorize aggrieved employees to "file complaints" with federal agencies, the phrase "file complaints" has an employment-related connotation (Id. at 583).

+aC9: *A contrario*. The phrase "to bear Arms" carries the idiomatic meaning "to serve as a soldier, do military service, fight" only when followed by the preposition "against." Lack of indication of this preposition allows the inference that the legislation did not intend this meaning (Id. at 586).

+aC10: Absurdity argument. Giving "bear Arms" its idiomatic meaning would cause the protected right to consist of the right to be a soldier or to wage war – an absurdity that no commentator has ever endorsed (Id. at 586).

+aC11: Analogy used as an underminer. State constitutions of the founding period routinely grouped multiple (related) guarantees under a singular "right."

Dissenting opinion

–aC1: Ordinary meaning (authority of dictionaries). "Bear arms" is a familiar idiom; when used unadorned by any additional words, its meaning is "to serve as a soldier, do military service, fight" (Id. at 646).

–aC2: Economic argument. The absence of any reference to civilian uses of weapons tailors the text of the Amendment to the purpose identified in its preamble (Id. at 669).

–aC3: *A contrario*. Had the Framers wished to expand the meaning of the phrase "bear arms" to encompass civilian possession and use, they could have done so by the addition of phrases such as "for the defense of themselves" (Id. at 647).

–aC4: Analogy. In the Pennsylvania and Vermont Declarations of Rights phrases such as "for the defense of themselves" were added to "bear arms" (Id. at 647).

–aC5: Systematic argument. In case of doubt, the preamble disambiguates (Id. at 647).

–aC6: *A contrario*. The unitary meaning of "keep and bear Arms" is established by the Second Amendment's calling it a "right" (singular) rather than "rights" (plural). It does not describe a right "to keep arms" and a separate right "to bear arms." Rather, the single right that it does describe is both a duty and a right to have arms available and ready for military service, and to use them for military purposes when necessary (Id. at 651).

–aC7: Ordinary meaning (induction from texts of the drafters' time). A number of state militia laws in effect at the time of the Second Amendment's drafting used the term "keep" to describe the requirement that militia members store their arms at their homes, ready to be used for service when necessary (Id. at 650).

Underminer
–aC8: Qualifications of the historical and authoritative arguments. The interpretations of the preceding sources were adopted in a different historical and political context and framed in markedly different language and tell us little about the meaning of the Second Amendment (Id. at 663).

The structure of this argumentation can be represented in Figure 3.8.

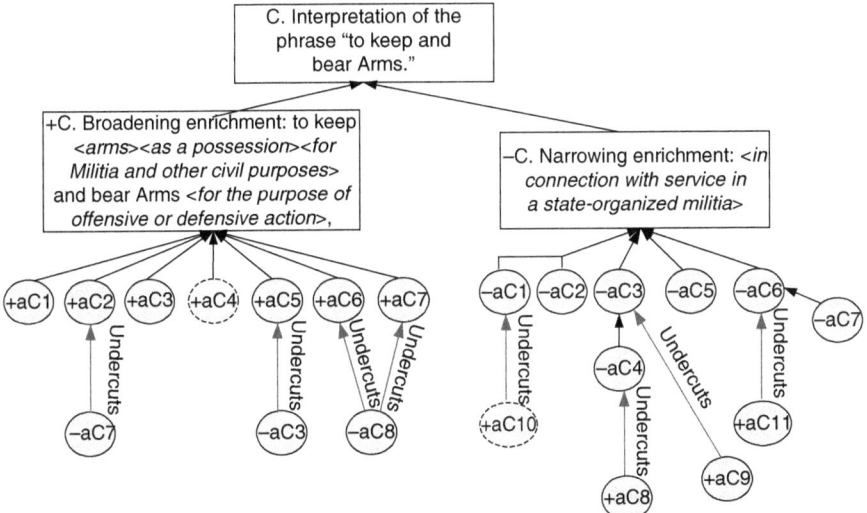

FIGURE 3.8 Arguments and counterarguments in the third issue of *Heller*

In Figure 3.8, we notice that the arguments on both sides can be compared and weighted one against the other. The ordinary meaning arguments in favor of the broadening explicature of the two verbs "keep" and "bear" (+aC1, +aC2, and +aC3) are countered by contrary arguments (–aC1 and –aC7). However, the pragmatic reasoning in the dissenting opinion is much more complex and supported by distinct backing reasons. Justice Stevens underlines the relevance dimension of the prefatory clause, also underscored in his arguments in Issue 1, which guarantees the use of the

R-principle (say no more than necessary). This pragmatic reasoning is combined with an *a contrario* argument that, based on the Q-principle (say no more than you can), excludes the enrichment of the majority opinion. In this sense, while both parties enrich the semantic representation based on pragmatic principles, only the dissenting opinion provides all the needed backings for the pragmatic inferences.

3.3.4 *The Missing Dimension of the "Original Meaning"*

The most striking aspect of the *Heller* dispute is the disproportion between the arguments provided concerning the first issue and those advanced in relation to the second and especially the third issue. In particular, the economic argument – pointing out the need of looking for relevance of the "prefatory" clause – used by the dissenting opinion is only vaguely addressed by Scalia, who draws a hypothesis about the legislator's intention by relying on the interpretation of the adjunct as a "preamble." Scalia relies on a principle of interpretation that regards the preamble as an unessential part of the statute, used only in cases of ambiguity of the "enacting clause" to interpret the clause based on the intention of the legislator made explicit in the preamble (Black, 1896, 253–254). In this view, "it is well settled, by the decided preponderance of authority, that general words in the body of the statute, if free from ambiguity, are not to be restrained or narrowed down by particular, or less comprehensive, recitals in the preamble" (Black, 1896, 179), "for, in such cases, there is no room for construction and no need to resort to the preamble" (Black, 1896, 178). This reasoning is aimed at excluding a narrowing enrichment based on specific contextual information, namely a section of the statute whose presumed purpose is to set out the premises of the enactment. However, this pragmatic principle aimed at excluding the application of the R-principle presupposes in turn a pragmatic enrichment of the adjunct as a preamble. Usually the preamble is marked by the conjunction "whereas"; in this case, the enrichment of the clause with this conjunction functions as an enrichment that needs to be justified. Scalia does not advance any argument: instead, he acknowledges that "this structure of the Second Amendment is unique in our Constitution" (*Heller* at 577). To support his enrichment, he draws an analogy with different types of documents (individual-rights provisions of state constitutions) based on the authority of one expert, who advanced two arguments:

1. the gerundive expresses a justification as two cases drawn from oral discussions at the time of the drafting can be interpreted as having a justificatory role; and

2. the justification clause may *aid* construction of the operative clause but may not *trump* the meaning of the operative clause (Volokh, 1998, 810).

Based on these two reasons (which are only implicitly referred to in the judgment), Scalia argues that, since the "operative clause" is unambiguous and since the "justificatory clause" is the same as a preamble, which can be taken into account only to disambiguate the meaning (*Heller* at 577), the meaning of the operative clause shall not be "restrained or narrowed down" (or, as Scalia put it, its scope shall not be "limited or expanded"). But limiting the scope of a clause is very different from claiming that the "justificatory clause" should not *trump* the meaning of the operative one. And, as Schiffer pointed out clearly, the assimilation of limiting and trumping amounts to an absurdity. Rejecting any limitation through justificatory clauses would entail for instance that "[I]f I say 'Having noticed there was no milk in the house, I went to the supermarket,' what I said is true if I noticed there was no milk in the house today but went to the supermarket three weeks ago" (Schiffer, 2016, 46).

Scalia's arguments, however, seem to be based on presumptions very different from purely "textual" considerations. First and foremost, the whole interpretative argument boils down to the analogy between the (personal) interpretation of two oral examples and the Second Amendment. This argument is used as a reason for a pragmatic enrichment (R-based inference) (Horn, 1984, 20–21):

1. the speaker used a present participle phrase ("being necessary to the security of a free State") without any further indications of time, purpose, or justification;
2. an inference to an abnormal conclusion is normally not drawn unless there are specific indications to that effect (Atlas and Levinson, 1981, 50);
3. it was abnormal to use a present participle phrase to express something different from a justification (such as providing a temporal or conditional restriction);
4. therefore, the speaker intended to mean that the present participle phrase is a justificatory phrase (setting out a general purpose without any restrictions).

Regardless of the acceptability of premise (3), the same reasoning could be used for the exactly contrary conclusion: as the legislator did not intend to provide an ambiguous meaning in the operative clause, and since it is abnormal to include a useless clause (a surplusage), in lack of explicit indications the present participle phrase cannot be interpreted as merely justificatory (Williams, 1998, 829).

Thus, the most evidently missing arguments are those that are actually textualist, namely the arguments that can establish the usual linguistic behavior. The Supreme Court does not cite any linguistic work that addressed the problem of adjuncts (such as the "prefatory clause"). In linguistics, a specific distinction is commonly drawn between strong and weak adjuncts (Stump,

2012, 42–43) and between the different types of "conversational background." Strong adjuncts such as the "prefatory clause" (presupposing the truth of the adjunct) set out a conversational background that can be of different type (such as deontic, epistemic, or teleological) (Kratzer, 2002). However, in modal contexts (such as those in which an obligation is expressed), the adjunct modifies the interpretation of the modal, which is used relationally, "in view of" the circumstances expressed in the adjunct (Kratzer, 1977, 341). Therefore, the "logical connection" that Scalia points out cannot be one of simple justification. Rather, in linguistics the most common interpretation is that of "logical consequence" or "compatibility" (Rocci, 2008, 175; Stump, 2012, 46).

Considering how it is used in one of the most important and controversial cases of the twentieth century, the appeal to the "original meaning" or more generally to the "plain meaning" does not entail a rejection of the pragmatic principles or the "intention of the legislator." Scalia interprets the Second Amendment by enriching it pragmatically, exactly as Stevens does. The difference lies in the justifications for the enrichment. Stevens focuses on textual arguments – the "systematic argument" based on the relevance of one clause to another; the "economic argument" excluding interpretations in which parts of the statute are useless, irrelevant, or uninformative. In contrast, Scalia resorts to the reconstruction of an intention of the legislator based on extratextual elements – the evidence provided in other documents by different legislators, a completely different type of communication (verbal speeches), other documents written by other authors of the period of the legislators. The "textualist" approach, in terms of arguments, is in fact a philological approach aimed at retrieving the *use* of the lexical items at the time of the drafting. While these arguments can shed light on some aspects of the meaning of the Amendment, they do not relieve the interpreter of the burden of proving the needed enrichments, which ultimately depend on the reconstruction of the intention made manifest in the text.

In the perspective of the arguments of interpretation, the concept of "original meaning" seems to be a rhetorical strategy more than a theoretical position. It resulted in avoiding the defense of some crucial premises:

1. that "the original meaning of the Constitution is a function of the original public meaning" – or conventional semantic meaning – of a given constitutional provision at the time the provision was framed and ratified (Solum, 2009, 946);
2. that the audience for the Constitution is not "the collection of citizens and officials who would be governed by its provisions for an indefinite period of time" but the people living at that specific time (Solum, 2009, 949–950);

3. that there is an equation between the use of a term to refer to or mean certain things and the correctness (or noncontroversiality) of such uses (Schiffer, 2016, 47);

4. finally, that the use of a term or a syntactic form with a specific meaning in certain contexts by certain speakers guarantees that a different speaker in a different context intends such a meaning.

In particular, most of the arguments used by Scalia are mere analogies drawn from some more or less similar texts; they are not evidence of how a word or construction was *commonly* used, let alone commonly used by the *specific* legislator, or commonly understood by the public, or *intended* by the legislator to have that specific meaning. The passage from the first argument to the last conclusion is a matter of inferences, none of which was proven. Rather, all such inferences were all presented as belonging to the theory of the "original meaning."

3.4 SEMANTIC AMBIGUITY IN *MUSCARELLO V. UNITED STATES*

The last case analyzed in this chapter concerns one of the most discussed problems of interpretation resulting from the polysemy of a predicate. The U.S. Federal Criminal Code imposes a five-year mandatory prison sentence on any person who uses or carries a firearm in relation to a drug-related crime. In *Muscarello v. United States*, 524 U.S. 125 (1998), the issue was whether the phrase "carries a firearm" used in the statute should be interpreted in a broader way as including carrying a firearm in a vehicle, or whether it should be used in a narrower way to mean carrying a firearm on one's person. The Supreme Court ruled that a firearm found in a vehicle, including the glove compartment or trunk, would fall under the broad (ordinary) meaning of the term "carry" as used in the statute.

3.4.1 *The "Linguistic" Arguments*

Muscarello had a handgun in the locked glove compartment of his truck in which he was transporting marijuana to make a drug deal. The Supreme Court consolidated this case with another one where the defendants carried several guns in the trunk of their car when they traveled to the location proposed as a drug sale point. On the way they were stopped by federal agents who searched the trunk of the car and arrested them. Muscarello and the other two defendants argued that carrying firearms in a glove compartment or the trunk of a car should not be included in the statutory definition of the word "carry" as used in the Federal Criminal Code. Their argument was based on the narrow interpretation of the expression "carry a firearm."

In Section A of his summary of the argumentation in the case, Justice Breyer, writing for the majority, began by stating that the opposed parties agreed that Congress intended the phrase "carries a firearm" to convey its ordinary meaning in natural language as opposed to some special legal meaning. The problem was that the parties disagreed about whether, according to that ordinary meaning, the expression "carry" should be interpreted in this case broadly or narrowly. Much linguistic evidence was cited arguing that in a most natural meaning of this expression, people do generally speak about carrying firearms in vehicles such as wagons, cars, or trucks. However, it was pointed out that in a secondary and more special meaning, such as in the slang expression "packing a gun," the expression specifically refers to carrying a firearm on one's person, for example in a coat pocket. The two positions addressed a crucial pragmatic issue, namely the disambiguation of the polysemy of the tokened phrase. The disagreement can be represented as concerning the choice between the following enriched representations of the scope of 18 U.S.C. § 924(c)(1), in the federal criminal code:

1. any person who, during and in relation to any crime of violence or drug trafficking crime [...] uses or carries a firearm *<in a wagon, car, truck, or other vehicle that one accompanies>*, or who, in furtherance of any such crime, possesses a firearm, shall, in addition to the punishment provided for such crime of violence or drug trafficking crime.
2. any person who, during and in relation to any crime of violence or drug trafficking crime [...] uses or carries a firearm *<on the person>*, or who, in furtherance of any such crime, possesses a firearm, shall, in addition to the punishment provided for such crime of violence or drug trafficking crime.

As described above, these two enrichments concern the representation of utterances, not of "syntactic structures" (Jaszczolt, 2007, 42). Both enrichments are drawn through pragmatic inferences, which are based not only on the word meaning and sentence structure, but also other type of information, first and most importantly background knowledge, among which are cultural, social, scientific knowledge, and default interpretations resulting from heuristic processes (also called "cognitive" defaults), and contextual information (Jaszczolt, 2005a, 48–57). The background assumptions and the contextual information become crucial sources of premises for supporting either interpretative conclusion (Nunberg, 1979, 148; Soames, 2009, 407).

The arguments for a broad interpretation provided by the majority opinion are based on different types of arguments. The first is the authority of dictionaries, which established the meaning made explicit by the enriched semantic representation 1. Both the synchronic and diachronic definitions are quoted, resorting to a series of quotations from such sources as the *Oxford English Dictionary, Barnhart Dictionary of Etymology* (tracing the word "carry" to its origin from the Latin word *carrus*), the *King James Bible,* and the *New York Times Manual of Style and Usage.* The most important argument concerns the possible counterargument, namely evidence of the most common use of the *phrase,* and not the isolated verb (*Muscarello* at 130):

> (+1a) Black's Law Dictionary defines the entire phrase "carry arms or weapons" as "To wear, bear or carry them upon the person or in the clothing or in a pocket, for the purpose of use, or for the purpose of being armed and ready for offensive or defensive action in case of a conflict with another person." Black's Law Dictionary 214 (6th ed. 1990).
> These special definitions, however, do not purport to limit the "carrying of arms" to the circumstances they describe. No one doubts that one who bears arms on his person "carries a weapon." But to say that is not to deny that one may also "carry a weapon" tied to the saddle of a horse or placed in a bag in a car.

These arguments provided only the evidence in favor of the background presumptions that could govern the pragmatic inferences (Atlas and Levinson, 1981, 46). The first type of inference is normally represented in pragmatics as based on the "quantity" maxim, developed as the "Q-principle": "Make your contribution sufficient; say as much as you can." Thus, if the legislator intended a more specific way, he should have indicated so (*Muscarello* at 128). Therefore, the more specific reading is excluded. Since the alternative is a less specific one, it should be preferred. The second type of inference is grounded on the aforementioned pragmatic R-principle (called I-principle in Levinson's theory) of "informativeness" or "relevance": Make your contribution necessary; say no more than you must (given the Q-principle). The reasoning is the following:

1. the speaker used a verb phrase without any further indications of purpose or location;
2. the speaker provided the necessary quantity of information, which is not enough in this specific circumstance;
3. a more informative proposition is preferred as an interpretation unless it contradicts what is commonly considered as stereotypical (called background conventions of noncontroversiality);
4. the more informative phrase "carry a firearm <*on the person or in a wagon, car, truck, or other vehicle that one accompanies*>" would allow the application of the law;
5. the more informative phrase "carry a firearm <*on the person or in a wagon, car, truck, or other vehicle that one accompanies*>" would not lead to inferring an abnormal conclusion;
6. therefore, the legislator should have intended this meaning.

The second "linguistic" strategy used by the court is expressed in two specular arguments (identified as –2a and –2b) (*Muscarello* at 135; numbers added):

> (–2a) The dissent refers to § 926A and to another statute where Congress used the word "transport" rather than "carry" to describe the movement of firearms. 18 U.S.C. § 925(a) (2)(B); *post*, at 146–147. According to the dissent, had Congress intended "carry" to have the meaning we give it, Congress would not have needed to use a different word in these provisions. But as we have discussed above, we believe the word "transport" is broader than the word "carry."

The dissent's argument (–2a) is based on the use of the Q-principle (make your contribution sufficient) (Atlas and Levinson, 1981, 47):

1. the speaker used a verb phrase without any further specifications of purpose or location;
2. if the legislator did not use the more specific term "transport," the legislator was in no position to make that claim;
3. therefore, the legislator did not intend to mean "transport."

This argument, however, is rejected based on the greater specificity of "to carry" ("to transport" is broader, namely less informative, than "to carry"). The rejection of this Q-based inference leads to the possibility of the alternative option, namely R-based inferences. The court in particular rejected the possibility of specifying the meaning of "to carry a firearm" as "carry *<on the person>*" based on its conflict with background conventions of noncontroversiality (Atlas and Levinson, 1981, 48) (at 138):

> (–2b) At the same time, the narrow interpretation creates its own anomalies. The statute, for example, defines "firearm" to include a "bomb," "grenade," "rocket having a propellant charge of more than four ounces," or "missile having an explosive or incendiary charge of more than one-quarter ounce," where such device is "explosive," "incendiary," or delivers "poison gas." 18 U.S.C. § 921(a)(4)(A). On petitioners' reading, the "carry" provision would not apply to instances where drug lords, engaged in a major transaction, took with them "firearms" such as these, which most likely could not be carried on the person.

The refutation of this enrichment resulted from an R-based inference (Horn, 1984, 20–21):

1. the speaker used a verb phrase without any further indications of purpose or location;
2. the speaker provided the necessary quantity of information, which is not enough in this specific circumstance;

3. a more specific proposition is preferred as an interpretation unless it contradicts what is commonly considered as stereotypical (background conventions of noncontroversiality);
4. the more specific phrase "carry <*on the person*>" is not stereotypical;
5. the more specific phrase "carry <*on the person*>" would lead to inferring an abnormal conclusion;
6. therefore, the inference to the more informative phrase "carry <*on the person*>" should be excluded.

These "linguistic" arguments are presented by the court as concerning the "ordinary meaning." However, the arguments used are aimed at developing the generic semantic representation of the provision according to specific pragmatic principles. The notion of "ordinary meaning" in this context is extremely problematic and even self-contradictory if it is taken to indicate an a-contextual interpretation (Solan, 2010, 74). Moreover, the arguments on both sides refer to the intention of the legislator, which is argumentatively reconstructed through textual evidence.

3.4.2 *Argumentative Inferences in* Muscarello

The pragmatic inferences indicated above can be represented as arguments (for a detailed analysis of these arguments, see our Chapter 5). In particular, both parties ground their reasoning on two opposing types of reasoning: an argument based on an inference in lack of evidence (from ignorance), and an ampliative reasoning based on the abduction of a further property based on those made explicit.

The Q-based inferences are aimed at inferring a specific negative intention of the speaker (or the legislator) based on the lack of an explicit indication to the contrary. This type of reasoning is commonly represented as follows (Macagno and Walton, 2011; Walton et al., 2008, 327):

ARGUMENTATION SCHEME *Argument from Ignorance*

Premise 1:	If A were true, then A would be known to be true.
Premise 2:	It is not the case that A is known to be true.
Conclusion:	Therefore, A is not true.

This type of argumentative reasoning, which in law is commonly referred to as an *a contrario* argument, applies to the aforementioned inferences aimed at excluding a specific interpretation:

Premise 1:	If the legislator intended to mean "to transport," he would have indicated his intention explicitly by using a verb different from "to carry" ("to transport").
Premise 2:	It is not the case that the legislator has indicated explicitly his intention to mean *"to transport."*
Conclusion:	Therefore, the legislator did not intend to mean *"to transport."*

The alternative type of pragmatic inference can be represented as an abductive type of argument (Atlas and Levinson, 1981; Fodor, 1983; Harman, 1965, 1992; Macagno and Walton, 2014; Walton, 2002; Walton et al., 2008, 172):

ARGUMENTATION SCHEME *Argument from Best Explanation*

Premise 1:	F (an utterance) is an observed fact.
Premise 2:	E_1 is a satisfactory ascription of meaning to F.
Premise 3:	No alternative interpretations $E_{2 \ldots n}$ given so far is as satisfactory as E_1.
Conclusion:	Therefore, E_1 is a plausible interpretation, based on what is known so far.

This type of reasoning can explain the enrichment of the provision defended in the majority opinion:

Premise 1:	The legislator used a verb phrase ("to carry a firearm") without any further indications of purpose or location and provided the necessary quantity of information, which is not enough in this specific circumstance.
Premise 2:	The more Informative phrase "carry a firearm *<on the person or in a wagon, car, truck, or other vehicle that one accompanies>*" would allow the application of the law, without leading to inferring an abnormal conclusion.
Premise 3:	The alternative enrichment "carry *<on the person>*" would lead to inferring an abnormal conclusion (it would not cover carrying bombs on a car) without being signaled.
Conclusion:	Therefore, "carry a firearm *<on the person or in a wagon, car, truck, or other vehicle that one accompanies>*" is the most plausible enrichment intended by the legislator.

The reconstruction of the interpretative reasoning in terms of argument allows analyzing different types of interpretative strategies considering their probative force and the nature of their premises. While the canons of interpretation tend to mirror the theoretical approach underlying the preference for a specific type of argument (ordinary meaning, naturalistic argument, etc.), the analysis of the interpretative reasons in terms of argumentation schemes allows bringing to light the premises of each argument and combining and comparing the pragmatic analyses with other types of reasoning.

For example, while the aforementioned examples were grounded on the analysis of the text of the legal statement, with a minimal consideration of the context, other arguments involved a broader analysis of the other relevant provisions of law, such as the following (*Muscarello* at 135):

> (–2c) And, if Congress intended "carry" to have the limited definition the dissent contends, it would have been quite unnecessary to add the proviso in § 926A requiring a person, to be exempt from penalties, to store her firearm in a locked container not immediately accessible. See § 926A (quoted in full, *post*, at 146) (exempting from criminal penalties one who transports a firearm from a place where "he may lawfully possess and carry such firearm" but not exempting the "transportation" of a firearm if it is "readily accessible or is directly accessible from the passenger compartment of such transporting vehicle"). The statute simply could have said that such a person may not "carry" a firearm. But, of course, Congress did not say this because that is not what "carry" means.

This reasoning can be represented in terms of an argument from consequences (Walton et al., 2008, 332):

ARGUMENTATION SCHEME *Argument from Consequences*

Premise 1:	If A is brought about, good (bad) consequences will plausibly occur.
Premise 2:	What leads to good (bad) consequences shall be (not) brought about.
Conclusion:	Therefore, A should be (not) brought about.

In this circumstance, this type of reasoning is applied to a contextual (in the sense of co-textual) consequence, namely the irrelevance of another provision, and can therefore be classified as an economic argument. Again, this type of inference is essentially pragmatic, as a specific intention of the speaker (in this case, the legislator) is inferred from the exclusion of a consequence whose undesirability is based on the pragmatic principle of relevance (Grice, 1975, 47; Sperber and Wilson, 1995, 158). This specific premise leads to the following argument:

Premise 1:	If the legislator intended to mean "carry *<on the person>*," the proviso in § 926A in the same text would be unnecessary (irrelevant).
Premise 2:	Irrelevance in a text is abnormal (the legislator cannot issue a useless statement of law).
Conclusion:	Therefore, the legislator did not intend to mean "carry *<on the person>.*"

The textual and contextual type of evidence used in the pragmatic arguments needs to be compared with the extratextual evidence that is used for inferring an intention from other similar cases or other documents that are different from the statute. Such evidence is, more than "contextual," it is rather external to the text. An example is the following argument provided by Justice Breyer, who drew a conclusion about the statute's purpose from the quoted remarks of the members of Congress about how they saw the purpose of the statute (*Muscarello* at 132–133):

> (+1b). This Court has described the statute's basic purpose broadly, as an effort to combat the "dangerous combination" of "drugs and guns." *Smith* v. *United States*, 508 U.S. 223, 240 (1993). And the provision's chief legislative sponsor has said that the provision seeks "to persuade the man who is tempted to commit a Federal felony to leave his gun at home" … From the perspective of any such purpose (persuading a criminal "to leave his gun at home"), what sense would it make for this statute to penalize one who walks with a gun in a bag to the site of a drug sale, but to ignore a similar individual who, like defendant Gray-Santana, travels to a similar site with a similar gun in a similar bag, but instead of walking, drives there with the gun in his car? How persuasive is a punishment that is without effect until a drug dealer who has brought his gun to a sale (indeed has it available for use) actually takes it from the trunk (or unlocks the glove compartment) of his car?

This type of reasoning can be represented as a practical argument, in which the means needed for pursuing the purpose are selected according to their consequences (Macagno and Walton, 2018; Walton et al., 2008, 323):

ARGUMENTATION SCHEME *Argument from Practical Reasoning*

Premise 1:	I have a goal G.
Premise 2:	Carrying out this action A is the best means to realize G.
Conclusion:	Therefore, I ought (practically speaking) to carry out this action A.

In our case, the reasoning can be represented as follows:

Premise 1:	The statute's basic purpose is to combat the "dangerous combination" of "drugs and guns," persuading the man who is tempted to commit a federal felony to leave his gun at home.
Premise 2:	The enrichment "carry a firearm *<on the person or in a wagon, car, truck, or other vehicle that one accompanies>*" allows the application of the law to cases in which people bring the gun with them.
	The alternative enrichment "carry *<on the person>*" would make the law without effect until a drug dealer who has brought his gun actually places it on his person.
Conclusion:	Therefore, the legislator's intended enrichment is "carry a firearm *<on the person or in a wagon, car, truck, or other vehicle that one accompanies>*."

This type of argument is especially interesting from an argumentation point of view because it goes back to the evidence from the congressional record, by quoting the remarks of the members of Congress who were deliberating on how to frame the legislation. Here we are moving to the level of a metadialogue, where the argumentation in the trial moves back to a secondary level to consider the evidence furnished by the argumentation of the members of Congress as they engaged in deliberations with each other on how to frame the wording of the legislation. This type of argumentation is based on quotations, where one group of arguers in a trial setting is trying to interpret words used in that setting by going back to a prior problem-solving dialogue that was conducted on how to formulate the statute. The argumentation scheme used here is that of argument from commitment, where the actual language of the legislators is quoted so that a reasonable person can extract what are presumed to be their commitments from the natural language quotations (Macagno and Walton, 2017; Walton et al., 2008, 132):

ARGUMENTATION SCHEME *Argument from Commitment*

Premise 1:	If arguer *a* has committed herself to proposition A at some point in a dialogue, then it may be inferred that she is also committed to proposition B, should the question of whether B is true become an issue later in the dialogue.
Premise 2:	Arguer *a* has committed herself to proposition A at some point in a dialogue.
Conclusion:	At some later point in the dialogue, where the issue of B arises, arguer *a* may be said to be committed to proposition B.

This is a kind of argument we use all the time in everyday conversational argumentation and it is clearly a mainstay of legal argumentation. How it works is that one arguer who is attempting to interpret the argumentation of another arguer expressed in natural language draws implications concerning what the second arguer thinks the first arguer is saying. Suppose an arguer has gone on record as making some statements that constitute an argument and another arguer is trying to draw out a proposition that the first arguer is supposedly committed to in virtue of having made these remarks. The remarks are taken to be fairly represented as statements that commit him to some proposition. But natural language is inherently prone to using words that are vague and ambiguous, and even that change in meaning over time. So, although argument from commitment seems trivial, in practice there can be different opinions about what some spoken or written text actually commits the speaker or writer to. But according to the scheme, if a speaker or writer has gone on record as committing herself by saying something, she may also be arguably committed to some other proposition that appears to logically follow from it. Although the argument from commitment is a defeasible form of argument, it can ground a presumption, and consequently oblige the other party to offer evidence for the rebuttal of the presumption. Often, the evidence for or against a commitment is linguistic evidence based on a quotation of what the speaker actually said or wrote. This argument can be classified in argumentation theory as a form of inference to the best explanation. Different explanations can be given of the text attributed to the speaker or writer, and different interpretations pro or con a hypothesis about what the speaker may be taken to have meant are possible. These arguments underlie the arguments from authority described at Section 5.7.

An overview of the main argument in Muscarello is shown in the argument graph in Figure 3.9. PR stands for the argumentation scheme for goal-directed practical reasoning, reasoning from a goal and means to achieve the goal to a conclusion representing a proposal for action. The notation EH stands for the argumentation scheme for argument from evidence to a hypothesis. Both arguments are pro arguments as indicated by the plus sign in the argument nodes, shown as rectangles with rounded corners. The propositions constituting the premises and conclusions of the arguments are shown in the rectangles with sharp corners.

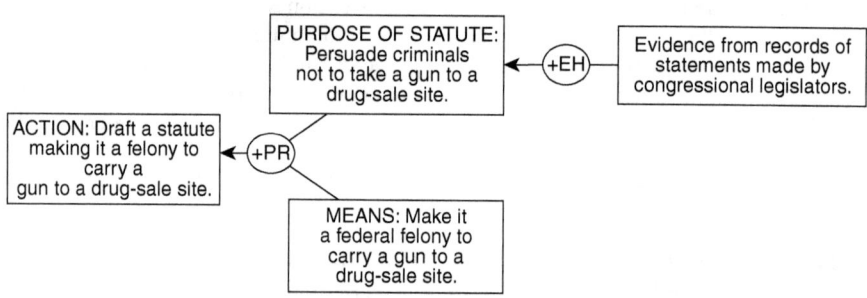

FIGURE 3.9 An argument graph illustrating argument from the purpose of a statute

The analysis of the different types of interpretative arguments in *Muscarello* shows three levels of evidence used for enriching the semantic representation of the legal provision. The "ordinary meaning" arguments, which both parties developed based on dictionary definitions and proofs of common use, are defeasible arguments that are grounded on presumptive patterns of reasoning. As both analyses of such arguments as pragmatic inferences and as argumentative ones highlight, the force of the "ordinary meaning" arguments lies in the possibility of rejecting the alternative reconstruction. From a pragmatic perspective, the majority opinion provided evidence that allowed both the exclusion of the alternative enrichment and the support of the defended reconstruction of the "ampliative" enrichment (resulting from an R-based inference). In argumentative terms, the reasoning from best explanation was justified in the argument of Justice Breyer by showing the unacceptability of the other alternatives. The role that other types of argument play depends on their defeasibility conditions. The relationship between the disputed statement or phrase and the co-textual information used as evidence is crucial for determining the defeasibility of an argument. The context provided by the text of the provision (the relevance of its parts) is less defeasible than the context of the surrounding provisions. For example, the systematic argument (the negative consequence of the irrelevance of a provision) can be rebutted by a different interpretation of the allegedly redundant provision, or of its purpose, or of its role within the legal system. This second type of context, i.e., the co-text is much less defeasible than the appeal to extratextual evidence, such as quotations. The use of such evidence presupposes a further argumentative reasoning (the argument from commitment), and other considerations such as the function of the individual who expressed the specific intention in drafting the text. The more the evidence becomes distant from the object of interpretation, the more reasoning steps are needed, and the more presumptions are subject to criticisms or counterarguments.

3.5 CONCLUSION

The analysis of four distinct cases of legal ambiguity – *Holy Trinity, HUD v. Rucker, Heller,* and *Muscarello* – brings to light the crucial role of pragmatics in legal interpretation. In legal theory, pragmatics is sometimes excluded from the realm of statutory interpretation (Poggi, 2011, 2016) due to the institutionalized and particular nature of statutes (Moore, 1980, 186–187): "As utterances, statutes lack many of the non-linguistic, contextual features which constitute the foundation for a pragmatics analysis. Statutes are institutionalized utterances. Consequently, the richness of time and circumstance which the pragmatic approach embraces to interpret the intent of an ambiguous expression is eliminated by this institutionalized nature of statutes."

This view could be somehow defended if pragmatics concerned only one type of implicature, the particularized conversational implicature (PCI), which are intended inferences that depend on the fact that the utterance is made in a specific context in which it can be perceived as uncooperative or less cooperative than expected in some respect. In order not to reject the presumption that the speaker is uncooperative (Grice, 1975, 28), the hearer draws an inference about what he meant. In this sense, "a PCI from saying p would leave no room for the idea that an implicature of this sort is NORMALLY carried by saying that p" (Levinson, 2000, 16–17). It is strictly bound to the specific context intended as the conversational setting. This type of inference is clearly not likely to be drawn in case of statutes, as it depends also on extratextual elements, which would make it much more defeasible than other inferences commonly used in interpretation.

As shown in this chapter, pragmatics is not only about the conversational setting. We need pragmatic considerations for any type of interpretation, and most "linguistic" arguments that the courts can bring for and against enrichments are indeed pragmatic. The context on which these pragmatic inferences are based consists of co-textual and contextual evidence and presumptions (Slocum, 2016a). The type of context is crucial for determining their acceptability. In order to show how pragmatic inferences can be assessed, we have represented them in terms of defeasible arguments, whose defeasibility depends on the type of their premises (first and foremost the nature of their presumptions) and the arguments that they presuppose. The "linguistic" arguments are thus not the arguments that are based on the "ordinary" or "plain" meaning regardless of the context or the intention of the speaker (Slocum, 2016a). Instead, they are defeasible arguments whose premises correspond to a specific type of evidence and specific types of presumptions, which make them less subject to being rebutted or criticized than other arguments, such as those grounded on quotations or analogy.

The crucial difference between the generalized implicatures analyzed in pragmatics and the inferences made explicit in legal arguments does not seem to lie in the special nature of the legal context (Morra, 2016). Rather, the difference lies in the purpose of the inferences themselves and thus in the nature of the maxims. Pragmatic maxims are presumptions used for describing the interpretation of an utterance, showing how the speaker's meaning is related to an utterance. This approach shows regularities that can provide hypotheses on how our minds work (Sperber and Wilson, 1995), or at least our interpretative tendencies. In contrast, the interpretative canons are maxims in the dialectical sense, namely elements of a repository of arguments used for justifying an interpretation. Their role is "rhetorical" (Tarello, 1980), or, to use a less loaded word, argumentative. This difference is mirrored also at the level of the structure of the two distinct types of maxims. Interpretative canons are expressed as dialogical presumptions: their conclusions concern what a legal text is presumed to mean (or how it should be interpreted, according to some formulations) based on specific linguistic or extralinguistic premises. Gricean maxims are worded as *meta*dialogical presumptions, as they concern the speaker's behavior. For example, the most famous principle that Grice sets out, the cooperative principle, is a presumption (indication) about how the speaker is expected to behave: "Make your conversational contribution such as is required, at the stage at which it occurs, by the accepted purpose or direction of the talk exchange in which you are engaged" (Grice, 1975, 45). For this reason, pragmatic inferences are hypotheses about the speaker's behavior – why he or she decides to flout or to comply with a maxim.

The last distinction concerns the difference between interpretative canons and argumentation schemes. Interpretative canons are principles that can be used dialectically to support an interpretative conclusion. However, they do not provide instruments for assessing and comparing interpretative arguments. The success of one argument over another, however, is not a matter of the nature of the canon itself. Rather, it is a matter of the whole argumentation brought for and against the interpretative conclusions by both parties. In this perspective, both the textualist and the intentionalist theories of interpretation can be regarded as reasonable rhetorical strategies for defending the force of specific types of arguments, both are pragmatic, but they are based on different types of evidence drawn from different dimensions of the "context." This is why argumentation schemes can be useful for the purpose of inter-pretative discussions. As we will show in the next chapters (and in particular in Chapter 5), argumentation schemes are abstract structures that allow the identification of the different types of premises used, and the assessment of both the acceptability of the inference and the strength of the evidence used.

REFERENCES

Alexy, Robert, and Ralf Dreier. 1991. "Statutory interpretation in the Federal Republic of Germany." In *Interpreting Statutes. A Comparative Study*, edited by Neil MacCormick and Robert Summers, 73–121. Aldershot, UK: Dartmouth.

Asgeirsson, Hrafn. 2012. "Textualism, pragmatic enrichment, and objective communicative content." *Monash University Faculty of Law Legal Studies Research Paper*, no. 2012/21. https://doi.org/10.2139/ssrn.2142266.

Atlas, Jay David. 1989. *Philosophy without Ambiguity: A Logico-Linguistic Essay*. Oxford, UK: Clarendon Press.

Atlas, Jay David. 2005. *Logic, Meaning, and Conversation*. Oxford, UK: Oxford University Press.

Atlas, Jay David, and Stephen Levinson. 1981. "It-clefts, informativeness and logical form: radical pragmatics (revised standard version)." In *Radical Pragmatics*, edited by Peter Cole, 1–62. New York, NY: Academic Press.

Bach, Kent. 2000. "Quantification, qualification and context a reply to Stanley and Szabó." *Mind and Language* 15 (2 and 3): 262–283. https://doi.org/10.1111/1468-0017.00131.

Barnett, Randy. 2011. "Interpretation and construction." *Harvard Journal of Law and Public Policy* 34: 65–72.

Baude, William, and Ryan Doerfler. 2017. "The (not so) plain meaning rule." *University of Chicago Law Review* 84(2): 539–566.

Bench-Capon, Trevor, and Henry Prakken. 2010. "Using argument schemes for hypothetical reasoning in law." *Artificial Intelligence and Law* 18(2): 153–174. https://doi.org/10.1007/s10506-010-9094-8.

Bezuidenhout, Anne. 1997. "Pragmatics, semantic undetermination and the referential/attri-butive distinction." *Mind* 106(423): 375–409. https://doi.org/10.1093/mind/106.423.375.

Black, Henry Campbell. 1896. *Handbook on the Construction and Interpretation of the Laws*. St. Paul, MN: West Publishing Company.

Bosanac, Paul. 2009. *Litigation Logic: A Practical Guide to Effective Argument*. Chicago, IL: American Bar Association.

Capone, Alessandro. 2009. "Are explicatures cancellable? Toward a theory of the speaker's intentionality." *Intercultural Pragmatics* 6(1): 55–83. https://doi.org/10.1515/IPRG.2009.003.

Capone, Alessandro. 2011. "The attributive/referential distinction, pragmatics, modularity of mind and modularization." *Australian Journal of Linguistics* 31(2): 153–186. https://doi.org /10.1080/07268602.2011.560827.

Carston, Robyn. 2002. *Thoughts and Utterances: The Pragmatics of Explicit Communication*. Oxford, UK: Blackwell Publishing Ltd.

Carston, Robyn. 2004. "Explicature and semantics." In *Semantics: A Reader*, edited by Steven Davis and Brendan Gillon, 817–845. Oxford, UK: Oxford University Press.

Carston, Robyn. 2013. "Legal texts and canons of construction: A view from current pragmatic theory." In *Law and Language: Current Legal Issues*, edited by Michael Freeman and Fiona Smith, 15:8–33. Oxford, UK: Oxford University Press.

Cowper, Elizabeth. 2009. *A Concise Introduction to Syntactic Theory: The Government-Binding Approach*. Chicago, IL: University of Chicago Press.

Dascal, Marcelo, and Jerzy Wróblewski. 1988. "Transparency and doubt: Understanding and interpretation in pragmatics and in law." *Law and Philosophy* 7(2): 203–224. https://doi.org /10.1007/BF00144156.

Endicott, Timothy. 2000. *Vagueness in Law*. Oxford, UK: Oxford University Press.

Farnsworth, Ward, Dustin Guzior, and Anup Malani. 2010. "Ambiguity about ambiguity: An empirical inquiry into legal interpretation." *Journal of Legal Analysis* 2(1): 257–300. https://doi.org/10.1093/jla/2.1.257

Fodor, Jerry. 1983. *The Modularity of Mind*. Cambridge, MA: MIT Press.

Gibbs, Raymond. 1992. "When is metaphor? The idea of understanding in theories of metaphor." *Poetics Today* 13(4): 575–606. https://doi.org/10.2307/1773290.

Grice, Paul. 1975. "Logic and conversation." In *Syntax and Semantics 3: Speech Acts*, edited by Peter Cole and Jerry Morgan, 41–58. New York, NY: Academic Press.

Guastini, Riccardo. 2011. *Interpretare e Argomentare*. Milano, Italy: Giuffrè.

Gullvåg, Ingemund, and Arne Naess. 1996. "Vagueness and ambiguity." In *Philosophy of Language*. Vol. 2, edited by Marcelo Dascal, Gerhardus Dietfried, Kuno Lorenz, and Georg Meggle, 1407–1417. Berlin, Germany, and New York, NY: De Gruyter.

Harman, Gilbert. 1965. "The inference to the best explanation." *The Philosophical Review* 74 (1): 88–95. https://doi.org/10.2307/2183532.

Harman, Gilbert. 1992. "Inference to the best explanation (review)." *Mind* 101(403): 578–580. https://doi.org/10.1093/mind/101.403.578.

Hart, Herbert Lionel Adolphus. 1958. "Positivism and the separation of law and morals." *Harvard Law Review* 71(4): 593–629.

Heine, Bernd, Heiko Narrog, and Kasia Jaszczolt. 2015. "Default semantics." In *The Oxford Handbook of Linguistic Analysis*, edited by Alex Barber and Robert Stainton, 193–221. Oxford, UK: Oxford University Press.

Horn, Laurence. 1984. "Toward a new taxonomy for pragmatic inference: Q-based and R-based implicature." In *Meaning, Form, and Use in Context*, edited by Deborah Schiffring, 11–42. Washington, DC: Georgetown University Press.

Horn, Laurence. 1991. "Given as new: When redundant affirmation isn't." *Journal of Pragmatics* 15(4): 313–336. https://doi.org/10.1016/0378-2166(91)90034-U.

Horn, Laurence. 1995. "Vehicles of meaning: Unconventional semantics and unbearable interpretation." *Washington University Law Quarterly* 73: 1145–1152.

Jaszczolt, Kasia. 1999. *Discourse, Beliefs and Intentions*. Oxford, UK: Elsevier.

Jaszczolt, Kasia. 2005a. *Default Semantics: Foundations of a Compositional Theory of Acts of Communication*. Oxford, UK: Oxford University Press.

Jaszczolt, Kasia. 2005b. "Default semantics." In *Concise Encyclopedia of Philosophy of Language and Linguistics*, edited by Alex Barber and Robert Stainton, 128–130. Oxford, UK: Oxford University Press.

Jaszczolt, Kasia. 2006. "Meaning merger: Pragmatic inference, defaults, and compositionality." *Intercultural Pragmatics* 3(2): 195–212. https://doi.org/10.1515/IP.2006.012.

Jaszczolt, Kasia. 2007. "The syntax-pragmatics merger: Belief reports in the theory of default semantics." *Pragmatics & Cognition* 15(1): 41–64. https://doi.org/10.1075/pc.15.1.06jas.

Jaszczolt, Kasia. 2011. "Salient meanings, default meanings, and automatic processing." In *Salience and Defaults in Utterance Processing*, edited by Kasia Jaszczolt and Keith Allan, 11–33. Berlin, Germany: De Gruyter.

Kaplan, Jeffrey, and Georgia Green. 1995. "Grammar and inferences of rationality in interpreting the child pornography statute." *Washington University Law Review* 73: 1223–1251.

Kecskes, Istvan. 2013. *Intercultural Pragmatics*. Oxford, UK: Oxford University Press.

Kissine, Mikhail. 2012. "Sentences, utterances, and speech acts." In *Cambridge Handbook of Pragmatics*, edited by Keith Allan and Kasia Jaszczolt, 169–190. New York, NY: Cambridge University Press.

Klein, Dan, and Christopher Manning. 2003. "Accurate unlexicalized parsing." In *Proceedings of the 41st Annual Meeting on Association for Computational Linguistics-Volume 1*, 423–430. Stroudsburg, PA: Association for Computational Linguistics.

Kratzer, Angelika. 1977. "What 'must' and 'can' must and can mean." *Linguistics and Philosophy* 1(3): 337–355. https://doi.org/10.1007/BF00353453.

Kratzer, Angelika. 2002. "The notional category of modality." In *Formal Semantics: The Essential Readings*, edited by Paul Portner and Barbara Partee, 289–323. Oxford, UK: John Wiley & Sons.

Langendoen, D Terence, Dana McDaniel, and Yedidyah Langsam. 1989. "Preposition-phrase attachment in noun phrases." *Journal of Psycholinguistic Research* 18(6): 533–548. https://doi.org/10.1007/BF01067157

Levinson, Stephen. 2000. *Presumptive Meanings: The Theory of Generalized Conversational Implicature*. Cambridge, MA: MIT Press.

Lyons, John. 1977. *Semantics, Vol. 1*. Cambridge, UK: Cambridge University Press.

Macagno, Fabrizio. 2017. "Defaults and inferences in interpretation." *Journal of Pragmatics* 117: 280–290. https://doi.org/10.1016/j.pragma.2017.06.005.

Macagno, Fabrizio, and Sarah Bigi. 2018. "Types of dialogue and pragmatic ambiguity." In *Argumentation and Language*, edited by Steve Oswald, Jérôme Jacquin, and Thierry Herman, 191–218. Cham, Switzerland: Springer.

Macagno, Fabrizio, and Alessandro Capone. 2016. "Interpretative disputes, explicatures, and argumentative reasoning." *Argumentation* 30(4): 399–422. https://doi.org/10.1007/s10503-015-9347-5.

Macagno, Fabrizio, and Douglas Walton. 2011. "Reasoning from paradigms and negative evidence." *Pragmatics & Cognition* 19(1): 92–116. https://doi.org/10.1075/pc.19.1.04mac.

Macagno, Fabrizio, and Douglas Walton. 2014. *Emotive Language in Argumentation*. New York, NY: Cambridge University Press.

Macagno, Fabrizio, and Douglas Walton. 2017. *Interpreting Straw Man Argumentation. The Pragmatics of Quotation and Reporting*. Amsterdam, Netherlands: Springer.

Macagno, Fabrizio, and Douglas Walton. 2018. "Practical reasoning arguments: A modular approach." *Argumentation* 32(4): 519–547. https://doi.org/10.1007/s10503-018-9450-5.

MacCormick, Neil. 1995. "Argumentation and interpretation in law." *Argumentation* 9(3): 467–480. https://doi.org/10.1007/BF00733152.

MacCormick, Neil. 2005. *Rhetoric and the Rule of Law*. Oxford, UK: Oxford University Press.

Marmor, Andrei. 2014. *The Language of Law*. Oxford, UK: Oxford University Press.

Moore, Michael S. 1980. "The semantics of judging." *Southern California Law Review* 54: 151–294.

Morra, Lucia. 2016. "Conversational implicatures in normative texts." In *Interdisciplinary Studies in Pragmatics, Culture and Society*, edited by Alessandro Capone and Jacob Mey, 537–562. Cham, Switzerland: Springer.

Naess, Arne. 2005a. "Basic terms." In *The Selected Works of Arne Naess*, edited by Alan Drengson, 5–82. Dordrecht, Netherlands: Springer.

Naess, Arne. 2005b. "Definitoid statements." In *The Selected Works of Arne Naess*, edited by Alan Drengson, 161–208. Dordrecht, Netherlands: Springer Netherlands.

Naess, Arne. 2005c. "Precization and definition." In *The Selected Works of Arne Naess*, edited by Alan Drengson, 1403–1433. Dordrecht, Netherlands: Springer.

Nunberg, Geoffrey. 1979. "The non-uniqueness of semantic solutions: Polysemy." *Linguistics and Philosophy* 3(2): 143–184. https://doi.org/10.1007/BF00126509.

Pantel, Patrick, and Dekang Lin. 2000. "An unsupervised approach to prepositional phrase attachment using contextually similar words." In *Proceedings of the 38th Annual Meeting on Association for Computational Linguistics*, 101–108. Stroudsburg, PA: Association for Computational Linguistics.

Patterson, Dennis. 1993. "Poverty of interpretative universalism: Toward the reconstruction of legal theory." *Texas Law Review* 72: 1–56.

Patterson, Dennis. 2005. "Interpretation in law." *San Diego Law Review* 42: 685–710.

Poggi, Francesca. 2011. "Law and conversational implicatures." *International Journal for the Semiotics of Law-Revue Internationale de Sémiotique Juridique* 24(1): 21–40. https://doi.org/10.1007/s11196-010-9201-x

Poggi, Francesca. 2016. "Grice, the law and the linguistic special case thesis." In *Pragmatics and Law: Philosophical Perspectives*, edited by Alessandro Capone and Francesca Poggi, 231–248. Cham, Switzerland: Springer.

Recanati, François. 1987. *Meaning and Force: The Pragmatics of Performative Utterances*. New York, NY: Cambridge University Press.

Recanati, François. 2002. "Unarticulated constituents." *Linguistics and Philosophy* 25(3): 299–345. https://doi.org/10.1023/A:1015267930510.

Recanati, François. 2012. "Pragmatic enrichment." In *Routledge Companion to Philosophy of Language*, edited by Gillian Russell and Delia Graff Fara, 67–78. New York, NY, and London, UK: Routledge.

Rocci, Andrea. 2008. "Modality and its conversational backgrounds in the reconstruction of argumentation." *Argumentation* 22(2): 165–189. https://doi.org/10.1007/s10503-007-9065-8.

Sadock, Jerrold. 1978. "On testing for conversational implicature." In *Syntax and Semantics: Pragmatics*, edited by Peter Cole, 281–297. New York, NY: Academic Press.

Scalia, Antonin, and Bryan Garner. 2012. *Reading Law: The Interpretation of Legal Texts*. Eagan, MN: Thomson West.

Schiffer, Stephen. 2016. "Philosophical and jurisprudential issues of vagueness." In *Vagueness and Law: Philosophical and Legal Perspectives*, edited by Geert Keil and Ralf Poscher, 23–48. Oxford, UK: Oxford University Press.

Slocum, Brian. 2016a. "Conversational implicatures and legal texts." *Ratio Juris* 29(1): 23–43. https://doi.org/10.1111/raju.12114.

Slocum, Brian. 2016b. *Ordinary Meaning: A Theory of the Most Fundamental Principle of Legal Interpretation*. Chicago, IL: University of Chicago Press.

Slocum, Brian. 2017. "The contribution of linguistics to legal interpretation." In *The Nature of Legal Interpretation : What Jurists Can Learn about Legal Interpretation from Linguistics and Philosophy*, edited by Brian Slocum, 14–45. Chicago, IL: Chicago University Press.

Soames, Scott. 2009. "Interpreting legal texts: What is, and what is not, special about the law." In *Philosophical Essays*, 1: 403–424. Princeton, NJ: Princeton University Press.

Solan, Lawrence. 2004. "Pernicious ambiguity in contracts and statutes." *Chicago-Kent Law Review* 79: 859–888.

Solan, Lawrence. 2010. *The Language of Statutes: Laws and Their Interpretation*. Chicago, IL: University of Chicago Press.

Solum, Lawrence. 1987. "On the indeterminacy crisis: Critiquing critical dogma." *The University of Chicago Law Review* 54: 462–503.

Solum, Lawrence. 2009. "*District of Columbia v. Heller* and originalism." *Northwestern University Law Review* 103(2): 923–982.

Solum, Lawrence. 2013. "Originalism and constitutional construction." *Fordham Law Review Rev.* 82(2): 453–537.

Solum, Lawrence. 2015. "Intellectual history as constitutional theory." *Virginia Law Review*, 1111–1164.

Solum, Lawrence. 2017. "Originalism, hermeneutics, and the fixation thesis." In *The Nature of Legal Interpretation: What Jurists Can Learn about Legal Interpretation from Linguistics and Philosophy*, edited by Brian Slocum, 130–155. Chicago, IL: University of Chicago Press.

Sperber, Dan, and Deirdre Wilson. 1995. *Relevance: Communication and Cognition*. Oxford, UK: Blackwell Publishing Ltd.

Strauss, David. 1996. "Why plain meaning." *Notre Dame Law Review* 72(5): 1565–1582.

Stump, Gregory Thomas. 2012. *The Semantic Variability of Absolute Constructions*. Dordrecht, Netherlands: Reidel.

Swanson, James, and Roger Pilon, eds. 2002. *Cato Supreme Court Review*. Washington, DC: Cato Institute.

Tarello, Giovanni. 1980. *L'interpretazione della Legge*. Milano, Italy: Giuffrè.

Tiersma, Peter. 1995. "The ambiguity of interpretation: Distinguishing interpretation from construction" *Washington University Law Review* 73(3): 1095–1101.

Tiersma, Peter. 2001. "A message in a bottle: Text, autonomy, and statutory interpretation." *Tulane Law Review* 76: 431–482.

Volokh, Eugene. 1998. "The commonplace Second Amendment." *New York University Law Review* 73: 793–821.

Waismann, Friedrich. 1951. "Verifiability." In *Logic and Language*, edited by Gilbert Ryle and Antony Flew, 35–68. Oxford, UK: Blackwell.

Walton, Douglas. 1996. *Fallacies Arising from Ambiguity*. Dordrecht, Netherlands: Springer.

Walton, Douglas. 2002. *Legal Argumentation and Evidence*. University Park, PA: The Pennsylvania State University Press.

Walton, Douglas. 2006. *Fundamentals of Critical Argumentation*. New York, NY: Cambridge University Press.

Walton, Douglas, Christopher Reed, and Fabrizio Macagno. 2008. *Argumentation Schemes*. New York, NY: Cambridge University Press.

Weinstock, Charles B., John B. Goodenough, and Ari Z. Klein. 2013. "Measuring assurance case confidence using Baconian probabilities." In *2013 1st International Workshop on Assurance Cases for Software-Intensive Systems (ASSURE)*, 7–11. San Francisco, CA: IEEE. https://doi.org/10.1109/ASSURE.2013.6614264.

Williams, David C. 1998. "The unitary Second Amendment." *New York University Law Review* 73: 822–830.

Williamson, Timothy. 2002. *Vagueness*. London, UK: Routledge.

Wilson, Deirdre, and Dan Sperber. 2004. "Relevance theory." In *Handbook of Pragmatics*, edited by Laurence Horn and Gregory Ward, 607–632. Oxford, UK: Blackwell.

Wyner, Adam, and Trevor Bench-Capon. 2007. "Argument schemes for legal case-based reasoning." In *Proceedings of the 2007 Conference on Legal Knowledge and Information Systems: JURIX 2007: The Twentieth Annual Conference*, edited by Arno Lodder and Laurens Mommers, 139–149. Amsterdam, Netherlands: IOS Press.

Zipf, George Kingsley. 1949. *Human Behavior and the Principle of Least Effort: An Introduction to Human Ecology*. Cambridge, UK: Addison-Wesley.

CASES CITED

Church of the Holy Trinity v. *United States* 1892 143 U.S. 457.

Department of Housing & Urban Development v. *Rucker* 2002 535 U.S. 125.

District of Columbia v. *Heller* 2008 554 U.S. 570.

Moskal v. *United States* 1990 No. 498 U.S. 103.

Muscarello v. *United States* 1998 no. 524 U.S. 125.

Smith v. *United States* 1993 508 U.S. 223.

United States v. *Missouri Pacific R.R. Co.* 1929. 278 U.S. 269.

4

Pragmatic Maxims and Presumptions in Legal Interpretation

4.1 INTRODUCTION

In our previous chapter on ambiguity, we underscored how the mere logical form of a legal statement does not provide the proposition expressed. The meaning of an utterance – the product of a verbal act performed in a specific context (Leech, 1983, 14) – cannot be the simple output of a decoding process (Sperber and Wilson, 1995, 182; Recanati, 2003, 56), or "semantic interpretation" (Leech, 1983, 5). The logical form (also called "semantic representation") that can be recovered by the mere decoding of an utterance through the application of the rules of grammar (Sperber and Wilson, 1995, 9–10) does not deliver complete propositions, but only "semantic schemata" (Recanati, 2003, 56). As Recanati put it, "semantic interpretation by itself cannot determine what is said by a sentence containing such an expression: for the semantic value of the expression – its own contribution to what is said – is a matter of speaker's meaning, and can only be determined by pragmatic interpretation" (Recanati, 2003, 57).

In our chapter on ambiguity we pointed out how disambiguation cannot be solved through the instruments of the linguistic structure, but needs to take into account elements external thereto, namely the co-text and the context in which a sentence is used. The same applies to the problem of reference assignment: in order to determine what "Bill is tall" means, we need to consider the context of the utterance, and not only the compositional meaning. The relationship between pragmatic processes and interpretation is much more pervasive and complex than the phenomena of disambiguation and reference assignment (Carston, 1988). The literature in pragmatic labels differently a set of operations that determine the explicit meaning of an utterance together with the rules of grammar, which we refer to generally with the terms "enrichments" or "explicatures" (regardless of the theoretical differences between these two concepts, see Bezuidenhout, 1997; Sperber and Wilson, 1995, 176–183; Carston, 2002, 116–118; Recanati, 2003, Chapter 3).[1] Such operations consist

---

[1] In relevance theory, explicature is defined as the development of the logical form: "An assumption communicated by an utterance U is *explicit* [an explicature] if and only if it is a development of a logical form encoded by U" (Sperber and Wilson, 1995, 182). The relationship between logical form

in the narrowing, loosening, or specification of the meaning of some lexical units in function of the context (Recanati, 2010, 3–12); ellipsis unpacking, indexical resolution, and reference identification (Levinson, 2000, 174–186); and determination of the existential presuppositions (Bezuidenhout, 1997, 394). The possibility of recovering the proposition expressed depends essentially on such processes, which operate together with those characterizing a purely "semantic" interpretation (Bezuidenhout, 1997, 387).

This chapter[2] addresses the relationship between pragmatics and legal interpretation, starting from the role and the possibility of a pragmatic dimension of legal texts. The goal is to analyze how the different interpretative canons used in legal theory can be integrated within a broader linguistic theory (Smolka and Pirker, 2016). Several approaches to statutory interpretation (see, for instance, Tarello, 1980; Hutton, 2009, 74–79; MacCormick, 2005; MacCormick, 1995; MacCormick and Summers, 1991; Guastini, 2011) advance sets of interpretative arguments (also referred to as "canons" or "maxims"), which are framed as isolated arguments militating for or against a given interpretation. Such arguments, however, are not related to any linguistic framework of interpretation, and appear as independent and unconnected instruments that judges and legal practitioners can use either to support or rebut an interpretation. Building on the modern theories of pragmatics (Levinson, 2000; Atlas, 2007) and argumentation (Walton, Sartor, and Macagno, 2016; Macagno, Walton, and Sartor, 2014), we will try to develop a framework of linguistic interpretation based on the structure of an inference to best explanation (Atlas and Levinson, 1981). We will show how, in this framework, the possible interpretations are grounded on presumptions, which can be classified using Gricean conversational maxims (listed in the following section) and to which the interpretative canons can be connected. We will illustrate how Gricean pragmatic presumptions, and more importantly the argumentative distinction between levels of presumptions, can produce an integrated conception of statutory interpretation in which the different maxims and cannons of statutory interpretation are no longer seen as isolated arguments, but distinct types of pragmatic inferences used in a specific interpretative activity. This approach can allow the analyst (or more generally a legal practitioner involved in an interpretative discussion) to understand the presumptions underlying the various interpretative arguments, and to compare and order them hierarchically.

---

and the pragmatic processes is controversial in pragmatics; we will use this term neutrally, without necessarily upholding the philosophical position of relevance theory.

[2]   This chapter is based on a paper by Macagno, F., Walton, D., and Sartor, G. (2018): "Pragmatic maxims and presumptions in legal interpretation." *Law and Philosophy*, 37(1), 69–115. https://doi.org /10.1007/s10982-017-9306-4, whose content this chapter integrates and updates.

4.2 A PRAGMATICS OF LEGAL INTERPRETATION: IS IT THEORETICALLY POSSIBLE?

The relationship between pragmatics and legal interpretation is an extremely controversial topic. Pragmatics has been defined according to its broadest definition as the study of how utterances have meanings in speech situations (Leech, 1983, viii), where "situation" is constituted by the addresser and addressee, the context, the goals, the illocutionary act, and the utterance (Leech, 1983, 15). Pragmatics is distinguished from semantics as the latter is rule-governed and addresses the properties of expressions in a language in abstraction from particular contexts, speakers, or bearers (Leech, 1983, 5–6). The problem is to understand whether and how a discipline (pragmatics) that considers the meaning as a result of linguistic "activities" in a specific context (situation) and that analyzes how speakers mean more (or other) than what they say can be related to legal texts, which typically try to avoid the dependence of their meaning on their context (Marmor, 2008, 426), which in turn is commonly considered as much more "opaque" (less rich) than the ordinary one.

This issue becomes more complex if we consider two crucial aspects of statutory interpretation: on the one hand, the content communicated by legal texts goes beyond the "meaning of the words and sentences uttered" (Slocum, 2016a, 24); on the other hand, legal texts are required and expected to be understandable to the general public, and not only to legal practitioners (Slocum, 2016a, 24). A clear example of the difference between the prescriptive content of the law and its semantic meaning is the famous enactment considered by Fuller (Fuller, 1957, 664): "It shall be a misdemeanor, punishable by a fine of five dollars, to sleep in any railway station." The semantic representation of this prohibition underdetermines its meaning, which needs to be specified to exclude contextually absurd cases of passengers dozing off. The prescriptive content could be generally phrased as "Using or attempting to use a railway station as a place to sleep" (Soames, 2009, 416). As Soames maintains, despite this case being fictional, it shows clearly that the semantic meaning does not correspond to the content of the law, which is the result of pragmatic processes.

The crucial aspect is to understand the role of pragmatics in legal interpretation, and to what extent it is compatible with the specific activity considered. In particular, one of the most controversial issues in the contemporary debate on pragmatics and legal interpretation concerns the Gricean theoretical framework (discussed below) and the possibility of using it in legal interpretation. The arguments against this possibility (in addition to the unsupported claim that cases in which the content the legislature prescribes is not exactly what it says are very rare or do not exist at all, see Marmor, 2008, 429) focus on three dimensions of Gricean pragmatics (a speaker with communicative intentions, a conversational context shared by the interlocutors, and the conversational maxims) and can be summarized in the following three claims (Marmor, 2008, 2011):

1. The very notion of the intention of the legislator is controversial, as the lawmaking process is a collective activity involving negotiations between different parties and often characterized by "tacitly acknowledged incomplete decisions," namely decisions whose implications are left deliberately undecided (Marmor, 2008, 436).

2. Statutory interpretation (and the legislative process in general) is a strategic, and not a cooperative, activity, and for this reason the fundamental Gricean cooperative principle does not hold.

3. The Gricean maxims of conversation are *normative* instantiations of the general purpose of a conversation seen as a cooperative exchange of information. Legislation is a different kind of conversation (Marmor, 2008, 438).

The first argument captures a problem that has been debated in philosophy of language since the beginning of Grice's theory of meaning (Davis, 1998, 2007a; Margolis, 1973; Neale, 1992; Ziff, 1967; Schiffer, 1972, Chapter 2), and is not a peculiarity of legal discourse, but rather of ordinary conversation. The problem of a psychological theory of meaning implied by the concept of the speaker's intention does not undermine the whole project, which is aimed at providing an explanation of how the meaning of an utterance can be reconstructed through the relevant rules and regularities of language that exceed purely linguistic conventions. Grice's theory is based on the presupposition that one cannot unintentionally say something (Neale, 1992), and that the intentions can be reconstructed through linguistic and conversational conventions. In this sense, "it is reasonably clear that the speaker must intend his hearer to understand the meaning of his utterance by the use of the relevant rules and regularities of language" (Margolis, 1973, 684). As Neale put it (Neale, 1992, 552), "the formation of genuine communicative intentions by U is constrained by U's expectations": based on the assumptions that the interlocutors act in accordance with the cooperative principle and the maxims (and share the same linguistic conventions) and can access the same relevant background information, it is possible to convey a specific meaning by uttering a sentence that would not conventionally convey it. The focus of many pragmatic theories has been placed not on the intentional dimension of meaning (often compared to the perlocutionary act of getting the addressee to believe or do something as consequences of the utterance, see Levinson, 2000, 23; Neale, 1992, 547), but on the process of understanding, namely the reconstruction of the utterance meaning (Brown and Levinson, 1987, 8; Levinson, 2000, 25) and the analysis of the mechanisms that cause a divergence between the meaning of an utterance and what is communicated by it in a particular context (Levinson, 1983, 18). In this

sense, pragmatics has focused on the reasons that are necessary for recognizing the speaker's intention (also called "m-intention"), not primarily on the
intentions themselves. As Carston put it (2013, 24):

> The m-intention is a special kind of fully overt intention which, roughly, consists
> of a higher-order intention that a lower-order intention to provide a certain
> content or information is made evident to the addressee. When producing an
> utterance, a speaker will often have several intentions; for instance, an utterance
> of the sentence "I hope you will" in a particular context, may come with (at least)
> the following intentions: that the addressee should recognize that the speaker
> intends him to think that she hopes that he will win a certain contest, that the
> addressee should feel supported and encouraged by her, that he should think the
> speaker is a good friend to him, that he should confide in her, and perhaps more.
> But only the first of these intentions has the overtness of an m-intention and
> a correct interpretation of the utterance will consist in recovery of the content of
> just this intention. Correlatively, in the interpretation of legal language, whether
> a contract, a will, a statute, or a constitution, the only intention that is of interest
> is the m-intention.

The speaker's intention (or m-intention) is indeed a crucial dimension of interpretation, including legal interpretation, as it underlies the distinction between the
meaning of a sentence and what the sentence was *used to say or stipulate* (Soames,
2011, 236–237), a distinction that characterizes legal language just like the ordinary
one (Soames, 2011):

> The content of a legal text is determined in essentially the same way that the
> contents of other texts or linguistic performances are, save for complications
> resulting from the fact that the agent of a legislative speech act is often not
> a single language user but a group, the purpose of the speech act is not usually
> to contribute to the cooperative exchange of information, but to generate
> behavior-modifying stipulations, and the resulting stipulated contents are
> required to fit smoothly into a complex set of pre-existing stipulations generated
> by other actors at other times.

Contrary to Marmor's point, the speaker's intention is more important in law than in
ordinary conversation. In Grice's view, the speaker's intention involves both the
intention to produce a certain response r in the interlocutor through the utterance of
x, and to allow the interlocutor to recognize the intention of producing r through
some features of the utterance of x (Schiffer, 1972). In this sense, Marmor's case
against the speaker's intention is actually contradicted by the evidence provided by
the interpretative activities. First, the identification of the legislator's illocutionary
act is a fundamental epistemological part of the interpretative task (Soames, 2011).
Second, unlike ordinary conversation, in legal interpretation evidence of the possible "perlocutionary" intention of the legislators is taken into account and becomes
an argument in favor of a specific interpretation in cases of vagueness, conflicting

laws, and absurd results. The problem lies in what is intended by "intention" (Soames, 2011):

> The search for legislative rationale is *not* a search for causally efficacious factors that motivated the required number of lawmakers to enact the law or legal provision ... The purposes of a law or other legal provision, sought in the adjudication of hard cases for which a constitutive judicial decision is needed, are *not* the causally efficacious motivators that produced the law or provision, but the chief *reasons* publically offered to *justify* its adoption.

While ordinary conversation does not offer evidence of the reasons of the speaker for uttering *x* to produce a specific response, in the law this evidence is available, and thus becomes sometimes crucial for interpretative purposes.

The second argument (statutory interpretation is strategic rather than cooperative) is more problematic. Marmor points out that while ordinary conversation is cooperative, namely based on the assumption that the interlocutors make relevant contributions to the conversation and comply with the maxims, legislation is a complex strategic activity aimed at generating rules that modify behavior. For this reason, Grice's cooperative principle, and consequently the maxims, do not apply (Marmor, 2008, 429–431). Again, this problem has been debated quite extensively in the pragmatic tradition. Grice described this principle in a vague fashion, as the interlocutors' sharing of a common communicative purpose, a common goal characterizing their verbal interaction (Grice, 1975, 45): "Our talk exchanges do not normally consist of a succession of disconnected remarks, and would not be rational if they did. They are characteristically, to some degree at least, cooperative efforts; and each participant recognizes in them, to some extent, a common purpose or set of purposes, or at least a mutually accepted direction." This claim can be interpreted in a purely formal way as principle "regulating what we say so that it contributes to some assumed illocutionary or discoursal goal(s)" (Leech, 1983, 82). This interpretation makes the cooperative principle closer to the principle of relevance, whose central role was acknowledged by Sperber and Wilson, who pointed out clearly how the degree of cooperation described by Grice does not correspond to what the interlocutors actually expect and comply with (Sperber and Wilson, 1995, 162). In this sense, legal discourse is a specific type of discourse, but still has a specific and shared goal (generating behavior-modifying stipulations) that makes the interaction between the interlocutors possible (Slocum, 2016a, 37). Moreover, the cooperative principle does not apply in the same way in all societies and in all the activity types (Levinson, 1992). In certain societies and in certain types of activities, some maxims have precedence over others (Leech, 1983, 80), leading to different interpretative strategies in which the maxims are applied in different ways or in different degrees, or can be simply contravened (Leech, 1983, 8). The conflict between the interlocutors' individual goals (Sarangi and Slembrouck, 1992, 128) that is normal in legal discourse simply characterizes a type of interaction (or activity type) that affects the hierarchy of the maxims and the presumptions on which the interlocutor rely (Macagno and Walton, 2017, 74–75; Sinclair, 1985; Tiersma, 1990; Solan and Tiersma, 2005; Horn 2009; Shuy, 2011; Solan, 2002; Jacobs and Jackson, 2006).

The third argument concerns the nature of the maxims (and submaxims) that Grice presented as "principles that participants will be expected (ceteris paribus) to observe," which can be summarized as follows (Grice, 1975, 26–27):

Quantity: Make your contribution as informative and no more informative than is required
1. Make your contribution as informative as is required (for the current purposes of the exchange).
2. Do not make your contribution more informative than is required.

Quality: Try to make your contribution one that is true.
1. Do not say what you believe to be false.
2. Do not say that for which you lack adequate evidence.

Relation: Be relevant.

Manner: Be perspicuous.
1. Avoid obscurity of expression.
2. Avoid ambiguity.
3. Be brief (avoid unnecessary prolixity).
4. Be orderly.

Marmor maintains that these maxims are normative principles (Marmor, 2011) characterizing a type of conversation defined by the cooperative principle (Marmor, 2014, 37). Thus, he argues that since legal discourse is strategic and not cooperative (a terminological opposition that results only from a specific interpretation of the notion of "cooperation"), the maxims do not apply. This argument is grounded on a misconception of the nature of the maxims (Bach, 2006, 24). Grice clearly excluded the idea of a quasi-contractual nature of the maxims (Grice, 1975, 48), pointing out how they are related instead to the expectations of the interlocutors (Grice, 1975, 47; 49):

> As one of my avowed aims is to see talking as a special case or variety of purposive, indeed rational, behavior, it may be worth noting that the specific expectations or presumptions connected with at least some of the foregoing maxims have their analogues in the sphere of transactions that are not talk exchanges . . .
>
>   So I would like to be able to show that observance of the [cooperative principle] and maxims is reasonable (rational) along the following lines: that anyone who cares about the goals that are central to conversation/

communication (e.g., giving and receiving information, influencing and being influenced by others) must be expected to have an interest, given suitable circumstances, in participation in talk exchanges that will be profitable only on the assumption that they are conducted in general accordance with the [cooperative principle] and the maxims.

Conversational maxims are not normative (Davis, 2007b); they are presumptions about utterances that are used to explain how speakers often mean more than they say (Leech, 1983, 8–9), or heuristics that the hearers rely on to interpret the speaker's intention (Levinson, 2000, 29–35).

Marmor's arguments do not prove that legal discourse (and the process of statutory interpretation) is extraneous to pragmatic considerations, or that pragmatic theories (and the Gricean maxims) cannot be used for interpreting statues or other types of legal texts. However, his attack brings to light a crucial issue, namely whether the Gricean maxims are the best instruments for analyzing the pragmatic dimension of legal texts and recovering their meaning. The maxims encode expectations of verbal behavior, not of textual features. In the literature in pragmatics, the maxims have been adapted, modified, and reduced to heuristic principles of interpretation (Levinson, 2000, 31–33; Horn, 1984) to better provide an explanation for phenomena such as the generalized conversational implicatures, a type of pragmatic inference that is normally drawn unless there are unusual specific contextual assumptions that defeat it. The problem of the pragmatic dimension of statutory interpretation concerns determining the pragmatic instruments that can be used for the specific goal of the interpreter, namely justifying an interpretative decision. The evidence that the interpretative practice provides is that the maxims are not used as justificatory principles; in this context, other principles (the canons of interpretation) are applied and invoked as the reasons in support or against a specific attribution of meaning to a legal statement (Marmor, 2014, 54). The crucial questions are whether these maxims – or at least some of them – can be conceived as pragmatic principles (Kaplan, 2019, Chapter 6), what relation they have with Gricean pragmatics, and whether they are more effective instruments for pursuing this specific goal within the specific legal context (Slocum, 2016a, 25).

The answers to these questions are not simple, as they involve comparison between presumptive principles of verbal behavior (or heuristics used for understanding the implicit meaning of an utterance) and canons conceived as argumentative (or rather dialectical) maxims (Everardus, *Loci argumentorum legales*). To this purpose, we will first show where argumentation and pragmatics meet for the goal of justifying an interpretation, and how the interpretative canons are related to the Gricean maxims. We will then analyze what the two paradigms share, namely their presumptive nature.

4.3 PRAGMATICS AND ARGUMENTATION THEORY IN STATUTORY INTERPRETATION

The possibility of developing a pragmatic framework for legal interpretation is rooted in the argumentative dimension of interpretative reasoning, and in the pragmatic dimension of legal communication and legal texts.

4.3.1 *Interpretation as Argumentative Reasoning*

Legal interpretation, broadly understood as the attribution of a meaning to a legal source, is argumentative in two respects, since interpretation is both the output and the input of legal argumentation. On the one hand, when the meaning of the legal source at issue is controversial in a specific context, the interpretations advanced by the various parties to the interpretative discussion need to be supported though appropriate reasons (Dascal and Wróblewski, 1988, 204). For instance, in the case *Dunnachie* v. *Kingston-upon-Hull City Council* (see MacCormick, 2005), the issue concerned whether the term "loss" in Section 117 of the Employment Rights Act 1996 referred only to pecuniary losses, or rather included also emotional loss. To determine the correct interpretation of this term, the judges used various interpretative arguments, backed by references to legislative history, the labor law system, and the intentions of the legislator.

On the other hand, interpretative decisions provide the input to classificatory arguments aimed at applying the law to specific cases (Walton and Macagno, 2009). This type of reasoning is used when a legal rule, obtained by reconstructing the meaning of the relevant legal sources, needs to be applied to the particular case at issue. For instance, the argument according to which an unjustly dismissed employee, Mr. Jones, has no right to be compensated for emotional "loss" is based on a legal rule according to which workers unjustly dismissed are entitled to compensation only for *pecuniary* loss. In the law of the United Kingdom, this rule was obtained by interpreting the term "loss" in Section 117 of the Employment Right Act 1996 as excluding non-pecuniary loss (case discussed in MacCormick, 2005).

In interpretative legal disputes, the implicit and presumptive reasoning that is commonly used in interpreting texts (Slocum, 2016b) needs to be represented in terms of argumentative reasons advanced pro and against a given meaning attributed to the text (Perelman, 1976). Interpretative argumentation is indeed "a particular form of practical argumentation in law, in which one argues for a particular understanding of authoritative texts or materials as a special kind of (justifying) reason for legal decisions" (MacCormick, 1995). The specific characteristics of this specific type of argumentation can be pointed out by considering the linguistic (pragmatic) dimension of interpretation.

4.3.2 *The Pragmatics of Legal Interpretation*

Pragmatics addresses the relationship between the linguistic code (the linguistic means used in the interaction), the producers-interpreters of the code, and the context of the interaction (Kecskes, 2013, 22). In the most general definition, pragmatics focuses "on how meaning is shaped and inferred during social interaction." In linguistic-philosophical pragmatics, the core of communication is the speaker's intention (meaning), as it is recognized and reconstructed through pragmatic inferences that are the focus of linguistic investigation (Kecskes, 2013; Capone, 2016). The discrepancy between sentential (semantic and syntactic) meaning and utterance meaning is bridged by pragmatic processes that involve enrichment (Butler, 2016a), disambiguation (Horn, 1995; Kaplan et al., 1995), and implicatures (Sinclair, 1985; Miller, 1990; Atlas, 2005).

The pragmatic analysis of statutory texts rests on a basic presupposition, namely that the processes governing the relationship between sentential meaning and utterance (speaker's) meaning in ordinary conversation can also apply to legislative speech (Smolka and Pirker, 2016). Conversation and legislation have in common that in both cases: (1) language (and in particular, ordinary language) is used (Kaplan and Green, 1995); (2) communication is confined by topic or subject matter; and (3) utterances are purposive, namely their interpretation is constrained by considering the purpose of the speaker. However, the use of pragmatic principles for reconstructing the meaning of a piece of legislation needs to take into account relevant peculiarities, since legislative speech is one-sided (there is nobody who can immediately answer back), and legislative utterances are not truth-functional. Thus, legislative communication "must wear its discursive heart on its sleeve" (Sinclair, 1985, 390). Despite the differences between the two types of communication, the pragmatic principles (even though adapted and modified accordingly) constitute a dimension of rationality that is necessary for the understanding of legal texts (Sinclair, 1985, 401):

> All the pragmatic maxims for statutes are justified in the same way. It is reasonable that a legislature should act in accordance with them; they are among the characteristics of rationality in legislation. From the point of view of the "hearer" – the reader of a statute – the propriety of the maxims is a precondition to the possibility of sensibly understanding, making use of, and guiding behavior by legislative speech. Being pragmatic constraints, they in fact may be violated on occasion, but the entire enterprise of legislation would fail if they were to be generally disregarded.

This (imperfect and partial) correspondence between ordinary and legal communication and the central importance of pragmatics in understanding and interpreting texts leads to the problem connecting the studies in linguistic pragmatics with the theories of legal interpretation.

The theoretical framework that seems to best bridge the two fields of studies is the three-layered analysis of communication of Levinson (Levinson, 2000, 93), complemented by the idea of inference to the best interpretation. Levinson distinguishes between: (1) sentence meaning, based on grammar; (2) utterance-type meaning, based on general expectations about how language is normally used; and (3) speaker meaning, based on nonce (once-off) inferences made in actual contexts by actual recipients with all of their rich particularities. The construction of the utterance-type meaning is based on generalized conversational implicatures, namely, implicatures that hold "unless unusual specific contextual assumptions defeat them." On the contrary, the construction of speaker meaning is based on specific contextual information that would "not invariably or even normally obtain."

As an example of a generalized conversational implicature, consider the heuristics according to which statements matching the pattern "some X are Y" defeasibly licenses the implicature "not all X are Y." This implicature is to be retracted given the information that "all X are Y," an assertion that is consistent with the statement "some X are Y" but contradicts the implicature "not all X are Y." For instance, the statement "some guests have left" defeasibly licenses the implicature "not all guests have left." The implicature, however, is defeated by a subsequent precization "yes, all guests have indeed left," which is consistent with the previous statement, but contradicts the implicature. Similarly, in the normative domain, the statement that "action X is permitted" implicates that also that "the omission of X is permitted." Had the X omission not been permitted, then one would have stated that X is obligatory. For instance, the statement "it is permitted to bring a laptop to the classroom" implicates that it is also permitted not to bring one. Had the professor meant that bringing a laptop was compulsory, she would have stated that explicitly.

As an example of a particularized implicature, let us consider how the statement "some guests have left" may implicate "it is late." This implication only works in particular contexts (e.g., an evening dinner). Also, particularized implicatures are defeasible, since they may be rejected, while retaining their premises, on the basis of further information (e.g., the clock shows that it is still early, there was a fight among the guests, and so this must have been the reason for some of them to leave).

Our focus will be on the utterance-type meaning, and specifically on the idea that the hearer, and in particular the addressee of legal sources, draws implicatures by using generalized heuristics, in other words, defeasible inference patterns, corresponding to stereotypical instantiations of the utterance. We will assume that such heuristics can be explained by using (variants of) Grice's maxims (Miller, 1990; Sinclair, 1985). The fact that such inferences are defeasible does not make them irrelevant, since they hold as long as prevailing incompatible information is not provided. In other words, they indicate prima facie interpretations (Jaszczolt, 2005; Huang, 2014; Mey, 2001; Simons, 2013) that carry a burden of disproof on the party that challenges it.

4.3.3 *Where Pragmatics and Argumentation Meet: Inference to the Best Interpretation*

Atlas and Levinson (1981) complement the idea that interpretation is governed by heuristics leading to conversational implicatures with the idea that when different possible interpretations are available (in other words, when doubts arise), then preference should go to the "best interpretation." An interpretation can be considered the best one when it best "fits" both the shared background presumptions in the context and the communicative intention attributable to the speaker in the light of "what he has said" (Atlas and Levinson, 1981, 42). Thus, on the one hand, conversational implicatures constrain the search for abductive explanations, avoiding time-consuming critical assessments of alterative interpretation. However, on the other hand, in case of unsolved conflicts between incompatible heuristics, a critical process of interpretation is needed, which can be represented as the inference to the best interpretation (Macagno and Walton, 2013; Macagno, 2012).[3] For instance, let us assume that the interpretation of "loss" as pecuniary loss is indicated by the heuristics that commands the ascription of stereotypical meanings. This provides us with a convenient interpretation that is also an explanation of why the legislator used the word "loss" without further specification: the legislator presumably did so exactly in order to convey the meaning of pecuniary loss (given this stereotypical background, had the legislator also wanted to address non-pecuniary losses, he would have included a corresponding specification).

In order to analyze this type of inference, various logical models for defeasible reasoning have been provided over the years (for a review, see Levinson, 2000). All of them provide for nonmonotonic inference, namely, reasoning processes where by adding additional information to an available set of premises, some defeasible conclusions of the original set may no longer hold. In our approach, the "best interpretation" is modeled by using defeasible argumentation (Walton, 2011; Walton, Sartor, and Macagno, 2016). The idea is that an argument that defeasibly supports a conclusion can also be attacked without challenging its premises, in other words, by providing a stronger argument having an incompatible conclusion or by arguing that, in the particular case at stake, the argument's premises fail to support its conclusion (Pollock, 1987).

For example, let us consider again the implicature from "some guests are leaving" to "not all guests are leaving," which can be viewed as an instantiation of Grice's first principle of quantity (make your contribution as informative as required). This implicature will be understood as an argument that, given (a) the statement "some

---

[3] Our notion of "best interpretation" does not coincide exactly with the use of the notion of "best interpretation" in interpretivist legal theory (Dworkin, 1986), where the "best interpretation" is the one that best balances the need to fit the legal material and to puts the law in its best light (which includes contributing to values of political morality). Our analysis is rather meant to provide the interpretation that better captures the pragmatic meaning of the legislative communication, considering the alternative interpretations and their defeasibility conditions.

guests are leaving" and (b) the defeasible heuristics "if it is stated that some X are Y then presumptively it is meant that not all X are Y," supports the defeasible conclusion that "not all guests are leaving." This inference could be defeated by the additional statement (the counterargument) that "all guests are leaving," which undercuts the inference, as in this particular situation (all are leaving), the original premise (some are leaving) no longer supports the conclusion (not all are leaving).

Grice's defeasible heuristics can be used to explain the interpretation of our running example, the "loss" case. The second maxim of quantity, "Do not make your contribution more informative than is required," can be considered as underlying the inference to the stereotypical meaning. In our case, considering that the term "loss" is stereotypically used to mean *pecuniary* (or *material*) loss, the reader can interpret the provision, "the amount of the compensation shall be such as the tribunal thinks fit having regard to the *loss* sustained by the complainant … " as referring to *pecuniary* loss. The defeasible reasoning can be represented as follows:

1. The provision claims that "losses consequent to unfair dismissals have to be compensated."
2. Stereotypical losses have a pecuniary or material nature.
3. Words are generally to be understood as addressing stereotypical cases.
4. Therefore, the statement shall be read as stating that "only pecuniary or material losses have to be compensated."

This reasoning is clearly defeasible, as it can be objected that in labor law the stereotypical meaning can be different, or within the context the first maxim applies instead (if the legislator had intended a narrow meaning, he would have said so).

4.4 PRIMA FACIE AND DELIBERATIVE INTERPRETATIVE REASONING

The heuristics and the legal canons of interpretation can be investigated within an argumentative approach. We can distinguish two ways of getting to an interpretation. The interpretation may be obtained directly, without consciously addressing doubts and assessing alternatives, or it may be obtained dialectically, namely by assessing the reasons for and against adopting the chosen interpretation and the defeasibility of other possible interpretations. Thus, we may distinguish the following two kinds of interpretative reasoning:

1. *Prima facie* interpretative reasoning, which attributes directly, through uncritical computation, a prima facie meaning to the utterance at issue;
2. *Deliberative* interpretative reasoning, which intervenes:
   a. when prima facie interpretative reasoning fails to provide a single, undoubted output, namely, when no prima facie meaning is obtained directly; or
   b. when multiple incompatible prima facie meanings are provided; or

c. when the prima facie meaning fails to satisfy immediately the concerns of the interpreter, so some doubts need to be addressed (Kennedy, 2007, 303–304).

Some authors prefer to use the term "interpretation" in a broader sense, to cover both kinds of reasoning, while other prefer to use it in a more restrictive sense, covering only the second (see Chapter 1). The first position is advocated by Tarello and Guastini (Tarello, 1980; Guastini, 2011), according to whom an interpretation is the necessary step leading from a sentence in a legal text to a rule (the meaning). In this perspective, there are no rules of law (obligations, prohibitions …) without interpretation.

Others prefer to use the term "understanding" (Patterson, 2005) or "direct understanding" (Dascal and Wróblewski, 1988), to refer to prima facie interpretative reasoning, while the term "interpretation" is intended to mean critical ascription of meaning. According to the latter position, which underlies the traditional saying that "in clear things, no interpretation takes place" (*in claris non fit interpretatio*), interpretation only covers the argumentative process that is aimed at resolving a doubt concerning the meaning of a text. For instance, Dascal and Wróblewski (1988, p. 204) define interpretation *sensu stricto* as "an ascription of meaning to a linguistic sign in the case its meaning is doubtful in a communicative situation, i.e. in the case its 'direct understanding' is not sufficient for the communicative purpose at hand."

According to Dascal and Wróblewski, clarity is a pragmatic notion, corresponding to the state in which no reasonable doubt can be raised concerning the meaning of the text (Dascal and Wróblewski, 1988, 214). A text can be clear from the beginning, or clarity may be achieved at a subsequent point through interpretative arguments. In cases of unclarity, namely when there is an "eventual 'mismatch' between the 'computed' utterance-meaning and some contextual factor" resulting from the background or the specific case to which the law is applied (Dascal and Wróblewski, 1988, 213; 216), the interpretation needs to be justified.

Considering the argumentative nature of interpretation, the challenge is to provide a framework for assessing interpretative arguments, namely a theoretical model in which the various and unrelated legal canons and the pragmatic maxims can be regarded in terms of defeasible reasons, grounded on different types of presumptions. In the sections below we will show how it is possible to outline an argumentative framework for analyzing interpretation building on the notion of a nonmonotonic and abductive mechanism of reasoning from best interpretation (Atlas, 2008; Atlas and Levinson, 1981; Dascal, 2003, 635). The structure of this type of reasoning can be explained using presumptive arguments (Macagno and Capone, 2016). The interpreter needs to assess the possible alternative explanations, or interpretations, of the evidence consisting of the utterance, the context, and the common ground. To this end, the alternatives are compared and evaluated through considering the presumptions each conflicts with (Macagno, Walton, and Sartor, 2014).

4.5 THE PRAGMATICS OF INTERPRETATION

The interpretation of a statement of law guarantees the inferential passage from a text (a legal text or statement) to its meaning (a rule of law). It can be analyzed as an instance of natural language interpretation aimed at retrieving what the text was intended to mean (namely the "objectified" speaker's meaning) (Skoczeń, 2016; Grice, 1975). As mentioned above, this reconstruction can lead to a prima facie interpretation that is reached by implicitly relying on uncontroversial common expectations about language and regarding the utterance as expressed in a stereotypical context (Huang, 2014). However, this "utterance type" is defeasible at various levels. The "prima facie" interpretation of indexicals and lexical items (Mel'cuk, 1997; Macagno, 2011; Hamblin, 1970; Macagno, 2012) can differ from the intended use thereof. Sentence types (such as declarative, interrogative, expressive, etc.) can be used to perform speech acts different from those prototypically associated with them (Capone, 2010; Kecskes and Zhang, 2009; Kecskes, 2013; Kissine, 2012). In this sense, the preferential and prototypical uses of linguistic elements or syntactic constructions can be considered as facilitating the reconstruction of what is meant, but they are always subject to defeat.

The prima facie and deliberative processes of interpretation can be explained using a well-known example in both legal theory and pragmatics, the sign in front of Lincoln Park (Horn, 1995, 1146): "All vehicles are prohibited from Lincoln Park." Based on the commonly shared definition of "vehicle" and the ordinary expectations about language, this statement can be interpreted prima facie as follows (understanding): "entities having wheels and used for the transportation of people are prohibited from Lincoln Park." In a prototypical context, characterized by specific background assumptions (Searle, 1979, 135), the presumptive reasoning leading to the default explanation can be accepted or considered as acceptable. However, sometimes the actual context is different from the stereotypical one characterizing the "utterance type." For example, push scooters of children may not count as vehicles as one foot continues to touch the ground; a wheelchair of a disabled person may not count as a vehicle, given its function of providing a person mobility aid. In other cases, the prima facie interpretation is subject to an exception. For example, while it is hard to deny that an ambulance is a vehicle, it may still be argued that the prohibition does not apply to ambulances when deployed in emergencies.

In such cases, the presumptive inference providing the prima facie interpretation of the text can be challenged and lead to a dialectical reconstruction of meaning, grounded on an analysis of the possible alternative interpretations. The whole structure of the reasoning process underlying interpretation (*sensu stricto*) can be summarized in the following sequence of actions:

1. A statement is used within a specific context, leading to a prima facie understanding.

2. A doubt is raised; namely, it is shown that the prima facie understanding is somehow inadequate.
3. The doubt leads to the search for alternative meaning.
4. The various candidate interpretations are assessed, examining pros and cons of each of them.
5. An interpretation is selected as the best one.

When the semantic meaning (legal text) is vague or ambiguous, so that understanding delivers alternative clues, or when it needs to be applied to a specific case instantiating reasons for *not* using the prima facie meaning, the prima facie interpretation is subject to defeat. The prima facie meaning thus becomes one of the possible interpretations. As a consequence, it is compared with the alternatives, and is assessed, challenged, and eventually accepted or rejected. In the example above, the prima facie meaning of "vehicles" is subject to defeat when the statement of law needs to be interpreted and applied to the specific case of ambulances. Can a law be unreasonable and protect a value (safety; peace and quiet) that is less important than human life? This circumstance and the presumption that the law shall not lead to absurd results (Brewer, 2011, 114) defeats the prima facie meaning (Hutton, 2009, 72–73). Thus, the interpreter looks for alternative explanations of meaning ("unauthorized transportation means," "transportation means with an engine," etc.). The least controversial interpretation – namely that which is comparatively less conflicting with countering presumptions and more fully supported by favorable presumptions – is chosen as the most acceptable one.

The distinction between prima facie and deliberative interpretation is relevant in law as it involves the allocation of the burden of argument. An unchallenged prima facie interpretation (understanding) does not involve a burden of argument, as it holds until it is challenged. Should the prima facie interpretation be questioned without bringing a reason against it, it may be supported by pointing to some heuristics underlying it (e.g., an appeal to stereotypical meaning). However, if an alternative interpretation is proposed, based on a different heuristic or on an alternative nonprototypical context, the prima facie interpretation becomes only one of the possible interpretations. As such, it becomes considered as potentially controversial and needs to be grounded in arguments. The various arguments advanced to support an interpretation need to defeat the other possible alternatives. They need to show that the advocated explanation of meaning is better (more adequate, more suitable) than the others.

4.6 REASONING FROM BEST INTERPRETATION AND ARGUMENTATION SCHEMES

The distinction between prima facie and deliberative interpretation has a psychological (Jaszczolt, 2006, 201; Wilson, 2005) and a dialogical foundation (Prakken and Sartor, 1996), since the transition from the first to the second takes place as soon as plausible doubts or alternatives are raised. However, it also has a logical aspect that can be addressed by analyzing the inferential and dialectical relations involved in the two interpretative processes.

The interpreter will be satisfied with a prima facie interpretation when the information available leads the interpreter directly to a single unquestioned output, according to the semantic meaning of the expression, coupled with the relevant interpretative heuristics. Critical interpretation is needed when additional and distinct heuristics, or specific reasons, are applicable, resulting in conflicting interpretations or potential flaws of the prima facie output.

To this purpose, the developments in pragmatics can be integrated using the tools of argumentation theory (Walton, 2002). A specific current within argumentation investigates the structures of defeasible arguments, namely arguments not proceeding from the meaning of quantifiers or connectors only, but from the semantic relations between the concepts involved. This account, rooted in Toulmin's notion of warrant (Toulmin, 1958; Toulmin, Rieke, and Janik, 1984), aims to represent the combination between a semantic principle (such as classification, cause, consequence, authority) and a type of reasoning, such as deductive, inductive, or abductive reasoning. Such patterns of argument are called argumentation schemes (Walton, Reed, and Macagno, 2008; Macagno and Walton, 2015) and can be used to bring to light the different inferential structures, defeasibility conditions, and dialectical effects of the inferences characterizing interpretation.

Prima facie interpretation can be conceived of as the inferential and automatic association between an utterance and its communicative effects. Interpretative heuristics, which underlie the implicatures that are stereotypically triggered in a communicative setting (Atlas, 2005; Levinson, 1983), can be viewed as defeasible inference schemes (Levinson, 2000; Atlas and Levinson, 1981; Walton, 1995; Macagno and Walton, 2014). Such schemes have the following structure (Rescher, 2006, 33):

Premise 1: *P* (the proposition representing the presumption) obtains whenever the condition *C* obtains unless and until the standard default proviso *D* (to the effect that countervailing evidence is at hand) obtains (Rule).

Premise 2: Condition *C* obtains (Fact).

Premise 3: Proviso *D* does not obtain (countervailing evidence is not at hand) (Exception).

Conclusion: *P* obtains.

In this pattern, the inference scheme (a heuristic, in Levinson's terms) is distinguished from the conclusion itself (the implicature), which obtains in case contrary evidence is not provided. In particular, the scheme leads to a meaning ("what is meant") that is a proposition compatible both with assumptions in the context and with "what is said" (Atlas, 2005, 91). The presumptive meaning is guided by two basic complementary metapresumptions (Atlas, 2005, 91):

> *Speaker-centered:* Do not say what you believe to be *highly* noncontroversial – that is, to be *entailed* by the presumptions of the common ground in context K.
>
> *Hearer-centered:* Take what you hear to be *lowly* noncontroversial – that is, *consistent* with the presumptions of the common ground in context K.

When such presumptions, usually operating as unconscious computations, do not lead to a single unquestioned outcome, it is necessary to assess the reasons underlying the conflicting interpretations, including the grounds of the meaning obtained presumptively.

In this perspective, the mechanisms (including primarily Grice's maxims and neo-Gricean heuristics) underlying the processing of implicit or incomplete meaning are made explicit and represented as defeasible arguments in favor of one interpretation over another. This representation of the processing and assessment of the possible interpretations can be modelled by integrating the presumptive arguments with reasoning from the best interpretation, which can be viewed as an instance of the more general pattern of reasoning from the best explanation (Atlas and Levinson, 1981). In argumentation theory, this type of reasoning is represented by the nonmonotonic (Oaksford and Chater, 1998, 131) and abductive structure (Walton, Reed, and Macagno, 2008; Macagno and Capone, 2016; Walton, 2002; Harman, 1992, 1965; Fodor, 1983; Macagno and Walton, 2014) that we introduced as "Argumentation scheme 2" in Chapter 3:

Premise 1:	F (an utterance) is an observed event.
Premise 2:	E_1 is a satisfactory ascription of meaning to F.
Premise 3:	No alternative interpretations $E_{2 \ldots n}$ given so far is as satisfactory as E_1.
Conclusion:	Therefore, E_1 is a plausible interpretation, based on what is known so far.

In particular, in cases of interpretation, the "bestness" of an explanation (an interpretative hypothesis)[4] can be established according to the pragmatic principle of informativeness (Atlas and Levinson, 1981, 40–41; Atlas, 2005, 95):

---

[4] A distinction needs to be drawn between the best explanation of a factual event and the best interpretation of a statement of law (used within a specific context). In the first case, the assumption is that an outcome is known (the grass is wet) and possible antecedent explanations of why this outcome holds (rain, sprinkler, etc.) are provided. In interpretation, we do not know the outcome (the right interpretation) in advance, and so it follows that we cannot engage in abductive explanations of why an expression should be interpreted in a certain way. However, the interpretative process needs to be thought of as a type of reasoning aimed at reconstructing an objectified communicative intention (the speaker's meaning) from the linguistic and contextual evidence that the speaker provides us with (Scalia, 1998, 17; 144; Soames, 2009, 415). The evidence we need to take into account is not the effect of a cause, but rather a reasonable sign of the speaker's communicative intention.

Suppose a speaker S addresses a sentence A to a hearer H in a context K. If H has n competing interpretations U_i ($1 \leq i \leq n$) of A in the context K with ... information contents $INF(U_i)$, and $G^H_{A,K}$, is the set of propositions that H takes to be noncontroversial for S in K with respect to A at the stage in the conversation at which A is uttered, then the "best" interpretation U^* of A for H in K is the most informative proposition among the competing interpretations U_i that are consistent with the common ground CG_K in the context and with the noncontroversial propositions $G^H_{A,K}$, associated with the uttering of A in the context K.

In this sense, the best interpretation is the one that is less controversial, namely less subject to defeat based on conflicting propositions contained in the common ground. A set of critical questions is associated with this pattern, pointing out its defeasibility conditions:

CQ_1: How satisfactory is E_1 as an interpretation of F, apart from the alternative interpretations $E_{2...n}$ available so far in the dialogue?

CQ_2: How much better an interpretation is E_1 than the alternative interpretations $E_{2...n}$ available so far in the dialogue?

CQ_3: How far has the dialogue progressed? If the dialogue is an inquiry, how thorough has the investigation of the case been?

CQ_4: Would it be better to continue the dialogue further, instead of drawing a conclusion at this point?

This scheme corresponds to an argumentation scheme used in a dialectical process aimed at determining the most acceptable conclusion. The critical questions are instruments for evaluating a conclusion through dialectical means. The acceptability of the conclusion of this abductive scheme consists in an evaluation of the possible alternative interpretations, namely in an analysis of their defeasibility conditions (underminers, undercutters, or rebuttals) that can affect the acceptability of the conclusion (Weinstock, Goodenough, and Klein, 2013; Walton, 2016, 246).

In many cases, the most important critical questions are the first and the second ones. The first one points to whether the interpretation considered is acceptable. The second question is the most complex one, as it requires a comparative assessment of the interpretations available. E_1 is compared with the possible alternatives, and the default conditions of each interpretation are evaluated. The one that is the least subject to attack and that is better supported by the evidence that can be marshalled on both sides of the disputed issue is chosen as the best. The competing hypotheses are eliminated by this procedure. While the first critical question can be used to encourage the proponent to provide further arguments or reasons in support of the goodness (coherence, sufficiency, etc.) of the interpretation, the second question shifts a burden of proof onto the respondent. The respondent has to show that an alternative interpretation is better, and provide arguments and evidence supporting it.

4.7 THE FUNCTION OF THE CONVERSATIONAL MAXIMS IN IMPLICATURES

The aforementioned argumentative framework, combining presumptive reasoning and reasoning from best interpretation, can be used to integrate the heuristics investigated in pragmatics and the legal canons of interpretation.

Grice's maxims are heuristics that guide natural language interpretation and more precisely the "amplification" of the semantic meaning of an utterance when considering contextual factors (Levinson, 1995, 96). They have been described as "general default heuristics, frameworks of assumption that can be taken to amplify the coded content of messages in predictable ways unless there is an indication that they do not apply" (Levinson, 1995, 96). As mentioned above, Grice collected such presumptions (or expectations) under four general categories, namely the maxims of quantity, quality, relation, and manner, subsumed under a more general rule, the so-called cooperative principle. We can show how they are used considering the following famous case of implicature (Case 4.1, see Grice, 1975, 52):

> ### CASE 4.1: RECOMMENDATION LETTER
>
> A is writing a testimonial about a pupil who is a candidate for a philosophy job, and his letter reads as follows: "Dear Sir, Mr. X's command of English is excellent, and his attendance at tutorial has been regular. Yours, etc."

In this example, the "utterance type," resulting from the semantic meaning and the generalized conversational implicatures, is subject to default. The conventional, stereotypical meaning conflicts with clear contextual information, resulting in a further interpretative step. The addressee of the letter retrieves the meaning of the sentence "*Mr. X's command of English is excellent ...*" not only by using his lexical and syntactic knowledge of English, but by combining this information with

1. a set of expectations and presumptions concerning the act of writing a recommendation letter (Grice, 1975, 47); and
2. some basic communication principles, such as the presumption that one should provide as much information as required or needed.

In this case, the fact that the professor does not mention more relevant skills of the applicant does not mean that the student does not have them. However, the fact that the professor did not mention such skills when it was requested constitutes a prima facie case for inferring that the student does not possess such abilities.

A crucial question is whether these maxims can be used in a very specific context, the legal one, which has often been characterized by being highly strategic and uncooperative (see the position of Marmor, 2014, 42–44, 2008 and the analysis thereof in Morra, 2016a). More precisely, legal dialogues are characterized by a specific goal, persuading the judge of the acceptability of a conclusion (Levinson, 1992; Macagno and Bigi, 2017). For this reason, the process of interpreting utterances made by the opposing party (or witnesses) is presumed to be aimed at supporting a viewpoint. They are relying on presumptions that are different from the Gricean maxims, in order to get some advantage in interpreting a statement in a more favorable way (Marmor, 2014, 46–47). One of the most famous examples is the following one (Case 4.2, *United States* v. *Bronston*, 453 F.2d 555 (2d Cir. 1971)):

CASE 4.2: PRESUMPTION OF EVASION

"Q. Do you have any bank accounts in Swiss banks, Mr. Bronston?"
"A. No, sir."
"Q. Have you ever?"
"A. The company had an account there for about six months, in Zurich."

In this famous cross-examination case (Sinclair, 1985; Tiersma, 1990; Solan and Tiersma, 2005; Horn, 2009; Shuy, 2011; Solan, 2002; Jacobs, and Jackson, 2006), the witness actually held a bank account in a Swiss bank, but was found to have testified truthfully, as he had never stated the contrary. The witness in fact only evaded the question; however, the lawyer examining Bronston relied on the prosecutor's adherence to the maxim of relevance, and gave to the answer an interpretation maximally relevant to the context.

This case sheds light on two fundamental aspects of Gricean maxims. First, Gricean maxims are hermeneutic principles (Poggi, 2011), presumptive principles (heuristics) for retrieving what the speaker means (his communicative intention) from what he says. They provide general patterns for accounting for the relationship between a statement's literal understanding (conventional meaning) and the propositional and implicated meaning that the speaker intends to convey (Morra, 2016b, 2016a). In this sense, they do not *provide* an interpretation, but rather *account for* an interpretation, bringing to light reasons to support it (Slocum, 2016b; Walton, 2002). Second, these conversational heuristics are defeasible, in the sense that they are defeated by stronger assumptions concerning the goal of the cooperative activity the interlocutors are carrying out (in this case, the goal of cross-examination is to elicit specific answers, to which the witness shall be considered committed, and avoid evasions). For this reason, the maxims need to be ordered and analyzed together with other types of presumptions governing conversation, the foremost being the purpose of the dialogue in which the interlocutors are engaged (Grice, 1975, 45; Morra, 2016a, 555; Butler, 2016b, 520).

In this view, the fact that the parties to a legal dispute are engaging in a type of dialogue different from ordinary conversation does not mean that they do not rely on hermeneutic principles. The apparent failure to adhere to the cooperative maxim in some cases does not mean that cooperation is excluded from legal discussion. In case of statutory interpretation, the lawmaker cannot exclude the interpreter's cooperation in processing the semantic meaning and inferring the conversational one. More simply, different hermeneutic principles apply, which are more adequate to the purpose of the dialogue, aimed at providing the strongest reasons in favor or against a controversial interpretation (Sinclair, 1985).

Gricean maxims can be used for analyzing legal interpretation, even though they need to be adapted to the specific conversational purpose. Grice's conversational presumptions (or heuristics) are extremely general principles (Lyons, 1977, 594) that can be used to calculate and support an interpretation, which can be extremely useful in the context of legal interpretative disputes. Despite the differences, the principles underlying the reconstruction of what is said and what is meant in everyday conversation and in the understanding and interpretation of legal texts can be compared (Hutton, 2009, 71). In the next two sections, we will show how the presumptions guiding the process of legal interpretation can be captured using the most generic (the neo-Gricean version of the maxims) and the more specific heuristics (the Gricean maxims) as the basis of the nonmonotonic processes aimed at establishing the speaker's meaning (Brewer, 2011, 114–115; Miller, 1990).

4.8 LEGAL INTERPRETATION AND THE HEURISTICS UNDERLYING GENERALIZED IMPLICATURES

In order to show that ordinary and legal interpretation can be framed within a common and abstract argumentative model of interpretation, we need to show how maxims and canons can be conceived as presumptions that differ from the level of abstraction. In particular, the first step is to show how the more generic Gricean maxims can be used for describing the reasoning underlying legal interpretation.

Legal interpretation, like everyday interpretation, needs to face a twofold concern. On the one hand, a communicative intention (a rule of law) cannot go beyond what is said (a statement of law), as the intention needs to be retrievable from what is made explicit. On the other hand, it is impossible to state everything (Levinson, 1995, 95); more importantly, the semantic content of a sentence doesn't always determine what is asserted and conveyed by literal uses of it (it needs to be specified and enriched) (Hutton, 2009; Soames, 2009, 408). For this reason, implicatures work not only to infer unstated information starting from the propositional content of an utterance and the context (particularized implicatures), but also (as seen in Chapter 3) to enrich the (undetermined) propositional content specifying it based on general expectations about how language is normally used. This level corresponds to the reconstruction of the utterance type, achieved through generalized implicatures and other pragmatic phenomena. These mechanisms are usually presumptive, and are relevant from an argumentative perspective when they are subject to default, namely when the best interpretation needs to be provided based on linguistic evidence.

As mentioned above, legal interpretative disputes arise when the understanding of the law is challenged (Slocum, 2016b). The passage from the statement of law to the legal rule is subject to defeat because an entity falling under (or not falling under) the presumptive rule of law is claimed to be excluded from (or included in) the category to which the legal predicate normally applies. For example, consider the following leading case of interpretation (Harris and Hutton, 2007, 164; Butler, 2016b; Soames, 2009) concerning the meaning of "to use a firearm" (whether it meant "to use a firearm for its intended purpose" or "to employ it somehow" (Case 4.3):

> **CASE 4.3: *SMITH V. UNITED STATES*, 508 U.S. 223 (1993)**
>
> Smith offered to trade an automatic weapon to an undercover officer for cocaine. He was charged with numerous firearm and drug trafficking offenses. Title 18 U.S.C. § 924(c)(1) requires the imposition of specified penalties if the defendant, "during and in relation to … [a] drug trafficking crime[,] uses … a firearm."

This case is particularly interesting because it involves a dispute about the reconstruction of the ordinary meaning of "using a firearm" (Slocum, 2016b; Morra, 2016a). The statutory language was incomplete relative to how the aforementioned phrase was to be interpreted (Soames, 2009, 414). The undetermined (namely, potentially vague or controversial) semantic meaning was thus interpreted by the opposing parties in a different fashion in order to support their goals. They had to convince the court of the higher acceptability of their interpretation, while the court had to assess the reasons and interpretation, in order to infer pragmatically *what uses* of a firearm Congress intended as an aggravating circumstance (which results in harsher sentencing). Both the majority and the dissenting opinions relied on the same pragmatic heuristics (or rather rules of presumption), completing the expression relying on what can be considered the stereotypical context and the presumptive intention of the speaker (the legislator) as inferable from the linguistic evidence.

The two rules of presumption accounting for this processing have been expressed in the neo-Gricean pragmatics (Horn, 1984, 1995; Levinson, 2000, 35–38) as the following two principles and the corresponding interpretative heuristics mentioned in Chapter 3 (see also Skoczeń 2019, Ch. 3):

Q-principle:
Say as much as you (truthfully and relevantly) can.

Interpretative heuristic (Q):
What isn't said, isn't the case.

I-principle (corresponding to Horn's R-principle mentioned in Chapter 3):
Say no more than you must.

Interpretative heuristic (I):
What is simply/briefly described is the stereotypical or normal (default) instance.

The first heuristic corresponds to the interpretative canon of *expressio unius*: what is not stated should be considered as excluded. The second principle corresponds to the canons of the plain meaning rule and *ejusdem generis*, the first providing for the use of a default or stereotypical meaning, the second for the enrichment of meaning based on what is commonly considered as falling under a concept.

According to the first canon, a statement of law, or an expression in a statement, needs to be interpreted according to its ordinary meaning in natural language, unless a statute explicitly defines some of its terms otherwise. The second canon provides that the meaning of a term can be enriched (made more precise) according to its context. Its meaning can be made more specific in a way that it fits with (it falls under the same general category of) the other words around it (or rather the instances of the concept enumerated). The classical example (Gifis, 2010) is the interpretation of "dangerous weapons" in a statute forbidding the concealment on one's person of "pistols, revolvers, derringers, or other dangerous weapons." The term "dangerous weapons" can be made more specific (enriched) by considering the general nature of the listed weapons, namely firearms or handguns. These two heuristics can be used as generic strategies for determining the semantic meaning of a statement of law, relying on a stereotypical context or the linguistic evidence of the speaker's intention. For example, we consider Case 4.2 above to see how such principles apply to draw distinct implicatures:

I(R)-implicature: Narrowing the meaning	Petitioner argues that the word "uses" has a somewhat reduced scope in § 924(c)(1) because it appears alongside the word "firearm." Specifically, petitioner contends that the average person on the street would not think immediately of a guns-for-drugs trade as an example of "us[ing]" a firearm."
Q-implicature: Narrowing the meaning	Just as adding the direct object "a firearm" to the verb "use" narrows the meaning of that verb (it can no longer mean "partake of"), so also adding the modifier "in the offense of transferring, selling, or transporting firearms" to the phrase "use a firearm" expands the meaning of that phrase (it then includes, as it previously would not,

(continued)

	nonweapon use). Congress did not add "in the offense of transferring . . . " and therefore intended the narrow meaning.
I(R)-implicature: Broadening the meaning	The next subsection of the statute, § 924(d), provides for the confiscation of firearms that are "used in" referenced offenses, which include the crimes of transferring, selling, or transporting firearms in interstate commerce. The Court concludes from this that whenever the term appears in this statute, "use" of a firearm must include nonweapon use.
	Surely petitioner's bartering of his firearm can be described as "use" within the everyday meaning of that term.
Q-implicature: Broadening the meaning	The words "use as a weapon" appear nowhere in the statute. Rather, § 924(c)(1)'s language sweeps broadly, punishing any "use" of a firearm, so long as the use is "during and in relation to" a drug-trafficking offense. Had Congress intended the narrow construction petitioner urges, it could have so indicated.

These heuristics can be used to understand the strategies based on linguistic evidence to support a specific interpretation. However, they provide little ground for assessing which interpretation is the best one. If we want to understand the mechanism of reasons in support of conflicting interpretations and bring to light the presumptions underlying them, it is necessary to go back to Grice's maxims and compare them with the "hermeneutic principles" used in legal interpretation. By bringing to light the various presumptions it is possible to analyze interpretative conflicts as argumentative discussions, which can be solved by comparing the opposite arguments and assessing them.

4.9 THE MAXIMS IN LEGAL INTERPRETATION

Legal interpretation, a conscious and reflective activity, aimed at providing contextual evidence to support a given interpretation, needs to be supported by explicit arguments based on presumptive (defeasible) premises. Such premises, made explicit in law as interpretative canons or "arguments," are presumptions governing the understanding or interpretation of a language, even though a very specific and technical one (Brewer, 2011, 114–115). By illustrating this correspondence between interpretative arguments and pragmatic maxims it is possible to pursue a twofold goal. On the one hand, the number of legal arguments can be reduced to a limited number of rules of presumption that can be compared and assessed. On the other hand, it is possible to show how the maxims can be made more specific by including contextual elements carrying different weight. More importantly, the comparison between maxims and canons can shed light on the possibility of ordering the presumptions underlying interpretation, providing generic criteria for describing the priority chosen in determining the best interpretation.

4.9.1 *Maxims and Interpretative Arguments*

In statutory interpretation, an interpretation is justified by providing arguments that are usually based on specific maxims of interpretation, which can be translated into formal language (Hage, 1997). MacCormick, Summers, and Tarello, among many others, provide sets of interpretative arguments (MacCormick and Summers, 1991; Tarello, 1980; Scalia and Garner, 2012; Greenawalt, 2015), which we summarized to a list of eleven arguments in Chapter 1 (Macagno, Walton, and Sartor, 2014) discussed in Chapter 1 and reported below:

1. Argument from the exclusion of what is not stated (*argumentum a contrario*). In lack of any other explicit rules, if a rule attributes any normative qualification to an individual or a category of individuals, any additional rule attributing the same quality to any other individual or category of individuals should be excluded.
2. Arguments from analogy (requiring the similarity of meaning between similar provisions):
   a. Extending a category to a similar case (*analogia legis*). The application of a *written* law applied to case C should be applied to a different, similar case D.
   b. Argument from general principles (*analogia iuris*). An abstract *principle of law, which provides explanation and justification to* stated laws and past decisions should be applied to new cases.
   c. Other analogical arguments. *Ejusdem generis:* Where general words follow an enumeration of two or more things, they should only apply to persons or things of the same general kind or class as those which are specifically mentioned. *Noscitur a sociis:* Words grouped in a list should be given related meanings.
3. Argument *a fortiori*. If a rule attributes any normative qualification Q to an individual or a category of individuals C, then Q can also be applied to another individual or another category of individuals D, based on the fact that, in the specific situation, the reasons for attributing Q to D are stronger than those for attributing A to C.
4. Authoritative arguments:
   a. Psychological argument. A statement of law shall be attributed the meaning that corresponds to the intention of its drafter or author, that is, the historical legislator.
   b. Historical argument. A statement of law should be interpreted according to the interpretation that has been developed historically.

    c. Authoritative argument. A statement of law should be interpreted according to a previous interpretation, or rather on the authority of the product of a previous interpretation.

    d. Naturalistic argument (or natural meaning argument). A term should be interpreted according to the commonly accepted "nature" of the things (or its commonly used definition).

5. Absurdity argument (*reductio ad absurdum*). The possible interpretations of a statement of law leading to an unreasonable or "absurd" rule should be rejected.

6. Equitative argument. Interpretations leading to (un)fair or (un)just consequences should be (excluded) accepted.

7. Argument from completeness of the law. The legal system is complete and without gaps; therefore, from the lack of a specific rule governing a case, it is possible to infer the existence of a generic one attributing a legal qualification to such a case.

8. Teleological (or purposive) argument. A statement of law should be given the interpretation that corresponds to its intended purpose.

9. Economic argument. The interpreter needs to exclude an interpretation of a statement of law that corresponds to the meaning of another (previously enacted or hierarchically superior) statement of law, as the legislator cannot issue a useless statement of law.

10. Systematic argument. If a term has a certain meaning in a statement of law, such a term should be interpreted as having such a meaning in all the statements of law in which it appears.

11. Arguments from coherence of the law. If a term has a certain meaning in a statement of law, such a term should be interpreted as having such a meaning in all the statements of law in which it appears; interpretations that do not engender conflicts between different legal rules should be preferred.

Some of these canons can be considered as "presumptions that are drawn from the drafter's choice of words, their grammatical placement in sentences, and their relationship to other parts of the 'whole' statute" (Slocum, 2016b). For this reason, such presumptions can be translated (even though imperfectly) into canons of legal interpretation (Miller, 1990, 1226), and the canons into arguments for statutory interpretation. In particular, while the psychological and historical argument and the argument from *analogia legis* rely on a context different from the one of the statute, the other canons can be considered as presumptions that can underlie the reconstruction of the propositional content that the legislator intends to convey. The set of correspondences is represented in Table 4.1:

TABLE 4.1 *Maxims, canons, and interpretative arguments*

Grice's Maxims	Legal Canons	Legal Arguments
Quantity 1. Make your contribution sufficiently informative.	*Expressio unius est exclusio alterius.* The plain meaning of a statute ordinarily governs.	A *contrario* Natural meaning argument
2. Do not make your contribution excessively informative.	*Ejusdem generis.*	A *fortiori;* a *simili*
Quality 1. Do not say anything false.	Interpret statutes to avoid absurdity.	Absurdity argument
2. Do not say anything meaningless.	Give effect, if possible, to every word of the statute.	Economic argument
3. Do not say anything self-contradictory.	Reconcile conflicting statutes if reasonably possible.	Coherence of the law
Relation Do not say anything irrelevant.	*In pari materia* (laws of the same matter and on the same subject must be construed with reference to each other)	Systematic argument
	Statutes should be interpreted in light of the legislature's purposes.	Teleological argument
Manner 1. Avoid obscurity.	Courts should interpret words according to their ordinary, common senses.	Natural meaning argument
	Courts should give legal words their established technical meanings.	Technical meaning argument
2. Avoid ambiguity.	The plain meaning of a statute ordinarily governs.	Natural meaning argument
3. Be brief.	Give effect to every word the legislature used.	Economic argument
	Expressio unius est exclusio alterius.	A *contrario*
4. Be orderly.		

The case of *Smith* v. *United States* can be analyzed using the aforementioned maxims and their corresponding arguments of statutory interpretation. We will indicate the proponents of the distinct arguments (the majority opinion advanced by O'Connor – also referred to as "the Court," which were opposed by the arguments of the petitioner [Smith] and Scalia in his dissenting opinion) in parentheses (Table 4.2).

TABLE 4.2 *Maxims and canons of interpretation in* Smith v. United States

Quantity 1 A *contrario*	1. Just as adding the direct object "a firearm" to the verb "use" narrows the meaning of that verb (it can no longer mean "partake of"), so also adding the modifier "in the offense of transferring, selling, or transporting firearms" to the phrase "use a firearm" expands the meaning of that phrase (it then includes, as it previously would not, nonweapon use). In Section 924(c)(1), the modifier "in the offense of transferring . . . " is not added to the phrase "use a firearm;" therefore, the narrow meaning should be intended. (Dissenting opinion, Scalia)
	2. The words "use as a weapon" appear nowhere in the statute. Rather, § 924(c)(1)'s language sweeps broadly, punishing any "use" of a firearm, so long as the use is "during and in relation to" a drug-trafficking offense. Had Congress intended the narrow construction, petitioner urges, it could have so indicated. (Majority opinion, O'Connor)
Quantity 2 A *simili*	3. The normal usage is reflected, for example, in the United States Sentencing Guidelines, which provide for enhanced sentences when firearms are "discharged, brandished, displayed, or possessed," or "otherwise used." See, e.g., United States Sentencing Commission, Guidelines Manual § 2B3.1(b)(2) (November 1992). As to the latter term, the Guidelines say: "Otherwise used" with reference to a dangerous weapon (including a firearm) means that the conduct "did not amount to the discharge of a firearm but was more than brandishing, displaying, or possessing a firearm or other dangerous weapon." USSG § 1B1.1, comment, n.1(g) (definitions). "Otherwise used" in this provision obviously means "otherwise used as a weapon." (Dissenting opinion, Scalia)
	4. Section 2B3.1(b)(2) clarifies that between the most culpable conduct of discharging the firearm and less culpable actions such as "brandishing, displaying, or possessing" lies a category of "other use[s]" for which the Guidelines impose intermediate punishment. It does not by its terms exclude from its scope trading, bludgeoning, or any other use beyond the firearm's "intended purpose." (Majority opinion, O'Connor)
Quality 1 Absurdity argument	5. The phrase "uses . . . a firearm" will produce anomalous applications. It would also be reasonable and normal to say that he "used" it to scratch his head. (Dissenting opinion, Scalia)
Quality 2 Economic argument	6. The words "use as a weapon" appear nowhere in the statute. Rather, § 924(c)(1)'s language sweeps broadly, punishing any "use" of a firearm, so long as the use is "during and in relation to" a drug-trafficking offense. (Majority opinion, O'Connor)
	7. § 924(c)(1) provides increased penalties not only for one who "uses" a firearm during and in relation to any crime of violence or drug-trafficking crime, but also for one who "carries" a firearm in those circumstances. The interpretation I would give this language produces an eminently reasonable dichotomy between "using a firearm" (as a weapon) and "carrying a firearm" (which in the

TABLE 4.2 *(continued)*

	context "uses or carries a firearm" means carrying it in such a manner as to be ready for use as a weapon). The Court's interpretation, by contrast, produces a strange dichotomy between "using a firearm for any purpose whatever, including barter," and "carrying a firearm." (Dissenting opinion, Scalia)
Relation Systematic argument	8. The next subsection of the statute, § 924(d) provides for the confiscation of firearms that are "used in" referenced offenses, which include the crimes of transferring, selling, or transporting firearms in interstate commerce. Therefore, whenever the term appears in this statute, "use" of a firearm must include nonweapon use. (Majority opinion, O'Connor)
Relevance Teleological argument	9. The fact that a gun is treated momentarily as an item of commerce does not render it inert or deprive it of destructive capacity. Rather, as experience demonstrates, it can be converted instantaneously from currency to cannon. We therefore see no reason why Congress would have intended courts and juries applying § 924(c)(1) to draw a fine metaphysical distinction between a gun's role in a drug offense as a weapon and its role as an item of barter; it creates a grave possibility of violence and death in either capacity. (Majority opinion, O'Connor)
Manner 1 Natural meaning argument	10. The words "uses" has a somewhat reduced scope in § 924(c)(1) because it appears alongside the word "firearm." Specifically, the average person on the street would not think immediately of a guns-for-drugs trade as an example of "us[ing]" a firearm." (Petitioner)
	11. It is one thing to say that the ordinary meaning of "uses a firearm" *includes* using a firearm as a weapon, since that is the intended purpose of a firearm and the example of "use" that most immediately comes to mind. But it is quite another to conclude that, as a result, the phrase also *excludes* any other use … That one example of "use" is the first to come to mind when the phrase "uses … a firearm" is uttered does not preclude us from recognizing that there are other "uses" that qualify as well. (Majority opinion, O'Connor)

The arguments used in this dispute about the meaning of "to use a firearm" are thus reconstructed according to the conversational maxims (presumptions). We notice that some maxims, such as the first and the second maxim of quantity, can be used to support contradictory conclusions (argument 1 vs. argument 2; argument 3 vs. argument 4). Other arguments can be defeated by using a different argument grounded on a different presumption. For example, the absurdity argument based on the first quality maxim (argument 5) can be defeated by an argument grounded on the second quality maxim (argument 6, economic argument). Similarly, the economic argument based on the second quality maxim (argument 7) can be defeated by a systematic argument grounded on the relevance maxim (argument 8). Moreover, some maxims are used to undermine an argument grounded on an unaccepted generalization. For example, in argument 10 the petitioner claims that the phrase "to use a firearm" is stereotypically intended as using the firearm as a weapon, concluding that therefore it cannot be intended to mean "to use for trade." However, the Court used the same maxim (and argument) to defeat the generalization (it is stereotypically interpreted *only* as . . .) and thereby to undermine the petitioner's conclusion.

4.9.2 *Maxims, Arguments, and Presumptions on Interpretation*

Smith is a crucial case for analyzing the presumptions and the levels of presumptions underlying the interpretation of a statutory text, which can be applied to the analysis of other cases. The "infamous decision" (Slocum, 2016b) to interpret "to use a firearm" as meaning "use a firearm for any purpose related to drug trafficking" can be regarded as grounded on different types of evidence that the canons of interpretation rely on and that the corresponding maxims bring to light.

The whole dispute is grounded on the fact that the intended meaning of the phrase at issue needs to be reconstructed using contextual evidence and pragmatic principles. The semantic meaning (the heuristic interpretation, or prima facie understanding) can be contextually enriched by considering a stereotypical context (resulting in the interpretation "using as a weapon") or the context of the statute. However, this interpretative controversy stems from two fundamental presumptions governing the legal system, namely that (1) the law needs to be understood by citizens and in criminal law, if a text is ambiguous, it should be interpreted in favor of the defendant, and (2) the law should not be unreasonable or absurd. Interpretative disputes concerning a nontechnical term typically arise if such a term is ambiguous (see also *Garner* v. *Burr* 1 KB 31 at 33 (1951), in which the interpretational dispute was allowed by the fact that "competent speakers of the English language presumably share a knowledge of the meaning of the word 'vehicle,' yet they disagree – apparently sincerely – over how to use the word" [Endicott, 2010]). However, in criminal law, doubts should be solved in favor of the defendant. Therefore, if the defendant is able to show that the provision being interpreted is ambiguous, he will obtain the interpretation favoring him (it will be excluded that using a firearm includes selling it). In contrast, if it is shown that the provision is not ambiguous, then the interpretation against the defendant (using a firearm also includes selling it) can possibly be successful.

Thus, arguments of the defendant and of the court (see Table 4.2) address two parallel issues: (1) which one of the alternative interpretations is based on stronger reasons; and (2) whether or not the statute can be considered as ambiguous.

The petitioner in *Smith* argued that selling should be excluded from the scope of using, through an argument of natural meaning (argument 10 in Table 4.2) (the presumption that the semantic meaning of the statute can be interpreted as within its stereotypical meaning). This argument, however, was rejected by the Court (majority opinion), which pointed out that the stereotypical context can be different and, for this reason, this argument could not be used for supporting the intended interpretation.

The petitioner also presented arguments aimed at establishing the ambiguity of the *contextual* meaning of the statute based on textual presumptions and textual evidence (*a contrario*; *a simili*; economic argument) (Easterbrook, 1984). All these arguments were rebutted by contrary arguments based on the same maxims (canons) and supported by contrary contextual evidence (see, for example, the conflict between the two *a contrario* arguments 1 and 2 in our table).

A more complex issue concerns the relationship between the context and the consequential or teleological arguments. Scalia, in his dissenting opinion, advanced an argument not directly based on contextual evidence (he used the absurdity argument, argument 5 in our table), aimed at excluding the Court's interpretation based on its possible foreseeable absurd consequences. This argument was grounded on another fundamental presumption underlying the legal system, namely that the law cannot be absurd or unreasonable. However, the argument simply provided an interpretation of the statute by taking into account a modified (stereotypical) context (to "use a firearm" would mean also "to use a firearm to scratch one's head"), which is easily undercut by the economic argument of the Court (argument 6 in our table), which placed the interpretation within the context of the statute (any use, *as long as* it is related to drug trafficking).

The conflict of interpretations was resolved by the Court using the teleological argument (argument 9 in Table 4.2), namely the intention of the law as it can be reconstructed from the context. Considering that the law is intended to punish violent drug-related crimes, it would be meaningless to construct it as punishing only some specific offenses (those resulting from the actual discharge of weapons) and excluding others (those related to the possible discharge of weapons). In this sense, the intention of the law would correspond to the prohibition of discharging weapons during drug crimes, which is suboptimal with regard to the goal of better protecting society. This argument is extremely problematic (Scalia, 1998, 39) as the line between what a law means and what a law ought to mean (according to the judge) risks being crossed. One way to interpret it from an argumentative perspective is to understand it as presupposing implicit contextual arguments. In this ideal perspective, this teleological argument is based on factual presumptions (e.g., that "weapons are used in drug trafficking") and also on other implicit legal arguments (such as economic arguments). In this view, the possible meaning alleged by the petitioner was claimed to be unacceptable because it would lead to a partially redundant and useless law (a presumption resulting from the contextual information). For this reason, the Court argued that the defendant's interpretation could not be accepted, and the statute could be considered as unambiguous.

This analysis shows how the arguments of legal interpretation and the conversational maxims represent distinct levels of analysis of the reasoning underlying an interpretative dispute. The legal arguments can be used to point out the various perspectives on the subject matter that can be used for and against a viewpoint, while the maxims can show the general strategies (relying on minimal context, or the most natural reading, or the existing context, or the contextual and co-textual effects and consequences). What emerges from this picture is that these two dimensions of interpretation can be integrated within an argumentative model. This model can represent the presumptive grounds on which such maxims and arguments are based. In this view, the reconstruction of the speaker's meaning can be analyzed through the categories of presumptions that can be used to support it. However, before integrating legal and ordinary interpretation within an argumentative model, and more importantly ordering the presumptions underlying arguments, canons, and maxims, it is necessary to analyze what is the goal of the interpretative process. To this purpose, we need to investigate the notion of the purpose of the law, show its relationships with the other interpretative presumptions, and point out how it can be integrated within a pragmatic approach to communication.

4.10 PRESUMPTIONS AND THE PURPOSE OF THE LAW

From an argumentative perspective, maxims, interpretative canons, and interpretative arguments can be regarded in terms of presumptions. However, so that we can order such presumptions and show the different strengths of the possible arguments based thereon, we need to identify the organizing principle. In this section, we will analyze the pragmatic presumption of legal interpretation, which is commonly referred to as the purpose of the law.

4.10.1 *The Purpose of the Law as a Presumption*

Both in ordinary conversation and legal interpretation, the addressees of the conversation (the hearer or the citizens) have access only to the text of the law, from which they need to reconstruct the speaker's meaning, or the legal meaning of the law. The psychological state of the speaker or lawmaker is inaccessible because it is unknown (in ordinary conversation) or attributable only to a group (the Congress), whose discussions are not easily accessible to the public (Easterbrook, 1984). The intention that is communicated is the one that is retrievable from the textual and contextual evidence provided (Carston, 2013, 24). The explicit content of a speech act (such as a statement of law) is the only accessible instrument for reconstructing the speaker's intention.

From the point of view of legal interpretation, the *Smith* case is an extremely clear illustration of the "textualistic" reconstruction of the speaker meaning. It underlies the essential relation between the contextual meaning and the purpose of the enactment, retrieved through other broader contextual information, including background knowledge (Greene, 2006, 1920). In the first place, what is reconstructed is the meaning that can be obtained from the co-text and the context.[5] The arguments can be classified into two general categories:

---

[5] This approach to meaning is in conflict with the approaches aiming at reconstructing the generic "intention of the actual legislator" (Scalia, 1998, 29–30; Tarello, 1980, 364), which, in lack of evidence of such an intention, amounts to the intention of the "historical legislator" (Tarello, 1980, 368) or the previous interpreters, such as in the argument *ab exemplo*.

1. those aimed at reconstructing the intention by means of co-textual clues; and

2. those that appeal to the purpose of the law, especially its relevance to the more general and basic goal of protecting the citizens' rights.

The first type of arguments can in turn be classified into linguistic and contextual arguments:

1(a). arguments grounded on the presumptively shared meaning of a linguistic expression; and

1(b). arguments based on the constraints imposed by the co-text onto the linguistic expressions.

The arguments from the purpose of the law are more complex, as they involve, in addition to linguistic and co-textual presumptions, also factual presumptions (what a weapon is used for) and more basic and generic pragmatic presumptions (what goals the law is supposed to pursue). The teleological argument (in *Smith* concerning the goal of reducing drug-related crimes and the goal of being understood by citizens) and the absurdity argument (in the same case, concerning the absurd consequences of punishing any possible "use" of a weapon) presuppose linguistic, co-textual, and contextual presumptions, but directly refer to overarching pragmatic presumptions. However, if we sever the argument from the contextualized and objective purpose of the law and also from the context and the evidence, we risk running into the problem of attributing to the laws the meanings they *ought* to have according to the judge (Scalia, 1998, 22).

In order to analyze the structure of pragmatic presumptions, it is useful to consider different types of reasoning in which the specific, "purpose of the law" is supported by various types of arguments. The most important one concerns the relevance of the possible effects of the article of law to the co-text (intended as the body of laws in which the article appears) and to the context (promoting equality and justice). One of the most famous examples is the Case 4.4. (Bentham, 1838, 313; Manning, 2003, 2388).

CASE 4.4: THE SURGEON AND THE WOUNDED MAN

"Whosoever draws blood in the streets shall be put to death"
I put three cases upon this law:

1. A surgeon, seeing a man drop down in a street in a fit of apoplexy, lets his blood and saves his life. Ought he for this to lose his own? Yet such must be the inevitable consequence of a strict execution of the letter of the law.
2. A man, waylaying his adversary, sets upon him in a street, and strangles him without shedding a drop of blood.
3. A man, waylaying his adversary, and meeting him in the street, draws blood from him, by giving him a stab, which however does not prove a mortal one.

The most basic interpretative reasoning grounded on the pragmatic intention of the law consists in comparing the actual goal pursued by the law and the basic pragmatic presumptions concerning the functions of the law. The afore-mentioned article of law contains a polysemic expression, "to draw blood," a phrase that is used differently in various contexts to mean different concepts, and that thus can lead potentially to ambiguity. Therefore, it is necessary to analyze whether the specific article of law is ambiguous, and how to resolve the ambiguity.

The reasoning can follow two distinct paths. The first is based on the argument from absurdity, which is aimed at excluding the broad interpreta-tion of "to draw blood." Since the law cannot be absurd, and killing a man for saving another man's life would be absurd, the interpretation supporting this consequence needs to be excluded. The other type of reasoning is grounded on the relevance of the law to the goal pursued by the body of laws (or the co-text) in which it is placed. Since the purpose of a criminal code is to punish criminal offenses, the statement of law needs to be inter-preted in a way that is relevant to pursue this general goal. For this reason, the meaning of "to draw blood" needs to be limited to the cases in which a criminal offense is committed (killing or stabbing). Moreover, putting a man to death for injuring another and acquitting a murderer would be an unreasonable consequence (contrary to equity or more specifically contra-dictory with other provisions of the criminal code). For this reason, the meaning of the phrase needs to be further reinterpreted. This can be done by resorting to metaphorical interpretations, which either extend its meaning ("to draw blood" in the sense of "to take someone's life"), or to restrict it ("to draw blood" in the sense of "to take someone's life by shedding his blood"). This last interpretation would pursue both the purpose of the criminal code and the presumption that the law needs to be understood by citizens (lenity rule). This case is only a hypothetical one, but it helps explain how the reasoning from the purpose of the law can work from an argumentative perspective as a fundamental (the highest) presumption.

4.10.2 *Ordering Interpretative Presumptions*

The argument from the purpose of the law can be considered as grounded on a metapresumption, governing the choice and the hierarchy of the arguments that can be advanced to support an interpretation. The purpose of the law can be regarded as a macrocontextual argument, in which the statute to be interpreted is placed within its broader context (the body of the laws), from which its intended generic or specific purpose can be retrieved. This context-based pragmatic presump-tion can overcome other types of presumptions or determine the hierarchy of the interpretative presumptions.

The purpose of the law can be a presumption stronger than the one raised by the instrument most frequently used by the legislator to avoid ambiguity, namely statutory definition. A clear example is *Bond* v. *United States*, 564 U.S. 211 (2011). In this case, a woman seeking revenge on her husband's mistress decided to spread chemicals on (among other things) her car, doorknob, and mailbox, causing only a minor burn that was easily treated with water. However, under the Chemical Weapons Convention Implementation Act, a "chemical weapon" is defined as follows:

CASE 4.5: TOXIC CHEMICAL

"[a] toxic chemical and its precursors, except where intended for a purpose not prohibited under this chapter." §229F(1) (A). A "toxic chemical" is "any chemical which through its chemical action on life processes can cause death, temporary incapacitation or permanent harm to humans or animals . . ." §229F (8)(A).

Mrs. Bond used chemicals that happened to be "toxic" as they resulted in her husband's mistress developing an uncomfortable rash. Moreover, since such chemicals were not used for any "peaceful purpose," they were classified as "chemical weapons" by the District Court, and the Court of Appeals confirmed such a decision. The US Supreme Court interpreted the statement of law by taking into account the co-text (a treaty on warfare and terrorism) and the context (the interpretation of the District Court would punish a local assault as an act of terrorism). The Supreme Court analyzed the purposes of the law in general (pursue equity, justice, etc.) and the specific purpose of the treaty in which the definition occurred (to punish crimes of warfare and terrorism). It concluded that the statement of law so interpreted would pursue a goal that was irrelevant and unreasonable (turning assaults into terrorism crimes). For this reason, the statute was interpreted by relying on a presumption stronger than the most obvious one (the statutory definition).

The purpose of the law can also overcome the presumption of the "plain" or stereotypical meaning. In *Garner* v. *Burr*, 1 KB 31 (1951), the dispute concerned the interpretation of a statement of law, making it an offense "to use a 'vehicle' on a road without pneumatic tires." The problem concerned the meaning of the term "vehicle," and more specifically the application thereof to the case of an empty chicken coop with wheels without rubber tires and towed by a tractor. The classification is controversial, because even though the dictionary defines a "vehicle" as "a means of conveyance provided with wheels or runners and used for the carriage of persons or goods," there is no agreement on how to use the term (Endicott, 2010). The court had to take into account two distinct arguments:

1. According to the dictionary definition, a "vehicle" is primarily to be regarded as a means of conveyance provided with wheels or runners and used for the carriage of persons or goods. The magistrates did not find that anything was carried in the vehicle at the time. Therefore, the coop was not a vehicle.

2. The Act was clearly aimed at anything that will run on wheels that is being drawn by a tractor or another motor vehicle. Therefore, the coop was a vehicle.

The second argument is based on the relevance of the statement of law to the body of laws in which it appears. What is essential for the law is that a vehicle is used "on a road without pneumatic tires," and the purpose thereof can be interpreted by resorting to contextual presumptions (heavy objects running on iron wheels can damage the roads). In this sense, the statement of law can contribute to a body of laws concerning the circulation of vehicles on public roads. The relevance of the statement of law (established by considering other types of co-textual and contextual presumptions) is to enact a rule for avoiding damages to the road.

The purpose of the law can be considered as a metapresumption resulting from the broader context of the legal system, within which all the other presumptions need to be ordered. In order to illustrate this point, it is useful to take into account another case from civil law, *Nix v. Hedden*, 149 U.S. 304 (1893). This case concerned the classification, or rather interpretation, of tomatoes as fruit or vegetable. The action was brought against the collector of the port of New York to recover back duties paid under protest on tomatoes imported by the plaintiff, which the collector classified as "vegetables" (resulting in a duty) and which the plaintiff contended should be classified as "fruit" (for which no duty had to be paid). The problem concerned the interpretation of the items listed on the Tariff Act of March 3, 1883, which provided that "fruits, green, ripe, or dried, not specially enumerated or provided for in this act" shall be duty free. The plaintiff relied on the dictionary (botanic) definition, which claimed to be the same as that used in trade in commerce, stating that "fruit" is the seed of plaints, or that part of plaints that contains the seed.

The dictionary definition, however, was considered as a presumption, which had to be assessed considering the context (or rather the purpose) of the article of law. The law concerned the commerce of goods (and not botany); for this reason, it had to be interpreted according to the recipient of the provision of law, namely "sellers or consumers of provisions." To a consumer or a seller of an article of food, the word "tomato" indicates a good consumed as a vegetable, "whether baked or boiled, or forming the basis of soup." In this case, the purpose of the law (regulating duties on commodities) determines what presumptions need to be relied on, the linguistic ones (related to a stereotypical context) or the ones concerning a specific context (trade and use of goods).

4.11 TYPES OF INTENTIONS AND LEVELS OF PRESUMPTIONS

The reconstruction of the "purpose of the law" can be examined within a pragmatic framework. The meaning of a single speech act is subordinated to dialogical intentions. Grice (Grice, 1975, 45) represented such a dialogical intention using the notion of the "direction" of the dialogue to which each speech act needs to be linked (Asher and Lascarides, 2003, Chapter 7). In order to retrieve this meaning, or a speaker's specific intention, it is necessary to retrieve the relationship between the speech act and the whole text, namely its relevance (Macagno and Walton, 2013; Walton and Macagno, 2007; Macagno, 2012; Walton and Macagno, 2016). This mechanism of retrieval of the speaker's intention is clearly at work in statutory interpretation. For example, in all the aforementioned criminal and civil cases, the purpose of the use of the statement of law was retrieved by taking into account the whole co-text of the provision in which it occurred, addressing a specific issue (the relationship between drug trafficking and other crimes; the commerce of consumable goods, etc.). The so-called purpose of the law can be regarded as a presumption to which other presumptions need to be subordinated, and which can be reconstructed through different types of arguments. In this perspective, the mechanism of interpretation crucially depends on the ordering of the presumptions underlying the different alternatives.

4.11.1 *Types and Levels of Presumptions*

Any reconstruction of a speaker's intention resulting from his or her speech act is grounded on several presumptions different in nature (Hamblin, 1970, 295):

> There is, as we might put it, a presumption of meaning-constancy in the absence of evidence to the contrary. The presumption is a methodological one of the same character as the legal presumption that an accused man is innocent in the absence of proof of guilt, or that a witness is telling the truth: it is not, of course, itself in the category of a reason or argument supporting the thesis of meaning-constancy, and least of all is it an argument for the impossibility of equivocation. Dialectic, however, has many presumptions of this kind, whose existence is related to the necessary conditions of meaningful or useful discourse. It is a presumption of any dialogue that its participants are sober, conscious, speak deliberately, know the language, mean what they say and tell the truth, that when they ask questions they want answers, and so on.

The presumptions that are at the basis of meaning reconstruction have different conditions of defeasibility (Kauffeld, 2003, 1998). The first kind of presumption (level 0) can be called "pragmatic". It connects the generic or specific illocutionary force of a speech act (assertive/assertion in the context of writing a recommendation letter) to its presumed generic or specific intention (informing the interlocutor/ providing information to support a decision to hire someone). The second type (level 1) consists in the conventional presumptive meaning of the lexical items (Grice, 1975; Levinson, 2000; Macagno, 2011; Hamblin, 1970). For instance, "attendance" is usually defined as "to be present at a place." However, in the case of the severe professor writing a recommendation letter, it could mean "to participate in classes actively, showing peculiar skills." The third type of presumption (level 2) concerns expectations about relations between facts or events that can be used to interpret a specific content or an action. For instance, attendance is not usually considered as an indicator of academic excellence. The last level (level 3) includes values or specific contextual knowledge (Macagno and Capone, 2016). For example, a specific professor may be presumed to be extremely severe, and that his recommendation letters are usually extremely concise.

These levels of presumptions are ranked contextually according to their distinct possibility of being subject to default, depending on the accessibility of information. Mutual information (concerning the specific context) is usually more accessible and less subject to default than encyclopedic information (concerning stereotypical events or facts) and the linguistic kind of information (concerning stereotypical contexts). For example, the shared presumption that a professor is famous for never writing anything at all (or anything positive) about his students overcomes the factual one that a recommendation letter indicating good attendance does not provide a reason for hiring. The semantic content of a speech act is usually employed to reconstruct the intention behind it, and may conflict with encyclopedic or shared information, which can rebut semantic presumptions. For example, the fact that a professor only uses the term "attendance" when a student is particularly active in class and shows exceptional skills can defeat the presumptive meaning of this term (see Saul, 2002).

In this case, the meaning of the statement is determined by the pragmatic presumption that the professor intended to provide information or an opinion relevant to the decision to hire the applicant. This presumption is drawn from contextual elements, namely the fact that the letter has been sent referring to an application (factual presumptions). However, this pragmatic presumption can be specified more by taking into account other presumptions. For example, the letter can be presumed to provide a *favorable* recommendation based on the presumptions associated with a stereotypical context of writing a recommendation letter. Alternatively, the same specific pragmatic presumption can be drawn from more contextual information, for example, the professor is expected to send either laconic recommendations or no recommendations at all. These two types of pragmatic presumptions have different defeasibility conditions. While the first can be rejected by relying on more contextual information, the second can hardly be subject to the default.

4.11.2 *Types and Levels of Presumptions in Statutory Interpretation*

This framework of hierarchies of presumptions can be applied to legal interpretation. Considering the interpretative disputes mentioned above, we identify four distinct levels of interpretative presumptions at work in statutory interpretation[6] (Figure 4.1).

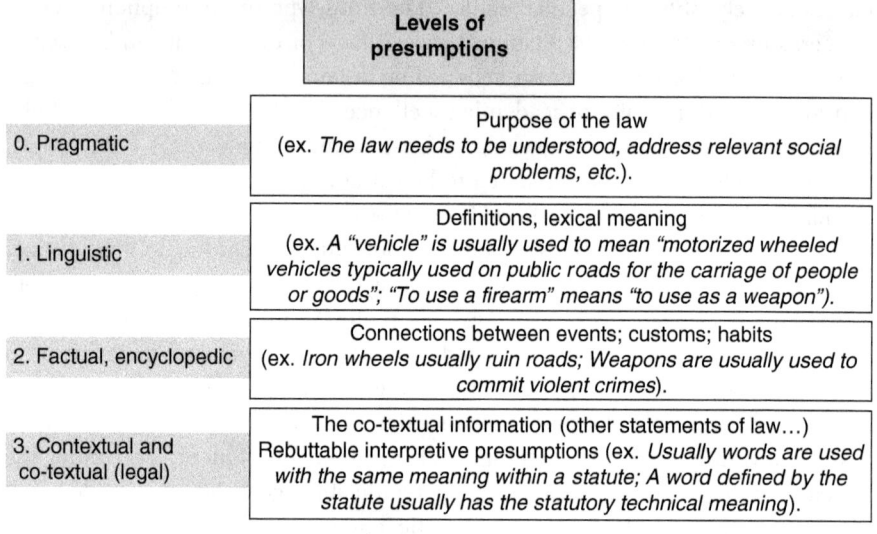

FIGURE 4.1 Levels of presumptions of legal interpretation

These different levels mirror the context-dependence of each presumption, namely their specificity. Presumptions can be classified according to their content and ordered and assessed based on their defeasibility conditions (Clark and Brennan, 1991; Clark, 1996, Chapter 4). The more likely that conflicting or defeating evidence can be added or be found, the more likely that a presumption is subject to default. Therefore, the presumptions that refer to a specific feature of the conversational situation in which the utterance (or the move) is performed are likely to be less subject to default than more generic presumptions. This principle for ordering the presumptions has been underscored also by Dascal, who distinguished between linguistic, extralinguistic, and metalinguistic clues that allow the addressee to interpret an utterance. These clues can be ordered in specific, shallow, and background "assumptions" depending on their relation and relevance to the utterance. However, only when the interpretation resulting from the linguistic and specific clues is

---

[6] The concept of presumption we are using in legal interpretation does not correspond to the legal one, which is highly controversial in itself (Gama, 2017; Macagno and Walton, 2012). Clearly some presumptions of law are essential for determining the purpose of the law (the law needs to be understood), and thus represent the strongest principles underlying interpretation.

contradicted by the presumptions concerning the conventions of use and background knowledge (namely more generic presumptions) are the other presumptions used for interpreting the utterance (Dascal, 2003, 173–177).

We can notice how the more general presumptions governing the overall purpose of the law (or a law) (pragmatic presumptions) are not related to specific type of evidence that can be found in a text. Thus, pragmatic presumptions are at the same time the most generic ones, to which all the others are subordinated. However, their use rests on the grounds that the use of the other types of presumptions can provide. The more specific presumptions are thus employed to back the reasonableness of the use of a presumption about "the purpose of the law," namely for specifying it within the specific context.

These levels of presumptions can be employed to model the structure of meaning reconstruction in statutory interpretation. For example, since the basic presumption concerning the purpose of the law is that the law needs to be understood by citizens, the linguistic presumptions (concerning the stereotypical use) will be the prevailing ones. In *Smith*, these presumptions concerned the ordinary meaning of "to use (a firearm)." However, once the everyday language ambiguity of a term has been established (two conflicting presumptions of level 1), the contextual presumptions will be used to establish whether it is also ambiguous within the specific provision of law. While the defense supported the interpretation based on the stereotypical context (linguistic presumptions, level 1), the prosecution grounded its conclusion relying on contextual elements. The majority opinion pointed out how the specific pragmatic intention of the law (level 0) was to avoid drug-related crimes and in particular any association between drug selling and weapons. This pragmatic presumption, however, needed to be justified. In particular, the justification was based on the other surrounding provisions of law (level 3) and the factual presumptions concerning the use of weapons in drug selling (factual presumptions, level 2). These presumptions defeated the more generic linguistic ones.

All the aforementioned cases can be analyzed using the same framework of presumptions. The possible ambiguity of the stereotypical (linguistic) meaning, considering the most generic pragmatic intention of setting out an obligation, leads to ascertaining the possible ambiguity of the contextual meaning (the ambiguity in pursuing the specific pragmatic intention). To this purpose, the presumptions relative to the specific context (factual and contextual) provide the strongest grounds for reconstructing the specific pragmatic presumption, which is in turn used to determine the univocal meaning of the contested statement (on the general principles of this defeasible reasoning see Walton, 2016, p. 246; Weinstock et al., 2013).

4.12 CONCLUSION

This chapter addressed a crucial issue in philosophy of law and linguistics, namely the relationship between pragmatics and statutory interpretation (or more generally, legal interpretation). One of the crucial problems underlying the possibility of this dialogue is the application of the pragmatic interpretative presumptions elaborated by Grice (and developed further by the neo-Gricean scholars) to legal interpretation, characterized by occurring in a strategic and uncooperative setting. This chapter showed how this relationship can be not only possible, but also highly useful for both fields of study. To this purpose, we showed how the mechanisms underlying ordinary and legal interpretation can be compared and included within a general same argumentative structure. We showed how the maxims and the canons of interpretation can be conceived as presumptions, which are used in a specific argumentative pattern called argument from best explanation. In this perspective, maxims and canons become the ground of the reasons advanced to support an interpretation.

The pragmatic approach to interpretative canons can also shed light on the different forces (or rather defeasibility conditions) of the various presumptions. The analysis of the intention of the law as an objectified intention can provide us with a first distinction between the presumptions concerning the authority of the legislator and the other presumptions. While the first ones are aimed at supporting the supposedly actual and subjective intention, the other (textual) presumptions are used to reconstruct the intention that the text can "reasonably be understood to mean" (Scalia, 1998, 144). Among these latter presumptions, it is possible to distinguish different types or classes, characterized by distinct goals and distinct overarching principles.

From a pragmatic point of view, the strongest presumptions are those directly related to the basic principles of the relationship between the lawmaker and the citizens (the law cannot be unreasonable, absurd, meaningless, incomprehensible, etc.). Clearly, such presumptions depend on the legal culture, even though they can be easily generalized to most legal systems characterized by democratic societies. The ordering of the presumptions can be analyzed by considering their defeasibility in the specific context and the specific purpose they are used to achieve. While the possibility of an ambiguity needs to be established based on linguistic presumptions (can the language used be expected to mean different concepts?), the presumptions underlying the specific interpretation can be ranked according to their relation to the specific context. In this sense, the so-called "intention of the lawmaker (or the law)" can be regarded as a specific pragmatic presumption that in turn is grounded on contextual and factual evidence and contextual and factual presumptions.

The legal interpretative dispute in this sense can be analyzed as a conflict of opinions concerning what the lawmaker meant by enacting a statement of law. The intended propositional content can be reconstructed by relying on the presumptions backing a stereotypical meaning (utterance type) or a specific contextual meaning (utterance token). The defeasibility conditions in these two cases are different. Contextual, specific evidence can be easily used to counter more generic presumptions (e.g., those underlying stereotypical interpretations).

REFERENCES

Asher, Nicholas, and Alex Lascarides. 2003. *Logics of Conversation*. Cambridge, UK: Cambridge University Press.

Atlas, Jay David. 2005. *Logic, Meaning, and Conversation*. Oxford, UK: Oxford University Press.

Atlas, Jay David. 2007. "Meanings, propositions, context, and semantical underdeterminacy." In *Context-Sensitivity and Semantic Minimalism: New Essays on Semantics and Pragmatics*, edited by Gerhard Preyer and Georg Peter, 217–239. Oxford, UK: Oxford University Press.

Atlas, Jay David. 2008. "Presupposition." In *The Handbook of Pragmatics*, edited by Laurence Horn and Gregory Ward, 29–52. Oxford, UK: Blackwell Publishing Ltd.

Atlas, Jay David, and Stephen Levinson. 1981. "It-clefts, informativeness and logical form: radical pragmatics (revised standard version)." In *Radical Pragmatics*, edited by Peter Cole, 1–62. New York, NY: Academic Press.

Bach, Kent. 2006. "The top 10 misconceptions about implicature." In *Drawing the Boundaries of Meaning: Neo-Gricean Studies in Pragmatics and Semantics in Honor of Laurence R. Horn*, edited by Betty Birner and Gregory Ward, 21–30. Amsterdam, Netherlands: John Benjamins Publishing.

Bentham, Jeremy. 1838. *The Works of Jeremy Bentham, Part IV*. Edinburgh, UK: William Tait.

Bezuidenhout, Anne. 1997. "Pragmatics, semantic undetermination and the referential/attributive distinction." *Mind* 106(423): 375–409. https://doi.org/10.1093/mind/106.423.375.

Brewer, Scott. 2011. *Logic, Probability, and Presumptions in Legal Reasoning*. New York, NY: Routledge.

Brown, Penelope, and Stephen Levinson. 1987. *Politeness: Some Universals in Language Usage*. Cambridge, UK: Cambridge University Press.

Butler, Brian. 2016a. "Law and the primacy of pragmatics." In *Pragmatics and Law: Philosophical Perspectives*, edited by Alessandro Capone and Francesca Poggi, 1–13. Cham, Switzerland: Springer.

Butler, Brian. 2016b. "Transparency and context in legal communication: Pragmatics and legal interpretation." In *Interdisciplinary Studies in Pragmatics, Culture and Society*, edited by Alessandro Capone and Jacob Mey, 517–535. Cham, Switzerland: Springer.

Capone, Alessandro. 2010. "On the social practice of indirect reports (further advances in the theory of pragmemes)." *Journal of Pragmatics* 42(2): 377–391. https://doi.org/10.1016/j.pragma.2009.06.013.

Capone, Alessandro. 2016. "The role of pragmatics in (re)constructing the rational law-maker." In *Pragmatics and Law. Philosophical Perspectives*, edited by Alessandro Capone and Francesca Poggi, 141–157. Cham, Switzerland: Springer.

Carston, Robyn. 1988. "Implicature, explicature, and truth-theoretic semantics." In *Mental Representations: The Interface between Language and Reality*, edited by Ruth Kempson, 155–181. Cambridge, UK: Cambridge University Press.

Carston, Robyn. 2002. *Thoughts and Utterances: The Pragmatics of Explicit Communication*. Oxford, UK: Blackwell.

Carston, Robyn. 2013. "Legal texts and canons of construction: A view from current pragmatic theory." In *Law and Language: Current Legal Issues*, edited by Michael Freeman and Fiona Smith, 15: 8–33. Oxford, UK: Oxford University Press.

Clark, Herbert. 1996. *Using Language*. Cambridge, UK: Cambridge University Press.

Clark, Herbert, and Susan Brennan. 1991. "Grounding in communication." In *Perspectives on Socially Shared Cognition*, edited by Lauren Resnick, John Levine, and Stephanie Teasley, 127–149. Washington, DC: American Psychological Association.

Dascal, Marcelo. 2003. *Interpretation and Understanding*. Amsterdam, Netherlands: John Benjamins Publishing Company.

Dascal, Marcelo, and Jerzy Wróblewski. 1988. "Transparency and doubt: Understanding and interpretation in pragmatics and in law." *Law and Philosophy* 7(2): 203–224. https://doi.org /10.1007/BF00144156.

Davis, Wayne. 1998. *Implicature: Intention, Convention, and Principle in the Failure of Gricean Theory*. New York, NY: Cambridge University Press.

Davis, Wayne. 2007a. "Grice's meaning project." *Teorema: Revista Internacional de Filosofía*, 41–58.

Davis, Wayne. 2007b. "How normative is implicature." *Journal of Pragmatics* 39(10): 1655–1672. https://doi.org/10.1016/j.pragma.2007.05.006.

Dworkin, Ronald. 1986. *Law's Empire*. Cambridge, MA: Harvard University Press.

Easterbrook, Frank. 1984. "Legal interpretation and the power of the judiciary." *Harvard Journal of Law and Public Policy* 7: 87–99.

Endicott, Timothy. 2010. "Law and language." *Stanford Encyclopedia of Philosophy*. https:// plato.stanford.edu/entries/law-language/

Everardus, Nicolaus. 1601. *Loci Argumentorum Legales*. Venice, Italy: Matthaeum Valentinum.

Fodor, Jerry. 1983. *The Modularity of Mind*. Cambridge, MA: MIT Press.

Fuller, Lon. 1957. "Positivism and fidelity to law – A reply to Professor Hart." *Harvard Law Review* 71(4): 630–672.

Gama, Raymundo. 2017. "The nature and the place of presumptions in law and legal argumentation." *Argumentation* 31: 555–572. https://doi.org/10.1007/s10503-016-9417-3.

Gifis, Steven. 2010. *Law Dictionary*. Hauppauge, NY: Barron's.

Greenawalt, Kent. 2015. *Interpreting the Constitution*. Oxford, UK: Oxford University Press.

Greene, Abner. 2006. "The missing step of textualism." *Fordham Law Review* 74(4): 1913–1936.

Grice, Paul. 1975. "Logic and conversation." In *Syntax and Semantics 3: Speech Acts*, edited by Peter Cole and Jerry Morgan, 41–58. New York, NY: Academic Press.

Guastini, Riccardo. 2011. *Interpretare e Argomentare*. Milano, Italy: Giuffrè.

Hage, Jaap. 1997. *Reasoning with Rules*. Dordrecht, Netherlands: Kluwer.

Hamblin, Charles Leonard. 1970. *Fallacies*. London, UK: Methuen.

Harman, Gilbert. 1965. "The inference to the best explanation." *The Philosophical Review* 74(1): 88–95.

Harman, Gilbert. 1992. "Inference to the best explanation (review)." *Mind* 101(403): 578–580. https://doi.org/10.1093/mind/101.403.578.

Harris, Roy, and Christopher Hutton. 2007. *Definition in Theory and Practice: Language, Lexicography and the Law*. London, UK: Continuum.

Horn, Laurence. 1984. "Toward a new taxonomy for pragmatic inference: Q-based and R-based implicature." In *Meaning, Form, and Use in Context*, edited by Deborah Schiffring, 11–42. Washington, DC: Georgetown University Press.

Horn, Laurence. 1995. "Vehicles of meaning: Unconventional semantics and unbearable interpretation." *Washington University Law Quarterly* 73: 1145–1152.

Horn, Laurence. 2009. "WJ-40: Implicature, truth, and meaning." *International Review of Pragmatics* 1: 3–34. https://doi.org/10.1163/187731009X455820.

Huang, Yan. 2014. *Pragmatics*. Oxford, UK: Oxford University Press.

Hutton, Christopher. 2009. *Language, Meaning and the Law*. Edinburgh, UK: Edinburgh University Press.

Jacobs, Scott, and Sally Jackson. 2006. "Derailments of argumentation: It takes two to tango." In *Considering Pragma-Dialectics*, edited by Peter Houtlosser and Agnes van Rees, 121–133. Mahwah, NJ: Lawrence Erlbaum Associates.

Jaszczolt, Kasia. 2005. *Default Semantics: Foundations of a Compositional Theory of Acts of Communication*. Oxford, UK: Oxford University Press.

Jaszczolt, Kasia. 2006. "Meaning merger: Pragmatic inference, defaults, and compositionality." *Intercultural Pragmatics* 3(2): 195–212. https://doi.org/10.1515/IP.2006.012.

Kaplan, Jeffrey. 2019. *Linguistics and Law*. New York, NY: Routledge.

Kaplan, Jeffrey, and Georgia Green. 1995. "Grammar and inferences of rationality in interpreting the Child Pornography Statute." *Washington University Law Review* 73: 1223–1251.

Kaplan, Jeffrey, Georgia Green, Clark Cunningham, and Judith Levi. 1995. "Bringing linguistics into judicial decisionmaking: Semantic analysis submitted to the US Supreme Court." *International Journal of Speech, Language and the Law* 2(1): 81–98. https://doi.org/10.1558/ijsll.v2i1.81,

Kauffeld, Fred. 1998. "Presumptions and the distribution of argumentative burdens in acts of proposing and accusing." *Argumentation* 12(2): 245–266. https://doi.org/10.1023/A:1007704116379.

Kauffeld, Fred. 2003. "The ordinary practice of presuming and presumption with special attention to veracity and the burden of proof." In *Anyone with a View: Theoretical Contributions to the Study of Argumentation*, edited by Frans van Eemeren, Anthony Blair, Charles Willard, and Francisca Snoeck-Henkemans, 133–146. Dordrecht, Netherlands: Kluwer.

Kecskes, Istvan. 2013. *Intercultural Pragmatics*. Oxford, UK: Oxford University Press.

Kecskes, Istvan, and Fenghui Zhang. 2009. "Activating, seeking, and creating common ground: A socio-cognitive approach." *Pragmatics & Cognition* 17(2): 331–355. https://doi.org/10.1075/pc.17.2.06kec.

Kennedy, Duncan. 2007. "A left phenomenological critique of the Hart/Kelsen theory of legal interpretation." *Kritische Justiz* 40(3): 296–305.

Kissine, Mikhail. 2012. "Sentences, utterances, and speech acts." In *Cambridge Handbook of Pragmatics*, edited by Keith Allan and Kasia Jaszczolt, 169–190. New York, NY: Cambridge University Press.

Leech, Geoffrey. 1983. *Principles of Pragmatics*. London, UK: Longman.

Levinson, Stephen. 1983. *Pragmatics*. Cambridge, UK: Cambridge University Press.

Levinson, Stephen 1992. "Activity types and language." In *Talk at Work: Interaction in Institutional Settings*, edited by Paul Drew and John Heritage, 66–100. Cambridge, UK: Cambridge University Press.

Levinson, Stephen. 1995. "Three levels of meaning." In *Grammar and Meaning: Essays in Honour of Sir John Lyons*, edited by Frank Palmer, 90–115. Cambridge, UK: Cambridge University Press.

Levinson, Stephen. 2000. *Presumptive Meanings: The Theory of Generalized Conversational Implicature*. Cambridge, MA.: MIT Press.

Lyons, John. 1977. *Semantics*, Vol. 1. Cambridge, UK: Cambridge University Press.

Macagno, Fabrizio. 2011. "The presumptions of meaning. Hamblin and equivocation." *Informal Logic* 31(4): 367–393 . https://doi.org/10.22329/il.v31i4.3326.

Macagno, Fabrizio. 2012. "Presumptive reasoning in interpretation. Implicatures and conflicts of presumptions." *Argumentation* 26(2): 233–265. https://doi.org/10.1007/s10503-011-9232-9.

Macagno, Fabrizio, and Sarah Bigi. 2017. "Analyzing the pragmatic structure of dialogues." *Discourse Studies* 19(2): 148–168. https://doi.org/10.1177/1461445617691702.

Macagno, Fabrizio, and Alessandro Capone. 2016. "Interpretative disputes, explicatures, and argumentative reasoning." *Argumentation* 30(4): 399–422. https://doi.org/10.1007/s10503-015-9347-5.

Macagno, Fabrizio, and Douglas Walton. 2012. "Presumptions in legal argumentation." *Ratio Juris* 25(3): 271–300. https://doi.org/10.1111/j.1467-9337.2012.00514.x.

Macagno, Fabrizio, and Douglas Walton. 2013. "Implicatures as forms of argument." In *Perspectives on Pragmatics and Philosophy*, edited by Alessandro Capone, Franco Lo Piparo, and Marco Carapezza, 203–225. Cham, Switzerland: Springer.

Macagno, Fabrizio, and Douglas Walton. 2014. *Emotive Language in Argumentation*. New York, NY: Cambridge University Press.

Macagno, Fabrizio, and Douglas Walton. 2015. "Classifying the patterns of natural arguments." *Philosophy and Rhetoric* 48(1): 26–53. https://doi.org/10.1353/par.2015.0005.

Macagno, Fabrizio, and Douglas Walton. 2017. *Interpreting Straw Man Argumentation. The Pragmatics of Quotation and Reporting*. Amsterdam, Netherlands: Springer.

Macagno, Fabrizio, Douglas Walton, and Giovanni Sartor. 2014. "Argumentation schemes for statutory interpretation." In *Proceedings of JURIX 2014: The Twenty-Seventh Annual Conference on Legal Knowledge and Information Systems*, edited by Rinke Hoekstra, 11–20. Amsterdam, Netherlands: IOS Press.

MacCormick, Neil. 1995. "Argumentation and interpretation in law." *Argumentation* 9(3): 467–480. https://doi.org/10.1007/BF00733152.

MacCormick, Neil. 2005. *Rhetoric and the Rule of Law*. Oxford, UK: Oxford University Press.

MacCormick, Neil, and Robert Summers, eds. 1991. *Interpreting Statutes: A Comparative Study*. Aldershot, UK: Dartmouth.

Manning, John. 2003. "The absurdity doctrine." *Harvard Law Review* 116(8): 2387–2486.

Margolis, Joseph. 1973. "Meaning, speakers' intentions, and speech acts." *The Review of Metaphysics* 26(4): 681–695.

Marmor, Andrei. 2008. "The pragmatics of legal language." *Ratio Juris* 21(4): 423–452. https://doi.org/10.1111/j.1467-9337.2008.00400.x.

Marmor, Andrei. 2011. "Can the law imply more than it says? On some pragmatic aspects of strategic speech." In *Philosophical Foundations of Language in the Law*, edited by Andrei Marmor and Scott Soames, 83–104. Oxford, UK: Oxford University Press.

Marmor, Andrei. 2014. *The Language of Law*. Oxford, UK: Oxford University Press.

Mel'cuk, Igor. 1997. "Vers une lnguistique sens-texte." In *Leçon Inaugurale, Collège de France, Chaire Internationale*. http://olst.ling.umontreal.ca/pdf/MelcukColldeFr.pdf

Mey, Jacob. 2001. *Pragmatics. An Introduction*. Oxford, UK: Blackwell.

Miller, Geoffrey. 1990. "Pragmatics and the maxims of interpretation." *University of Wisconsin Law*, 1179–1227.

Morra, Lucia. 2016a. "Conversational implicatures in normative texts." In *Interdisciplinary Studies in Pragmatics, Culture and Society*, edited by Alessandro Capone and Jacob Mey, 537–562. Cham, Switzerland: Springer.

Morra, Lucia. 2016b. "Widening the Gricean picture to strategic exchanges." In *Pragmatics and Law: Philosophical Perspectives*, edited by Alessandro Capone and Francesca Poggi, 201–229. Cham, Switzerland: Springer.

Neale, Stephen. 1992. "Paul Grice and the philosophy of language." *Linguistics and Philosophy* 15(5): 509–559. https://doi.org/10.1007/BF00630629.

Oaksford, Mike, and Nick Chater. 1998. *Rationality in an Uncertain World: Essays on the Cognitive Science of Human Reasoning*. Hove, UK: Psychology Press.

Patterson, Dennis. 2005. "Interpretation in law." *San Diego Law Review* 42: 685–710.

Perelman, Chaim. 1976. *Logique Juridique*. Paris, France: Dalloz.

Poggi, Francesca. 2011. "Law and conversational implicatures." *International Journal for the Semiotics of Law-Revue Internationale de Sémiotique Juridique* 24(1): 21–40. https://doi.org /10.1007/s11196-010-9201-x.

Pollock, John. 1987. "Defeasible reasoning." *Cognitive Science* 11(4): 481–518. https://doi.org /10.1207/s15516709cog1104_4.

Prakken, Henry, and Giovanni Sartor. 1996. "A dialectical model of assessing conflicting arguments in legal reasoning." *Artificial Intelligence and Law* 4: 331–368. https://doi.org/10 .1007/BF00118496

Recanati, François. 2003. *Literal Meaning*. Cambridge, UK: Cambridge University Press.

Recanati, François. 2010. *Truth-Conditional Pragmatics*. Oxford, UK: Oxford University Press.

Rescher, Nicholas. 2006. *Presumption and the Practices of Tentative Cognition*. Cambridge, UK: Cambridge University Press.

Sarangi, Srikant, and Stefaan Slembrouck. 1992. "Non-cooperation in communication: A reassessment of Gricean pragmatics." *Journal of Pragmatics* 17(2): 117–154. https://doi .org/10.1016/0378-2166(92)90037-C.

Saul, Jennifer M. 2002. "Speaker meaning, what is said, and what is implicated." *Nous* 36(2): 228–248. https://doi.org/10.1111/1468–0068.00369.

Scalia, Antonin. 1998. *A Matter of Interpretation: Federal Courts and the Law*. Princeton, NJ: Princeton University Press.

Scalia, Antonin, and Bryan Garner. 2012. *Reading Law: The Interpretation of Legal Texts*. Eagan, MN: Thomson West.

Schiffer, Stephen. 1972. *Meaning*. Oxford, UK: Oxford University Press.

Searle, John. 1979. *Expression and Meaning: Studies in the Theory of Speech Acts*. Cambridge, UK: Cambridge University Press.

Shuy, Roger. 2011. *The Language of Perjury Cases*. New York, NY:: Oxford University Press.

Simons, Mandy. 2013. "On the conversational basis of some presuppositions." In *Perspectives on Linguistic Pragmatics, Perspectives in Pragmatics, Philosophy & Psychology 2*, edited by Alessandro Capone, Franco Lo Piparo, and Marco Carapezza, 329–348. Cham, Switzerland: Springer.

Sinclair, Michael. 1985. "Law and language: The role of pragmatics in statutory interpretation." *University of Pittsburgh Law Review* 46: 373–420.

Skoczeń, Izabela. 2016. "Minimal semantics and legal interpretation." *International Journal for the Semiotics of Law* 29(3): 615–633. https://doi.org/10.1007/s11196-015-9448-3.

Skoczeń, Izabela. 2019. *Implicatures within Legal Language*. Cham, Switzerland: Springer.

Slocum, Brian. 2016a. "Conversational implicatures and legal texts." *Ratio Juris* 29(1): 23–43. https://doi.org/10.1111/raju.12114.

Slocum, Brian. 2016b. *Ordinary Meaning: A Theory of the Most Fundamental Principle of Legal Interpretation*. Chicago, IL: University of Chicago Press.

Smolka, Jennifer, and Benedikt Pirker. 2016. "International law and pragmatics. An account of interpretation in international law." *International Journal of Language & Law* 5: 1–40. https://doi.org/10.14762/jll.2016.001.

Soames, Scott. 2009. "Interpreting legal texts: What is, and what is not, special about the law." In *Philosophical Essays*, 1: 403–424. Princeton, NJ: Princeton University Press.

Soames, Scott. 2011. "Toward a theory of legal interpretation." *NYU Law School Journal of Law and Liberty* 6: 231–259.

Solan, Lawrence. 2002. "The Clinton scandal: Some legal lessons from linguistics." In *Language in the Legal Process*, edited by Janet Cotterill, 180–195. New York, NY: Palgrave.

Solan, Lawrence, and Peter Tiersma. 2005. *Speaking of Crime: The Language of Criminal Justice*. Chicago, IL: University of Chicago Press.

Sperber, Dan, and Deirdre Wilson. 1995. *Relevance: Communication and Cognition*. Oxford, UK: Blackwell Publishing Ltd.

Tarello, Giovanni. 1980. *L'interpretazione della Legge*. Milano, Italy: Giuffrè.

Tiersma, Peter. 1990. "The language of perjury: Literal truth, ambiguity, and the false statement requirement." *Southern California Law Review* 63: 373.431.

Toulmin, Stephen. 1958. *The Uses of Argument*. Cambridge, UK: Cambridge University Press.

Toulmin, Stephen, Richard Rieke, and Allan Janik. 1984. *An Introduction to Reasoning*. New York, NY: Macmillan Publishing Company.

Walton, Douglas. 1995. *Argumentation Schemes for Presumptive Reasoning*.Mahwah, NJ: Routledge.

Walton, Douglas. 2002. *Legal Argumentation and Evidence*. University Park, PA: The Pennsylvania State University Press.

Walton, Douglas. 2011. "Defeasible reasoning and informal fallacies." *Synthese* 179(3): 377–407. https://doi.org/10.1007/s11229-009-9657-y.

Walton, Douglas. 2016. *Argument Evaluation and Evidence*. Cham, Switzerland: Springer.

Walton, Douglas, and Fabrizio Macagno. 2007. "Types of dialogue, dialectical relevance and textual congruity." *Anthropology & Philosophy* 8(1–2): 101–119.

Walton, Douglas, and Fabrizio Macagno. 2009. "Reasoning from classifications and definitions." *Argumentation* 23(1): 81–107. https://doi.org/10.1007/s10503-008–9110-2.

Walton, Douglas, and Fabrizio Macagno. 2016. "Profiles of dialogue for relevance." *Informal Logic* 36(4): 523–556. https://doi.org/10.22329/il.v36i4.4586.

Walton, Douglas, Christopher Reed, and Fabrizio Macagno. 2008. *Argumentation Schemes*. New York, NY: Cambridge University Press.

Walton, Douglas, Giovanni Sartor, and Fabrizio Macagno. 2016. "An argumentation framework for contested cases of statutory interpretation." *Artificial Intelligence and Law* 24(1): 51–91. https://doi.org/10.1007/s10506-016–9179-0.

Weinstock, Charles B., John B. Goodenough, and Ari Z. Klein. 2013. "Measuring assurance case confidence using Baconian probabilities." In *2013 1st International Workshop on Assurance Cases for Software-Intensive Systems (ASSURE)*, 7–11. San Francisco, CA: IEEE.

Wilson, Deirdre. 2005. "New directions for research on pragmatics and modularity." *Lingua* 115(8): 1129–1146. https://doi.org/10.1016/j.lingua.2004.02.005.

Ziff, Paul. 1967. "On HP Grice's account of meaning." *Analysis* 28(1): 1–8. https://doi.org/10.1093/analys/28.1.1.

CASES CITED

Bond v. United States 2011 564 U.S. 211.

Dunnachie v. Kingston-upon-Hull City Council 2004 UKHL 36.

Garner v. Burr [1951] 1 KB 31.

Nix v. Hedden 1893 149 U.S. 304.

Smith v. United States 1993 508 U.S. 223.

United States v. Bronston 1971 453 F.2d 555.

5

Arguments of Statutory Interpretation and Argumentation Schemes

5.1 INTRODUCTION

As shown in the previous chapters, interpretation is at the crossroad between linguistics – and in particular pragmatics – and legal theory. When we analyzed the relationship between the Gricean and neo-Gricean pragmatic frameworks and the instruments used in legal interpretation, we pointed out the role of presumptions and defeasibility in assessing the strength of an interpretation. In this perspective, pragmatic maxims and interpretative canons are both useful tools for justifying an interpretation, but alone do not provide any criteria for establishing the superiority of an argument – and consequently of a justified interpretation – over another. In our previous chapter, we pointed out how a hierarchy of presumptions based on their defeasibility conditions can guide the process of assessment. In this view, the less defeasible arguments are those that are based on specific presumptions, namely defeasible generalizations linking an interpretation to specific features of a text or co-text. These presumptions ground an interpretative hypothesis directly on evidence that cannot be controversial, and thus they are less likely to be defeated by further evidence.

This framework, however, does not exhaust the concept of defeasibility of an argument. The strength of a presumption lies in the possibility of finding evidence that undercuts its probative strength (Bergmann, 2005; Pollock, 1984, 1986, 38–39) (the "standard default proviso"), but this possibility represents *one* of the aspects of the defeasibility of the argument that is based thereon. The conclusion can be defeasible not only because the presumption can be easily undercut by counter-evidence, but also because the inference that is drawn from it is weak or can be rebutted by stronger types of argument (Pollock, 1995). In this perspective, the evaluation of interpretative arguments becomes an essential aspect of the interpretative process, but neither pragmatics nor the theories of legal interpretation provide an account of how arguments are analyzed, and their defeasible dimensions brought to light. Both approaches focus on one dimension of interpretative arguments, namely the specific "maxim" or *idia* (the specific topics) in the dialectical tradition

(Macagno and Walton, 2014a; Rubinelli, 2009, 59–70; Stump, 1989, 29; de Pater, 1965, 134; Everardus *Loci Argumentorum Legales*). According to Aristotle, the specific topics represent generalizations that concern specific disciplines, such as ethics, law, or medicine, which are used to draw specific conclusions. However, their inferential force can be understood only by considering the category of generic topic they fall under. To this purpose, we need to resort to the tools provided by the modern development of ancient dialectics, namely argumentation theory, and in particular the modern interpretation of the ancient dialectical and rhetorical *topoi* or commonplaces (Balkin, 2018).

The relationship between the canons of interpretation used in legal theory and dialectics was clearly pointed out by Viehweg (1953), who related the former to the ancient theory of topics (Chiassoni, Feteris, and Kreuzbauer, 2016; Kreuzbauer, 2008). The dialectical and argumentative dimension of legal interpretation was underscored by several authors (Dascal and Wróblewski, 1988; MacCormick, 1995; Patterson, 2005; Perelman, 1980; Perelman, 1976), who stressed how the "best" interpretation of a legal statement should be based on the analysis and evaluation of the arguments on which it is grounded.

The purpose of this chapter[1] is to investigate and classify the structure of the generic arguments used in statutory interpretation, starting from the logical analysis of interpretative arguments provided in works by Macagno, Sartor, and Walton (Macagno, Walton, and Sartor, 2014; Walton, Sartor, and Macagno, 2016). We will first summarize the theoretical framework based on the relationship between argumentation, pragmatics, and legal interpretation that was defended in Chapter 1 and Chapter 4, to provide a clear ground for the terminology we will be using in the following sections as well as the reasons supporting a dialectical (argumentative) account of interpretative arguments. Then, we will reconstruct the structure of the legal arguments (Tarello, 1980) in civil law systems and in common law (MacCormick, 1995; MacCormick and Summers, 1991), translating them into argumentation schemes (Walton, Reed, and Macagno, 2008). By means of a series of examples, we will discuss how to classify these schemes, how to apply them to cases, and how to use them to bring to light the defeasibility conditions and inferential structures of interpretative arguments.

5.2 INTERPRETATION AND ITS ARGUMENTS

As maintained in Chapter 1 and Chapter 4, the activity of deliberative interpretation (interpretation in the strict sense, distinct from a broader concept of interpretation covering any meaning assignment, see Guastini, 2011; Tarello, 1980) presupposes

---

[1] This chapter is based on a paper by Macagno, F., and Walton, D. (2017), "Arguments of statutory interpretation and argumentation schemes." *International Journal of Legal Discourse*, 2(1), 47–83. Several positions defended in this earlier paper concerning several aspects of interpretative schemes and argumentations schemes have been modified and corrected in the present chapter.

a doubt, namely an implicit or explicit conflict of opinions, concerning the meaning of a word, a sentence or a text (Patterson, 2005; Slocum, 2016b). It starts when no prima facie understanding (Dascal and Wróblewski, 1988) is obtained directly, or when multiple incompatible prima facie meanings are provided, or also when the prima facie meaning fails to satisfy the concerns of the interpreter, so that doubts are raised and need to be addressed (Dascal and Wróblewski, 1988, 204; Kennedy, 2007, 303–304).

This concept of interpretation is grounded on the etymology of the term, which we outlined in Chapter 1. An interpretation addresses a lack of understanding, or more generally a doubt, which needs to be solved by resorting to special tools, such as another code or language, or other terms. For this reason, interpretation cannot have as an object uncontroversial content that does not need any justification. Rather, interpretation arises when the attribution of meaning to an utterance is doubtful or problematic (Slocum, 2016b, 4), namely in the cases in which the "direct understanding" of an utterance leads to different ascriptions of meaning, or conflicts with contextual or co-textual clues, including the expectations related to the communicative setting (Dascal, 2003, 13–17; Dascal and Wróblewski, 1988, 204).

In this perspective, the role of pragmatics becomes crucial. As pointed out in our previous chapters, pragmatics is involved in both the specification of "what is said," namely the enrichment of the logical form of an utterance, which is normally called "enriched representation" or in other theories, "utterance type" (see Levinson, 2000, 21–22), and the further inferences that are drawn in actual contexts by actual recipients with all of their particularities, which may result in an "utterance token" different from the "type." The intermediate level of "utterance type" (Atlas, 1989) is normally regarded as a kind of "default but defeasible inference" (Levinson, 1987, 723), which is based on stereotypes (Atlas, 2005, 29; Atlas and Levinson, 1981). This type of reasoning is local and prepropositional (Jaszczolt, 2008), consisting in the application of default rules associated with specific lexical items or syntactic constructions (e.g., "some" is usually interpreted as "not all"). These types of conventional implicatures, not based on linguistic conventions but rather on conventions of use, are called "generalized conversational implicatures" (Grice, 1975, 56), and are defaultive, as they are implicated by an utterance unless there are unusual specific contextual assumptions that defeat it (Levinson, 2000, 16). In contrast, indirect meaning (from Anna's utterance "I need to talk to Bob privately," it is possible to infer that the interlocutor needs to leave) is the result of a different type of reasoning. These "particularized" conversational implicatures are inferred from an utterance "on a particular occasion in virtue of special features of the context, cases in which there is no room for the idea that an implicature of this sort is normally carried by it" (Grice, 1975, 56).

The relationship between pragmatics and interpretation is thus more complex and broader than the prototypical cases of particularized implicatures, which, as Marmor pointed out (Marmor, 2008, 429), are very rare, as legal texts depend minimally on the norms of conversation and the "context." However, it is necessary to underscore also that a provision's legal meaning often deviates from its ordinary meaning (Slocum, 2016b, 7), due to the conflicts between what the law says and its purpose. Despite this difference of opinion, the cases in which "the content the legislature prescribes is not exactly what it says," namely the cases in which the prescribed content (utterance token or speaker's meaning) corresponds to a particularized conversational implicature, correspond only to the most prototypical case in which the pragmatic processes underlying the reconstruction of the "speaker's meaning" do not correspond to default inferences. As discussed in Chapters 3 and 4, the enrichment (specification) of the logical form of an utterance – a crucial dimension of the interpretation of legal texts (Slocum, 2016a) – is grounded on the same pragmatic principles underlying the reconstruction of indirect meaning but starting from conventions of use (Hutton, 2009, 72–73). However, such default inferences can be contradicted by textual, extratextual, or metatextual evidence or presumptions (Dascal, 2003, 15), making them doubtful or controversial. In these cases, the default reasoning becomes more complex, as the most acceptable interpretative hypothesis needs to be justified. Here is how Dascal and Wróblewski put it (1988, 214), where "L-interpretation" refers to *sensu lato* and "S-interpretation" refers to *sensu stricto*:

> [P]ragmatic interpretation cannot be restricted to working out indirect meaning. For, unless at least a summary contextual check of appropriateness is made, one can never know whether the utterance-meaning corresponds to the speaker's-meaning. Making such a check amounts to asking whether there are reasons not to accept the utterance-meaning at face value. If the answer is "No," one can say that the utterance is "transparent." If it is "Yes," a heuristic for generating and checking alternative interpretations is put to work until a "No" answer is reached for a given interpretative hypothesis which is then taken to be the speaker's-meaning of the utterance in that context. Though fallible in principle, since it is not algorithmic but heuristic, not deductive (nor inductive) but abductive, this process of interpretation is in general fairly reliable and convergent. Pragmatic interpretation is, thus, always required, even in the case of transparency. It corresponds, in a sense, to the notion of L-interpretation... In this framework, the notions of clarity and S-interpretation can be reconstructed as follows: clarity means "transparency," i.e., endorsement of the "computed" utterance-meaning or, if you wish, straightforward L-interpretation, while S-interpretation refers to a lack of transparency (a "yes" answer to the checking question) that leads to a search for an "indirect" meaning of the utterance or text.

Thus, as we explained in detail in Chapter 4.3, the linguistic conventions and the default inferences that result in an "utterance type" can be contradicted by specific evidence and presumptions, leading to a more complex type of reasoning.

As pointed out in our previous chapters, understanding does not involve a burden of proof, as it is the default explanation that holds until contrary evidence (i.e., challenges or a nonprototypical context) emerges. When these conditions do not apply, the default explanation ceases to be as such. It becomes one of the possible interpretations that are considered as potentially controversial and, therefore, need to be grounded on arguments. The various arguments advanced to support an interpretation need to defeat the other possible alternatives. They need to show that the advocated explanation of meaning is better (more adequate, more suitable) than the others.

Considering this background, this chapter will be devoted to analyzing the argumentative structure of legal interpretation, namely the arguments that are used in the nondefaultive (and automatic) process of meaning attribution. To this purpose, it is necessary to translate the linguistic terminology into a vocabulary that is specific to the interpretative activity under analysis. Following the account of Tarello and Guastini, we refer to the rule, which is the result of an interpretative process, as the "meaning" of a statement of law.[2] We can then distinguish the following objects we are dealing with:

- **Source statements**: Statements contained in legal sources, meant to express legal rules. They correspond to the "utterances" analyzed in pragmatics.
- **Prima facie understanding of a source statement**: The legal content, if any, that in a certain sociolinguistic context is attributed by default to the source statement (and the activity of grasping such a rule). In pragmatics, it would be referred to as "utterance type" or "specific semantic representation" or "enriched logical form."
- **Interpretative statement**: A statement affirming that a source statement has a certain meaning (expresses a certain legal content), made to overcome a doubt on its understanding (to select this one, among other possible meanings of the same source). Such statements would express the speaker's meaning (or utterance-token meaning) in pragmatics.
- **Interpretation**: The legal content that is attributed to a source statement, which amounts to an answer to a doubt on its understanding (and the activity of making and supporting such statement).
- **Arguments of interpretation**: The arguments provided to support a particular interpretation of a source statement.

As claimed in the Introduction, Walton, Macagno, and Sartor (Macagno, Walton, and Sartor, 2014; Walton, Macagno, and Sartor, 2014) compiled a list of interpretative arguments identified by MacCormick and Summers (MacCormick, 1995; MacCormick and Summers, 1991), and compared them with the fourteen types

---

[2] Interpretation reduces the vagueness of the statements of law, identifying the specific cases that are governed by such statements of law (Guastini, 2011, p. 18). In this view, the "meaning" corresponds to both *Sinn* and *Bedeutung* (Guastini, 2011, p. 6).

previously identified by Tarello (Tarello, 1980, Chapter 8) and the most important of the "semantic" and "contextual" canons described by Scalia and Garner (2012) and Balkin (Balkin, 2018). These arguments can be classified in five general categories, which we classify on the basis of their argumentative structure:

1. Argument from the Exclusion of what is not stated (*A Contrario* Arguments).
2. Argument from Analogy (requiring the similarity of meaning between similar provisions)

   a. *Extending a Category to a Similar Case (Analogia Legis).*
   b. *Argument from General Principles (Analogia Iuris).*
   c. *Other analogical arguments. Eiusdem Generis.*
   d. *Noscitur a sociis.*
   e. Argument *a fortiori*.

3. Arguments from Authority:

   a. Psychological Argument.
   b. Historical Argument.
   c. Authoritative Argument.
   d. Naturalistic Argument (or Natural Meaning Argument).

4. Practical Arguments:

   a. Absurdity Argument (*Reductio ad Absurdum*).
   b. Equitative Argument.
   c. Argument from Coherence of the Law.
   d. Economic Argument.
   e. Teleological (or Purposive) Argument.

5. Abductive Arguments

   a. Ordinary and Technical Meaning arguments.
   b. Systematic Argument.
   c. Argument from Completeness of the Law.

Some crucial problems concerning these types of interpretative arguments concern their use (in training legal practitioners or scholars) and their relations with the works in argumentation theory and logic on argument analysis and reconstruction. Recently, the canons or maxims that express the general principle characterizing each type of argument have been represented as defeasible rules, to be integrated within a prioritized defeasible logic system (Rotolo, Governatori, and Sartor, 2015). In this chapter, the aforementioned types of interpretative arguments (which clearly do not exhaust the interpretative canons used in law but represent the most used and debated in legal theory) are modeled as "patterns of argument" or argumentation schemes.

Argumentation schemes (Walton et al., 2008) are the modern development of the ancient dialectical maxims or *loci* (Macagno and Walton, 2014a; Macagno, Walton, and Tindale, 2014; Walton and Macagno, 2009a). They are stereotypical and quasi-formal patterns that bring to light the semantic principles connecting premises and conclusions and the logical structure of inferences (Bird, 1962). They allow identifying the type and assessing the strength of interpretative reasoning by providing a set of critical questions, or points of defeasibility, associated with the types of argument represented according to their most prototypical logical pattern (Macagno and Walton, 2015; Walton and Macagno, 2015). By translating the interpretative canons into argumentation schemes, interpretative reasoning is framed within a broader dialectical framework, involving a specific burden of bearing out and defeating a specific interpretation (Gizbert-Studnicki, 1990) and connecting legal theory with linguistics and argumentation.

5.3 ARGUMENTATION SCHEMES

Argumentation schemes represent the structure of defeasible arguments, namely arguments not proceeding from the meaning of quantifiers or connectors only, but rather from the semantic relations between the concepts involved. This account is rooted in Toulmin's notion of warrant, which he defines as "general, hypothetical statements, which can act as bridges, and authorize the sort of step to which our particular argument commits us" (Toulmin, 1958, 91). These warrants can be different in nature: they can be grounded on laws, principles of classification, statistics, authority, causal relations, or ethical principles. They have become the principle of classification of arguments (Toulmin, Rieke, and Janik, 1984, 199). Building on this approach, the idea of argumentation schemes was developed, representing the combination between a semantic principle (such as classification, cause, consequence, authority) and a type of reasoning, such as deductive, inductive, or abductive reasoning. Their main purpose as regards legal argumentation is to provide abstract patterns representing types of arguments that carry probative weight for supporting or attacking a conclusion, but in the most typical instances are defeasible. Such arguments do not lead to necessarily true conclusions and are not based on necessarily true premises.

Most of the argumentation schemes listed in the book *Argumentation Schemes* (Walton et al., 2008) have a defeasible *modus ponens* structure, grounded on a conditional defeasible generalization. A standard example is the following expanded scheme for argument from expert opinion, which we will discuss further in Section 5.7 (Walton et al., 2008, 19).

ARGUMENTATION SCHEME 3 *Argument from Expert Opinion*

Minor premise 1:	Source E is an expert in subject domain S containing proposition A.
Minor premise 2:	E asserts that proposition A (in domain S) is true (false).
Major premise:	If source E is an expert in a subject domain S containing proposition A, and E asserts that proposition A is true (false), then A may plausibly be taken to be true (false).
Conclusion:	A may plausibly be taken to be true (false).

It is readily visible that this version of the scheme for argument from expert opinion has a *modus ponens* structure as an inference. Since experts are generally not omniscient, and since in law it would be a great error to take what an expert says uncritically, this inference must be viewed as being defeasible.

Subsequent work on argumentation schemes has followed this general way of representing the logical structure of many defeasible argumentation schemes. Bench-Capon and Prakken view the application of defeasible rules (such as legal or moral norms) as instances of defeasible *modus ponens*. They represent any inference warranted by a defeasible rule of this sort by a semicolon connective (;). Below is their basic argument scheme for applying defeasible rules, called the Rule Application Scheme (Bench-Capon and Prakken, 2010, 159):

$$r: P_1, \ldots, P_n ; Q$$
$$P_1, \ldots, P_n$$
$$Q$$

The letter r indicates the name of the rule. The following two critical questions match this scheme (Bench-Capon and Prakken, 2010, 159):

CQ_1: Is r valid?

CQ_2: Is r applicable to the current case?

Critical questions concerning an inference scheme indicate situations that can be presumptively assumed when reasoning with the scheme, but whose nonexistence would put the application of the scheme into question. Negative answers to critical questions can be reformulated as counterarguments that undercut (make inapplicable) the concerned scheme or contradict (rebut) its premises (Walton and Sartor, 2013).

Now we can see, in general, that our conditional rule for framing interpretative arguments is a general pattern for defeasible rules or argument schemes that can be cast into this format. Below, this rule has been expanded into a defeasible *modus ponens* form of inference:

If a statement/term X has the property P, then X should (not) be given meaning M.
This statement/term X has the property P.
Therefore X should (not) be given meaning M.

This abstract structure of inference represents the most generic pattern that the interpretative arguments have. In this perspective, the different argumentation schemes can be adapted to the specific field of interpretation by specifying the abstract variables of the defeasible *modus ponens* pattern. This form of inference can be used to translate the aforementioned arguments described by Tarello into argumentation schemes.

The translation of the canons into the more general schemes is clearly extremely controversial and problematic. For example, the category of authoritative arguments in Tarello's list might relate to the scheme for argument from expert opinion. This leads to the more general problems of whether we should distinguish different kinds of arguments from authority. One is the "epistemic" kind, being based on superior knowledge, wisdom, or competence, as the authority of expert witnesses in legal proceedings, or the authority of legal scholars on matters concerning their expertise. Another is the "institutional" kind, being based on the capacity to enact statements that are legally or socially binding (this is the case for legislators, administrative authorities, and judges). We can acknowledge also a kind of authority of institutional statements that are not institutionally binding, but still are considered to have some weight, such as political commitments by legislators, guidelines by administrative authorities, or *obiter dicta* in binding precedents, or nonbinding precedents.

The nature of different claims based on authority is related to the problem of understanding how Tarello's version of interpretative argument from authority fits in with schemes from MacCormick and Summers' list, such as argument from precedent, argument from a legal concept, argument from general principles, and argument from history. None of these questions can be discussed in this chapter, for reasons of length, but they need to be recognized here as problems for future research. Another similar problem is how the interpretative argument from precedent, as it is called in MacCormick and Summers' list, is related to the general scheme for argument from precedent, already recognized in the argumentation literature. The problem is that there are great divisions of opinion on precisely how the scheme should be modeled. Argument from precedent is considered by some authors as always based on argument from analogy, that is, on a comparison between a source case and a target case. But this claim is opposed by the argument that the *legal* argument from precedent needs to be based on the *ratio decidendi*. Another question raised by this difference of opinion is whether the *ratio decidendi* represents some kind of analogy between the two cases where the rationale used to arrive at the conclusion in the source case is supposed to be similar to a comparable rationale that can fit the target case. For these reasons, the classification we are going to propose is only a tentative one, and can lead to several criticisms depending on the theoretical viewpoint from which it is read and analyzed. However, our overall goal is to show that it is possible to combine the instruments used in the disciplines of argumentation studies and legal theory to study how interpretations are argued for or against.

5.4 A CONTRARIO ARGUMENT

The argument *a contrario* can be summarized by the Latin principle *Ubi lex voluit, dixit; ubi noluit, tacuit* (what the law wants, it states, what the law does not want, it keeps silent upon). According to this maxim, if a rule attributes any normative property (such as a power, an obligation, or a status) to an individual or a category of individuals, in the absence of any other explicit rules, it shall be excluded that a different rule is in force (exists, is valid) attributing the same quality to any other individual or category of individuals (Tarello, 1980, 346). This argument excludes an interpretation wider than the literal one, and it rebuts any analogical or extensive interpretation (Guastini, 2011, 271). For instance, Article 17, paragraph 1 of the Italian Constitution provides that: "All citizens have the right to assemble peaceably and unarmed."

Is the legal predicate "to have the right of assembly" also attributable to foreigners and stateless people? If we use the argument *a contrario*, we proceed from the principle that if the law wished to vest such a right in foreigners and stateless people, it would have stated it (Guastini, 2011, 272). Since there are no legal provisions relative thereto, it shall be concluded that such a predicate is attributed *only* to citizens. As a consequence, foreigners and stateless people will be excluded from such a right.

The argument *a contrario* concerns what a law does not provide for. At common law, this argument is usually referred to as "*expressio unius est exclusio alterius.*" A clear case is the US Supreme Court case *Leatherman* v. *Tarrant County Narcotics Intelligence & Coordination Unit* (507 U.S. 163 (1992)). The issue concerned the interpretation of the rules for filing a claim for relief in a specific circumstance in which a claim for alleged unwarranted search of plaintiff for narcotics was brought against local officials acting in their official capacity, a county, and two municipal corporations. The plaintiff's complaint had been rejected for not including a detailed and particular description of the basis for the claim, as requested by the Court of Appeals in complaints against municipal corporations. The problem was that this standard conflicted with Rule 8(a)(2) of the Federal Rules of Civil Procedure, which provided that a claim for relief must contain only "a short and plain statement of the claim showing that the pleader is entitled to relief." The only exception is stated in Rule 9(b): "In alleging fraud or mistake, a party must state with particularity the circumstances constituting fraud or mistake," which does not include among the enumerated actions any reference to complaints alleging municipal liability. The Supreme Court reasoned as shown in Case 5.1. (507 U.S. 163, 168):

CASE 5.1: *A CONTRARIO*

Perhaps if Rules 8 and 9 were rewritten today, claims against municipalities under § 1983 might be subjected to the added specificity requirement of Rule 9(b). But that is a result which must be obtained by the process of amending the Federal Rules, and not by judicial interpretation. In the absence of such an amendment, federal courts and litigants must rely on summary judgment and control of discovery to weed out unmeritorious claims sooner rather than later.

This type of reasoning can be represented in Figure 5.1, in which the *a contrario* argument is used for undercutting the argument, namely attacking the application of the rule.

In this figure, the pro argument advanced by the respondent (Tarrant County Narcotics Intelligence and Coordination Unit) is grounded on the rule (established by a previous case) that requires a detailed description of the claim. This argument, however, is rebutted by the *a contrario* reasoning based on Rules 8 and 9 of the Federal Rules of Civil Procedure. Since a heightened pleading standard (a detailed description of the claim) is required only in cases of fraud or mistake, which do not correspond to the cause of complaint in the pleaded case, such a standard should not be considered as applicable to it.

The reasoning structure of this argument can be modeled according to argumentation scheme 1A.

ARGUMENTATION SCHEME 1A *A Contrario*

Major premise:	If x is P, then x has the right/is A.
Closed-world premise:	In lack of contrary provisions, if x is not P, then x does not have the right/ is not A.
Minor premise:	Individual a is not P.
Conclusion:	Therefore, individual a does not have the right/is not A.

In this case, we need to notice that the reasoning is effective only in a closed-world scenario. In other terms, the conclusion can be drawn only in conditions of lack of contrary evidence, that is, when no other laws setting out the attribution of the same predicate to other categories are known. For this reason, the crucial logical assumption behind this type of reasoning can be represented as a form of reasoning from ignorance, as shown in argumentation scheme 1B (Walton et al., 2008, 327).

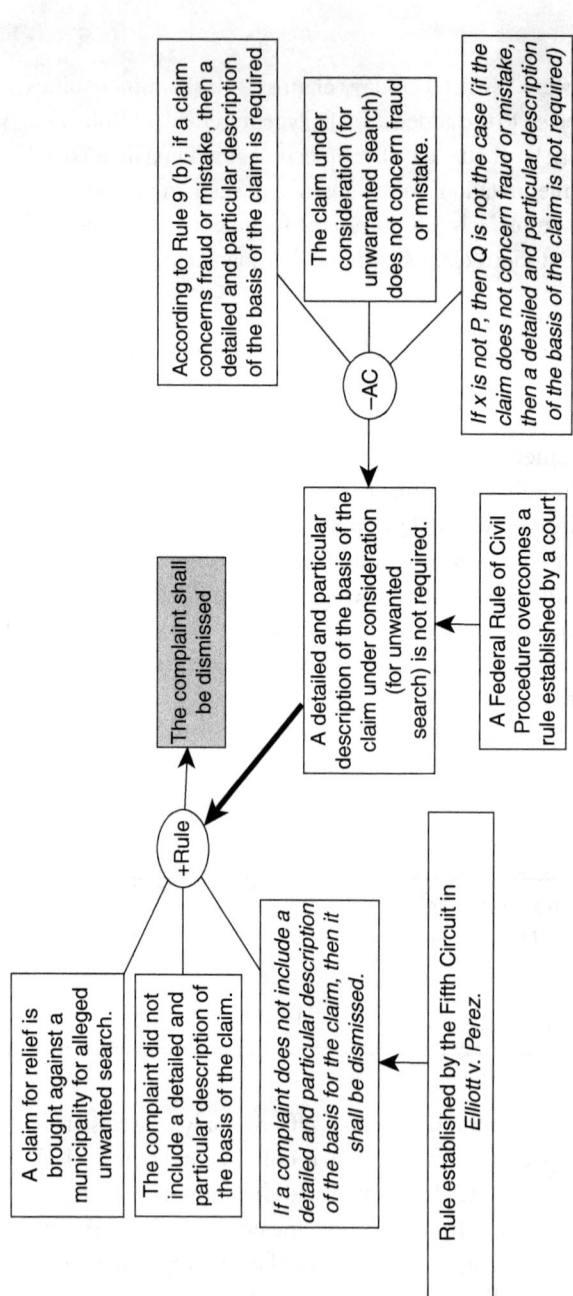

FIGURE 5.1 *A contrario* reasoning in *Leatherman v. Tarrant County*

ARGUMENTATION SCHEME 1B *Argument from Ignorance*

Major premise:	If *A* were true, then *A* would be known to be true.
Minor premise:	It is not the case that *A* is known to be true.
Conclusion:	Therefore, *A* is not true.

This argument represents the passage from lack of knowledge to negation. Similarly, the closed-world premise supports the inference from the absence of a provision for attributing a predicate to category of individuals to the negation of the predicate for such a category. Based on the critical questions of the argument from ignorance (Walton, 1996, 84–86) and the relationship between the Q and I(R) principles described in our previous chapter, the *a contrario* argument can be challenged as follows:

CQ$_1$: Are there reasons or evidence to conclude that *x* has not the right *A*?

CQ$_2$: Is there evidence or a reason to believe that *x* has the right *A*?

CQ$_3$: Are there evidence or reasons that justify a classification of *x* as *P*?

CQ$_4$: Is an analogical extension of *P* to include *x* based on more evidence than the narrow interpretation underlying the *a contrario* argument?

The critical questions allow analyzing the argument within the framework of the possible contrary arguments, and in particular the analogical ones that can be used to extend the meaning of the category *P*.

5.5 ARGUMENTS FROM ANALOGY

The argument from similarity (or *a simili*) can be considered as opposite (from an interpretative perspective) to the argument *a contrario* (Canale and Tuzet, 2018, 67–68). Instead of excluding the attribution of the legal predicate to the entities not belonging to the category mentioned in the law, it extends it. As Tarello put it, if a rule attributes any normative qualification to an individual or a category of individuals, an argument by analogy would support the conclusion that there is a different rule in force that attributes the same quality to another individual or category of individuals connected with the former class by a similarity or an analogy relation. Such a relationship is held to be relevant from the perspective of the applicable law, or the qualification to be attributed (Tarello, 1980, 351). In law, however, the notion of analogical arguments is extremely complex, as a distinction needs to be drawn in civil law between analogical arguments and extensive interpretation.

5.5.1 *Problems of Analogy in Law*

In this chapter, we are using the term "analogy" in a very broad sense, referring to the reasoning pattern that can be found at the basis of distinct interpretative arguments. However, in civil law, analogical reasoning is at the basis of two distinct and incompatible argumentative strategies. Analogical arguments refer to the arguments used for the purposes of construction, and more specifically for "filling" a normative gap arising from the lack of available interpretations of a valid legal provision that can cover the case under discussion (Canale and Tuzet, 2018, 77–78), which however falls under the purpose of a specific provision (Langenbucher, 1998, 483–484). In contrast, extensive interpretation refers to arguments that are used for interpreting an existing legal provision, extending its content to cover the case under discussion. Thus, in civil law, while it may be said that analogical arguments develop new norms, extensive interpretations broaden the scope of existing norms. Analogical arguments presuppose that the legal provision has already been interpreted (has already been assigned a meaning); in contrast, the extensive interpretation leads to an interpretation.

From our perspective, both analogy *sensu stricto* and extensive interpretation may be viewed as forms of analogical reasoning *sensu lato*, since they are both based on a similarity between the entities that prototypically fall under the scope of a provision, and different entities to which the provision's legal effect is applied, as a result of analogy or extensive interpretation. The difference between the two argumentative patterns can be very thin and subject to different evaluations. The difference is based on distinct core presuppositions concerning the scope of the provision being interpreted. In the case of extensive interpretation, the interpreter presupposes that the application of a provision to certain entities that fall outside of the core meaning is still compatible with the semantic meaning of that provision – even though such application can be considered as unusual and even bizarre. In contrast, this assumption does not underlie analogical reasoning *sensu stricto*, which, on the contrary, presupposes that the similar entities fall outside the scope of the provision being interpreted. An example can be the issue of whether sending radio waves should be sanctioned based on a provision that prohibits causing nuisance by "throwing things" (as in the *Italian Vatican Radio* case, Cass. Pen. no. 36845/2008, see Canale and Tuzet, 2018). If we want to argue from analogy, we just need to show that "sending radio waves" is similar to "throwing material objects," and that the rationale for the prohibition of "throwing material objects" (e.g., to enable people to safely enjoy their property) also applies to the case of "sending radio waves." If we want to build an extensive interpretation, we need to show also that the meaning of the phrase "throwing things" can also include the "sending of radio waves," namely, that the use of this phrase to refer to the sending of radio waves is consistent with the common understanding of this expression (for the problem of determining the "meaning" of an expression in a context, see Chapters 3 and 4).

Consider the issue of whether the strict liability of innkeepers for thefts in the guests' rooms also applies to steamboat operators for thefts in passengers' cabins

(*Adams* v. *New Jersey Steamboat Co.*, 151 N.Y. 163, 170 (1896)). If we want to use an analogical argument, we need to focus on the similarities between inn rooms and steamboat cabins, and on the reasons for strict liability that apply to both cases (in both cases the victims left their property in closed spaces, under the control of their hosts). If we argue from an extensive interpretation, we would need also to show that it would be linguistically correct to apply the term "inn" to steamboats. In some cases, extensive interpretations are implausible, while analogies can be successful. For example, consider the issue of how to share the costs for maintenance of an elevator in a condominium under the Italian law. In the Italian Civil Code, there was a provision (Article 1124) that determined the criterion for dividing the maintenance costs for stairs (based on the floor level of the apartments to be reached through the stairs). This rule was applied analogically to elevators, while an extensive interpretation of the term "stairs" to include also "elevators" would not be linguistically correct. (In 2012, the need to analogize was overcome by the amendment of Article 1124, which now explicitly refers to "stairs or elevators.")

The distinction is crucial in the interpretation of criminal provision (in particular, but not only, in civil law systems). "Analogical arguments" are prohibited in criminal law, according to the so-called principle of legality (there should be no crime without legal provision establishing it, *nullum crimen sine lege*), unless they are used in favor of the accused, that is, to argue for a justification or extenuating circumstance. On the contrary, arguments for extensive interpretations are allowed with regard to criminal provision (Canale and Tuzet, 2018). However, as Canale and Tuzet emphasize (66), these two types of arguments are often hard to distinguish:

> Indeed, if a trial court justifies a criminal decision arguing by analogy, the decision will be reasonably quashed on appeal because it is contrary to the law. The same decision is justified, however, when it can be considered an extensive interpretation of a criminal provision, even when this is the same provision that the court could have used analogically. The problem is that in legal practice one can hardly distinguish analogy from extensive interpretation. It is very unclear whether there is a real difference between the two and where it might lie. On the one hand, some scholars claim that they differ from a theoretical point of view, since they do not have the same argumentative structure. On the other hand, analogical reasoning and extensive interpretation come to the same result starting from the same legal materials: they justify the extension of a regulation to a case that is not explicitly considered by the law.

Considering the difference between analogy and extensive interpretation, we will distinguish two broad categories of analogical arguments: the "additive" ones, corresponding to the legal canons of *analogia iuris* (or rule-based analogy) and *analogia legis* (or principle-based analogy), and the merely interpretative ones, which include the principles of *ejusdem generis* and *noscitur a sociis*. In both categories, the result of the reasoning is the use of a provision beyond its prima facie "semantic representation." However, in the interpretative category, the starting point is compliance with the core meaning of the linguistic expressions used in the provision being interpreted, while in the additive category, an essential difference is presupposed, which makes it unreasonable to classify the new case under the intended legal predicate.

The analogy based on statutory provisions can be compared to the uses of analogical arguments when reasoning from precedents (rather than in statutory interpretation). This type of reasoning proceeds from two premises: the *ratio decidendi* that establishes that a specific legal consequence follows from the facts of case *x*, and the similarity between the facts of case *x* and the facts of the new case *y*. However, the way the similarity between the two cases is established brings closer the analogical reasoning from rules and from precedent closer (Langenbucher, 1998, 494):

> To establish a similarity between a precedent and a novel case, it is not sufficient to list the total number of ways in which two cases are similar. Instead, a standard has to be established according to which the similarity is measured. It has been convincingly demonstrated that this standard lies in the rationale underlying the decision in the first case or, more often, underlying the line of precedents. This brings common law and civil law reasoning very close, the one relying on the ratio of a line of precedents, the other on the ratio legis. Two cases are therefore relevantly similar if the principle which underlies the precedents indiscriminately applies to both of them.

In the following sections, we will present the general structure of the argument from analogy, and then we will focus on the distinctions between additive analogy and extensive interpretation. Finally, we will address the purely interpretative analogical arguments.

5.5.2 *The Structure of Analogical Arguments (Additive Analogy)*

In argumentation theory, the reasoning structure of arguments from analogy is normally represented through a very generic structure, corresponding to the following (Walton et al., 2008, 315):

ARGUMENTATION SCHEME 2 *Argument from Analogy*

Major premise:	Generally, case A_1 is similar to case A_2.
Minor premise:	Predicate P is true (false) in case A_1.
Conclusion:	Predicate P is true (false) in case A_2.

This pattern relies on two crucial aspects: the concept of "similarity" between the target subject (A_2) and the analogue (A_1) and the relationship between the similarity and the assigned predicate P (Juthe, 2005, 2–3). A fundamental problem in logic, law, and philosophy of science is how to assess analogical arguments, which amounts to how to describe the analogical inference and the similarity relation on which it is based (Ashley, 2006; Ashley and Rissland, 2003; Waller, 2001; Weinreb,

2005). The critical questions cited in *Argumentation Schemes* (Walton et al., 2008) point out some fundamental dimensions of defeasibility:

CQ_1: Is P true (false) in A_1?

CQ_2: Are A_1 and A_2 similar, in the respects cited?

CQ_3: Are there important differences (dissimilarities) between A_1 and A_2?

CQ_4: Is there some other case A_3 that is also similar to A_1 except that P is false (true) in A_3?

The defeasibility aspects mentioned, however, do not address two basic issues: (1) determining what is an important similarity/dissimilarity for the purpose of the inference; and (2) defining and assessing the *respects* under which the two terms are considered as similar. The argumentation scheme and the critical questions do not involve, in other words, the nature of the common features on which the comparison is grounded, and the nature of the inferences supporting the analogical conclusion.

The starting point for addressing these problems can be found in the concept of relevance that constitutes one of the acknowledged grounds of analogical reasoning. In the literature on analogical arguments, one of the requirements that the shared features of the terms of the comparison need to meet is to be relevant to the attribution of the property (Copi and Burgess-Jackson, 1992, 1992; Hesse, 1966; Russell, 1988; Waller, 2001, 201–202; Weinreb, 2005, 32). For this reason, the comparison is not between the shared features per se, but rather "between the causal or higher-order relationships in which the items in an analogy participate" (Shelley, 2003, 6). In this view, analogies can be thought of as abstractions, or rather as identities at an abstract level (Darden, 1982, 151–152). A "super-ordinate category" (Glucksberg and Keysar, 1990) is thus created, which includes the terms of the analogy for the purpose of guaranteeing the attribution of the relevant property. In order to analyze the strength and defeasibility conditions of analogical arguments, it is necessary to investigate the nature of such an "abstract category." What kind of features are drawn from the terms of the analogy? Such characteristics can be semantic (fundamental or peripheral), commonly shared (common knowledge), or merely abstracted from a state of affairs. These distinctions are crucial for understanding the nature and the force of an analogical conclusion.

Aristotle (*Topics*, 108a 7–108a 17) underscored the existence of two types of "likeness" or similarity, expressing two different types of relationships. The first is an identity of relations, which can be compared to a proportion: as A is to B, so is C to D. For example, using an Aristotelian example, "as knowledge stands to the object of knowledge, so is perception related to the object of perception." In the second type, the terms of the comparison share the same generic fundamental characteristics and are subject to the same predication. This latter type of similarity can be the basis of a different type of reasoning, aimed at attributing a predicate P to a target A based on the fact that A and its analogue B belong to the same generic category, which can be existing or simply inferred. For example, as the internal structure of a cuttlefish serves the same functions as the bones in an animal, they are both their skeleton.

The rhetorical tradition developed a type of analogical reasoning based on "accidental" similarities, namely relations that do not belong to the definitions of the terms of the analogy (Boethius, *De Topicis Differentiis*, 1191B 30–34). The third type of similarity consists in the accidental similarity of relations ("a sailor is to his ship as a ruler is to a city") used for attributing an assigned predicate (in this case, the speaker wanted to establish whether a ruler should be chosen by lot). The relation is not essential because the definition of "sailor" does not share other predicates apart from "being a human being" with "ruler" that can justify the attribution of the assigned predicate. The relationship is justified by a common feature (persons performing an activity involving a responsibility toward other people in virtue of specific skill or expertise), which can be conceived as a proximate "quasi" genus that is, however, not semantic (or definitional) (Lloyd, 1962; Macagno, Walton, and Tindale, 2017), but ad hoc necessary for justifying the attribution of the predicate. This type of similarity was distinguished from the similarity between instances or individuals, namely the *denotata*, the particular things referred to by predicates (in the logical sense) (Levin, 1982). For example, an analogy of this type would be based on a comparison between two specific cases occurring in two distinct places and times (it was bad for the Americans to fight in Vietnam; therefore, it is going to be bad for the Saudi Arabians to fight in Yemen). Here, a common property needs to be discovered through the comparison. For this reason, it is considered as an "empirical" type of analogy (Levin, 1982). For example, this analogy is grounded on an empirical generalization that "wars in difficult territories are unsuccessful" (Hesse, 1988). This type of similarity is the ground of a type of reasoning, the "example," that has been regarded in the Aristotelian and medieval tradition as a kind of "rhetorical induction."

The core of the reasoning in all these different types of analogy lies in the discovery of a common semantic or accidental feature that can be found through a process of abstraction (Darden, 1982; Genesereth, 1980; Gentner, 1980; Kakuta, Haraguchi, and Okubo, 1997), resulting in the identification of a generic, functional predicate that can be attributed to entities different in kind (Macagno and Walton, 2009). This predicate can be conceived as a genus, a logical-semantic construct that expresses the generic fundamental features of a concept, answering the question "what is it?," and is attributed to all the specifications of the concept (its species) (Aristotle, *Topics*, 102a 31–32). For this reason, it is predicated of what the species is predicated of (Stump, 1989, 36). This "functional genus" does not need to correspond to a predicate that is codified in natural language (Aristotle, *Posterior Analytics*, 98a 20-23). Rather, it can be (and often is) an ad hoc concept developed for identifying the *respect* under which distinct specific can be considered as the same, which justifies the attribution of the assigned predicate (Hesse, 1965, 329, 1966, Chapter 4).

The analysis of the types of similarity can be considered as a criterion for evaluating the "major premise" of the scheme (A_1 is similar to A_2) (Macagno et al., 2017). In particular, it is possible to distinguish whether the similarity is established based on semantic characteristics of the two terms of the analogy or on the features that their referents normally have. Thus, by providing a list of critical questions, it is possible to determine whether the force of the conclusion is consistent with the acceptability of the premise (essential similarities can warrant strong conclusions, but not accidental ones concerning individual cases):

CQ_1: What kind of similarity characterizes the relationship between the target and the analogue?

 a. Is it an essential (semantic) similarity or an accidental one (concerning the referents of the concept)?
 b. If it is essential, does it represent an existing category or a new (unnamed) one?
 c. If it is accidental, does it concern generalizations or specific instances (individual beings or events)?

The other dimension of analogy consists in the transfer of the predicate (the assigned predicate) from the analogue to the target based on the "functional genus" or common characteristic, namely the relationship between the "minor premise" of the scheme (P is true (false) in case A_1) and the conclusion (P is true (false) in case A_2). This relationship can be semantic (and thus guaranteed by some definitional rules) or grounded on a justification that may need further arguments to be acceptable (Canale and Tuzet, 2009). For example, though we may claim that a "steamboat" and a "hotel" are similar, it would be very hard to show that they are semantically related, as the common definition of the former (a "boat that is propelled by a steam engine") is not included in the definition of the latter (an "establishment that provides paid lodging on a short-term basis"). In this case, the common feature that is identified is "offers overnight accommodation," which justifies the attribution of the assigned predicate "to be strictly liable for the guest's losses." The general category under which we place the two concepts does not belong to their definition, but is an "accident" – or contingent feature – of the former. For this reason, this similarity (or rather, this new functional genus we proposed) needs to be backed by further arguments (e.g., stressing the common characteristics of the contracts governing the relationships between the carrier and the passenger and the innkeeper and his or her guests, related to the exclusive use of a room; see *Adams v. New Jersey Steamboat Co.*, 151 N.Y. 163, 170 (1896)).

These differences can be elicited by a second set of critical questions, aimed at analyzing whether the conclusion is warranted and how:

CQ_2: How is the common characteristic (functional genus) related to the predicate attributed to the analogue and the target (i.e., the assigned predicate)?

 a. Is this relationship semantic, or is it a rule?
 b. If it is a rule, is it a shared one or is it provided to explain the specific case?
 c. If it is a shared rule, what kind of rule is it?

The analysis outlined above can be used for interpreting the reasoning underlying legal analogical arguments. A first distinction can be drawn between two types of analogical reasoning. Aristotle distinguished the "proportional" analogy from the reasoning from example (paradigm) (Macagno and Walton, 2009). The former concerns a similarity of relations, which can be represented as an equation: A is to B like C is to D (Aristotle, *Prior Analytics*, II, 24; 68b38-69a19). The proportional analogy can be used for either "discovering" a new principle (general rule) or using an existing one from which a rule can be drawn that applies to target cases different from the analogue. For example, Aristotle provides the following example of analogy in the *Rhetoric* (Aristotle, *Rhetoric*, II, XIII, 17):

> as Iphicrates urged when they compelled his son to serve who was under the standard age, because he was tall, that "if they esteem great children as men, they assuredly will vote small men to be children." And Theodectes, in the oration respecting the law, asked, "Do ye make the mercenaries, such as Strabax and Charidemus, citizens on the account of their virtue, and will ye not make exiles of those among the mercenaries who have committed these intolerable acts?"

Here a general principle is abstracted from a decision (age depends on height; citizenship depends on virtue) and applied to a target case that is not governed by the rule that was used and was granted.

This type of reasoning is different from placing a concept or an entity under a common genus to which the assigned predicate applies. This latter process is aimed at extending an existing category or creating a new one, so that the assigned predicate can be predicated of the target. The difference between these two types of reasoning, mirrored in the dialectical tradition, can be represented as follows:

Paradigmatic analogy	Proportional analogy
A_1 is P.	If A_1 is P_1, then A_2 is P_2.
A_1 and A_2 belong to the same genus G.	What is G (property in common between A_1 and A_2) is P (property in common between P_1 and P_2).
If x is G, then x is P.	A_1 (as a type of G) is P_1 (as a type of P).
A_2 is G.	A_2 (as a type of G) is P_2 (as a type of P).
A_2 is P.	

Both types of analogy are characterized by a "super-ordinate category" (Glucksberg and Keysar, 1990) that justifies (is relevant for) the attribution of the assigned predicate (Brewer, 2018, 38–39; Copi and Burgess-Jackson, 1992, 1992; Hesse, 1966; Russell, 1988; Waller, 2001, 201–202; Weinreb, 2005, 32). In both cases, the abstract genus G (and the attributed predicate P) can be an existing predicate or a new one. However, in case of proportional analogy, the reasoning is based on the identity between two abstract relations, which in their turn proceed from the abstraction of generic properties (G and R), or higher genera (Hesse, 1965, 331) from the antecedents and the consequents of the two ratios.

In the case of *paradigma*, it is possible to redefine an existing category, by broadening or narrowing it. For example, as one of the provisions of the Italian Criminal Code on theft states that electric power, as any other energy with economic value, legally counts as a thing, thus electromagnetic waves are "things" according to the law (Canale and Tuzet, 2018, 74). Conversely, as in the US Federal Arbitration Act an exception is granted to "contracts of employment of seamen, railroad employees, or any *other class of workers engaged in foreign or interstate commerce* [emphasis added]," the phrase "other class of workers" shall be confined to the generic category of "transportation workers" abstracted from the other two types of workers (*Circuit City Stores, Inc.* v. *Adams*, 532 U.S. 105, 109 (2001)). In both cases, the category is specified through analogy ("thing" is broadened to include intangible entities, and "workers" is narrowed to a specific type of workers).

When the general predicate does not correspond to an existing category, the analogy creates a new one. In this sense, analogy is no longer an interpretative instrument, strictly speaking, but an instrument for developing new rules. The starting point is not the specification of a legal predicate to cover borderline cases, but the creation of a new rule to cover a case that clearly does not fall under the existing ones (Canale and Tuzet, 2018, 77–78). For example, according to Article 57 of the Italian Criminal Law, the editor in chief of a printed periodical is responsible for conducting the controls for preventing offenses through the published materials. However, there are no norms governing this responsibility in a case of the editors in chief of an online newspaper (Italian Court of Cassation, 5th criminal section, judgment no. 1275 of January 11 2019). By using analogical reasoning (rejected by the court), it would be possible to create a new norm: as an online newspaper is similar to a printed one, the new inferred category of "editors in chief of materials distributed to the public" can be created, leading to a new analogous norm governing the responsibility of editors of electronic publications (Amerio, 2019, 287).

As noted above in civil law systems, additive analogy is distinguished from extensive interpretation. The first is commonly characterized by three features: a lacuna in the code (a new case not covered in a statute but falling within its purpose), a lack of constitutional restrictions barring the analogy, and the relevant similarity between the new case and the scope of the original rule (Langenbucher, 1998, 483). This "type" of analogy can in turn be divided in a paradigmatic analogy aimed at introducing a new generic category, and a proportional analogy aimed at establishing a new generic principle, namely a relationship between two categories abstracted from an existing provision. The former often is used in *analogia legis*, or the application of a *written* law to a different, similar case (Colombo, 2003, 96–97), while the latter is employed for *analogia iuris*, or the application of an abstract and unexpressed principle of law from which the stated law is drawn (Guastini, 2011, 281). While in the first case analogical reasoning is used to fill a legal gap by *applying* an existing law to a case not covered by it, in the second case it is used to draw and support *a new unexpressed rule* covering a legal gap. In the following sections, we will show the uses in both systems of law, building on the accounts of analogy advanced in argumentation theory (Macagno and Walton, 2009; Macagno et al., 2017) and our previous works on specific interpretative schemes (Macagno, 2015b).

5.5.3 Analogia Legis (*Argument from Written Law*)

The argument from *analogia legis* is grounded on specific legislative rules, and is used in civil law where a "comprehensive set of enacted rules has omitted a class of case" (Langenbucher, 1998, 503). This reasoning can be illustrated in civil law by the following case from the Italian Constitutional Court (ECLI:IT:COST:2010:280). Article no. 180, 4th paragraph of the Legislative Decree n. 285 of 1992, allowed public transport (of persons) and vehicles for rental to keep on board only a photocopy of the registration document, authenticated by the owner. Police officers stopped the driver of a vehicle owned by a waste management company, who showed them the driving license and the photocopy of the registration document, authenticated by the company. Was the legal provision applicable in this case, even though the purpose of the vehicle was not transportation of people, but of objects? The Italian judges advanced an argument comparing the waste management service with public transport of people, pointing out that they are both characterized by two essential features, namely "providing an essential public service" and "using a large fleet of vehicles." These features provide a new genus, not codified as a legal concept, to which the relevant legal assigned predicate – normally referred to as "deontic quality" or "legal consequence" in legal analogy (Langenbucher, 1998, 488) (to be allowed to have only a photocopy of the documents related to the vehicle) – applies and is thus transferred to the target. This type of reasoning can be represented as follows (from Ashley, 1991, 758):

ARGUMENTATION SCHEME 2A *Argument from* Analogia Legis

Premise 1 (Rule):	$A_1 => P$ (a right or obligation, or other legal property).
Premise 2:	A_2 is different from A_1 (but it was not excluded from the Rule).
Premise 3 (Similarity):	A_2 is similar to A_1.
Premise 4 (Classification):	$A_1 => G$.
Premise 5 (Classification):	$A_2 => G$.
Premise 6 (Classification):	G supports P (even though $G => P$ is not a positive legal rule).
Conclusion:	Therefore, there is a norm $A_2 => P$.

The new predicate G allows extending an existing rule to a case that is not covered by it (A2); the new predicate includes the case that is covered by the existing rule (A_1), but expresses a broader rationale explaining why A_1 should lead to P, which also applies to A_2. This type of reasoning can be distinguished from the so-called *analogia iuris*.

5.5.4 Analogia Iuris *(Argument from General Principles)*

Analogia iuris (or principle-based analogy, Langenbucher, 1998, 504) represents the application of an implicit *ratio decidendi* governing a law to a different case. In civil law it represents the reasoning underlying the "construction of an unexpressed rule" (Guastini, 2011, 278), which can be illustrated by the following case (Guastini, 2011, 280):

CASE 5.2: ANALOGIA IURIS

According to art. 2038 of the Italian Civil code, whoever has unduly received some goods and has transferred them in good faith, being unaware of the obligation to return them, shall return the consideration thereof and not the very goods or their value. The *ratio decidendi* of the law is the principle of protecting good faith. In this view, in order to protect the good faith of the receiver of the goods, the law imposes on him only the restitution of the consideration and not more burdensome obligations. The undue receipt and the transferal subsequent thereof is similar to the purchase and sale of stolen goods when their illicit provenience is unknown. Therefore, art. 2038, 1st paragraph, shall be interpreted as applicable also to the case of purchase in good faith of stolen goods.

In this case, an unexpressed principle is abstracted from a law and applied to a case not possibly falling thereunder. From this perspective, the *analogia iuris* creates a new law.

This argument can be represented as follows (Canale and Tuzet, 2018, 69; Guastini, 2011, 280–281; Macagno and Walton, 2009, 173; Macagno et al., 2017):

ARGUMENTATION SCHEME 2B *Argument from* Analogia Iuris

Premise 1 (Target):	No law provides for A_2.
Premise 2 (Analogous rule):	$A_1 => P$ (a right or obligation).
Premise 2 (Similarity):	$A_1 => G$ (a more general predicate).
Premise 4 (Abstraction):	$G => P$.
Premise 5 (Species – Genus):	$A_2 => G$.
Conclusion:	A_2 implies P.

This type of reasoning is based on the abstraction of a new rule, of the kind "what is G has the right/obligation P," drawn from an existing rule "If something is A_1, then it has the right/obligation P" (it is its *ratio decidendi*). The abstract rule can provide for a legal qualification identical with the existing rule, or broader. This justification is not semantic, but purely functional or pragmatic (Canale and Tuzet, 2018; Macagno, 2017), and allows the attribution of the assigned predicate P to the other species of the generic predicate G, namely A_2. The assigned predicate can be the same as P or a specification thereof to the specific circumstance.

5.5.5 *Analogies and Precedents*

At common law, reasoning from precedents is used to "apply a precedential *ratio decidendi* to a new set of facts" (Langenbucher, 1998, 520). In this type of reasoning, the judge both applies and defines the legal rules based on previously decided cases (Friesen, 1996, 12–13). The holding of the case, however, is different both from its rationale (or justification, namely the binding element, see Marshall, 2016), and the principle or rule that is derived from the holding in light of its "underpinning reasoning or rationale" (Summers, 2016, 386; 391). These characteristics distinguish the analogy underlying the use of precedents from the two types of analogy used for constructive purposes at civil law. However, these distinctions can shed light on some different strategies used for applying a precedent. To this purpose, we will discuss two cases in which precedents are used.

The first case is *Popov* v. *Hayashi*, WL 31833731 (Cal. Super. Ct. 2002), in which the plaintiff, Popov (a baseball fan), stopped a ball hit by a famous player with his glove. The player who hit the ball had set a new record for home runs, making the ball very valuable. However, in order to reach for the ball, Popov lost his balance and was forced to the ground by the crowd, leaving the ball loose on the ground. Hayashi (the defendant) was involuntarily forced to the ground too, and when he saw the loose ball, he picked it up, rose to his feet, and put it in his pocket. Popov, who intended to establish and maintain possession of the ball, could not prove that he had secured it. An issue for both parties was the classification of Popov's act as possession: while there is a legal definition of possession, this definition could not cover the cases of incomplete possession. For this reason, the court used the analogy in Case 5.3 (at 8):

CASE 5.3: PRECEDENT AND ANALOGY

The hunting and fishing cases recognize that a mortally wounded animal may run for a distance before falling. The hunter acquires possession upon the act of wounding the animal not the eventual capture. Similarly, whalers acquire possession by landing a harpoon, not by subduing the animal.

The plaintiff compared the possession of the ball with the possession of an animal or a whale in hunting and fishing, cases that are covered by specific legal provisions. In these latter cases, possession is established based on the criterion, or rather factor, of "wounding" or "landing a harpoon." The analogical reasoning in *Popov* abstracted a generic predicate shared by the two existing rules from other areas of law and the present case (stopping the ball with a glove), creating a new category of "undertaking significant but incomplete steps to achieve possession of a piece of abandoned personal property." This new predicate supports the transfer of the legal qualification (or assigned predicate) "to acquire a qualified right to possession." In this case, the analogical reasoning concerns the factors that can be used for determining the "right to possession," namely specifying the definition of the legal predicate (Sorensen, 1991, 100), making it similar to the reasoning from paradigmatic analogy.

A different type of analogy is used further in the same case. As both Popov and Hayashi had a right to possession, the court had to determine which party the ball belonged to. Since there was no law governing this case, the court reasoned by analogy from a precedent case, namely *Arnold v. Producers Fruit Co.*, in which fruit was mixed from many different growers together in a single bin and much of it rotted because it was improperly treated. In *Arnold*, the court concluded that each grower had an undivided interest in the whole, and the responsibility was proportional to the amount of fruit each had originally contributed. In *Popov*, the court used the precedent not for redefining a predicate (possession), but rather to abstract from the precedent a new principle, according to which "where more than one party has a valid claim to a single piece of property, the court will recognize an undivided interest in the property in proportion to the strength of the claim." This type of reasoning is more similar to the proportional analogy described above.

The (subtle) difference between a paradigmatic (redefinitional) type of analogical reasoning and the proportional one consists in the inference of a relationship between the properties of a case and the legal predicate attributed to it, and not only in the extension or a redefinition of a predicate of an existing one. The *ratio decidendi* is used to abstract two predicates, both the "genus" and the assigned predicate, and not only the former. This reasoning, shown in a second analogy of *Popov*, can be illustrated also by the case 5.4 (*Adams v. New Jersey Steamboat Co.*, 29 N.Y.S. 56 (1894)):

CASE 5.4: ANALOGIA IURIS

The action was brought to recover a certain sum of money alleged to have been lost to plaintiff when a passenger upon one of defendant's steamboats ... The liability of a steamboat company is analogous to that of an innkeeper at common law, and proof of the loss from a stateroom of a sum of money which might reasonably be carried for traveling expenses renders the company liable therefor.

In this instance, there was no law governing the liability of steamboat operators. However, there was a law providing that innkeepers shall be liable as insurers for their guest's losses. The court decided to use the *ratio decidendi* underlying the liability of innkeepers, abstracting the properties motivating the application of the legal predicate. In this case, the *ratio decidendi* was the accessory consequence of the contract to feed, lodge, and accommodate a guest for a suitable reward. A new implicit category was created, namely "providers of a service of accommodation governed by contract," which comprised both innkeepers and steamboat operators, and led to the application of a generic assigned predicate "to be liable as insurers for their losses of the people accommodated." This new relation is more abstract than the rule of law used as an analogue and leads to a new rule of law that is applied to the target case (steamboat operators are liable as insurers for their passengers' losses) (Canale and Tuzet, 2018, 69).

5.5.6 *Interpretative Analogical Arguments:* Ejusdem Generis *and* Noscitur a Sociis

In Chapter 4, we pointed out how the pragmatic maxims are mirrored by textualistic canons, and underscored the use of analogy as a strategy for both narrowing and broadening the meaning of a legal term based on the context. Unlike the analogical arguments described above, analogy can be used also when the generic predicate G is codified in a rule of law, but the case under discussion is a borderline one. Analogy in this circumstance works as an interpretative principle: two cases are compared, but instead of abstracting a new generic predicate, the existing one is specified ("extended" or rather redefined, see Sorensen, 1991) by highlighting the factors that allow the classification of new entities. The analogy allows the specification of the characteristics (factors) of an already existing predicate that is used as a genus (G), which thus become essential to its meaning. In practice, it is possible to reinterpret the cases of *analogia legis* (and *iuris*) above as interpretative arguments. The concept of "public transport" can be extended analogically to cover the transporting of "things" for public purposes; the notion of "inn" can be extended to cover the "floating inns," namely steamboats. In this sense, the line between some uses of analogy to fill legal gaps and their function as an interpretative instrument is strategic and can be justified by providing arguments in support of or against the vagueness of a legal provision. This type of reasoning can be described as follows:

ARGUMENTATION SCHEME 2C *Interpretative Analogy* (A Simili)

Premise 1 (Rule):	If *x* is A, then *x* has the right/is P.
Premise 2 (Borderline):	It is not clear whether *a* (a borderline case) is A.

ARGUMENTATION SCHEME 2C *(continued)*

Premise 3 (Similarity):	*a* is similar to *b*.
Premise 4 (Classification):	*b* was classified as A because of the factors $f_1, f_2, \ldots, f_n$ (defining the generic predicate G).
Premise 5 (Redefinition):	If *x* has the factors $f_1, f_2, \ldots, f_n$ (is G), then *x* is A.
Premise 6:	*a* has $f_1, f_2, \ldots, f_n$ (*is G*).
Conclusion:	Therefore, *a* is A (and, therefore, is P).

The extensive interpretation is different from the analogical arguments described in the previous sections because here the starting point is not the absence of a rule covering the case, but rather the existence of a classificatory doubt concerning the application of an existing rule. The focus is on how a category should be interpreted, namely, how it should be defined. The analogy provides criteria for defining – or more precisely redefining or précising it (Naess, 2005a). In particular, the analogy provides an "implicit predicate" or functional genus that is used implicitly for specifying the meaning of A. This type of analogy is clearly paradigmatic, as it involves only one relation (between two terms) and can be either semantic (essential) or contingent and functional (accidental), namely, drawn for the sole purpose of justifying the attribution of the assigned predicate to the analogous (and the target). This generic structure of paradigmatic analogy used for interpretative purposes is further specified by two distinct subschemes, corresponding to two textualistic arguments used in interpretation (Slocum, 2016a, 41): the *ejusdem generis* and the *noscitur a sociis*.

The *ejusdem generis* argument can be illustrated by a very simple example. A law concerning the regulation of gin, bourbon, vodka, rum, and other beverages would not likely be interpreted as including a soft drink, even though a soft drink is still a beverage (Slocum, 2016a, 26). This principle of interpretation has been defined as follows (Scalia and Garner, 2012, 199): "Where general words follow an enumeration of two or more things, they apply only to persons or things of the same general kind or class specifically mentioned."

The fundamental feature of this type of argument is the explicit mentioning of the genus (Brannon, 2018, 54; Dickerson, 1975, 234; Slocum, 2016a, 26), which distinguishes it from the argument *noscitur a sociis*, according to which "words grouped in a list should be given related meanings" (Scalia and Garner, 2012, Chapter 31). An example of the latter canon is the example fo case 5.5. drawn from Scalia and Garner (ibid.) (*State v. Taylor*, 594 N.W.2d 533, 535–536 (Minn. Ct. App. 1999)):

According to the Minnesota Statutes, "a permit to carry is not required of a person: ... (5) to transport a pistol in a motor vehicle, snowmobile or boat if the pistol is unloaded, contained in a closed and fastened case, gunbox, or securely tied package" (Minn. Stat. § 624.714, subd. 9(e)). If, as Taylor argues, a "case" includes anything that encloses or contains [such as a purse], then the term "gunbox," referring to a particular type of "case," adds nothing to the statute.

The argument is analogical because the different listed items are redefined as belonging to a new "unessential" and unnamed genus, which justifies the attribution of the assigned predicate (to be allowed to carry a weapon) based on a legal principle. In the *Taylor* example, the unnamed genus of the listed items is "a container that does not make the gun readily retrievable," which is relevant to the principle of protecting the people.

In the *ejusdem generis*, the common genus is already provided, but it needs to be specified by analogy. Analogy works as an instrument for redefining the items of the list considering the general category already provided by the law. However, the specification of the genus can be carried out considering different types of features of the concepts listed. The distinction that we have drawn above between an essential and an accidental functional genus becomes of crucial importance in this type of reasoning. A clear example of the use of the *ejusdem generis* is *James* v. *United States*, 550 U.S. 192 (2007), which concerns the interpretation of the concept of "violent felony." This offense is defined in the US Code under the section titled "Penalties" as follows (18 U.S.C. § 924(e) (2)(B)): "[T]he term 'violent felony' means any crime ... that – (i) has as an element the use, attempted use, or threatened use of physical force against the person of another; or (ii) is burglary, arson, or extortion, involves use of explosives, or otherwise involves conduct that presents a serious potential risk of physical injury to another."

Petitioner James pleaded guilty to being in possession of a firearm while a felon, in violation of federal law; however, since he admitted three prior felony convictions, which included an attempted burglary, he was sentenced to the fifteen-year prison term provided by the Armed Career Criminal Act, § 924(e), for an armed defendant who has three prior "violent felony" convictions. The dispute was focused on the classification of "attempted burglary" as a "violent felony," which led to the conflicting arguments from analogy (*ejusdem generis*) presented in case 5.6:

Petitioner James: Under the *ejusdem generis* canon, the residual provision must be read to extend only to completed offenses because the specifically enumerated offenses – burglary, arson, extortion, and explosives crimes – all have that common attribute.

Majority opinion: The most relevant common attribute of the enumerated offenses is that, while not technically crimes against the person, they nevertheless create significant risks of bodily injury to others, or of violent confrontation that could lead to such injury.

Scalia, dissenting: The crimes listed involve *conducts* that present a serious potential risk of physical injury. Burglary, by its nature, involves a substantial risk that the burglar will use force against a victim *in completing the crime*. By definition, a perpetrator who has been convicted only of attempted burglary has failed to make it inside the home or workplace. Thus, the entry into the home that makes burglary such a threat to the physical safety of its victim is necessarily absent in attempted burglary.

The reasoning from analogy used by James was based on an analogy from an unstated "essential" genus, namely an abstraction from the definitions of the enumerated crimes of the elements common to them, and in particular the most generic one, which is their aspect (namely being completed (performed) acts). This new category, however, is highly defeasible, as it is not the proximate genus thereof – more specific and thus relevant characteristics can be found that are common to the listed items. Moreover, the generic feature of "completion" does not justify the predication of the assigned predicate (to be "violent felony").

The court used against this argument a similar type of *ejusdem generis*, but more specific. The enumerated crimes were considered to belong to the category of "offences that somehow may pose a risk of injury to persons." This type of reasoning fulfills the criterion of relevance, as it provides a justification for the attribution of the predicate and the resulting legal consequences; however, its defeasibility rests in the possibility of showing that it is not acceptable or not the best one. As Scalia objected, the only justification for the creation of this more generic category that includes also attempted – and thus not involving risk – crimes is that crimes displaying a similar degree of depravity need to be similarly deterred, which is not the principle underlying the law.

In contrast, the reasoning of the dissenting opinion (Scalia) followed a distinct path, not based on the existing definitions of the listed concepts, but on the feature that is spelled out in the new unessential genus that followed the list (to be crime that involves *conduct* that presents a serious potential risk of physical injury to another). The common characteristics that specify the stated genus are thus nonessential, as such crimes are defined by their elements, and not by the conduct that the crime involves in "the ordinary case" (*Johnson* v. *United States*, 576 U.S. 591 (2015)). In this sense, the common feature is "a criminal conduct that in normal cases leads to the possibility that risk of physical harm becomes a reality." Since attempted burglary cannot lead to this risk (as in normal cases of attempted burglary the burglar fails to enter the premises, which would be the only source of the risk of physical harm), Scalia concluded that it cannot be classified as "violent felony." This argument was later used in *Johnson* to overrule the judgment of *James*.

5.6 A PARTICULAR ANALOGICAL ARGUMENT: THE *A FORTIORI* ARGUMENT

The first analysis of *a fortiori* argument was undertaken by Aristotle in the *Topics* and in the *Rhetoric*. In both works he pointed out how this type of reasoning is grounded on the concept of likeness of predication. The negative *a fortiori* reasoning can be described as follows: if a predicate A cannot be attributed to an entity P, neither can it be attributed to an entity Q that it is less likely to be characterized as an A (*Topics*, II, 10). The positive *a fortiori* reasoning can be stated as follows: if a predicate A can be attributed to an entity, it must be attributed to another entity that it is more likely to be characterized as an A. In legal argumentation, the *a fortiori* argument can be considered as a kind of argument from similarity (Guastini, 2011, 282–283). In both negative and positive *a fortiori* the interpreter aims at supporting an unexpressed rule and presupposes a *ratio iuris*, which is applied to the case not judged yet (Horovitz, 1972, 96). The structure of the reasoning can be expressed as follows. If a rule attributes any normative qualification (such as a power, an obligation, or a status) to an individual or a category of individuals, it can be concluded that there is a different rule that attributes the same quality to another individual or category of individuals in a situation in which such a normative qualification should be all the more attributed (Tarello, 1980, 355). This argument is used to extend the application of a normative statement to categories of individuals or behaviors not falling within the scope of that statement. The standard cases of *a fortiori* can be illustrated through the following example: Alcohol is more damaging than marijuana: if alcohol is allowed, then marijuana should also be allowed. A more complex example is in Case 5.7. (*Bekteshi* v. *Mukasey*, 260 F. App'x 642 (5th Cir. 2007)):

CASE 5.7: A FORTIORI

Failure to satisfy the less demanding asylum standard was, *a fortiori*, a failure to demonstrate eligibility for withholding of removal.

According to this reasoning, two conditions can result in the legal consequences provided by the law, namely relief, i.e., the right not to be expelled from the US (A): satisfying the standard for asylum (P) and satisfying the standard for withholding of removal (Q), where the latter can be requested also by individuals who have committed crimes that exclude them from asylum. To obtain asylum the applicant must meet a specific standard (which we will refer to as D_1): he has to demonstrate more than a 50 percent risk that he will be persecuted in his home country on account of his race, religion, nationality, membership in a particular socia group, or political opinion (percent risk). The standard for withholding of removal (D_1+i) is higher than that for asylum applications. The reasoning can be represented as follows:

1. Condition *a* (characterized by a risk lower than the required one; say, 40 percent risk) entails the rejection of relief based on asylum request.
2. If a condition motivates the rejection of relief based on asylum request, it motivates even more the rejection of relief based on withholding removal request.
3. Condition *a* motivates the rejection of relief based on asylum request.
4. Condition *a* motivates even more the rejection of relief based on withholding removal request.
5. Condition *a* entails the rejection of relief based on withholding removal request.

By this reasoning, the failure to satisfy the standard for asylum implies the failure to demonstrate a more demanding standard.

For the purpose of being eligible for "relief" (A), the standard for "withholding of removal" (Q) is higher than the standard for "asylum" (P), in the sense that (1) to achieve respectively P and Q, different levels must be reached in the degree of satisfaction of a scalable dimension D (the level or risk) that justifies the attribution of A; (2) the level of D required for Q is greater than the level that is required for P; (3) therefore, failing to reach the level of D for P (failing to qualify for asylum) entails failing to reach the level of D for Q (failing to qualify for "withholding of removal"). Obviously, the converse does not hold: failing to reach the level of D for Q des not entail failing to reach the level of D for P. This type of reasoning is convertible for destructive purposes but not for constructive ones: if Q is A, then P is A, but if P is A, it does not follow that Q is A. On the other hand, if Q is not A, it does not follow that P is not A, while if P is not A, Q cannot be A. Thus we can consider the *a fortiori* argument an argument from analogy not as establishing a relation of equivalence (Q is the same as P), but as a relation of entailment between the two predicates (if Q, then P). We can represent the structure of the argument as follows:

ARGUMENTATION SCHEME 2D *Argument from Analogy – A Fortiori*

Premise 1 (Target):	There is legal norm that the Ps are As.
Premise 2 (Similarity):	The Ps are Gs and the Qs are Gs.

ARGUMENTATION SCHEME 2D *(continued)*

Premise 3 (Scalability):	The Qs satisfy to a higher degree than the Ps one or more binary or scalable dimensions $D+$ that proportionally favors the attribution of A to G, or to a lesser degree than the Ps one or more binary or scalable dimension $D-$ that proportionally disfavors the attribution of A to G.
Conclusion:	A *fortiori* the Qs are As (there is an implied legal rule according to which also the Qs are As).

In this type of argument, the classes being compared, namely the Ps and the Qs, share a genus G, and there is a norm that attributes the legal predicate A only to the Ps. It is claimed that the Qs should be attributed the predicate A for a stronger reason, namely based on the fact that the Qs under some aspect $(D+)$ require the legal predicate A more than the Ps. This aspect consists in the fact that the Qs satisfy to a higher degree than the Ps one or more binary or scalable dimensions (D) that proportionally favors A $(D+)$, *or to a lesser degree* one or more binary or scalable dimension that proportionally disfavors A $(D-)$. By a binary dimension we consider a Boolean yes–no predicate (e.g., being or not a human, or a citizen) and by a scalable dimension, a predicate susceptible to receive multiple values, continuous or discrete (age, size, etc.). Here are some examples:

1. Existing rule: Dogs (P) allowed in the restaurant (A).
2. Cats (Q) *a fortiori* are to be allowed since they are pets (G) (like dogs) and they do not bite (lack of a property D_i- disfavoring admission).
3. Rabbits (Q) *a fortiori* are to be allowed (A) since they are pets (G) (like dogs), they do not bite (lack of a binary disfavoring dimension D_i-) and they are silent (presence of a binary dimension D_j+ favoring admission).
4. Hamsters *a fortiori* are to be allowed since they are pets (like dogs) they do not bite, they are silent, and are smaller (higher degree of a scalable dimension D_k+ favoring admission).

An *a fortiori* inference that the Qs are *a fortiori* As can be countered by pointing to the fact that the Qs also possess some features that disfavors A (or lack some features favoring A). So, for instance, it could be argued that it is true that cats do not bite, but it also true that cats scratch, this being a feature that disfavors admission.

In civil law these inferences are used to interpret normative statements. For instance, we can consider Case 5.8 (from Guastini, 2011, 283).

In this case, the *a fortiori* inference is based on the principle that the lower a source, the more its operation can be limited by a constraint; so, if nonretroactivity

According to art. 11, 1st paragraph disp. prel. (disposition effective prior to constitution) of the Italian Civil Code, statutes cannot be retroactively effective; therefore, *a fortiori*, regulations, which are subordinated to statutes, cannot be retroactively effective.

constrains statutes, and regulations are inferior to statutes, then *a fortiori* nonretroactivity constrains regulations.

However, the same pattern of reasoning could not be used for concluding that, since the constitutional laws have to be approved by the absolute majority of the Parliament members, *a fortiori* ordinary legislation rules have to be approved by the absolute majority of such members. Guastini distinguishes between two types of *a fortiori* argument, depending on whether the reasoning is aimed at interpreting statements imposing an advantageous condition (such as a right) or a disadvantageous one (such as a duty or a prohibition). In the first case, the argument proceeds *a maiore ad minus* (from the greater to the lesser). For instance, if it is allowed to flash one's own headlights to warn other cars, then in such cases it is allowed to flash one's own dimmed headlights. In the second case, the argument is *a minore ad maius* (from the lesser to the greater). For instance, if bikes are prohibited from a park, then, *a fortiori*, motorbikes are prohibited. This distinction drawn by Guastini highlights the difference between the constructive predicates (rights) and the destructive ones (obligations and limitations). The difference affects the evaluation of the action at issue. If an action is prohibited, then any action that is of a similar kind but is worse (with regard to the law's values) is also *a fortiori* prohibited; if an action is permitted then anything that is better is *a fortiori* permitted. This type of reasoning is grounded on the legally relevant characteristics of an action. Something is regarded as legally bad when it has a certain feature or dimension legally assessed as negative. As a consequence, something is worse when it is characterized by a higher degree or level of such a negative feature, while it is better when it is characterized by a lower degree of such a negative property. On the contrary, something is regarded as legally good when it characterized by a property whose higher degree increases the goodness of the action, while the lower degree thereof worsens the action.

5.7 ARGUMENTS FROM AUTHORITY

The interpretative arguments from authority can be considered as a strategy for shifting the interpretative problem to a different context and to different types of evidence. The first distinction that needs to be drawn, however, is between the different types of authoritative arguments that can be used for backing an interpretation. Walton and Koszowy (Walton and Koszowy, 2015) have extended the study of arguments from authority by adding an argumentation scheme for arguments from administrative authority to the existing scheme for argument from expert opinion. An epistemic authority is defined as an expert in the field of knowledge, whereas an administrative authority has a right to exercise command or influence over another party subject to that authority (Bochenski, 1974, 71; Walton, 2010). The pronouncement of an administrative authority can be legally binding but can also be subject to appeal, and disobedience can have penalties. This distinction between administrative authority and expert opinion illustrates the difference between the various types of arguments grounded on the authority of the lawmaker and the ones based on the appeal to the expert witness. The use of a kind of authority characterizes also a third kind of argument used in statutory interpretation, whose force derives from the authority of the majority of the people or the common opinion.

5.7.1 *Psychological Argument (Intention of the Actual Legislator)*

The psychological argument is grounded on the intention of the actual, real drafter of the statement of law that needs to be interpreted. According to this line of reasoning, to a statement of law shall be attributed the meaning that allegedly corresponds to the intention of its drafter or author, that is, the historical legislator (Tarello, 1980, 364). This type of argument is based on the idea that a statement of law is the expression of a command from a superior authority. Therefore, the interpretation of a statement of law corresponds to the reconstruction of the intention of the authority. However, if the legislator is not a single authority, such as a king or an *imperator*, but a plurality of people (an assembly such as the Senate or the House of Representatives), this argument amounts to attributing a unique intention to a community of people, who may have voted the statement of law for different reasons and different intentions (Easterbrook, 1984).

This argument shifts the problem of supporting an intended interpretation to a different type of evidence. Instead of using the evidence from the text and the present context and co-text, the interpreter reconstructs the "speaker's intention" based on other types of clues, such as texts that were drafted during the lawmaking process. The psychological argument is thus not just a simple argument; rather, it is an argument that shifts the interpretative problem to another interpretative problem. The intention of the "actual" legislator is in fact established based on other interpretative arguments that are grounded on a historical context. Therefore the defeasibility of psychological arguments is twofold, as the weaknesses that characterize the interpretative arguments used to support the "intention" of the administrative authority combine with the potential criticisms that can arise from the use of texts external to the legislative ones and the controversial notion of the "intention of the legislator" (Marmor, 2008) (see pages 147–148 for our analysis of the arguments underlying this use of authority and their defeasibility).

This type of argument can be illustrated (see Case 5.9) using an example from the common law (*United States* v. *California*, 381 U.S. 139, 150, 151 (1965)). This controversy, concerning the possession of the submerged lands of California, was based on the definition of "submerged land," which in its turn amounted to the definition of "inland water." The object of the dispute was the determination of dominion over the submerged lands and mineral rights under the three-mile belt of sea off the California coast. According to the Submerged Lands Act (1953), the states have ownership of the lands beneath navigable waters within their boundaries, including the seaward boundaries considered as not exceeding three geographical miles into the Pacific Ocean from their "inland waters." The problem concerns the interpretation of this latter term, which according to the United States corresponded to the definition of inland waters that had been applied by the United States in its foreign relations since 1947, while according to California refered to what the states historically considered to be "inland" when they joined the Union.

The court used the following argument to decide on the issue, pointing out that the only way of recovering the definition was the legislative history, or rather the intention of the legislator. Since the Senate Committee excluded the definition set out in the proposed bill, their intention was not to define it, leaving its meaning to be determined by the courts:

CASE 5.9: PSYCHOLOGICAL ARGUMENT

As first written, the bill defined inland waters to include "all estuaries, ports, harbors, bays, channels, straits, historic bays, and sounds, and all other bodies of water which join the open sea." This definition was removed by the Senate Committee ... Removal of the definition for inland waters and the addition of the three-mile limitation in the Pacific, when taken together, unmistakably show that California cannot prevail in its contention that "as used in the Act, Congress intended inland waters to identify those areas which the states always thought were inland waters." By deleting the original definition of "inland waters" Congress made plain its intent to leave the meaning of the term to be elaborated by the courts, independently of the Submerged Lands Act.

In order to analyze the force and the characteristics of this type of argument, it is useful to distinguish between two kinds of authority. One is the classic form of argument from authority, corresponding to the authority of the expert (Argumentation Scheme 3) presented in Section 5.3 (Walton et al., 2008, 19). As mentioned above, the legislator can be considered as an administrative authority, characterized by the power deriving from a superior role or standing of some official who is entitled to make rulings that are binding within a legislative framework (Cicero, *Topica*, 24). This type of argument from authority has the argumentation scheme 3.4.

ARGUMENTATION SCHEME 3A *Administrative Authority*

Minor premise 1:	Source L is an authority involved in (passing, drafting, amending) the statement of law E.
Minor premise 2:	L (passed, drafted, amended) proposition E intending M.
Major premise:	If source L is an authority involved in (passing, drafting, amending) the statement of law E, and L intended the M, then E should presumably be interpreted as M.
Conclusion:	E shoudl presumably plausibly be interpreted as M.

In *Conroy* v. *Aniskoff* (507 U.S. 511, 519 (1993)), Justice Scalia pointed out some crucial critical dimensions of this scheme, related to the fact that attributing a specific intention to a body is extremely problematic, and depending on the viewpoint one wants to defend, one will choose the opinions of the personages better suiting one's own purpose. Building on the critical questions of the argument from expert opinion (Godden and Walton, 2006; Walton et al., 2008, 92–93), along with Tarello's analysis (Tarello, 1980, 366–367) and the aforementioned refutation of the psychological argument, this response can be summarized in the following defeasible dimensions:

1. *Authority question:* Shall L be considered as an authority (the law is independent from the will of the legislator)?
2. *Role question:* Who is L (the majority, the most influential, the representatives) and what role has L played?
3. *Evidence questions:* What did L assert that implies M? What is the textual evidence that L intended M?
4. *Consistency question:* Is M consistent with the intention of other Ls that passed the same law?
5. *Coherence question:* Does M lead to any antinomy or incoherence in the legal system?

One of the crucial and most controversial problems is how to determine a collective intention, especially if the statement of law has been voted by different political groups for different purposes. As Scalia put it, "There is no escaping the point: Legislative history that does not represent the intent of the whole Congress is nonprobative; and legislative history that does represent the intent of the whole Congress is fanciful" (*Bank One Chicago, N.A.* v. *Midwest Bank & Trust Co.*, 516 U.S. 264, 281 (1996)). Another problem is to determine the intention. The *travaux preparatoires*, or legislative history, are used for this purpose as evidence that is employed for analyzing the reasons given by the legislative bodies to support a statement of law. Obviously, the reconstruction of the intention needs to be supported by further arguments, one of which is the appeal to further authorities.

5.7.2 *Historical Argument (Presumption of Continuity or Conservative Legislator)*

The psychological argument is based on the legislator as an authority. However, the problem is to determine what the legislator intended in that specific case. The historical argument can be considered as a different form of argument from authority, where the authority is not directly the actual legislator but the traditional interpretation of a previous statement of law that governed the same case in the same legal system. This reasoning is based on the principle that the rules are constant in time, and that subsequent legislators used – and should use – the ancient rules as a model to be simply improved from a formal or lexical perspective (Tarello, 1980, 368). In this perspective, the previous interpretation works as an authority for the subsequent ones, and then the previous legislators can be thought of as the authorities on whom the actual ones base their intentions. Again, the defeasibility of this argument is twofold, as the inherent weakness of this argument (the controversial immutability of a law, see also our argument from commitment in Section 3.4.2) is combined with the weakness of the evidence that was provided in support of a specific interpretation.

The historical argument is used at common law to reconstruct the intention of the legislator in cases in which the intent is not clear. For instance, we consider the use of this argument in *People* v. *Davis*, 218 P.3d 718, 726 (Colo. App. 2008), concerning the interpretation of Section 12–47–901 of the Colorado statutes (Case 5.10):

CASE 5.10: HISTORICAL ARGUMENT

Because the legislative intent is not reasonably certain from the plain language of the 2005 version of Section 12–47–903(5), we look to the prior version of the law, the goal of the statutory scheme, the consequences of its construction, and the legislative history to determine legislative intent. In 1997, the General Assembly manifested its intent that violations of the liquor code proscription of providing liquor to a minor would also violate the general criminal code proscription against contributing to the delinquency of a minor. In doing so, the legislature explicitly provided that these violations of the liquor code could also be prosecuted under the criminal code. Thus, … the plain language of the 1997 statute explicitly reflected the legislature's intent to permit prosecution under the criminal code … In this context, we conclude that the 1997 amendment demonstrates that the General Assembly intended that liquor code violations pertaining to providing alcohol to minors could be punishable under the criminal code. Further, we conclude that the 2005 amendment, and the fact that the General Assembly did not, at the same time, amend Section 12–47–903(5) to reflect the addition of subsection (a.5) in 12–47–901(1), do not express or imply an intention to preclude prosecution of contributing to the delinquency of a minor under the criminal code.

In the absence of more powerful arguments clearly supporting the actual legislator's intent, the historical argument can be extremely effective, especially when the documents considered are close in time to the statement of law to be interpreted. However, this argument is grounded on the principle that the law should reflect the intent of the legislator, incurring the same weaknesses as the psychological argument. Moreover, it presupposes that the actual legislator is relying on the intentions of previous legislators. Finally, just as the psychological argument risks becoming a following of one's "friends," quoting Scalia's metaphor, the historical one risks turning into a potentially open-ended inquiry, in which "one could go back further in time to examine the Civil War-era relief Acts" (*Conroy v. Aniskoff,* 507 U.S. 511, 520, 521 (1993) (Scalia, concurring)).

5.7.3 *Authoritative Argument* (Ab Exemplo)

The authoritative argument is based on the authority of a previous interpretation, or rather on the authority of the product of a previous interpretation. This type of reasoning cannot be considered as the same as the argument from precedent, or analogy, because the authoritative argument applies when the previous interpretation or decision is not considered to be legally binding as a source of the law. The crucial aspect in arguments from previous interpretations concerns identifying the legal theory that is majoritarian or is the best one. The crucial dimension of the argument from a previous decision is the *ratio decidendi*, the reason why the precedent case was decided in a certain way. Such a reason, which corresponds to an argument or a combination of arguments, is applied to a similar case.

This type of argument can be represented as a variant of the aforementioned argument from expert opinion (our Argumentation Scheme 3) (Walton et al., 2008, 19):

ARGUMENTATION SCHEME 3B *Authority of Previous Interpretations*

Minor premise 1:	Source L (legal theory/previous case) is an authority in subject domain S containing proposition A.
Minor premise 2:	L asserts that proposition A (in domain S) is true (false).
Major premise:	If source L is an authority in a subject domain S containing proposition A, and L asserts that proposition A is true (false), then A may presumably be taken to be true (false).
Conclusion:	A is true (false).

The critical questions remain the same as in Argumentation Scheme from Administrative authority.

5.7.4 *Appeal to Popular Opinion: Naturalistic Argument*

The naturalistic argument is based on the so-called "nature" of humanity, social relations, or things. In this perspective, the law is directly drawn or taken from the nature of something, and the legislator cannot force it, it must be consistent with it. For instance, killing and torturing are objectively wrong, and therefore there are laws against homicide and torture (Guastini, 2011, 242). The fact that killing is wrong is not based on a decision of a legislator; on the contrary, the law is based on a natural value (killing is wrong), and consequently this statement of law can be said validated by nature. An example of a naturalistic argument, is the following Italian case (Corte Costituzionale, Sentenza n. 138/2010) concerning the constitutionality of the civil law prohibiting same-sex marriage. Such a law was allegedly in conflict with Article 3 of the Italian Constitution (prohibiting any discrimination) and Article 29, defining "family." The court found that the same-sex marriage ban was not unconstitutional, grounding its argument on the definition of family as a "natural society based on marriage" (Italian Constitution, Article 29). This definition is gender-neutral; however, what shall be considered as a "natural society" (Damele, 2016)? The argument provided by the court and supporting the unnaturalness of same-sex marriage proceeds from the "nature" of family, which seems to amount to the realistic idea that there are entities that fit natural kinds, and that the terms denoting them have a meaning that is not fixed by linguistic convention but rather by reference.

The argumentative structure of the naturalistic argument can be shown through its use in a very complex judgment, the recent *Obergefell* v. *Hodges* in which the concept of "marriage" in relation to same-sex unions is debated. The judges of the majority opinion did not discuss or debate the (controversial) definition of marriage. Instead, they described this concept as they were mirroring its "nature" (135 S. Ct. 2584, 2598 (2015)):

> ### CASE 5.11: NATURALISTIC ARGUMENT
>
> The nature of marriage is that, through its enduring bond, two persons together can find other freedoms, such as expression, intimacy, and spirituality. This is true for all persons, whatever their sexual orientation . . . There is dignity in the bond between two men or two women who seek to marry and in their autonomy to make such profound choices. Cf. Loving, supra, at 12, 87 S. Ct. 1817, 18 L. Ed. 2d 1010 ("[T]he freedom to marry, or not marry, a person of another race resides with the individual and cannot be infringed by the State").

The judges used the concept of "nature" of marriage to present their definition as the "true" one (Halldén, 1960), opposed to the traditional (alternative) one in which it describes the union of a man and a woman. The use of the appeal to the "nature" of things has primarily a dialectical consequence, namely the shifting of the burden of disproving the general acceptance and acceptability of the definition. The dissenting justices had to rebut the definition described as "natural," and defend the traditional definition of marriage and the fact that it is legally and commonly accepted (or is at least a matter for discussion). They had to argue against the fact that the new definition is commonly accepted; they attacked the argument from classification (Argumentation scheme 9 below) used by the majority judges providing arguments supporting its defeasibility conditions set out in the critical questions. This discussion would have been a simple dialectical discussion should the definition not be taken for granted. The concurring judges, however, evaded the burden of proving that it is the commonly shared and legally accepted definition. This resulted in a metadialogue on the conditions and rules of the dialogue itself. In this sense, the "naturalistic" argument is a strategy for taking the acceptability of a definition for granted. The reason for this effect needs to be found in the argument that it presupposes.

The naturalistic argument is clearly based on the concept of "nature," which is in itself highly problematic, as it sometimes corresponds to the biological (scientific) definition of a concept (Ohlin, 2016). More often it seems to point to some commonly shared view on "essence" of things (Focarelli, 2012, 253). Both accounts can be captured by the notion of "natural meaning" or "common sense," namely to commonly accepted principles that do not need to be further proved (*People v. Collins*, 214 Ill. 2d 206, 218 (2005)). Thus the naturalistic arguments can be represented using the argument from popular opinion (Walton et al., 2008, 311):

ARGUMENTATION SCHEME 4 *Argument from Popular Opinion*

General acceptance premise:	A is generally accepted as true.
Presumption premise:	If A is generally accepted as true, then A may presumably be taken to be true (false).
Conclusion:	A is true (false).

This argument can be assessed based on the following critical questions (Walton et al., 2008, 124):

CQ$_1$: Does a large majority of the cited reference group accept A as true?

CQ$_2$: Is there other relevant evidence available that would support the assumption that A is not true?

CQ$_3$: What reason is there for thinking that the view of this large majority is likely to be right?

In this perspective, we can conceive the structure of the interpretative naturalistic argument (i.e., an appeal to the "nature" of a concept that needs to be interpreted) as a specific case of an appeal to a shared consensus on a definition (the "true" or "real" meaning) (Halldén, 1960; Macagno and Walton, 2014b, Chapter 3; Schiappa, 1993).

Clearly, this shared definition needs to be supported by evidence, which is controversial in itself, as it would lead to other subquestions:

a. Are there different definitions?
b. What is the source for establishing that a definition is the commonly accepted one (dictionaries; newspapers; other texts; linguists; etc.)?
c. Is the evidence acceptable?
d. Has the definition changed in time? Does the "nature" of things correspond to the definition shared at the time the law was drafted, or the one used at present?

This type of authoritative argument does not avoid the production of interpretative evidence but allows the use of other types of evidence. Notwithstanding the high defeasibility of this type of reasoning, it is commonly used for rhetorical purposes (Damele, 2011).

5.8 ARGUMENTS FROM CONSEQUENCES

Four interpretative arguments can be traced back to instances or subtypes of argument from consequences: the *reductio ad absurdum* (apagogic or absurdity argument), the equitative argument, the ancillary argument of coherence of the law, and the economic argument (corresponding to the arguments indicated in our Section 5.2 in the category of "practical arguments," as arguments 4a–d). The other argument classified as a "practical argument" shows instead a different argumentative pattern, which will be discussed in Section 5.9.

5.8.1 Reductio ad Absurdum

The apagogic argument, also called *reductio ad absurdum*, may be grounded on the assumption of the reasonableness of the legislator. This argument is aimed at excluding the possible interpretations of a statement of law that would lead to an unreasonable or "absurd" rule (Tarello, 1980, 369). The apagogic argument is purely destructive, as it is aimed at excluding one or more possible alternatives without providing any positive grounds to support a specific interpretation. It can be particularly effective when there is only one possible alternative interpretation, as it turns into the pragmatic counterpart of the disjunctive syllogism, or reasoning from oppositions.

The force of this type of reasoning, however, lies on an ambiguous concept, absurdity, and in particular the absurdity of a rule of law. As Tarello emphasized (Tarello, 1980, 370), a rule of law can be absurd because of its application to a case (or the generalization of such an application) or because of the outcomes or effects of its application to a case (or the generalization thereof). Moreover, the nature of absurdity is ambiguous. Such applications or effects can be logically, practically, or ethically absurd. For this reason, Tarello suggests that the apagogic argument is an umbrella term covering different strategies of refutation, aimed at excluding a possible interpretation in order to affirm possible alternative ones.

At common law, this type of reasoning is called the "absurdity doctrine" (Gold, 2006; Manning, 2003). It can be illustrated through Case 5.12 (*Corley v. United States*, 556 U.S. 303, 317 (2009)):

CASE 5.12: ABSURDITY ARGUMENT

§ 3501(e) defines "confession" as "any confession of guilt of any criminal offense or any self-incriminating statement made or given orally or in writing." Thus, if the Government seriously urged a literal reading, (a) would mean that "[i]n any criminal prosecution brought by the United States ..., ['any self-incriminating statement' with respect to 'any criminal offense'] ... shall be admissible in evidence if it is voluntarily given." Thus would many a Rule of Evidence be overridden in case after case: a defendant's self-incriminating statement to his lawyer would be admissible despite his insistence on attorney–client privilege; a fourth-hand hearsay statement the defendant allegedly made would come in; and a defendant's confession to an entirely unrelated crime committed years earlier would be admissible. These are some of the absurdities of literalism that show that Congress could not have been writing in a literalistic frame of mind.

This type of reasoning can be represented with the argument from consequences (Macagno, 2015a; Walton et al., 2008, 332):

ARGUMENTATION SCHEME 5 *Argument from Consequences*

Premise 1:	If A is brought about, good (bad) consequences will plausibly occur.
Premise 2:	What leads to good (bad) consequences shall be (not) brought about.
Conclusion:	Therefore, A should (should not) be brought about.

The apagogical argument claims that, a legal interpretation of a statement of law would lead to outcomes that are bad (unacceptable) for different reasons. For instance, the rule created by such an interpretation would introduce a contradiction in the legal system (directly or indirectly conflicting with another provision) or contradict ethical rules. The critical questions that can be used to assess this scheme are the following (Walton et al., 2008, 102):

CQ$_1$: How strong is the likelihood that the cited consequences will (may, must) occur?

CQ$_2$: What evidence supports the claim that the cited consequences will (may, must) occur, and is it sufficient to support the strength of the claim adequately?

CQ$_3$: What evidence supports the claim that the cited consequences are bad (absurd)?

CQ_4: Are there other opposite consequences (bad as opposed to good, for example) that should be taken into account?

We now need to recall that the quotation from Tarello just above defined the "absurd" result as a result that is "contrary to perceived social values." As CQ_3 above points out, this classification of the consequences cannot be taken for granted, but needs to be established by providing evidence and arguments.

In argumentation, the classification of an action or consequence as good or bad is the result of the so-called argumentation schemes for arguments from values (Macagno and Walton, 2014b, Chapter 2, 2018). The first of the pair is the scheme for argument from positive value (Walton et al., 2008, 321).

ARGUMENTATION SCHEME 6 *Argument from Values – Positive Values*

Premise 1:	Value V is positive as judged by agent α.
Premise 2:	The commitment to goal G contributes to (is an instance of) value V.
Conclusion:	V is a reason for α to commit to goal G.

The second of the pair is the scheme for argument from negative value (Walton et al., 2008, 321).

ARGUMENTATION SCHEME 6 *Argument from Values – Negative Values*

Premise 1:	Value V is negative as judged by agent α.
Premise 2:	The commitment to goal G contributes to (is an instance of) value V.
Conclusion:	V is a reason for retracting commitment to goal G.

This scheme can be used for analyzing the "absurdity" of the results that justifies the rejection of a specific interpretation. Clearly, the fundamental defeasibility dimension of this scheme consists in the evidence that can be brought in favor of the classification of the commitment to the pursued goal as an instance of a "negative value." The critical questions that can capture this aspect are represented as follows:

CQ_1: What evidence is there that V is positive/negative?

CQ_2: What evidence is there that the commitment to G contributes to (is an instance of) V, as opposed to evidence indicating room for doubt about whether it should be so classified?

CQ_3: Can the commitment be classified otherwise?

Based on this scheme, the absurdity argument needs to be backed by further evidence, which needs to establish both the foundation of the absurdity (unless it is evident) and the classification of the consequence as an instance thereof.

5.8.2 *Equitative Argument*

One of the interpretative arguments that fall within the aforementioned argumentation scheme representing the Argument from values is the equitative one, an argument proceeding from a specific value that cannot be disputed, namely fairness. In analyzing legal argumentation based on appeal to justice, Perelman (1980, 11) argued that the notion of justice consists in an application of the notion of equality. Following Aristotle, who observed that there should exist a likeness between beings to whom justice is administered, Perelman (1980) defined the principle of formal or abstract justice as the principle of action in accordance with which beings in the same essential category must be treated in the same way.

One clear example comes from *Popov v. Hayashi*, WL 31833731 (Cal. Super. Ct. 2002). As mentioned above, both claimant and defendant had different reasons to claim possession of the home-run ball. Plaintiff Popov had first a prepossessory interest in the ball, as he tried to catch it, not achieving full possession. Defendant Hayashi achieved full possession of the ball, but it had a cloud on its title. The court proposed to apply the principle of equitable division, which, however, had to be supported by reasons. One of the arguments used was from the authority of Roman law, which is not considered as a source of law at common law (at 11):

CASE 5.13: EQUITATIVE ARGUMENT

Both men have a superior claim to the ball as against all the world. Each man has a claim of equal dignity as to the other. We are, therefore, left with something of a dilemma . . . The concept of equitable division has its roots in ancient Roman law. As Helmholz points out, it is useful in that it "provides an equitable way to resolve competing claims which are equally strong." Moreover, "[i]t comports with what one instinctively feels to be fair."

In the same case, the court had to justify the application of the principle. However, there were no California cases on such an issue and for this reason argument from analogy could not be used. The only argument was the authority of a previous case where the same principle ("where more than one party has a valid claim to a single piece of property, the court will recognize an undivided interest in the property in proportion to the strength of the claim") was used (at 11).

Since this was a civil case, it had to be decided on the basis of the preponderance of the evidence. But what happens if the argument of one side is not even provably stronger than the argument of the other side to justify awarding the ball to one of the sides? As Judge McCarthy put it, each man has a claim of equal worth, based on the facts that could be determined. On the evidence, there appears to be no way to arrive at a just decision. However, Judge McCarthy broke the deadlock by appealing to the principle of fairness. As it happens, this way of arriving at a legal decision is a form of argument that does fit in an argumentation scheme (Walton, 2014, 434), derived from Perelman's views on the principle of justice (Perelman, 1980, 10–11). In the formulation of this scheme below α and β are agents and φ is an action or policy being considered.

ARGUMENTATION SCHEME 6A *Argument from Values – Fairness as equality*

Premise 1:	Agents α and β are of the same kind.
Premise 2:	φ treats α and β equally.
Premise 3:	If φ treats α and β equally, then φ is fair.
Interim conclusion:	φ is fair.
Premise 4:	If φ is fair, then φ should be carried out.
Ultimate conclusion:	φ should be carried out.

The version of the argument from fairness models the scheme as a chaining together of two inferences. The first supports the conclusion that φ is fair. The second uses this conclusion as a premise in an argument supporting the action φ. Judge McCarthy's argument fits the scheme: since Popov and Hayashi are agents of the same kind, splitting the proceeds for the ball treats them both equally, and if splitting the proceeds treats both equally, then it is a fair policy. Moreover, if this is a fair policy, it should be carried out.

5.8.3 Ancillary Argument: Argument from Coherence of the Law

The argument from coherence of the law is an ancillary argument, or rather a rebuttal of arguments supporting an interpretation of a statement of law leading to conflict of rules. It is grounded on the principle that the law provides a coherent system regulating community life without antinomies. It leads to the conclusion that in cases of interpretative controversies involving interpretations resulting in a conflict of rules, a "corrective interpretation" needs to be found (Tarello, 1980, 361). Like the argument from completeness of the law (see Section 5.11.3 below), the argument from coherence is purely negative, as it is used to rebut a specific (interpretative) conclusion without advancing any interpretation. However, while the argument from completeness of the law simply supports the need for an interpretation of a statement of law, this argument, by rejecting one of the possible interpretations, indicates the paradigm of the acceptable ones. In particular, it is used to exclude the abrogation of one of the conflicting statements of law (e.g., as being older or hierarchically inferior), opening the way for possible interpretations that do not result in a conflict of rules. As Tarello put it, in the event that there are two statements of law (A and B) that allow for different interpretations ($a_1, a_2, a_3; b_1, b_2$), some of which are incompatible (a_2 and b_2, or a_3 and b_2), there are two possible scenarios (Tarello, 1980, 362):

Possible solutions	Argument from coherence	Possible solutions
1. Declaring B unenforceable, as inferior or prior to A.	$\Longrightarrow$	*Not possible*, or not opportune
2. Choosing nonconflicting interpretations (a_1 and $b_1/b_2/b_3$; a_2 and b_1; or a_3 and b_1).	$\Longrightarrow$	(a_1 and $b_1/b_2/b_3$; a_2 and b_1; or a_3 and b_1)

This type of argument can be considered a subtype of Arguments from Consequences – see Argumentation Scheme 5 above.

5.8.4 Economic Argument

This last argument from consequences is also called argument from the non-repetitive legislator, as it is based on the principle that the legislator cannot issue useless expressions or statements. This argument is used for destructive purposes and excludes an interpretation of a statement of law that corresponds to the meaning of another, older or hierarchically superior, statement of law, or an interpretation that would make certain expression redundant. This argument is particularly effective if the statements of law are issued by the same source. However, it is extremely weak if the laws are on different hierarchical levels (statutes versus laws; laws versus regional laws), as in these instances repetition is extremely frequent.

The economic argument is used for excluding "default" interpretations (or explicatures) of specific lexical items and indicating the need for a different interpretative criterion. A clear case is *State* v. *Taylor*, discussed above (Case 5.5), which addressed the problem of interpreting "case" in the Minnesota Statutes (624.714, subd. 9(e), 1996) providing an exception to the gun permit requirement in the event the weapon is "contained in a closed and fastened case, gunbox, or securely tied package." The court needed to determine whether a purse can be considered as a "case" and argued as shown in Case box 5.14.

CASE 5.14: ECONOMIC ARGUMENT

A court construes technical words in a statute according to their technical meaning and other words according to common and accepted usage ... The court must construe the statutory language in context rather than defining each word in isolation from the others ... Not only would it be anomalous to construe "case" as broadly as Taylor suggests, when it is followed in the statute by so specialized a term as "gunbox," but also to do so would render the term "gunbox" completely superfluous ... If, as Taylor argues, a "case" includes anything that encloses or contains, then the term "gunbox," referring to a particular type of "case," adds nothing to the statute.

Here, the interpretation that leads to a redundancy or a useless term is excluded. This type of reasoning can be considered as a specific application of the inference resulting from flouting the second Gricean maxim of quantity, "Make your contribution as informative as is required (for the current purposes of the exchange)" (Grice, 1975, 45). The m-intention is retrieved by excluding interpretations (based on the default "ordinary meaning") that would lead to uninformative contributions and enriching the semantic representation of the utterance in a way that can be considered as informative. In this case, the explicature of the legal provision consists in narrowing the term "case" to "a gun case expressly made to contain a firearm."

In the *Taylor* example, the economic argument is used only for excluding an interpretation based on the pragmatically unacceptable consequence of an uninformative (redundant) term. However, this interpretative argument can be used for constructive purposes when there is only one acceptable alternative. A clear example is *Healthkeepers, Inc.* v. *Richmond Ambulance Authority*, 642 F.3d 466 (4th Cir. 2011), which addressed whether ambulance services are encompassed within the definition of "emergency services." In the US Code, the phrase "emergency services" is defined as follows (42 U.S.C. § 1396u-2(b)(2)(B)):

CASE 5.15: ECONOMIC ARGUMENT

In subparagraph (A)(i), the term "emergency services" means, with respect to an individual enrolled with an organization, covered inpatient and outpatient services that –

(i) are furnished by a provider that is qualified to furnish such services under this subchapter, and

(ii) are needed to evaluate or stabilize an emergency medical condition (as defined in subparagraph (C)).

According to this argument, the words "In subparagraph (A)(i)" limit the application of the definition to the subparagraph mentioned; otherwise such a phrase would be superfluous. The argument excludes an interpretation and leads to the only possible alternative option, following a pattern slightly more complex than the basic argument from consequences.

ARGUMENTATION SCHEME 5A *Argument from Consequences – Dichotomy*

Premise 1:	If A_1 is brought about, bad consequences will plausibly occur.
Premise 2:	What leads to bad consequences shall be not brought about.
Premise 3:	The alternative to A_1 is A_2.
Premise 4:	A_2 does not lead to the bad consequences of A_1.
Conclusion:	Therefore, A_2 should be brought about.

This scheme is more complex, as a specific interpretation (A_2) is backed by the fact that it is the alternative to an interpretation that leads to unwanted consequences. However, its acceptability depends on the fulfillment of the requirements that characterize the practical reasoning argument (Argumentation Scheme 7), described next.

5.9 PRACTICAL REASONING AND TELEOLOGICAL ARGUMENT

The teleological, or "purpose of the law," argument is based on the idea of an abstract legislator who enacted the law for a specific purpose. The interpreter is not reconstructing the actual will of a real person, but the goal for which a statement of law was issued. According to this argument, a statement of law shall be given the interpretation that corresponds to its purpose. The purpose is reconstructed considering the text of the specific act under consideration or the interests and goals pursued by the law in general (Tarello, 1980, 370). By means of this argument, the interpreted text can extend the application of a certain act beyond the literary meaning of the terms used therein.

The teleological argument can be represented with the Argumentation scheme 7, called practical reasoning, which we previously mentioned in Chapter 3.4 (Walton et al., 2008, 323).

ARGUMENTATION SCHEME 7 *Practical Reasoning*

Premise 1:	I (an agent) have a goal G.
Premise 2:	Carrying out this action A is a means to realize G.
Conclusion:	Therefore, I ought to (practically speaking) carry out this action A.

This scheme is challenged through the following critical questions (Walton et al., 2008, 96):

CQ$_1$: *Goal question:* Why is G the goal in this specific circumstance? Based on what evidence?

CQ$_2$: *Other-goals question:* Do I have goals other than G whose achievement is preferable and that should have priority?

CQ$_3$: *Possibility question:* Is it possible to bring about G in the given circumstances?

CQ$_4$: *Side-effects question:* Would bringing about G have known bad consequences that ought to be taken into account?

CQ$_5$: *Other-means question:* Are there alternative possible actions to bring about G?

CQ$_6$: *Best-means question:* Is A the best (or most favorable) of the alternatives?

For instance, we can consider *Garner* v. *Burr* [1951] 1 KB 31, 33. In this case, a farmer put wheels without rubber tires on a chicken coop and towed it with his tractor. He was prosecuted pursuant to the Road Traffic Act 1930, which prohibited the use of vehicles without rubber tires on highways. The defense argued that the coop was not a vehicle, which the dictionary defined as "a means of conveyance provided with wheels or runners and used for the carriage of persons or goods." The wheeled coop was not used to transport any person or goods at that time and could not be classified as a "vehicle." The court applied teleological reasoning as shown in Case box 5.16 (*emphasis* added).

CASE 5.16: TELEOLOGICAL ARGUMENT

The regulations are designed for a variety of reasons, among them *the protection of road surfaces*; and, as this vehicle had ordinary iron tyres, not pneumatic tyres, it was liable to damage the roads ... It is true that, according to the dictionary definition, a "vehicle" is primarily to be regarded as a means of conveyance provided with wheels or runners and used for the carriage of persons or goods. It is true that the [magistrates] do not find that anything was carried in the vehicle at the time; but I think that the Act is clearly *aimed at anything which will run on wheels which is being drawn by a tractor or another motor vehicle*.

In the case above, the purpose of the law is drawn from the "social" effects of the law, namely, to protect road surfaces. The definition of vehicle in this sense is argued for as a means to pursue the original purpose of the law.

The argument from purpose can be supported also by a historical argument, showing how the purpose of the law should correspond to the purpose of the legislators. For instance, in *Smith* v. *United States* (extensively discussed in Section 4.9 above) the defendants were accused of drug trafficking aggravated by the alleged "use of weapons." However, the defendants were actually bartering weapons, not "using it [a weapon] for its intended purpose," as the defense defined the term to counter the prosecution's more generic definition as "to derive service from." The court supported the broader definition, refusing to attribute to the Congress an intention that was claimed to be unreasonable given the possibility of violence that weapons create in any case (*Smith* at 240). The argument from the purpose of the law is extremely effective also if associated with an argument aimed at excluding alternatives, such as the *reductio ad absurdum* (see Section 5.8.1). By claiming that the intended interpretation not only supports the purpose of the law, but also is the only one that does not lead to absurd results or contradictions with that purpose, it is also supported by denying all the alternatives (see, for example, *United States* v. *Barber*, 360 F. Supp. 2d 784, 788 (E.D. Va. 2005)).

5.10 THE LOGICAL ROLE OF DEFINITIONS – THE ARGUMENT FROM CLASSIFICATION

The arguments analyzed so far concern the interpretation of statements and expressions in the sense of the different operations of "pragmatic enrichment" of the semantic representation of a legal statement. A more complex problem concerns the choice of a definition, namely the decision to use a meaning that is coded, conventional, stated in a legal document, or can be retrieved from the context. In order to address the problem concerning the reasoning underlying the choice of a definition, it is useful to introduce broadly the reasoning on which the use of a definition is based.

Definitions are crucial instruments for applying rules – texts expressing a general obligation or prohibition – to cases. We can reprise our example of *James* v. *United States*, discussed at Section 5.6 (*ejusdem generis*):

> **CASE 5.17: CLASSIFICATION**
>
> According to the Armed Career Criminal Act § 924(e), a person who has three previous convictions for a violent felony or a serious drug offense shall be imprisoned not less than fifteen years. The petitioner, Alphonso James, was convicted of firearm possession after having been convicted of a felony. James had previously been convicted once for attempted burglary and twice for drug trafficking. Therefore, the government argued that he had the necessary three "countable" convictions for the increased sentence.

The "application of a rule to a case" can be represented as a twofold process of reasoning, having the following pattern (Marmor 2013, 60):

(a) According to the law in situation S (at time t, etc.) if fact X takes place, then legal result Y obtains.

(b1) Event E took place.

(b2) According to the law in S, E counts as X.

(c1) According to the law, X takes place (from b1 and b2).

(c2) According to the law, Y obtains (from a and c1).

The first premise (a) is a major directive premise (if X, then Y), leading from the occurrence of a fact (case) X to a normative judgment (obligation or prescription) Y, expressed in the conclusion. However, the "fact" is the result of a classification of an event or specific circumstances (E) under a legal category (X) based on the provisions of the relevant legal system (S). These two steps of reasoning can be represented as two distinct patterns of arguments, based on different rules of material inference.

5.10.1 *Reasoning from Rules*

The argument leading from a general rule of law to a normative judgment can be represented as an argument from rules having the following pattern (adapted from Walton, Reed, and Macagno, 2008, 71):

ARGUMENTATION SCHEME 8 *Argument from Rules*

Major premise:	If carrying out action A is the established rule for situations of type V and a case x is a situation of type V, then (unless the case is an exception), A ought to be carried out in x.
Minor premise 1:	Carrying out types of actions A is the established rule for a situation of type V.
Minor premise 2:	*Case c has been classified as a V.*
Conclusion:	Therefore, A ought to be carried out in c.

The application of this argumentation scheme to the aforementioned example can be represented as follows:

Premise 1: If carrying out action A is the established rule for situations of type V, and a case x is a situation of type V, then (unless the case is an exception) A ought to be carried out in x.

Premise 2: Imprisoning a convicted person for no less than fifteen years is the established rule for a situation in which that person has three previous convictions for a violent felony or a serious drug offense (V).

Premise 3: James, who was convicted of possessing a firearm while a felon, and who had previously been convicted once for attempted burglary and twice for drug trafficking (c), has three previous convictions for a violent felony or a serious drug offense (V).

Conclusion: Therefore, due to his crimes, James (c) should be punished by a term of imprisonment of not less than fifteen years (A).

This scheme is only apparently simple. The problems arise when we consider the defeasibility conditions, summarized in the following critical questions:

CQ_1: Does the rule require carrying out types of actions that include A as an instance?

CQ_2: Are there other established rules that might conflict with, or override this one?

CQ_3: Is this case an exceptional one, that is, could there be extenuating circumstances warranting an excuse for noncompliance?

The first critical aspect (CQ_1) concerns the second premise, in which the rule applicable to the state of affairs A is provided. The law, however, provides only statements of law, texts from which rules result. The passage from a statement of law to a rule is at the center of the very notion of interpretation, which we discussed in our previous chapters. The second defeasibility condition concerns the possible conflicts between rules (Premise 1), in the sense that rules can be subject to conflicts with other rules or values, or their application can be problematic in a specific case. The third defeasibility condition addresses the problem of exceptions: a rule may provide for exceptions, and the speaker needs to take into account whether the case is an exceptional one (Premise 3).

5.10.2 *Reasoning from Classification*

The argumentation scheme above presupposes in Premise 3 the classification of the relevant circumstances (the concerned state of affairs c) under a relevant legal category V (to be a felony; to be a burglary, etc.). This classification is the conclusion of a defeasible classificatory reasoning (Marmor, 2013, 60), grounded on the circumstances and the meaning attributed in the context to the relevant legal predicate (V) (Ross, 1944). For example, the argument of the court in Case 17 rests on the fact that James committed three crimes that can be classified as "violent felony" or "serious drug offense."

This classificatory reasoning can be represented as a pattern of defeasible reasoning called "argument from classification," in which a new property (or a name) is attributed to an entity on the basis of other properties detected (Hastings, 1963; Schiappa, 2003; Walton and Macagno, 2009b, 2010; Zarefsky, 1998, 2006). This argument can be represented as follows (Walton, Reed, and Macagno 2008, 319).

ARGUMENTATION SCHEME 9 *Argument from Classification*

Major premise:	If some particular thing *a* can be classified as falling under verbal category C, then *a* has property V (in virtue of such a classification).
Minor premise:	*a* can be classified as falling under verbal category C.
Conclusion:	Therefore, *a* has property V.

The classificatory premise can be drawn either from (1) a rule of language taken for granted and drawn from the ordinary use of language, or (2) (in statutory definitions) a legal norm (Guastini, 2011, 56, 168), namely a second-order rule governing the interpretation of the legal statements and the application of the legal rules (Macagno and Damele, 2016). An example can be drawn from *James*:

Premise 1: If an action is an "offense under State law, involving manufacturing, distributing, or possessing with intent to manufacture or distribute, a controlled substance," (C), then it is a serious drug offense (V) (18 U.S.C. § 924(e) (2)(A)).

Premise 2: James's convictions for drug trafficking (*a*) can be classified as convictions for offenses involving distributing a controlled substance (C).

Conclusion: Therefore, James's prior convictions (a) were for serious drug offense (V).

Apparently, the use of this reasoning is not problematic. However, its complexity emerges when we investigate its defeasibility conditions.

5.10.3 *Defeasibility Conditions of Argument from Classification*

The acceptability of argument from classification depends on the acceptability of the definition, and on whether it admits for possible exceptions or defaults. This scheme is defeasible for two reasons. First, Premise 1 is defeasible, as it depends on (1) whether the definition is accepted or acceptable, and (2) whether it is not subject to exceptions. The classificatory premise (2) is also defeasible, as it rests on a previous defeasible classificatory reasoning based on the definition of C (Ross, 1944). These defeasibility conditions are summarized in the following dialectical criteria for assessing the quality of a classificatory argument:

CQ_1: What evidence is there that *a* definitely has property C, as opposed to evidence indicating room for doubt about whether it should be so classified?

CQ_2: Is the verbal classification in the classification premise based merely on an assumption about word usage that is subject to doubt?

The second critical question can be specified further, pointing out the various defeasibility conditions concerning the classificatory premise:

CQ$_{2.1}$: According to the classificatory principle, is there room for exceptions (is it possible for an entity to be a *C* and not a *V*)?

CQ$_{2.2}$: Is the classificatory principle (if *C* then *V*) based on reasonable and sufficient grounds?

CQ$_{2.3}$: Are there alternative classificatory criteria for *C*?

CQ$_{2.4}$: In the given context, is there an alternative classificatory principle that is supported by stronger interpretative arguments?

The defeasibility of the argument from classification emerges clearly in *James*. While the classification of "drug trafficking" as a "serious drug offense" was undisputed, more problematic was the categorization of "attempted burglary" as a "violent felony." The petitioner used the aforementioned scheme by denying the classificatory premise:

Premise 1: If a crime "(i) has as an element the use, attempted use, or threatened use of physical force against the person of another; or (ii) is burglary, arson, or extortion, involves use of explosives, or otherwise involves conduct that presents a serious potential risk of physical injury to another" (*C*), then it is a violent felony (*V*) (18 U.S.C. § 924(e)(2)(B)).

Premise 2: James's conviction for attempted burglary (*a*) cannot be classified as a conviction for burglary (*not C*).

Conclusion: Therefore, James's conviction for attempted burglary (*a*) was not a conviction for a violent felony (*not V*).

However, the Court of Appeals for the Eleventh Circuit underscored the defeasibility of this reasoning, represented by CQ$_{2.3}$ (Are there alternative classificatory criteria for *C*?). The reasoning of the court was the following:

Premise 1: If a crime "(i) has as an element the use, attempted use, or threatened use of physical force against the person of another; or (ii) is burglary, arson, or extortion, involves use of explosives, or otherwise involves conduct that presents a serious potential risk of physical injury to another" (*C*), then it is a violent felony (*V*) (18 U.S.C. § 924(e)(2)(B)).

Premise 2: Attempted burglary (*a*) "presents a serious potential risk of physical injury to another" (*C*), as, according to Florida law, it "involves conduct that presents a serious potential risk of physical injury to another."

Conclusion: Therefore, James's conviction for attempted burglary (*a*) was a conviction for a violent felony (*V*).

The most complex aspect of the argument from classification, however, is partially captured by the first critical question, which concerns the relationship between *definiens* and *definiendum*. The argument is grounded on a principle of inference establishing that "What the definition is predicated of, also the *definiendum* is

predicated of" (Stump 2004, 184, 221). This principle is based on a semantic equivalence, thus a biconditional relation, between a "*definiendum* expression" and
a "*definiens* expression" (Naess, 2005b, 161). However, not all the instances of
reasoning from classification are grounded on a semantic equivalence. Rather, this
equivalence is one of the possible "definitory" statements that are used to establish
identity and difference (Aristotle, *Topics*, 102 a17). An example from *James* is the
following argument from classification by Justice Scalia's dissenting opinion. His
reasoning focused on Premise 2, and consisted in an argument based on the definitions of the concepts involved ("burglary" and "attempt").

Premise 1: If there is the risk that the burglar will use force against a victim in completing
the crime (namely in the house) (C), then the burglar's conduct "presents
a serious potential risk of physical injury to another" (V) (*Taylor v. United
States*, 495 U.S. 575, 600 (1990)).

Premise 2a: Burglary is the "unlawful or unprivileged entry into, or remaining in,
a building or structure, with intent to commit a crime" (*Taylor* at 599).

Premise 2b: A perpetrator who has been convicted only of attempted burglary (*a*) has
failed to make it inside the home or workplace (*not C*).

Conclusion: Therefore, a criminal convicted only of attempted burglary (*a*) almost
certainly injured no one (*not V*); otherwise, he would have been convicted
of something far more serious, such as assault or murder.

Scalia's reasoning is grounded on three classificatory premises. The definitions of
"burglary" and "to attempt" are uncontroversial, and lead to the conclusion that an
attempted burglary consists of failing to enter the house. However, Premise 1
expresses a principle for classifying "a serious potential risk of physical injury to
another" as "the risk that force is used against a victim in completing the crime."
This definitory statement, applied to burglary, leads to the conclusion that a burglar
needs to be in the house in order to complete the crime (otherwise he is only
attempting it), and, therefore, if he is not in the house, there cannot be a serious
potential risk of physical injury. While Premise 1 can be certainly used for guiding
the classification of crimes, it can be hardly considered as an accepted definition, as
it introduces a specification ("in completing the crime") that is not accepted by the
other members of the court. Moreover, since it is not a semantic definition, it is not
convertible. Even if James did not enter the house in attempting to commit burglary,
his behavior could have caused a serious potential risk of physical injury.

The problem of the choice of a definition to be used in an argument from rules
leads to the crucial issue of justifying a definition. "Burglary" can be defined in
different ways, according to the meaning given by contemporary dictionaries,
statutory definitions, or dictionaries of the time the statute was drafted. The choice
of one of these possible definitions leads to legal consequences and needs to be
backed by arguments when it is controversial. This leads to the category of

"abductive" arguments, a broad category that groups the reasons that can be given to support the choice of a definition.

5.11 ABDUCTIVE ARGUMENTS

The category of "abductive arguments" includes arguments used for formulating a hypothesis that best explains or accounts for data describing a state of affairs, an event, or a verbal activity and its units – such as statements or use of specific lexical item (Harman, 1965; Hobbs, Stickel, Appelt, and Martin, 1993; Josephson and Josephson, 1996, 5–8). Abduction is commonly considered as a theory-forming or interpretative inference, which has been used in pragmatics to represent the reasoning underlying the formation of an interpretative hypothesis informativeness (Atlas, 2005, 95; Atlas and Levinson, 1981, 40–41) (see our discussion of the concept of reasoning from the best interpretation in Chapter 4). As we pointed out in our previous chapter, the structure of the reasoning proceeds from a set of findings or data and a set of possible explanations to the determination of the "best" one. This type of inference was adapted in pragmatics to describe the inferences used in interpreting statements. In this event, the "best" interpretation of an utterance is assessed considering its informativity (the best interpretation is the most informative one among the competing interpretations) and its consistency with the common ground associated to the context. An interpretation is thus regarded as a dialectical process (Miller, 2019; Van Fraassen, 1980, 134).

In this perspective, an interpretation of a statute should be understood as a hypothesis about what the word, phrase, sentence, or other unit of language, should best be taken to mean representing the speaker's intention in a dialogue, given the textual and contextual evidence in the case. Provided that such a hypothesis can be classified as a species of explanation, as it could be on the dialectical approach, it is possible to have an argumentation scheme for inference to the best interpretation that is a modified version of the scheme for inference to the best explanation presented in Section 3.4.2 and in Chapter 4. This is the new scheme we propose for legal interpretation.

ARGUMENTATION SCHEME 10 *Abductive Scheme for Inference to the Best Interpretation*

Premise 1:	S is a sentence (or lexical item) used in a legal document such as a statute (generally, in context K).
Premise 2:	I_1 is a satisfactory interpretation of S.
Premise 3:	No alternative interpretation $I_2 \ldots I_n$ given so far is as satisfactory as I_1.
Conclusion:	Therefore, I_1 is a plausible interpretation of S, as a defeasible hypothesis.

This type of inference is characterized by an adaptation of the critical questions we described in Chapter 4 and developed in the pragmatics literature.

CQ_1: How satisfactory is I_1 as an interpretation of S, apart from the alternative interpreta-tions $I_2 \ldots _n$ available so far in the dialogue?

CQ_2: How much better an interpretation is I_1 than the alternative interpretations $I_2 \ldots _n$ available so far in the dialogue?

CQ_3: How far has the dialogue progressed? If the dialogue is an inquiry, how thorough has the investigation of the case been?

CQ_4: Would it be better to continue the dialogue further, instead of drawing a conclusion at this point?

This abductive and critical type of reasoning is, however, often used in its simplified version for drawing a plausible interpretation of a linguistic expression, called "argument from sign." This type of argument associates a fact to the most common possible explanation thereof, disregarding the competing alternatives. In this sense, the fact becomes a signal, and the explanation is heuristically drawn. The pattern of argument proceeds from the occurrence of B to the occurrence of A, based on the generalization that normally, if A occurs, then B will (might) occur (Walton et al., 2008, 170). This type of argument can be reinterpreted for representing the interpretation of a legal expression in a legal text as follows.

ARGUMENTATION SCHEME 11 *Argument from Sign*

Premise 1:	S is a sentence (or lexical item) used in a legal document such as a statute.
Premise 2:	When S is used, the speaker normally intends I.
Conclusion:	Therefore, the speaker intended I by using S.

This pattern of reasoning is an uncritical version of the argument to the best interpretation. While this latter scheme represents the overall interpretative activity, aimed at reaching the best explanation of a legal statement based on the analysis of the arguments provided in support of the alternatives, the argument from sign represents a heuristic association between the *explanandum* and its most prototypical interpretation, in the case of statutory interpretation the coded or conventional meaning (Jaszczolt, 2007,50–52, 2011, 13). In this sense, the argument from sign can be one of the possible alternative hypotheses of the argument from best explanation.

The strength of the argument from sign lies in the frequency of the association between *explanans* and *explanandum*, in our case the statement or more specifically the lexical item and its interpretation. In legal interpretation, there are three distinct criteria for attributing the meaning to a linguistic expression:

1. Ordinary meaning (the meaning that a speaker would attribute to an expression at the time the law is interpreted).
2. Ordinary "original" meaning (the meaning that a speaker would ascribe to an expression at the time the law was drafted).
3. Technical meaning (the specific definition that a term receives in a text or the meaning that the individuals who are expert in or familiar with the specific relevant technical/professional context would attribute to it).

These three possibilities represent common ways to attribute a specific meaning to an expression: when a term S occurs, it usually means I (based on linguistic conventions in force at present, in the past, or in the specific contextually relevant field of activities); therefore, if the legislator used S, he probably meant I (Hobbs, Stickel, Appelt, and Martin, 1993). In the reasoning grounded on these three usual explanations, we notice that the contextual evidence is limited to its role in supporting the choice of a type of convention (i.e., definition). A different basis for meaning is constituted of the evidence from the surrounding text: according to this type of sign, the meaning of an expression should be determined based on the meaning it received in the "system" of the law or the co-text of the other legal statements or provisions. While in the cases a–c above the regularities are conventions, in the case of systematic argument the explanation is either a convention established elsewhere in the legal system or a regularity abstracted from the uses of the term in the co-text (broadly considered). The conflict between these explanations of meaning can be thought of in terms of presumptions, in which those associated with ordinary or technical meaning conflict with the ones associated with the system of the law (the absurdity of an incoherent legal system; the purpose of the law) (De Sloovere, 1936, 233).

5.11.1 *Ordinary and Technical Meaning Arguments*

According to the rule of the ordinary meaning, "words are to be understood in their ordinary, everyday meanings – unless the context indicates that they bear a technical sense" (Scalia and Garner, 2012, Chapter 6). This argument is aimed at providing an explanation in the event that no statutory definition is provided, nor the context supports a technical interpretation (Slocum, 2016b, 3). The "best explanation" or best interpretation of the speaker's (or legislative) intention expressed in legal texts is commonly considered the ordinary meaning of the language in a statutory text (Slocum, 2016b, 8). The force of this type of clue does not, however, eliminate the inherent defeasibility of this pattern of argument (Slocum, 2016b, 11, 15–20): in addition to the fact that legal language differs from the ordinary one due to its vocabulary and syntax (Tiersma, 1999), the intention expressed by the "plain meaning" can be contradicted by other types of argument in support of a different intention or challenging its consequences.

The force of this argument lies in its backings, namely (a) the reasons for excluding other competing definitions, and (b) the reasons for accepting a specific definition as that which mirrors the "ordinary meaning" of the term. The first type of backing is an argument from ignorance (Argumentation Scheme 1B), which leads from the absence of evidence of a legal definition to the need of an ordinary meaning one. The second is more complex, as it normally corresponds to an argument from expertise (the authority of dictionaries or linguists), or an argument from popular opinion, namely the evidence of a common and shared use of the term (Slocum, 2016b, Chapter 3).

An example of the role of the authority argument is the argument used by Scalia in *James* v. *United States* (our Case 5.6), in which he argues in favor of a specific interpretation of the notion of "violent felonies" at 18 U.S.C. § 924(e)(2)(A).

CASE 5.18: ORDINARY-MEANING ARGUMENT

First to invite analysis is the word Congress placed at the forefront of the residual provision: "otherwise." When used as an adverb (as it is in § 924(e)(2) (B)(ii), modifying the verb "involves"), "otherwise" is defined as "[i]n a different manner" or "in another way." *Webster's New International Dictionary* 1729 (2d ed. 1954). Thus, the most natural reading of the statute is that committing one of the enumerated crimes (burglary, arson, extortion, or crimes involving explosives) is *one way* to commit a crime "involv[ing] conduct that presents a serious potential risk of physical injury to another"; and that *other ways* of committing a crime of that character similarly constitute "violent felon[ies]." In other words, the enumerated crimes are examples of what Congress had in mind under the residual provision, and the residual provision should be interpreted with those examples in mind.

This argument could be used because a more specific meaning – the technical one provided by the statute, or by the context of other legal texts, or the specific context of the subject matter at hand – was not available. However, concerning the term "burglary," the court used arguments only based on the definitions given at common law (since it concerns a federal offense) and the relevant state laws. These definitions provide the "technical" meaning, which is thus more relevant than the ordinary one.

The presumed lower defeasibility of the technical meaning leads to the burden of proving the higher acceptability of a different type of meaning. A clear example is the aforementioned *Taylor* v. *United States*, in which the common law definition of the disputed term "burglary" (the most relevant definition for the interpretation of the statute) is challenged based on the "ordinary" meaning that the term has in the criminal codes of the States (*Taylor* at 593–594, emphasis added):

CASE 5.19: TECHNICAL VERSUS "ORDINARY" MEANING

Some Courts of Appeals, see n. 2, supra, have ruled that 924(e) incorporates the common-law definition of burglary [(a breaking and entering of a dwelling at night, with intent to commit a felony)], relying on the maxim that a statutory term is generally presumed to have its common-law meaning ... The problem with this view is that the contemporary understanding of "burglary" *has diverged a long way from its common-law roots.* Only a few States retain the common-law definition, or something closely resembling it. Most other States have expanded this definition to include entry without a "breaking," structures other than dwellings, offenses committed in the daytime, entry with intent to commit a crime other than a felony, etc. ...

The relationship between the ordinary-meaning and the authority arguments emerges in cases of conflicts of authorities – namely what kind of authorities can be used to support a given interpretation. In particular, the ordinary-meaning argument can be attacked by another type of authority argument, the one based on the "ordinary" meaning shared by the people *at the time when the law was drafted.* This conflict is at the basis of one of the crucial issues of dissent in *District of Columbia* v. *Heller,* 554 U.S. 570 (2008) analyzed in our Section 3.3. The majority opinion used the following argument (at 584):

CASE 5.20: ORDINARY-MEANING ARGUMENT – MODERN USE

We turn to the phrases "keep arms" and "bear arms." Johnson defined "keep" as, most relevantly, "[t]o retain; not to lose," and "[t]o have in custody." Johnson 1095. Webster defined it as "[t]o hold; to retain in one's power or possession." No party has apprised us of an idiomatic meaning of "keep Arms." Thus, the most natural reading of "keep Arms" in the Second Amendment is to "have weapons." ... At the time of the founding, as now, to "bear" meant to "carry." See Johnson 161; Webster; T. Sheridan, *A Complete Dictionary of the English Language* (1796); 2 *Oxford English Dictionary* 20 (2d ed. 1989) (hereinafter Oxford). When used with "arms," however, the term has a meaning that refers to carrying for a particular purpose – confrontation.

The authority of contemporary dictionaries is here used to support a specific interpretation of "to keep arms" and "to bear arms," which is shown to be similar to the one found in the dictionaries at the time of drafting.

This argument was challenged by a contrary one, focused on the meaning that the phrase and its components had for the citizens in the eighteenth century. The argument of the dissenting opinion reads as follows (*Heller* at 646–647):

CASE 5.21: "FIXED" MEANING ARGUMENT – ORIGINAL USE

The term "bear arms" is a familiar idiom; when used unadorned by any additional words, its meaning is "to serve as a soldier, do military service, fight." *Oxford English Dictionary* 634 (2d ed. 1989). It is derived from the Latin *arma ferre*, which, translated literally, means "to bear *[ferre]* war equipment *[arma]*." Brief for Professors of Linguistics and English as *Amici Curiae* 19. One 18th-century dictionary defined "arms" as "weapons of offence, or armour of defence," 1 S. Johnson, A *Dictionary of the English Language* (1755), and another contemporaneous source explained that "[b]y *arms*, we understand those instruments of offence generally made use of in war; such as firearms, swords, & c. By *weapons*, we more particularly mean instruments of other kinds (exclusive of fire-arms), made use of as offensive, on special occasions." 1 J. Trusler, The Distinction Between Words Esteemed Synonymous in the English Language 37 (1794). Had the Framers wished to expand the meaning of the phrase "bear arms" to encompass civilian possession and use, they could have done so by the addition of phrases such as "for the defense of themselves," as was done in the Pennsylvania and Vermont Declarations of Rights. The *unmodified* use of "bear arms," by contrast, refers most naturally to a military purpose, as evidenced by its use in literally dozens of contemporary texts.

In addition to the authority of the dictionaries, the dissenting judge provided the authority of experts (professors of linguistics) and specific works on the semantic distinctions between apparent synonyms. Moreover, this argument from ordinary meaning also provided an inductive line of proof, collecting the relevant texts in which the phrase occurred and generalizing the common meaning.

5.11.2 *Systematic Argument*

The systematic argument is a strategy of harmonization (Groppi and Spigno, 2017, 535; Raitio, 2003, 333), grounded on the concept of legal system, according to which the meaning of a statement of law (or a term) shall correspond to the meaning imposed (and not excluded) by the legal system. Tarello points out that, due to the ambiguity of "legal system," the systematic argument is actually an umbrella term under which several types of arguments are collected, all characterized by the fact that co-textual evidence is used to draw a conclusion about the interpretation of a term, a phrase, or an expression (see also Groppi and Spigno, 2017). A systematic argument consists in drawing the intention of the legislator from the evidence of the legal system: the co-text is taken as a sign of the speaker's intention (the intention of the legislator) (De Sloovere, 1936, 232). This argument can be simple or associated with other schemes, and in particular with the analogical ones. The occurrence of the same term in another statement of law of the same statute is considered as a sign of the same communicative intention. When the term is defined in its other occurrence, the reasoning is simply an abductive argument. However, when the meaning is not defined, it needs to be abstracted from the various occurrences and applied to the controversial one. In this sense, the argument from sign is mixed with an analogical argument. Another variant is the practical argument: different interpretations of the same term or expression would lead to an incoherence; therefore, the best way to avoid this consequence is to assign the same meaning to the different occurrences of the same term or expression. Its force lies in the possible negative or absurd consequences caused by an alleged inconsistency of the legal system.

The systematic argument can have a broader or narrower scope, namely it can be grounded on a broader or narrower type of "co-text." The broadest type of systematic argument is based on a meaning of "system" that corresponds to the whole set of legal concepts. In this view, the meaning of a term shall be determined based on the definition it acquires based on the whole legal system. However, since legal concepts are often conflicting with each other, this argument is often weak (Tarello, 1980, 378). A narrower interpretation of the notion of "system" corresponds to the order or place of statement of law or term within a *code*. For instance, Guastini provides the following example (Guastini, 2011, 48–49). Article 49 of the Italian Constitution reads as follows:

CASE 5.22: SYSTEMATIC ARGUMENT

All citizens have the right to freely associate in political parties in order to contribute by democratic methods to determine national policy.

Considering the rights of the immigrants, how shall be the concept of "citizen" interpreted in this article? According to the systematic argument, the placement of this term in an article of the Constitution is a sign that the legislator intended its meaning to be retrievable from the other provisions of this text. In this perspective, its meaning can be drawn from the article that governs the inviolable human rights (Article 2): "The republic recognizes and guarantees the inviolable human rights, be it as an individual or in social groups expressing their personality, and it ensures the performance of the unalterable duty to political, economic, and social solidarity."

The interpreter can establish that the right of political association is a human right, and then claim that the inviolable rights are guaranteed not only to citizens, but to all human beings. Therefore, the concept of "citizen" should not be interpreted according to its legal meaning of "legally recognized subject or national of a state," but extensively as "human being." The reasoning is abductive, as the occurrence of the regulation of a specific right with another provision governing more general rights is only a sign of a common intention. This reasoning can also be interpreted as abductive in the practical sense: the best way to avoid inconsistencies is to interpret the term "citizen" as "human being."

In Chapter 2, we noted that in the EU case *Google Spain SL, Google Inc. v. Agencia Española de Protección de Datos (AEPD), Costeja Gonzalez* (2014, C-131/12, ECLI:EU:C:2014:317), the "purpose of the law" was determined based on the textual evidence. In particular, one of most important arguments of the court was based on the purpose of Directive 95/46/EC, namely "to ensure a high level of protection of the fundamental rights and freedoms of natural persons, in particular their right to privacy, with respect to the processing of personal data." This goal was supported by the indications provided in the preamble of the directive and in a previous article thereof, which were considered as signs of the "speaker's intention." The argument of the court for supporting the "purpose of the law" was presented as follows (*Google Spain* at 54):

> **CASE 5.23: SYSTEMATIC ARGUMENT – PURPOSE OF THE LAW**
>
> It is to be noted in this context that it is clear in particular from recitals 18 to 20 in the preamble to Directive 95/46 and Article 4 thereof that the European Union legislature sought to prevent individuals from being deprived of the protection guaranteed by the directive and that protection from being circumvented, by prescribing a particularly broad territorial scope.

The court interpreted the recitals (stating the goal "to ensure that individuals are not deprived of the protection to which they are entitled under this Directive") and Article 4 ("Member States shall protect the fundamental rights and freedoms of natural persons, and in particular their right to privacy") as related and indicating the intention of ensuring a "high level of protection" that is pursued by "a broad territorial scope." The relationships between the legal statements and the purpose of the law, and between this goal and the right that is disputed in the aforementioned case (the right to object, provided for at Article 14 of the Directive) are drawn abductively as default explanations (signs). The court reasoned that the intention expressed in different statements should be related, and that the intention expressed in previous articles and whereas clauses underlies all the specific articles.

The systematic argument can also correspond to the argument grounded on a terminological consistency. According to a second interpretation of "legal system," it shall be considered as the set of concepts used by the legislator (in a code, in an act). For this reason, based on the presumption that there is a rigid correspondence between legal concepts and legal terms, if a term has a certain meaning in a statement of law, such a term shall be interpreted as having such a meaning in all the statements of law in which it appears. This type of reasoning can be explained with an example from the aforementioned case *Healthkeepers, Inc.* v. *Richmond Ambulance Authority*, in which the concept of "emergency services" was defined in a paragraph, but the definition provided was limited to its use in a previous paragraph. According to the systematic argument, such a definition shall be applied also for all the uses within the statute. In this case, in particular, the systematic argument is reinforced by an argument from absurd consequences (*Healthkeepers* at 472):

> CASE 5.24: SYSTEMATIC ARGUMENT – TERMINOLOGICAL CONSISTENCY
>
> Here, were emergency services given two different meanings in two parts of the statute, there would be inconsistencies in its application to various services.

Also in this case, the systematic argument is used in its simple form, as the term has been previously defined.

The systematic argument, in its variant of terminological consistency, can be used in combination with an abstraction of the common features from the occurrences of the same term in the relevant context. An example can be found in the aforementioned *Taylor* v. *United States*, which hinged on the interpretation of "burglary" for the purposes of determining the number of prior "violent felonies" committed by a defendant. Since the crime has different definitions according to the criminal laws of each state, the term "burglary" could mean both the crime classified as such, and the behavior that led to prior convictions. The doubt concerned whether the classification of a specific case of burglary as a violent felony shall be established considering the features of the specific conduct, or the features of each state's definitions of this category of conducts. The court reasoned by considering the text of the relevant statute, as shown in Case box 5.23 (*Taylor* at 601, emphasis added):

CASE 5.25: SYSTEMATIC ARGUMENT – ANALOGY WITH OTHER TERMS

First, the language of [Armed Career Criminal Act §] 924(e) generally supports the inference that Congress intended the sentencing court to look only to the fact that the defendant had been convicted of crimes falling within certain categories, and not to the facts underlying the prior convictions. Section 924(e) (1) refers to "a person who ... has three previous *convictions*" for – not a person who has *committed* – three previous violent felonies or drug offenses. Section 924(e)(2)(B)(i) defines "violent felony" as any crime punishable by imprisonment for more than a year that "has as an *element*" – not any crime that, in a particular case, *involves* – the use or threat of force. Read in this context, the phrase "is burglary" in 924(e)(2)(B)(ii) most likely refers to the elements of the statute of conviction, not to the facts of each defendant's conduct.

The evidence from the surrounding text is taken as a sign of the speaker's intention. As underscored in our previous chapter, the pragmatic principle at work in this argument is the maxim of relation. According to this principle, the statements and the lexical items are not disconnected remarks, but are related to each other to pursue a common purpose (Grice, 1975, 45; 51). However, the argument from sign provides only the indication of the evidence to look at; it does not provide the definition for determining the enriched semantic representation of the statement. To this purpose, the common features need to be abstracted from the various uses of "crime" and "felony," two terms that represent generic categories of "burglary." Since these two terms are both used to refer to *categories* of crime and not to conducts, the relevant feature is to be an "abstract category" or "type of conduct," which is then transferred to the controversial terms being interpreted (in a kind of *noscitur a sociis*). Thus, the use of "burglary" together with the other terms is a sign that it should be interpreted in the same way, namely as a category of crime.

In our previous chapter, we pointed out how the systematic argument has a strong relationship with the pragmatic maxim of relevance (see our Section 4.2), and more precisely with the cognitive principle aimed at maximizing informativity and minimizing effort (Nunberg, 1979, 167–168; Sperber and Wilson, 1995; Zipf, 1949). The systematic argument provides the default explanation for the interpretation of a term that occurs in different sections or statements in a statute: if the speaker (the legislator) has used a term with a specific meaning elsewhere, then it is a sign that he intends to use the term with that specific meaning in the statute. The systematic argument is thus a sign justified by the pragmatic structure of the text. An example is the case introduced in Chapter 4 and briefly mentioned above, *Smith* v. *United States* (at 233–236; emphasis in original, see Case box 5.26).

[T]he next subsection of the statute, § 924(d) . . . provides for the confiscation of firearms that are "used in" referenced offenses which include the crimes of transferring, selling, or transporting firearms in interstate commerce. The court concludes from this that *whenever* the term appears in this statute, "use" of a firearm must include nonweapon use.

The systematic argument represents a crucial example of the relationship between pragmatic principles, legal canons, and argumentation. The principle of a text as a "coherent whole" is firstly a pragmatic principle (Giora, 1985; Macagno, 2018; Reinhart, 1980), justified based on the economy principle and the assumption that the speaker intends to be maximally efficient in identifying the meaning of the terms used (Nunberg, 1979; Wilson and Sperber, 2004). The use of a term with a specific meaning or the expression of the "purpose of the law" in the co-text is thus taken as a sign of a global intention that is generalized to the whole text, and that shall apply to the interpretation of the other legal statements or occurrences of the same term.

In the systematic argument, the weakness of the sign argument is offset by the general acceptance of the principle of relevance (or more limitedly, of text coherence). The strength of this type of argument lies in its combination with other types of reasoning, which can be explicit or implicit. In our Case 24, the court explicitly mentioned the negative (absurd) consequences of having a term used with different definitions. In Case 25, the court backed the abductive argument with an argument from ignorance ("If Congress had meant to adopt an approach that would require the sentencing court to engage in an elaborate factfinding process regarding the defendant's prior offenses, surely this would have been mentioned somewhere in the legislative history," *Taylor* at 602). The exclusion of the competing explanations makes the interpretative hypothesis proposed the only one that is based on evidence and is acceptable, thus the "best" one.

5.11.3 *Ancillary Argument: Argument from Completeness of the Law*

This argument is ancillary, in the sense that it supports the need for an interpretation, without providing it. It is based on the idea that the legal system is complete and without gaps and it is aimed at inferring, from the lack of a specific rule governing a case, the existence of a generic principle attributing to such a case a legal qualification (a subtype of argument from best explanation, see Argumentation Scheme 10). This argument is grounded on the fact that it is impossible to explicitly regulate every specific category of individuals and specific behavior by attributing precise legal qualifications, but the law implicitly provides a regulation for every case. For this reason, if no legal qualifications are explicitly attributed to a certain behavior, then it is still possible to argue for the existence of an implicit rule governing such behavior. This argument is used to reject any arguments leading to the conclusion that if a specific behavior is not governed by a specific rule, then no legal qualification is attributed by law to such behavior.

5.12 CONCLUSION

In this chapter we have shown how it is possible to translate the arguments of interpretation into informal patterns of argument, namely argumentation schemes. By identifying the semantic and logical structure of the prototypical inferences used to support the interpretation of a source statement, it is possible to reduce the arguments of interpretation to six argumentation schemes (as preliminarily shown in Macagno, Walton, and Sartor 2014): the scheme for argument from lack of evidence, the scheme for argument from analogy, the scheme for argument from authority (including the scheme from a "democratic" authority, i.e., popular opinion), the scheme for argument from consequences (including the argument from values), the scheme for practical reasoning, and the scheme for abductive arguments. The interpretative arguments can be conceived as subtypes of these generic patterns, each representing a specific characterization of the semantic principle underlying the use of the scheme. The summary of this translation can be represented in Figure 5.2, which comprises the eleven interpretative arguments that we listed in the introduction and the arguments from ordinary and technical meaning.

This correspondence between interpretative arguments and argumentation schemes can be important for several reasons. First, it provides a common vocabulary, which can be shared in the fields of law, argumentation theory, artificial intelligence, and pragmatics (Macagno, Walton, and Sartor, 2018) for referring to maxims usually named differently in the various common law or civil law traditions or schools. Second, it is crucial for assessing the grounds of statute interpretation (formalized in artificial intelligence, see Bench-Capon and Prakken, 2010; Gordon, 2010; Verheij, 2003) and detecting the potential critical dimensions of each construction. Third, schemes can be further classified, providing tree-models that allow the interpreter to select the most suitable argument by means of disjunctive questions (Macagno, 2015a; Macagno and Walton, 2015; Walton et al., 2016, 57), depending on the type of conclusion the interpreter intends to pursue (or the interpretative text advocates). As we have shown, what is also important is the categorization of the maxims of judicial interpretation by the types of reasoning that justify their application.

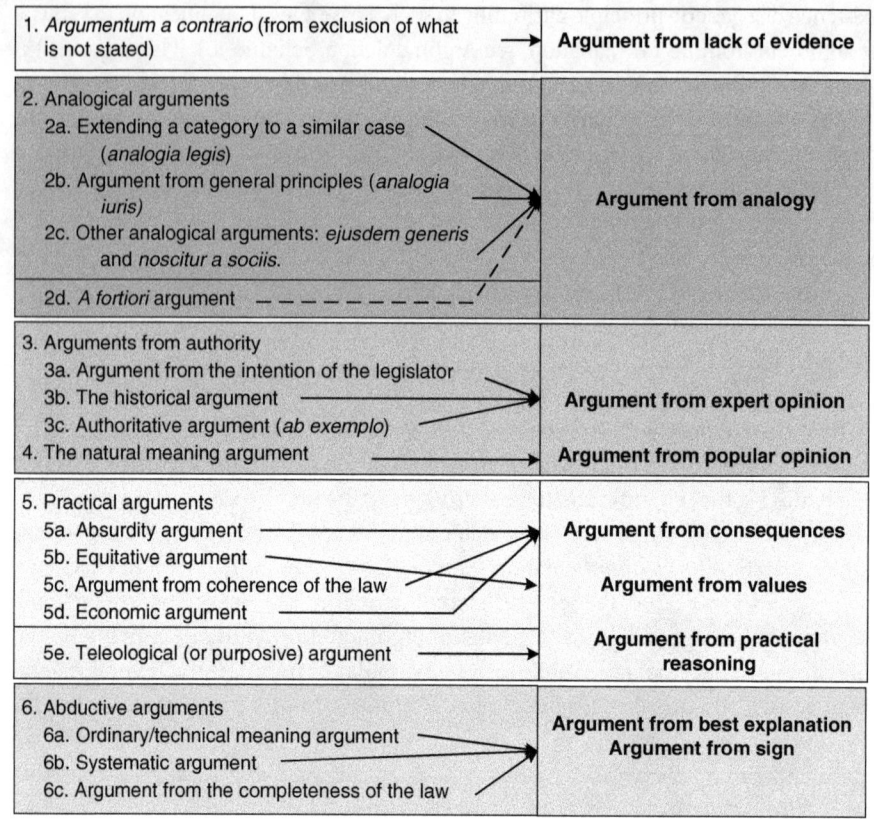

FIGURE 5.2 The arguments of interpretation

REFERENCES

Amerio, Lucilla. 2019. "La responsabilità ex art. 57 c.p. del direttore di testate telematiche: tra estensione interpretativa ed analogia in malam partem." *Media Laws* (2): 283–292.

Aristotle. 1991a. "Posterior analytics." In *The Complete Works of Aristotle, Vol. I*, edited by Jonathan Barnes. Princeton, NJ: Princeton University Press.

Aristotle. 1991b. "Prior analytics." In *The Complete Works of Aristotle, Vol. I*, edited by Jonathan Barnes. Princeton. NJ: Princeton University Press.

Aristotle. 1991c. "Rhetoric." In *The Complete Works of Aristotle, Vol. II*, edited by Jonathan Barnes. Princeton, NJ: Princeton University Press.

Aristotle. 1991d. "Topics." In *The Complete Works of Aristotle, Vol. I*, edited by Jonathan Barnes. Princeton, NJ: Princeton University Press.

Ashley, Kevin. 1991. "Reasoning with cases and hypotheticals in HYPO." *International Journal of Man-Machine Studies* 34(6): 753–796. https://doi.org/10.1016/0020-7373(91)90011-U.

Ashley, Kevin. 2006. "Case-based reasoning." In *Information Technology and Lawyers*, edited by Arno R. Lodder and Anja Oskamp, 26–60. Amsterdam, Netherlands: Springer.

Ashley, Kevin, and Edwina Rissland. 2003. "Law, learning and representation." *Artificial Intelligence* 150(1): 17–58. https://doi.org/10.1016/S0004-3702(03)00109-7.

Atlas, Jay David. 1989. *Philosophy without Ambiguity: A Logico-Linguistic Essay*. Oxford, UK: Clarendon Press.

Atlas, Jay David. 2005. *Logic, Meaning, and Conversation*. Oxford, UK: Oxford University Press.

Atlas, Jay David, and Stephen Levinson. 1981. "It-clefts, informativeness and logical form: Radical pragmatics (revised standard version)." In *Radical Pragmatics*, edited by Peter Cole, 1–62. New York, NY: Academic Press.

Balkin, Jack. 2018. "Arguing about the constitution: The topics in constitutional interpretation." *Constitutional Commentary* 33: 145–255.

Bench-Capon, Trevor, and Henry Prakken. 2010. "Using argument schemes for hypothetical reasoning in law." *Artificial Intelligence and Law* 18(2): 153–174. https://doi.org/10.1007/s10506-010-9094-8.

Bergmann, Michael. 2005. "Defeaters and higher-level requirements." *The Philosophical Quarterly* 55(220): 419–436. https://doi.org/10.1111/j.0031-8094.2005.00408.x.

Bird, Otto. 1962. "The tradition of the logical topics: Aristotle to Ockham." *Journal of the History of Ideas* 23(3): 307–323. https://doi.org/10.2307/2708069.

Bochenski, Innocent Marie-Joseph. 1974. "An analysis of authority." In *Authority*, edited by Frederick Adelman, 58–65. The Hague, Netherlands: Martinus Nijhoff.

Brannon, Valerie. 2018. *Statutory Interpretation: Theories, Tools, and Trends*. Washington, DC: Congressional Research Service.

Brewer, Scott. 2018. "Indefeasible analogical argument." In *Analogy and Exemplary Reasoning in Legal Discourse*, edited by Hendrik Kaptein and Bastiaan van der Velden, 33–48. Amsterdam, Netherlands: Amsterdam University Press.

Canale, Damiano, and Giovanni Tuzet. 2009. "The a simili argument: An inferentialist setting." *Ratio Juris* 22(4): 499–509. https://doi.org/10.1111/j.1467-9337.2009.00437.x.

Canale, Damiano, and Giovanni Tuzet. 2018. "Analogical reasoning and extensive interpretation." In *Analogy and Exemplary Reasoning in Legal Discourse*, edited by Hendrik Kaptein and Bastiaan van der Velden, 65–86. Amsterdam, Netherlands: University of Amsterdam Press.

Chiassoni, Pierluigi, Eveline Feteris, and Hanna Maria Kreuzbauer. 2016. "Taking stock of the past: Rhetoric, topics, hermeneutics." In *A Treatise of Legal Philosophy and General Jurisprudence*, edited by Enrico Pattaro and Corrado Roversi, 1693–1713. Amsterdam, Netherlands: Springer.

Cicero, Marcus Tullius. 2003. *Topica*, edited by Tobias Reinhardt. Oxford, UK: Oxford University Press.

Colombo, Giovanna Maria. 2003. *Sapiens Aequitas*: L'Equità nella Riflessione Canonistica tra i Due Codici. Rome, Italy: Pontificia Università Gregoriana.

Copi, Irving, and Keith Burgess-Jackson. 1992. *Informal Logic*. New York, NY: Macmillan Publishing Company.

Damele, Giovanni. 2011. "Rhetoric and persuasive strategies in high courts' decisions: Some remarks on the recent decisions of the Portuguese Tribunal Constitucional and the Italian Corte Costituzionale on same-sex marriage." In *Argumentation*, edited by Michał Araszkiewicz, Matej Myška, Terezie Smejkalová, Jaromír Šavelka, and Martin Škop, 81–93. Brno, Czech Republic: Masarykova UP.

Damele, Giovanni. 2016. "Adventures of a metaphor. Apian imagery in the history of political thought." In *Metaphor and Communication*, edited by Elisabetta Gola and Francesca Ervas, 173–188. Amsterdam, Netherlands-Philadelphia, PA: John Benjamins Publishing Company.

Darden, Lindley. 1982. "Artificial intelligence and philosophy of science: Reasoning by analogy in theory construction." In *PSA: Proceedings of the Biennial Meeting of the Philosophy of Science Association*, 147–165. Chicago, IL: University of Chicago Press.

Dascal, Marcelo. 2003. *Interpretation and Understanding*. Amsterdam, Netherlands: John Benjamins Publishing Company.

Dascal, Marcelo, and Jerzy Wróblewski. 1988. "Transparency and doubt: Understanding and interpretation in pragmatics and in law." *Law and Philosophy* 7(2): 203–224. https://doi.org/10.1007/BF00144156.

de Pater, Wilhelmus. 1965. *Les Topiques d'Aristote et la Dialectique Platonicienne*. Fribourg, Germany: Éditions de St. Paul.

De Sloovere, Frederick, 1936. "Contextual interpretation of statutes." *Fordham Law Review* 5 (2): 219–239.

Dickerson, Reed. 1975. *The Interpretation and Application of Statutes*. Boston, MA: Little, Brown and Company.

Easterbrook, Frank. 1984. "Legal interpretation and the power of the judiciary." *Harvard Journal of Law and Public Policy* 7: 87–99.

Everardus, Nicolaus. 1601. *Loci Argumentorum Legales*. Venice, Italy: Matthaeum Valentinum.

Focarelli, Carlo. 2012. *International Law as Social Construct: The Struggle for Global Justice*. Oxford, UK: Oxford University Press.

Friesen, Jeffrey. 1996. "When common law courts interpret civil codes." *Wisconsin International Law Journal* 15: 1–27.

Genesereth, Michael. 1980. "Metaphors and models." In *Proceedings of the National Conference on Artificial Intelligence*, 208–211. Stanford, CA: Morgan-Kaufmann.

Gentner, Dedre. 1980. *The Structure of Analogical Models in Science*. Cambridge, UK: Bolt Beranek and Newman.

Giora, Rachel. 1985. "Notes towards a theory of text coherence." *Poetics Today* 6(4): 699–715. https://doi.org/10.2307/1771962.

Gizbert-Studnicki, Tomasz. 1990. "The burden of argumentation in legal disputes." *Ratio Juris* 3(1): 118–129. https://doi.org/10.1111/j.1467-9337.1990.tb00075.x.

Glucksberg, Sam, and Boaz Keysar. 1990. "Understanding metaphorical comparisons: Beyond similarity." *Psychological Review* 97(1): 3–18. https://doi.org/10.1037/0033-295X.97.1.3.

Godden, David, and Douglas Walton. 2006. "Argument from expert opinion as legal evidence: Critical questions and admissibility criteria of expert testimony in the American legal system." *Ratio Juris* 19(3): 261–286. https://doi.org/10.1111/j.1467-9337.2006.00331.x.

Gold, Andrew. 2006. "Absurd results, scrivener's errors, and statutory interpretation." *University of Cincinnati Law Review* 75: 25–86.

Gordon, Thomas. 2010. "An overview of the Carneades argumentation support system." In *Dialectics, Dialogue and Argumentation. An Examination of Douglas Walton's Theories of Reasoning and Argument*, edited by Christopher Reed and Christopher Tindale, 145–156. London, UK: College Publications.

Grice, Paul. 1975. "Logic and conversation." In *Syntax and Semantics 3: Speech Acts*, edited by Peter Cole and Jerry Morgan, 41–58. New York, NY: Academic Press.

Groppi, Tania, and Irene Spigno. 2017. "The Constitutional Court of Italy." In *Comparative Constitutional Reasoning*, edited by András Jakab, Arthur Dyevre, and Giulio Itzcovich, 516–559. Cambridge, UK: Cambridge University Press.

Guastini, Riccardo. 2011. *Interpretare e Argomentare*. Milano, Italy: Giuffrè.

Halldén, Sören. 1960. *True Love, True Humour and True Religion: A Semantic Study*. Lund, Sweden: Gleerup.

Harman, Gilbert. 1965. "The inference to the best explanation." *The Philosophical Review* 74 (1): 88–95. https://doi.org/10.2307/2183532.

Hastings, Arthur. 1963. *A Reformulation of the Modes of Reasoning in Argumentation.* Evanston, IL: Ph.D. Dissertation, Northwestern University.

Hesse, Mary. 1965. "Aristotle's logic of analogy." *The Philosophical Quarterly* 15(61): 328–340. https://doi.org/10.2307/2218258.

Hesse, Mary. 1966. *Models and Analogies in Science.* Notre Dame, IN: University of Notre Dame Press.

Hesse, Mary. 1988. "Theories, family resemblances and analogy." In *Analogical Reasoning,* edited by David Helman, 317–340. Dordrecht, Netherlands: Springer.

Hobbs, Jerry, Mark Stickel, Douglas Appelt, and Paul Martin. 1993. "Interpretation as abduction." *Artificial Intelligence* 63(1–2): 69–142. https://doi.org/10.1016/0004-3702 (93)90015-4.

Horovitz, Joseph. 1972. *Law and Logic: A Critical Account of Legal Argument.* Vienna, Austria: Springer-Verlag.

Hutton, Christopher. 2009. *Language, Meaning and the Law.* Edinburgh, UK: Edinburgh University Press.

Jaszczolt, Kasia. 2007. "The syntax-pragmatics merger: Belief reports in the theory of Default Semantics." *Pragmatics & Cognition* 15(1): 41–64. https://doi.org/10.1075/pc.15.1.06jas.

Jaszczolt, Kasia. 2008. "Psychological explanations in Gricean pragmatics and Frege's legacy." In *Intentions, Common Ground, and the Egocentric Speaker-Hearer,* edited by Istvan Kecskes and Jacob Mey, 9–45. Berlin, Germany: Mouton de Gruyter.

Jaszczolt, Kasia. 2011. "Salient meanings, default meanings, and automatic processing." In *Salience and Defaults in Utterance Processing,* edited by Kasia Jaszczolt and Keith Allan, 11–33. Berlin, Germany: De Gruyter.

Josephson, John, and Susan Josephson. 1996. *Abductive Inference: Computation, Philosophy, Technology.* Cambridge, UK: Cambridge University Press.

Juthe, Andre. 2005. "Argument by analogy." *Argumentation* 19(1): 1–27. https://doi.org/10.1007 /s10503-005-2314-9.

Kakuta, Tokuyasu, Makoto Haraguchi, and Yoshiaki Okubo. 1997. "A goal-dependent abstraction for legal reasoning by analogy." *Artificial Intelligence and Law* 5(1–2): 97–118. https:// doi.org/10.1023/A:1008272013974.

Kennedy, Duncan. 2007. "A left phenomenological critique of the Hart/Kelsen theory of legal interpretation." *Kritische Justiz* 40(3): 296–305.

Kreuzbauer, Guenther. 2008. "Topics in contemporary legal argumentation: Some remarks on the topical nature of legal argumentation in the continental law tradition." *Informal Logic* 28(1): 71–85. https://doi.org/10.22329/il.v28i1.515.

Langenbucher, Katja. 1998. "Argument by analogy in European law." *The Cambridge Law Journal* 57(3): 481–521.

Levin, Samuel. 1982. "Aristotle's theory of metaphor." *Philosophy & Rhetoric* 15(1): 24–46.

Levinson, Stephen. 1987. "Implicature explicated?" *Behavioral and Brain Sciences* 10(4): 722–723. https://doi.org/10.1017/S0140525X00055473.

Levinson, Stephen. 2000. *Presumptive Meanings: The Theory of Generalized Conversational Implicature.* Cambridge, MA: MIT Press.

Lloyd, Anthony. 1962. "Genus, species and ordered series in Aristotle." *Phronesis* 7(1): 67–90.

Macagno, Fabrizio. 2015a. "A means-end classification of argumentation schemes." In *Reflections on Theoretical Issues in Argumentation Theory,* edited by Frans van Eemeren and Bart Garssen, 183–201. Cham, Switzerland: Springer.

Macagno, Fabrizio 2015b. "Arguments of interpretation and argumentation schemes." In *Studies on Argumentation and Legal Philosophy. Further Steps Towards a Pluralistic Approach*, edited by Maurizio Manzin, Federico Puppo, and Serena Tomasi, 51–80. Trento, Italy: Università degli studi di Trento.

Macagno, Fabrizio 2017. "The logical and pragmatic structure of arguments from analogy." *Logique et Analyse* 60(240): 465–490. https://doi.org/10.2143/LEA.240.0.3254093.

Macagno, Fabrizio 2018. "Assessing relevance." *Lingua* 210–211: 42–64. https://doi.org/10.1016/j .lingua.2018.04.007.

Macagno, Fabrizio, and Giovanni Damele. 2016. "The hidden acts of definition in law – Statutory definitions and burden of persuasion." In *Logic in the Theory and Practice of Lawmaking*, edited by Michal Araszkiewicz and Krzysztof Pleszka, 225–251. Cham, Switzerland: Springer.

Macagno, Fabrizio, and Douglas Walton. 2009. "Argument from analogy in law, the classical tradition, and recent theories." *Philosophy and Rhetoric* 42(2): 154–182. https://doi.org/10 .1353/par.0.0034.

Macagno, Fabrizio, and Douglas Walton. 2014a. "Argumentation schemes and topical relations." In *Language, Reason and Education*, edited by Giovanni Gobber and Andrea Rocci, 185–216. Bern, Switzerland: Peter Lang.

Macagno, Fabrizio, and Douglas Walton. 2014b. *Emotive Language in Argumentation*. New York, NY: Cambridge University Press.

Macagno, Fabrizio, and Douglas Walton.2015. "Classifying the patterns of natural arguments." *Philosophy and Rhetoric* 48(1): 26–53. https://doi.org/10.1353/par.2015.0005.

Macagno, Fabrizio, and Douglas Walton. 2018. "Practical reasoning arguments: A modular approach." *Argumentation* 32(4): 519–547. https://doi.org/10.1007/s10503-018-9450-5.

Macagno, Fabrizio, Douglas Walton, and Giovanni Sartor. 2014. "Argumentation schemes for statutory interpretation." In *Proceedings of JURIX 2014: The Twenty-Seventh Annual Conference on Legal Knowledge and Information Systems*, edited by Rinke Hoekstra, 11–20. Amsterdam, Netherlands: IOS Press.

Macagno, Fabrizio, Douglas Walton, and Giovanni Sartor. 2018. "Pragmatic maxims and presumptions in legal interpretation." *Law and Philosophy* 37(1): 69–115. https://doi.org/10 .1007/s10982-017-9306-4.

Macagno, Fabrizio, Douglas Walton, and Christopher Tindale. 2014. "Analogical reasoning and semantic rules of inference." *Revue Internationale de Philosophie* 270(4): 419–432. https://doi.org/10.3917/rip.270.0419.

Macagno, Fabrizio, Douglas Walton, and Christopher Tindale. 2017. "Analogical arguments: Inferential structures and defeasibility conditions." *Argumentation* 31(2): 221–243. https://doi .org/10.1007/s10503-016-9406-6.

MacCormick, Neil. 1995. "Argumentation and interpretation in law." *Argumentation* 9(3): 467–480. https://doi.org/10.1007/BF00733152.

MacCormick, Neil, and Robert Summers, eds. 1991. *Interpreting Statutes: A Comparative Study*. Aldershot, UK: Dartmouth.

Manning, John. 2003. "The absurdity doctrine." *Harvard Law Review* 116(8): 2387–2486. https://doi.org/10.2307/1342768.

Marmor, Andrei. 2008. "The pragmatics of legal language." *Ratio Juris* 21(4): 423–452. https:// doi.org/10.1111/j.1467-9337.2008.00400.x.

Marmor, Andrei. 2013. "Truth in law." In *Law and Language*, edited by Michael Freeman and Fiona Smith, 45–61. Oxford: UK: Oxford University Press.

Marshall, Geoffrey. 2016. "What is binding in a precedent." In *Interpreting Precedents: A Comparative Study*, edited by Neil MacCormick and Robert Summers, 503–518. London, UK, and New York, NY: Routledge.

Miller, Tim. 2019. "Explanation in artificial intelligence: Insights from the social sciences." *Artificial Intelligence* 267: 1–38. https://doi.org/10.1016/j.artint.2018.07.007.

Naess, Arne. 2005a. "Precization and definition." In *The Selected Works of Arne Naess*, edited by Alan Drengson, 1403–1433. Dordrecht, Netherlands: Springer.

Naess, Arne. 2005b. "Definitoid statements." In *The Selected Works of Arne Naess* edited by Alan Drengson, 161–208. Dordrecht, Netherlands: Springer.

Nunberg, Geoffrey. 1979. "The non-uniqueness of semantic solutions: Polysemy." *Linguistics and Philosophy* 3(2): 143–184. https://doi.org/10.1007/BF00126509.

Ohlin, Jens David. 2016. "Is the concept of the person necessary for human rights?" In *International Legal Personality*, edited by Fleur Johns, 437–478. London, UK, and New York, NY: Routledge.

Patterson, Dennis. 2005. "Interpretation in law." *San Diego Law Review* 42, 685–710.

Perelman, Chaïm. 1980. *Justice, Law and Argument*. Dordrecht, Netherlands: Reidel.

Perelman, Chaïm. 1976. *Logique Juridique*. Paris, France: Dalloz.

Pollock, John. 1984. "Reliability and justified belief." *Canadian Journal of Philosophy* 14(1): 103–114. https://doi.org/10.1080/00455091.1984.10716371

Pollock, John. 1986. *Contemporary Theories of Knowledge*. Savage, MD: Rowman and Littlefield.

Pollock, John. 1995. *Cognitive Carpentry*. Cambridge, MA: MIT Press.

Raitio, Juha. 2003. *The Principle of Legal Certainty in EC Law*. Amsterdam, Netherlands: Springer.

Reinhart, Tanya. 1980. "Conditions for text coherence." *Poetics Today* 1(4): 161–180. https://doi.org/10.2307/1771893.

Ross, Alf. 1944. "Imperatives and logic." *Philosophy of Science* 11(1): 30–46. https://doi.org/10.1086/286823.

Rotolo, Antonino, Guido Governatori, and Giovanni Sartor. 2015. "Deontic defeasible reasoning in legal interpretation: Two options for modelling interpretative arguments." In *Proceedings of the 15th International Conference on Artificial Intelligence and Law*, 99–108. New York, NY: ACM Press.

Rubinelli, Sara. 2009. *Ars Topica: The Classical Technique of Constructing Arguments from Aristotle to Cicero*. Amsterdam, Netherlands: Springer.

Russell, Stuart. 1988. "Analogy by similarity." In *Analogical Reasoning*, edited by David Helman, 251–269. Dordrecht, Netherlands: Springer.

Scalia, Antonin, and Bryan Garner. 2012. *Reading Law: The Interpretation of Legal Texts*. Eagan, MN: Thomson West.

Schiappa, Edward. 1993. "Arguing about definitions." *Argumentation* 7(4): 403–417. https://doi.org/10.1007/BF00711058.

Schiappa, Edward. 2003. *Defining Reality. Definitions and the Politics of Meaning*. Carbondale and Edwardsville, IL: Southern Illinois University Press.

Shelley, Cameron. 2003. *Multiple Analogies in Science and Philosophy*. Amsterdam-Philadelphia: John Benjamins Publishing.

Slocum, Brian. 2016a. "Conversational implicatures and legal texts." *Ratio Juris* 29(1): 23–43. https://doi.org/10.1111/raju.12114.

Slocum, Brian. 2016b. *Ordinary Meaning: A Theory of the Most Fundamental Principle of Legal Interpretation*. Chicago, IL: University of Chicago Press.

Sorensen, Roy. 1991. "Vagueness and the desiderata for definition." In *Definitions and Definability: Philosophical Perspectives*, edited by James Fetzer, David Shatz, and George Schlesinger, 71–109. Dordrecht, Netherlands: Springer.

Sperber, Dan, and Deirdre Wilson. 1995. *Relevance: Communication and Cognition*. Oxford, UK: Blackwell Publishing Ltd.

Stump, Eleonore. 1989. *Dialectic and Its Place in the Development of Medieval Logic*. Ithaca, IL and London, UK: Cornell University Press.

Stump, Eleonore. 2004. *Boethius's "De topicis differentiis."* Ithaca, IL, and London, UK: Cornell University Press.

Summers, Robert. 2016. "Precedent in the United States (New York State)." In *Interpreting Precedents: A Comparative Study*, edited by Neil MacCormick and Robert Summers, 355–406. London, UK, and New York, NY: Routledge.

Tarello, Giovanni. 1980. *L'Interpretazione della Legge*. Milano, Italy: Giuffrè.

Tiersma, Peter. 1999. *Legal Language*. Chicago, IL: University of Chicago Press.

Toulmin, Stephen. 1958. *The Uses of Argument*. Cambridge, UK: Cambridge University Press.

Toulmin, Stephen, Richard Rieke, and Allan Janik. 1984. *An Introduction to Reasoning*. New York, NY: Macmillan Publishing Company.

Van Fraassen, Bas. 1980. *The Scientific Image*. Oxford, UK: Oxford University Press.

Verheij, Bart. 2003. "Deflog: on the logical interpretation of prima facie justified assumptions." *Journal of Logic and Computation* 13(3): 319–346. https://doi.org/10.1093/logcom/13.3.319.

Viehweg, Theodor. 1953. *Topik und Jurisprudenz: Ein Beitrag zur rechtswissenschaftlichen Grundlagenforschung*. München, Germany: C. H. Beck.

Waller, Bruce. 2001. "Classifying and analyzing analogies." *Informal Logic* 21(3): 199–218. https://doi.org/10.22329/il.v21i3.2246.

Walton, Douglas. 1996. *Arguments from Ignorance*. University Park, PA: Pennsylvania State University Press.

Walton, Douglas. 2010. *Appeal to Expert Opinion: Arguments from Authority*. University Park, PA: The Pennsylvania State University Press.

Walton, Douglas. 2014. "Baseballs and arguments from fairness." *Artificial Intelligence and Law* 22(4): 423–449. https://doi.org/10.1007/s10506-013-9151-1.

Walton, Douglas, and Marcin Koszowy. 2015. "Two kinds of arguments from authority in the *ad verecundiam* fallacy." In *Proceedings of the 8th Conference of the International Society for the Study of Argumentation*, edited by Frans van Eemeren, Bart Garssen, David Godden, and Gordon Mitchell, 1483–1492. Amsterdam, Netherlands: Sic Sat.

Walton, Douglas, and Fabrizio Macagno. 2009a. "Enthymemes, argumentation schemes and topics." *Logique et Analyse* 52(205): 39–56.

Walton, Douglas, and Fabrizio Macagno. 2009b. "Reasoning from classifications and definitions." *Argumentation* 23(1): 81–107. https://doi.org/10.1007/s10503-008-9110-2.

Walton, Douglas, and Fabrizio Macagno. 2010. "Defeasible classifications and inferences from definitions." *Informal Logic* 30(1): 34–61. https://doi.org/10.22329/il.v30i1.692.

Walton, Douglas, and Fabrizio Macagno. 2015. "A classification system for argumentation schemes." *Argument and Computation* (3): 219–245. https://doi.org/10.1080/19462166.2015.1123772.

Walton, Douglas, Fabrizio Macagno, and Giovanni Sartor. 2014. "Interpretative argumentation schemes." In *JURIX 2014: The twenty-seventh annual conference*, edited by Rinke Hoekstra, 271: 21–22. New York, NY: IOS Press.

Walton, Douglas, Christopher Reed, and Fabrizio Macagno. 2008. *Argumentation Schemes*. New York, NY: Cambridge University Press.

Walton, Douglas, and Giovanni Sartor. 2013. "Teleological justification of argumentation schemes." *Argumentation* 27(2): 111–142. https://doi.org/10.1007/s10503-012-9262-y.

Walton, Douglas, Giovanni Sartor, and Fabrizio Macagno. 2016. "An argumentation framework for contested cases of statutory interpretation." *Artificial Intelligence and Law* 24(1): 51–91. https://doi.org/10.1007/s10506-016-9179-0.

Weinreb, Lloyd. 2005. *Legal Reason: The Use of Analogy in Legal Argument*. New York, NY: Cambridge University Press.

Wilson, Deirdre, and Dan Sperber. 2004. "Relevance theory." In *Handbook of Pragmatics*, edited by Laurence Horn and Gregory Ward, 607–632. Oxford, UK: Blackwell.

Zarefsky, David. 1998. "Definitions." In *Argument in a Time of Change: Definitions, Frameworks, and Critiques*, edited by James Klumpp, 1–11. Annandale, VA: National Communication Association.

Zarefsky, David. 2006. "Strategic maneuvering through persuasive definitions: Implications for dialectic and rhetoric." *Argumentation* 20(4): 399–416. https://doi.org/10.1007/s10503-007-9030-6.

Zipf, George Kingsley. 1949. *Human Behavior and the Principle of Least Effort: An Introduction to Human Ecology*. Cambridge, UK: Addison-Wesley.

CASES CITED

Adams v. New Jersey Steamboat Co. 1896. 151 N.Y. 163.

Arnold v. Producers Fruit Co. 1900. 61 P 283.

Bank One Chicago, N.A. v. Midwest Bank & Trust Co. 1996. 516 U.S. 264.

Bekteshi v. Mukasey 2007. 260 F. App'x 642.

Cassazione penale, sez. III, sentenza 26/09/2008 n° 36845

Cassazione penale, sez. V, sentenza 11/01/2019 n° 1275

Circuit City Stores, Inc. v. Adams 2001. 532 U.S. 105.

Conroy v. Aniskoff 1993. 507 U.S. 511.

Corley v. United States 2009. 556 U.S. 303.

Corte Costituzionale. Sentenza n. 138/2010. ECLI:IT:COST:2010:138.

Corte Costituzionale. Sentenza n. 280/2010. ECLI:IT:COST:2010:280.

District of Columbia v. Heller 2008. 554 U.S. 570.

Garner v. Burr [1951] 1 KB 31.

Google Spain SL, Google Inc. v. Agencia Española de Protección de Datos (AEPD), *Costeja Gonzalez* 2014. ECLI:EU:C:2014:317.

Healthkeepers, Inc. v. Richmond Ambulance Authority 2011. 642 F.3d 466.

James v. United States 2007. 550 U.S. 192.

Johnson v. United States 2015. 576 U.S. 591.

Leatherman v. Tarrant County Narcotics Intelligence & Coordination Unit 1992. 507 U.S. 163.

Obergefell v. Hodges 2015. 135 S. Ct. 2584.

People v. Collins 2005. 214 Ill. 2d 206.

People v. Davis 2008. 218 P.3d 718.

Popov v. Hayashi 2002. WL 31833731.

State v. Taylor 1999. 594 N.W.2d 533.

Taylor v. United States 1990. 495 U.S. 575.

United States v. Barber 2005. 360 F. Supp. 2d 784.

United States v. California 1965. 381 U.S. 139.

6

Classification and Formalization of Interpretative Schemes

6.1 INTRODUCTION

In our previous chapters, we underscored the role of interpretative arguments in the passage from a legal text to a legal rule (Hage, 1996, 214; Tarello, 1980), where the latter is intended as a normative premise under which an individual case can be "subsumed" or classified (Moreso and Chilovi, 2018). Legal interpretation can be compared to the common understanding and processing of utterances in ordinary conversation (Smolka and Pirker, 2016), in which semantic content is only a vehicle for getting to the "speaker's meaning," i.e., what is communicated – a richer content to which semantic "meaning and obvious background assumptions have both contributed" (Soames, 2009, 411; see also Butler, 2016; Carston, 2013; Horn, 1995; Miller, 1990). As we maintained in Chapters 3, 4, and 5, legal (and more precisely statutory) interpretation does not differ essentially from ordinary interpretation, even though legislative speech is one-sided and the basic presumptions governing legislative texts may differ from the ones characterizing everyday conversation (Sinclair, 1985, 390). Despite such differences, pragmatic principles constitute a dimension of rationality that is necessary for the understanding of legal texts (Sinclair, 1985, 401).

In Chapter 5, we pointed out the boundaries of legal interpretation. Interpretation is regarded as a specific activity within the attribution of meaning to an utterance (a statement of law, in our case). We normally reconstruct the "speaker's" meaning by relying on semantic meaning, social and cultural conventions, or cognitive principles, which lead to default "interpretations" (in the broad sense of the term, see Heine, Narrog, and Jaszczolt, 2015; Jaszczolt, 2005). Such meaning reconstructions are based on defeasible inferences to the first unchallenged alternative: "we reason by default, unless we have evidence that we should not" (Jaszczolt, 2005, 46). This automatic, default process needs to be distinguished from the more complex process of interpretation strictly understood, which is defined as "an ascription of meaning to a linguistic sign in the case its meaning is doubtful in a communicative situation, i.e. in the case its 'direct understanding' is not sufficient for the communicative purpose at hand" (Dascal and Wróblewski, 1988, 204). In this latter case, the reconstruction of the "m-intention" (speaker's meaning intention) needs to be justified, as a doubt needs to be overcome or a different reconstruction needs to be rejected. In legal theory, this twofold process is addressed through the concepts of understanding and interpretation.

In our previous chapters, we addressed the problem of representing and assessing the reasons provided in favor of a specific interpretation, i.e., the reasons justifying why and how one interpretation is more acceptable than others (Macagno, 2017). At this functional level, such interpretative reasons are regarded as arguments (Macagno and Capone, 2016) aimed at showing why a particular rule representing the meaning of a legal statement should be preferred to another on the basis of the available evidence (Hage, 1996, 215). In this chapter,[1] we will show how the canons of interpretation, represented as argumentation schemes in the previous chapter, can be formalized as patterns of defeasible argument (Hage, 1997) advanced in support of the interpretation of a text (or part thereof). This formalization can be then used to bridge the gap between legal interpretation and argumentation theory. More specifically, the argumentation schemes can be used for representing and evaluating arguments (Macagno and Walton, 2015; Walton, Reed, and Macagno, 2008).

The functional analysis of legal interpretation in terms of arguments, and the formalization of the interpretative arguments as schemes (advanced in Sections 6.2 and 6.3) allows modeling legal interpretation combining the formal argumentation system such as Carneades or ASPIC$^+$ with a logical language (Sartor, Walton, Macagno, and Rotolo, 2014). After introducing the Carneades Argumentation System (Section 6.3) and applying it to two cases, we will devote the remainder of the chapter to developing a logical model for reasoning with interpretative canons, conceived as defeasible rules (Sartor, 2018). The logical structure developed will not be framed in deontic terms, but rather will concern terminological assertions on what should count as the best interpretations of the contested or potentially contested expressions.

6.2 INTERPRETATIVE ARGUMENTS

The justification of an interpretation will be modeled as an argumentation-based procedure in which the best interpretation is that which is supported by the strongest arguments (Atlas and Levinson, 1981; Macagno, Walton, and Sartor, 2018). In this perspective, the "canons" or maxims of interpretation are reframed as argument schemes (Macagno and Walton, 2017), which can be classified according to their communicative purpose and types of warrants. This classification allows for detecting the relationship between interpretative canons and the schemes commonly used in argumentation theory. In this chapter, we recognize the existence of problems concerning the classification of interpretative argument schemes without delving

---

[1] This chapter is based on a paper by Walton, D., Sartor, G., and Macagno, F. (2016), "An argumentation framework for contested cases of statutory interpretation." *Artificial intelligence and law*, 24(1), 51–91. https://doi.org/10.1007/s10506-016–9179-0, which this chapter expands, corrects, and updates.

into a detailed analysis thereof, so that we can forge ahead with building a framework for interpretative argumentation schemes that can later be applied to studying specific schemes and issues. The starting point is to provide a general classification of interpretative arguments, identifying the more generic identities between them. Then we move through a sequence of examples of legal arguments where interpretation of a statute or law is at issue, applying the model to the examples. As always, the work of applying formal structures to real cases of argumentation in natural language discourse raises problems and difficulties in its own right.

6.2.1 *Classifying Interpretative Arguments*

MacCormick (2005, 124–125) proposes that there are three main categories of interpretative argument acknowledged as persuasive in grounding a selected interpretation of a text in a disputed case in a broad variety of legal systems (see Chapter 1). *Linguistic arguments* appeal to the general linguistic context, as provided by ordinary language or by technical languages, to support an interpretation. *Systemic arguments* take the special context of the authoritative text within the legal system into account; such schemes merge the authority of the legal sources with the reconstruction of the definition from their texts. *Teleological-evaluative arguments* make sense of the text in light of its aims or goals (which we can refer to as pragmatic arguments, see Macagno and Walton, 2015). A fourth category is what MacCormick (2005) calls *appeal to the lawmaker's intention*. Because of the ambiguity and indeterminacy of the notion of intention, MacCormick does not consider this type of interpretative argument alongside the other main categories of interpretative argument. He rather views it a transcategorical type of argument that ranges across all the other categories and their types, as linguistic, systemic, or teleological-evaluative considerations can support the attribution of intentions to legislators.

The classification categories that MacCormick uses can be reinterpreted considering the types of argument that we have described in our Chapter 5. The first distinction that can be drawn is between families of reasoning patterns: arguments from ignorance, from authority, analogical, practical, and abductive (or best explanation) arguments. Each group of arguments is defined by specific logical-semantic features, and more importantly by specific defeasibility conditions. Such critical questions vary depending on the specific argument used. The differentiation between the different strategies needs to be combined with a pragmatic criterion, namely the goal an argument was presumably put forward to fulfill.

Arguments are pragmatic constructs – they are used for achieving a specific communicative goal (Walton, 1990). Thus, if we try to analyze the lists of arguments in terms of patterns of argument – explaining the arguments of legal interpretation using the categories of argumentation schemes – we need to draw a first crucial distinction between arguments that support an interpretation and arguments that reject an interpretation. Some interpretative canons, however, are bivalent, in the sense that they provide for two interpretative schemes: one (positive or negative) when the canon's condition is satisfied, and the opposite (negative or positive) when the canon's condition is not satisfied. For instance, while the contextual coherence of an interpretation supports the adoption of an interpretation, lack of contextual coherence supports rejection. In such cases we use the symbols "+" and "–" to denote the use of a scheme to support and reject an interpretation. For instance, as we shall see, +*SA* (where *SA* stands for systematic argument, dealing with contextual coherence) denotes an argument for an interpretation based on its coherence with the legal corpus, while – *SA* denotes an argument that rejects an interpretation based on its incoherence with the legal corpus.

The characteristics of the schemes can be merged with their preferential use – namely the goal of supporting or rejecting an interpretation (Macagno, 2015). The combination of these criteria leads to the diagram that represents a classification of the schemes in Figure 6.1.

MacCormick (2005) recognized that there can be conflicts between interpretative arguments, pitting one form of interpretative argument against another (Rotolo, Governatori, and Sartor, 2015). Some legal traditions provide general criteria for dealing with conflicts of this sort based on certain kinds of priorities. Alexy and Dreier (Alexy and Dreier, 1991, 95–98) have cited criteria such as the following: (1) in criminal law, arguments from ordinary meaning have priority over arguments from technical meaning; (2) in criminal law, generic arguments based on the intention of the legislator have priority over arguments not based on authority, but do not have priority over linguistic arguments. We have observed that explicitly made pragmatic arguments often prevail over linguistic arguments. However, it is unclear whether this is due to a general priority criterion endorsed in the legal community, or because pragmatic arguments are made explicit only when they are likely to prevail over the default linguistic considerations.

The classification of interpretative arguments can be the starting point for translating the arguments (and canons or maxims) into formal (or rather, quasi-formal) schemes representing how a conclusion is supported by premises. In particular, we will provide the schemes for the general categories of interpretative schemes – used for both supporting and challenging an interpretation – including the definition-based arguments (in particular, from ordinary and technical meaning). These schemes will be the ground for the further formal representations in Section 6.3, and the logical formalization in the remaining sections.

6.2.2 *The Association between Language and Meaning*

Statutes are written in natural language. Our concern is with the interpretation of sentences expressed in natural language that are susceptible to differing interpretations (Atlas, 2005; Horn, 1995). The major philosophical concern is how the notion of meaning is to be defined in relation to the task of finding the evidential basis for

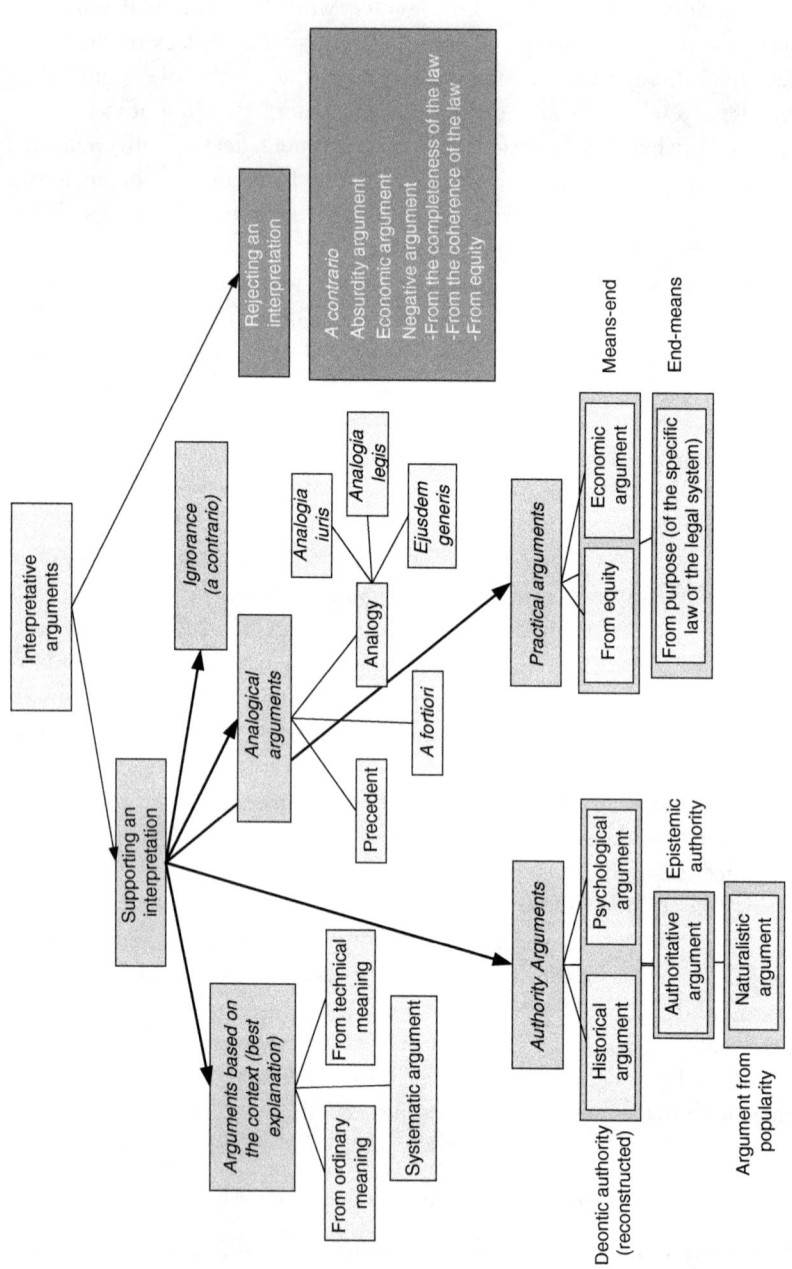

FIGURE 6.1 Classifying the arguments of interpretation

preferring one interpretation or another (Atlas, 2005; Atlas and Levinson, 1981; Dascal, 2003, 635). We adopt a pragmatic approach to meaning, namely to understand statutory meaning as the intention expressed through the legal text (Carston, 2013), an approach that corresponds to the transcategorial understanding of interpretation in MacCormick (2005).

The syntax representing the structure of the sentence being interpreted, as well as the individual semantic meanings of each term contained in it, is important. But over and above such factors, it needs to be acknowledged that in legal interpretation the sentence and its elements need to be placed in the context of a broader text or corpus in which it is embedded. For example, the issue of whether a contested word should be taken as expressing an ordinary meaning as opposed to a technical meaning is a dispute about whether the word can be interpreted one way or the other in a special context of use. For these reasons, although we acknowledge the importance of semantics and syntax in matters of statutory interpretation, we need to study the notion of meaning in a broad manner, to include not only these aspects but also the aspect of the placement of the sentence in a broader context of use in different kinds of discourse.

From our perspective, making an interpretation consists in associating a linguistic occurrence and a meaning within a specific context and use, that is, in claiming that a certain expression E in a certain document D has a certain meaning M. Interpretations are not necessarily correct, according to the different perspectives at stake. Typically, the parties in a legal case argue that certain interpretations are right or wrong, preferable or not to other interpretations.

6.2.3 *Common Template*

We shall model the application of interpretation canons by using a uniform template, so that for each canon we obtain an argument scheme including a major premise, a minor premise, and an interpretative conclusion:

- The major premise is a general canon: If interpreting an expression (word, phrase, sentence) in a legal document (source, text, statute) in a certain way satisfies the condition of the canon, then the expression should/should not (depending on whether the canon is a negative or positive one) be interpreted in that way.
- The minor premise is a specific assertion: Interpreting a particular expression in a particular document in a certain way does satisfy the condition of the canon.
- The conclusion is a specific claim: The particular expression in that document indeed should/should not be interpreted in that way.

In this chapter we shall apply this template to provide schemes in particular for the following canons:

(1) argument from ordinary language (OL),

(2) argument from technical language (*TL*),

(3) *a contrario* argument (*AC*),

(4) systematic argument (contextual harmonization) (*SA*),

(5) argument from the authority of previous interpretations (precedent) (*PR*).

This list of schemes will be expanded as new schemes are formulated.

Here is our system of notation for labeling the nodes in an argument diagram to indicate a scheme. In the diagrams we use "**+**" for schemes used to argue for an interpretation, "**–**" for schemes used to argue against an interpretation, "*e*" for exclusion, and "*i*" for inclusion. Thus for instance *+eOL* would denote a scheme of ordinary language being used in favor of exclusion (for the exclusionary conclusion), while *+iPr* labels a pro argument from precedent used for inclusion purposes.

6.2.4 *Positive Uses of Interpretative Schemes*

As mentioned above, two uses of interpretative argument schemes need to be distinguished: the positive use to support an interpretation, and the negative use to reject an interpretation. Here is the template for positive use of interpretative argument schemes. In presenting this template we shall use uppercase letters for variables and lowercase letters for constants.

Major Premise	C: If the interpretation of *E* in *D* as *M satisfies canon C's condition*, then *E* in *D* should be interpreted as *M*.
Minor Premise	The interpretation of *e* in *d* as *m satisfies canon C's condition*.
Conclusion	*e* in *d* should be interpreted as *m*.

In applying this template, we need to add into the major premise the condition that characterizes a particular canon, for instance, fitting "ordinary meaning" (see our Section 5.11.1) if we consider the canon from ordinary language (*OL*).

In order to show how positive interpretative canons can be applied with this pattern, we use the case of *Dunnachie* v. *Kingston-upon-Hull City Council* UKHL 36, 2004, also used by MacCormick (2005), as a running example. This case concerns an employee who claimed to have been unfairly dismissed, and as a result to have suffered humiliation, injury to feelings, and distress. The employer argued that the relevant section of the current UK legislation, called the Employment Rights Act 1996, only permits recovery of *pecuniary (financial) loss*. The employee argued that a proper construction of all the relevant section of the statute allows for recovery of *losses* other than pecuniary loss narrowly construed. The question posed was whether the term "*loss*," as used in the statute, referred only to pecuniary loss or could be given a more extended meaning so that it included emotional damage and harm to feelings.

If we use the ordinary language canon, we obtain the following structure:

Major Premise	+*OL*: If the interpretation of *E* in *D* as *M* fits ordinary language, then *E* in *D* should be interpreted as *M*.
Minor Premise	The interpretation of *"loss"* in the *Employment Rights Act* as *PecuniaryLoss* fits ordinary language.
Conclusion	*"Loss"* in the *Employment Rights Act* should be interpreted as *PecuniaryLoss*.

Note that we use quotation marks with italics for linguistic occurrences (*"loss"*) and a single italicized word with capitalized initials for meanings (*PecuniaryLoss*).

By substituting the *OL* canon with other canons listed above it is possible to generate other interpretation schemes. For instance, we can obtain the following scheme for the positive use of technical language (+*TL*) (see for an analysis of this canon our Section 5.11.1.):

Major Premise	+*TL*: If the interpretation of *E* in *D* as *M* fits technical language, then *E* in *D* should be interpreted as *M*.
Minor Premise	The interpretation of *"loss"* in the *Employment Rights Act* as *PecuniaryLossOrEmotionalDamage* fits technical language.
Conclusion	*"Loss"* in the *Employment Rights Act* should be interpreted as *PecuniaryLossOrEmotionalDamage*.

Obviously, our interpretative schemes provide only the top-level step in the reasoning that is needed to apply an interpretative canon. For supporting the application of a canon, we need to establish the minor premise of the corresponding scheme, namely, to show that the interpretation we are proposing satisfies the canon we are considering. This requires specific arguments, according to the particular scheme being considered. For instance, for establishing that interpretation *"pecuniary loss"* of expression *"loss"* in document Employment Rights Act fits the ordinary language canon, we will have to establish, by providing adequate evidence, that this interpretation matches the current linguistic usage. Thus, for instance, to support the application of the ordinary language canon, we would need an inference like the following:

Major Premise	If *E* is commonly understood as *M*, then the interpretation of *E* in *D* as *M* fits ordinary language.
Minor Premise	*"Loss"* is commonly understood as *PecuniaryLoss*.
Conclusion	The interpretation of *"loss"* in the *Employment Rights Act* as *PecuniaryLoss* fits ordinary language.

Here the minor premise is a substitution instance of the antecedent of the major premise.

6.2.5 *Negative Uses of Interpretative Schemes*

According to the negative use of a canon, if an interpretation meets the canon's condition, then it is to be rejected.

Major Premise	−C: If the interpretation of E in D as M *satisfies canon C's conditions*, then E in D should not be interpreted as M.
Minor Premise	The interpretation of e in d as m *satisfies C's conditions.*
Conclusion	e in d should not be interpreted as m.

For instance, the *a contrario* (AC) scheme (see Section 5.4) is often used to reject an interpretation that is over- or underinclusive with regard to the usual semantic meaning of an expression, according to the idea that *ubi lex voluit, dixit; ubi noluit, tacuit* (what the law wishes, it states, what the law does not want, it keeps silent upon). As noted in Chapter 5, the *a contrario* canon can also be viewed as a counterfactual appeal to the intention of the legislator: if the legislator had meant to express a meaning that is different from the usual meaning (the semantic meaning) of the expression at issue, it would have used a different expression. Here is an example of application of the *a contrario* canon.

Major Premise	−AC: If the interpretation of E in D as M conflicts with the usual meaning of E (is over- or underinclusive), then E in D should not be interpreted as M.
Minor Premise	The interpretation of the expression "*loss*" in the *Employment Rights Act* as *PecuniaryLossOrEmotionalDamage* conflicts with the usual meaning of "*loss.*"
Conclusion	"*Loss*" in the *Employment Rights Act* should not be interpreted as *PecuniaryLossOrEmotionalDamage*.

There is also a more specific kind of *a contrario* argument, which we may call subclass *a contrario*: rather than rejecting an interpretation as a whole, it addresses the exclusion or inclusion of a certain subclass S in the interpretation at issue, on the basis of the fact that the subclass is included in or excluded from the usual meaning. These two variants are the exclusionary *a contrario* (eAC) and the inclusionary *a contrario* (iAC). Note that the *iAC* has a positive interpretative conclusion, as the nonexclusion – that is, the non-non-inclusion – is an inclusion.

Here is the first variant, namely, the exclusionary *a contrario* argument.

Major Premise	+eAC: If the interpretation of E in D as including S conflicts with the usual meaning of E, then E in D should be interpreted as excluding S.
Minor Premise	The interpretation of "*loss*" in the *Employment Rights Act* as including *EmotionalDamage* conflicts with the usual meaning of "*loss.*"
Conclusion	"*Loss*" in the *Employment Rights Act* should be interpreted as excluding *EmotionalDamage*.

Here is the second variant, the inclusionary *a contrario* argument.

Major Premise	+*iAC*: If the interpretation of *E* in *D* as excluding *S* conflicts with the usual meaning of *E*, then *E* in *D* should be interpreted as including *S*.
Minor Premise	The interpretation of "*loss*" in the *Employment Rights Act* as excluding *EmotionalDamage* conflicts with the usual meaning of "*loss*."
Conclusion	"*Loss*" in the *Employment Rights Act* should be interpreted as including *EmotionalDamage*.

The *a contrario* scheme can also be used in a metadialogical sense, one that concerns the choice of the scheme. A clear example is the following argument taken from *R. v. Barnet London Borough Council* [2004] 1 All ER 97:

> The words "ordinarily residing with" are common English words and here there is no context requiring that they should be given other than their natural meaning in accordance with the accepted usage of English. Even in such circumstances, however, there can be difficulty and doubt as to their applicability to particular sets of facts, because the conception to which the words have reference does not have a clearly definable content or fixed boundaries.

This reasoning can be represented as follows, where –*mAC* stands for the negative use of meta *a contrario*.

Major Premise	–*mAC*: If *E* is an ordinary English expression, and *E* in *D* has no context requiring a technical meaning, then the technical language canon is inapplicable to expression *E* in a document *D*.
Minor Premise 1	"*Ordinarily residing with*" is an ordinary English expression.
Minor Premise 2	"*Ordinarily residing with*" in the *Local Education Authority Awards Regulations* has no context requiring a technical meaning.
Conclusion	The technical language canon is not applicable to expression "*ordinarily residing with*" in the *Local Education Authority Awards Regulations*.

In this case, the absence of a context requiring a technical language (such as a definition, or the technical nature of the object of the regulation at issue) leads to the inapplicability of the technical language canon. This scheme is not a mere rebuttal (exclusion of a determinate meaning), but an undercutter (an attack against the use of argument, in this case against the possibility of using the argument's major premise in the given context) (Pollock, 1995; Walton, 2015). Thus, the fact that the technical language argument cannot be used to support a certain interpretation – in this case interpretation does not exclude that the same interpretation can be successfully proposed through a different argument, such as the teleological one (argument from purpose).

The metadialogical analysis of the *a contrario* argument raises two issues concerning its nature. The first is the relationship between the exclusion of alternative canons of interpretations and the idea of default. According to Alexy and Dreier (1991, 95–98), the ordinary language scheme should be taken as the default setting. The general principle at work here is the following general principle: any expression in a legislative document should be interpreted using the ordinary language scheme, unless there are superior reasons to interpret the expression as fitting one of the other schemes. However, all interpretative canons are defaultive. The difference here is that for any expression we can raise the defeasible claim that it should be interpreted according to its ordinary language meaning, while claims based on other canons can only be raised under specific conditions (e.g., a technical context is required to substantiate the claim that a term should be interpreted in a technical meaning).

The second controversial issue about the *a contrario* argument is whether it ought to be treated only as an argumentation scheme or also as a metalevel principle that can be applied in conjunction with interpretative argumentation schemes. The argument from ignorance has traditionally been treated as an argumentation scheme in logic (Macagno and Walton, 2011; Walton, 1995), whereas the closed-world assumption has been treated in artificial intelligence as a metalevel principle rather than as a specific form of argument in its own right (Reiter, 1980). The *a contrario* argument is similar to the argument from lack of evidence as it supports an inference from a negative finding to a positive conclusion.

6.3 ATTACKING, QUESTIONING, AND DEFENDING INTERPRETATIVE ARGUMENTS

In this section we shall consider how interpretative arguments can be challenged through counterarguments. After introducing counterarguments and linking them to critical questions, we shall focus on modeling opposed arguments in the Carneades argumentation framework, which will be applied to two extensive examples.

6.3.1 *From Critical Questions to Counterarguments in Formal Argumentation Systems*

Since the basic defeasible schemes provide a general pattern for interpretative arguments, there is no need to formulate critical questions for each of these schemes individually. The critical questions for each of them follow the general pattern indicated by the following three critical questions:

CQ1: What alternative interpretations of expression E in document D should be considered?

CQ2: What reasons are there for rejecting alternative explanations?

CQ3: What reasons are there for accepting alternative explanations as better than (or equally good as) the one selected?

The function of the critical questions is to probe into an interpretative argument and provide an initial idea of its weak points. They have a heuristic function of suggesting to an arguer who is at a loss as to how to respond by suggesting possible avenues of attack. Relatively to this objective, the three critical questions are not independent of one another, and they have an ordering: CQ_1 should be asked first.

The way we will analyze interpretative arguments, as well as critical questions matching them and counterarguments attacking them, is to build an argumentation tree that includes a contested interpretative argument and provides an analysis of how the chains of argumentation on both sides of the dispute connect with each other and to the ultimate claim at issue. This can be done using tools from formal argumentation systems such as Carneades or ASPIC$^+$. Both Carneades and ASPIC$^+$ are based on a logical language comprising both strict and defeasible inference rules that can be used to build arguments, and both systems use argumentation schemes. In this section, we will use a simplified version of Carneades, which will prove to have some tools that can be applied to examples illustrating the distinctive argumentation approach to interpretative arguments. In Section 6.4 we will use ASPIC$^+$ to build a logical analysis of interpretative schemes (Sartor et al., 2014).

Both Carneades and ASPIC$^+$ use a scheme called defeasible *modus ponens*, also used in the DefLog argumentation system of Verheij (2008). This scheme is a variant of *modus ponens* in which the antecedent of the conditional premise takes the form of a conjunction. Verheij (2008, 24) observes that if you look at the typical argumentation scheme with eyes slightly narrowed, it appears to have a *modus ponens* format in outline. In the formalism that will be used in the second part of this chapter, each scheme fits the following type of argument structure, where the major premise is a defeasible conditional with a conjunctive antecedent.

Major premise: $A, B, C, \ldots \Rightarrow Z$

Minor premises: $A, B, C, \ldots$

Conclusion: Z

It was shown in Walton (2004, 134–139) that a majority of the schemes recognized in the argumentation literature can be tailored to fit this defeasible *modus ponens* form. In both ASPIC$^+$ and Carneades, arguments are modeled as graphs containing nodes representing propositions from the logical language and link from nodes to nodes. In these systems an argument can be supported or attacked by other arguments, which can themselves be supported or attacked by additional arguments. The outcome in a typical case of argumentation is a graph structure representing a series of supporting arguments, attacks, and counterattacks in a sequence that can be represented using an argument map, also often called an argument diagram.

In both ASPIC$^+$ and Carneades there are ways in which one argument can attack and defeat another. An opponent can attack one or more of the premises of an argument. This is called an undermining attack. Or an opponent can attack the conclusion of an argument by arguing that the attacked conclusion is false or unacceptable. This type of attack is called a rebutter. Thirdly, the opponent can attack the inferential link joining an argument's step to its conclusion. This type of attack is called an undercutter. For example, if an argument's inference is based on a rule, the attacker could claim that there is an exception to the rule, and that the exception applies in the present case at issue. This way of modeling argumentation is based on Pollock's distinction (Pollock, 1995, 40) between rebutters and under-cutters. In Pollock's view, a rebutter is a counterargument that attacks the conclusion of a prior argument, whereas an undercutter is a counterargument that attacks the link between the premises and the conclusion of the attacked argument. For example, an argument that fits the argumentation scheme for argument from expert opinion can be critically questioned by asking whether the expert is biased. This critical question can be modeled as an undercutter: if there is evidence that the expert is biased, then the expert testimony fails to support the conclusion of the expert, and therefore this instance of the expert opinion scheme is defeated.

6.3.2 *Argument Graphs in Carneades*

Carneades models arguments as directed graphs consisting of argument nodes connected to statement nodes, which provide for premises and conclusions (Gordon, 2010). In the argument maps below, the name of the argumentation scheme is inserted in the node (the circle) joining the premises to the conclusion. As shown in the figures, there can be two kinds of arguments shown in the node, a pro (supporting argument) or a con (attacking) argument. The nodes contain argumentation schemes such as *modus ponens*, argument from expert opinion, and so forth.[2] Conflicts between pro and con arguments can be resolved using proof standards such as including preponderance of the evidence (Gordon and Walton, 2009b). Argument graphs are evaluated, relative to audiences, modeled as a set of assumptions and an assignment of weights to argument nodes. An audience is defined as a structure <*assumptions, weight*>, where *assumptions* is a consistent set of propositions assumed to be acceptable by the audience and *weight* maps argu-ments to real numbers in the range [0,1], representing the relative weights assigned by the audience to the arguments (Gordon and Walton, 2011).

In Carneades, compound arguments consist of several argument nodes linked together in the graph so that an argument represents a chain of reasoning from the supporting premises down to the ultimate proposition to be proved, the so-called statement at issue. Arguments are evaluated on the basis of whether the audience accepts the premises or not, and on the strength of the various arguments making up the graph.

---

[2] For more details and a specific description on how the software works, see Carneades Argumentation System, http://carneades.github.com.

A very simple example of how an argument evaluation works in the Carneades system is shown in Figure 6.2. The circular nodes represent argumentation schemes accepted by the audience. A pro argument is indicated by a plus sign in its node; a con argument is represented by a minus sign in its node. The square nodes contain propositions that can be premises or conclusions of arguments. The arguments are chained together so that the conclusion of one argument can become a premise of another argument. The colors indicate the acceptance of a proposition: light grey means the proposition is accepted by the audience, and dark grey means the proposition is rejected by the audience. If the node is white (no color), the proposition is neither accepted nor rejected.[3]

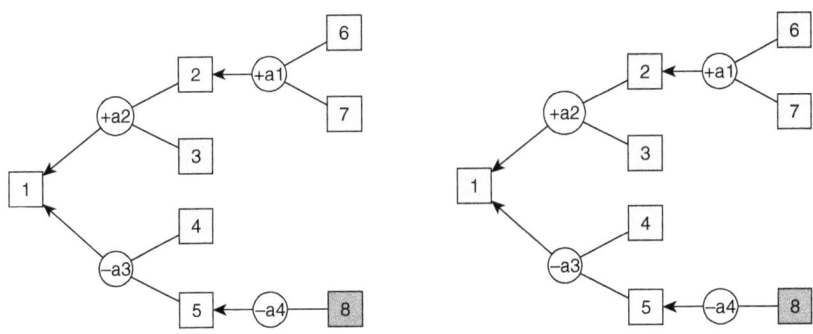

FIGURE 6.2 Carneades graphs displaying an argument evaluation

In both argument diagrams shown in Figure 6.2, the ultimate conclusion, statement 1, is shown on the far left of the diagram. First, let's consider which premises the audience accepts or rejects, as shown in the argument diagram on the left. Argument a2 is a pro argument supporting statement 1, while argument a3 is a con argument attacking statement 1. The audience accepts proposition 3 as a premise in argument a2, but the other premise, statement 2, is neither accepted nor rejected by the audience. Both premises of an additional argument, argument a1, are accepted by the audience. Argument a3 is a con argument but one of its premises, statement 5, is not accepted. Moreover, this premise is attacked by a con argument (argument a4), but the only premise in this con argument, statement 8, is rejected.

To see how this conflict is resolved, look at the diagram on the right. Since both statements 6 and 7 are accepted by the audience, Carneades automatically calculates that statement 2 is accepted. However, what about the con argument against statement 1 shown at the bottom, namely argument a3? This con argument could defeat statement 5, but its premise 8 is rejected by the audience. Therefore, pro argument a2 wins out over con argument a3, and so the ultimate conclusion 1 is shown in light grey as acceptable.

---

3   In the software, light grey appears as green and dark grey as red.

Carneades also formalizes argumentation schemes. Schemes can be used to construct or reconstruct arguments, as well as to determine whether a given argument properly instantiates the types of argument deemed normatively appropriate according to the scheme requirements.

The critical questions matching an argumentation scheme cannot be modeled in a standard argument graph straightforwardly by representing each critical question as an additional implicit premise of the scheme. The reason is that there are two different variations on what happens when a respondent asks a critical question (Walton and Gordon, 2005). These variations concern the pattern of how the burden of proof shifts from the proponent to the respondent and back as each critical question is asked by the respondent in a dialogue. With some critical questions, merely asking the question is enough to defeat the proponent's argument, because the burden of proof is shifted onto the proponent's side, and if the proponent fails to meet this burden of proof, the initial argument is immediately defeated. With other critical questions, merely asking the critical question is not enough by itself to defeat the proponent's argument. For example, if the respondent asks the bias critical question when the proponent has put forward an argument from expert opinion, the proponent can simply reply, "What proof do you have that my expert is biased?" In this approach, merely asking the question does not defeat the proponent's argument until the respondent offers some evidence to back it up. Carneades deals with this problem of burden of proof for critical questioning by distinguishing three types of premises in an argumentation scheme, called assumptions, exceptions and ordinary premises. Assumptions are assumed to be acceptable unless called into question. Exceptions are modeled as premises that are not assumed to be acceptable and that can block or undercut an argument as it proceeds. Hence an exception, which is modeled in Carneades as an undercutter, defeats the argument it was attacking only if it is supported by other arguments that offer reasons to back up the undercutting argument. Ordinary premises of an argumentation scheme are treated as assumptions. They are assumed to be acceptable in case they are put forward, but must be supported by further arguments to remain acceptable after being challenged by critical questions or counterarguments.

For any one of these critical questions to be effective in defeating the original interpretative argument, the respondent must give some indication of what he or she takes this alternative interpretation to be. Thus, it would appear that each of these critical questions defeats the original interpretative argument only if some evidence is presented by the respondent pinpointing an alternative interpretation that might challenge the one originally appealed to by the proponent's argument.

6.3.3 *The Education Grants Example: Modeling Judicial Interpretation*

In this section we use Carneades to show how interpretative schemes can be applied to an extended sequence of argumentation in a typical legal case, using a large argument graph to connect the individual interpretative arguments to each other.

According to the account of the following case described in Cross (2005, 90), section 1 of the Education Act 1962 required local education authorities to make grants to students who were "ordinarily resident" in their area, so that the student could attend higher education courses. A requirement in the Education Act stipulated that in order to be eligible, the student had to have been *ordinarily resident* in the United Kingdom for three years prior to his or her application. The following issue arose: Could someone who had come to the United Kingdom for education count the period spent in education as ordinary residence in order to qualify for a mandatory grant under the Education Act?

There were two sides to the issue. The Court of Appeal held that such a person could not count this period as ordinary residence, offering the following argument quoted from Cross (2005, 90):

> Lord Denning MR and Everleigh LJ were impressed by the need to relate this Act to the policy of the Commonwealth Immigrants Act 1962 and its successor, the Immigration Act 1971. Under the latter Act, students coming only for study had a conditional leave to stay in the country limited to the purpose of study and this conditional leave did not involve ordinary residence for the general purposes of everyday life. They considered that consistency with this Act required the term "ordinarily resident" in the Education Act to be interpreted as living as an ordinary member of the community would, which could not include residence for the limited purpose of study.

Arriving at a different interpretation, the House of Lords unanimously reversed this decision. They felt that the Court of Appeal had given too much weight to arguments drawn from the Immigration Act. They offered the following argument, quoted from Cross (2005, 91):

> Parliament's purpose expressed in the Education Act gave no hint of any restriction on the eligibility for a mandatory award other than ordinary residence in the United Kingdom for three years and a satisfactory educational record. There was nothing expressed in the Immigration Act which gave guidance as to the interpretation of the Education Act and, indeed, despite a series of immigration measures since 1962, nationality had not formed part of the regulations under the Education Act until 1980. Accordingly, the ordinary natural meaning of the Education Act prevailed to make the students eligible for a mandatory grant if they had resided in the United Kingdom for the purposes of study.

In this case it was concluded that the role of the judge should not be to reconcile legislative provisions. Instead, it was proposed that the basis for interpretation should be that of the ordinary language meaning of the expression "ordinarily resident." The argumentation in this case can be analyzed as an interpretative argument put forward by its proponents Denning and Everleigh, countered by an interpretative argument put forward in the House of Lords. Below we use a sequence of three argument maps to model the structure of the argumentation sequence in the case.

The first argument, shown in Figure 6.3, cites the Immigration Act 1971, which stated that students coming to a country for study only had a conditional leave to stay in the country, adding that this conditional leave does not involve ordinary residence for the general purposes of everyday life. Because a related document is cited as the basis for drawing a conclusion in support of statutory interpretation, the argumentation scheme that is the basis of this argument is an abductive one, proceeding from the "system of the law." This type of systematic argument (which we will refer to as "SA"), labeled by MacCormick and Summers as "contextual harmonization," is taken to represent here the following kind of argument: a certain expression that occurs in a document is best interpreted as fitting with its usage in a set of related documents, therefore in this document it will be interpreted in the same way. In other words, if there is an issue about how to interpret an expression in a given document, such as a statute, then it can be argued that the best way to interpret it is within a context of related documents so that it fits with the way the term has been interpreted in these other documents.

Let us apply this abductive scheme for the systematic argument to the first part of this example. The notation +SA, referring to a supporting use of the systematic argument, has been inserted in the node linking the two premises in the middle of Figure 6.3 to the ultimate conclusion shown at the left. Here is a textual representation of the arguments, which corresponds to the graph of Figure 6.3. Let us first examine the initial argument, by Lord Denning.

Major Premise	+SA: If the interpretation of E in D as excluding C fits the context, then E in D should be interpreted as excluding C.
Minor Premise	The interpretation of *"residence"* in the *Education Act* as excluding *ResidenceForTheLimitedPurposeOfStudy* fits the context.
Conclusion	*"Residence"* in the *Education Act* should be interpreted as excluding *ResidenceForTheLimitedPurposeOfStudy*.

The supporting argument may appeal to the fact that in other pieces of legislation, *"ordinary residence"* indeed excludes *"residence for the limited purpose of study."*

Major Premise	+SA: If an expression E in document D_1 also occurs in a related document D_2, and the meaning of E in D_1 excludes a concept C, then the interpretation of the expression E in D_2 as excluding C fits the context.
Minor Premise	The expression *"residence"* in the *Education Act* also occurs in the related document *Immigration Act*.
Minor Premise	The meaning of *"residence"* in the *Immigration Act* excludes the concept *ResidenceForTheLimitedPurposeOf Study*.
Conclusion	The interpretation of an expression *"residence"* in the *Education Act* as excluding *ResidenceForTheLimitedPurposeOf Study* fits the context.

The structure of this complex argument can be represented in Figure 6.3. The types of arguments are indicated in the elliptical nodes, while the principles of inference are marked in italics. For graphical reasons, we abbreviated in all the following figures "*ResidenceForTheLimitedPurposeOfStudy*" as "*ResidenceFLPS.*"

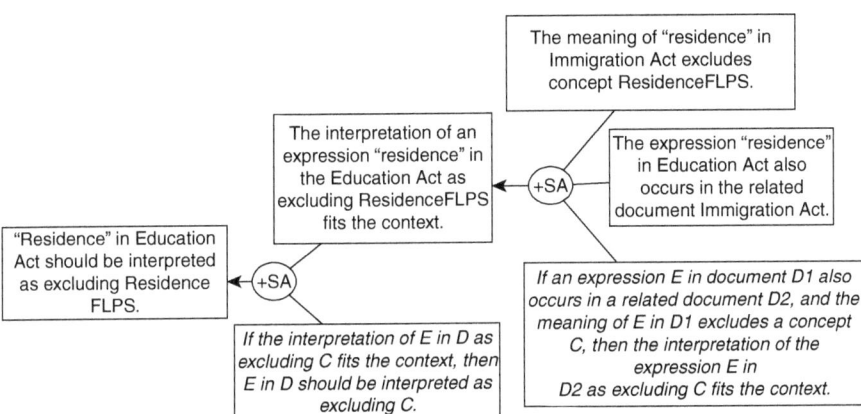

FIGURE 6.3 Proponent's argument in the educational grants example

The ultimate conclusion is the statement that non-UK students cannot count the period as ordinary residence.

Next we turn to an analysis of the argumentation in the second quoted text above, where the opponent, in this instance the House of Lords, put forward a counterargument.

> Parliament's purpose expressed in the Education Act gave no hint of any restriction on the eligibility for a mandatory award other than ordinary residence in the United Kingdom for three years and a satisfactory educational record.

This authoritative argument (a kind of argument from authority in our classification of Chapter 5) is a complex scheme where two arguments are combined, namely an *a contrario* argument and an authoritative argument from the intention of the legislator. The first argument is aimed at including an interpretation ("residence" includes *ResidenceForTheLimitedPurposeOfStudy*) based on the fact that the legislator did not provide hints that this interpretation was to be excluded (+iAC). The second argument leads from the intention of the legislator to a judgment on the exclusion of an interpretation (namely, the interpretation of "residence" to exclude *ResidenceForTheLimitedPurposeOfStudy* is contrary to the legislator's intentions) (–eIL). The first argument can be represented as follows.

Major Premise	+*iAC*: If the linguistic meaning of E in D includes S, and there are no hints that the legislator intended to exclude S from the meaning of E in D, then the legislator intends to include S in E.
Minor Premise 1	The linguistic meaning of "*residence*" in the *Education Act* includes *ResidenceForTheLimitedPurposeOfStudy*.
Minor Premise 2	There are no hints the legislator intended to exclude *ResidenceForTheLimitedPurposeOfStudy* from the meaning of "*residence*" in the *Education Act*.
Conclusion	The legislator intended to include *ResidenceForTheLimitedPurposeOfStudy* in the meaning of "*residence*" in the *Education Act*.

The second argument draws a conclusion from the intention of the legislator and the incompatibility of the two interpretations to the unacceptability of the exclusionary interpretation. The overall argument can be modeled as follows.

Major Premise	+*iIL/–eIL*: If the interpretation of E in D as excluding S conflicts with legislative purpose, then this exclusionary interpretation should be rejected, and the contrary interpretation should rather be accepted, i.e., E in D should be interpreted as including S.
Minor Premise	The interpretation of "*residence*" in the *Education Act* as excluding *ResidenceForTheLimitedPurposeOfStudy* conflicts with the legislative intention.
Conclusion	"*Residence*" in the *Education Act* should be interpreted as including *ResidenceForTheLimitedPurposeOfStudy*.

The minor premise of this argument is based on the opposition (incompatibility) between two interpretations. The reasoning underlying this conclusion can be represented as an argument from classification (our Argumentation Scheme 9 in Chapter 5) (Macagno and Walton, 2010).

Major Classification Premise	The inclusion of a specific property S in the meaning of E is contrary to the exclusion of S from E for the purpose of D.
Minor Classification Premise	The legislator intended to include *ResidenceForTheLimitedPurposeOfStudy* in the meaning of "*residence*" in the *Education Act*.
Conclusion	+*Class*: The exclusion of *ResidenceForTheLimitedPurposeOfStudy* from the meaning of "*residence*" in the *Education Act* conflicts with the legislative intention.

This argument is shown in Figure 6.4 as a counterargument to the one in Figure 6.3.

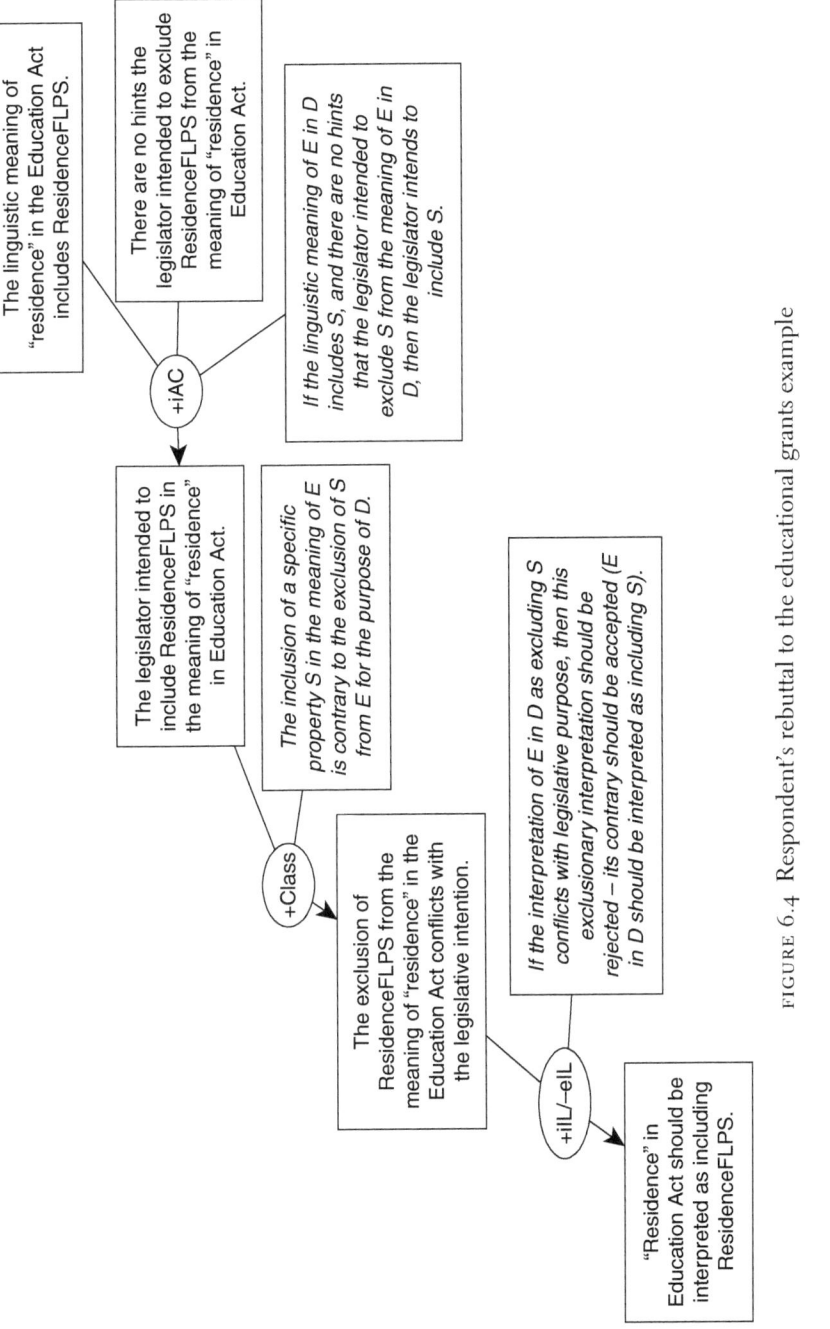

FIGURE 6.4 Respondent's rebuttal to the educational grants example

Next let's look at the first side of the issue again. Denning and Everleigh held in the Court of Appeal that, for consistency with the Immigration Act 1971 – which stated that students coming only for study did not have "ordinary residence" for the general purposes of everyday life – the term "residence" in the Education Act should be interpreted as "ordinary residence," that is, as living as an ordinary member of the community, which excludes staying in the United Kingdom for the limited purpose of study.

In the following we make fully explicit this argument by developing it into three steps. The initial step, as noted above, concludes that "residence" should be interpreted as excluding residence for the limited purpose of study, since this interpretation fits the systematic argument (contextual harmonization). This argument contradicts the opposite argument presented in Figure 6.4.

Major Premise	+*iSA*: If the interpretation of *E* in *D* as excluding *S* fits with the interpretations of other related documents, then *E* in *D* should be interpreted as excluding *S*.
Minor Premise	*ResidenceForTheLimitedPurposeOfStudy* is excluded from the interpretation of "*residence*" according to the *Immigration Act 1962*.
Conclusion	"*Residence*" in the *Education Act* should be interpreted as excluding *ResidenceForTheLimitedPurposeOfStudy*.

The minor premise of this argument can be established through a further supporting argument, proceeding from a verbal classification grounded on the opposition between two interpretations.

Major Classificatory premise	+*Class*: If *E* means P_1, and satisfying property P_1 entails not satisfying property P_2, according to document *D*, then P_2 is excluded from the interpretation of expression *E*, according to document *D*.
Premise 1	"*Residence*" means *OrdinaryResidence* according to the *Immigration Act 1962*.
Premise 2	Satisfying *ResidenceForTheLimitedPurposeOfStudy* entails not satisfying *OrdinaryResidence*, according to the *Immigration Act 1962*.
Conclusion	*ResidenceForTheLimitedPurposeOfStudy* is excluded from the interpretation of "*residence*" according to the *Immigration Act 1962*.

This complex argument is represented in Figure 6.5.

The figure shows a rebuttal because it presents an argument that attacks the ultimate conclusion of the argument shown in Figure 6.4.

As with all arguments found in natural language texts, it is possible to analyze the given text in further depth by bringing out more implicit assumptions and more subtle inferences. However, building an argument map of a real argument expressed in natural language is very often a difficult interpretative task, and often itself provides many challenges of textual interpretation. Generally, one finds there are alternative interpretations opened up as the text of the cases is analyzed in greater

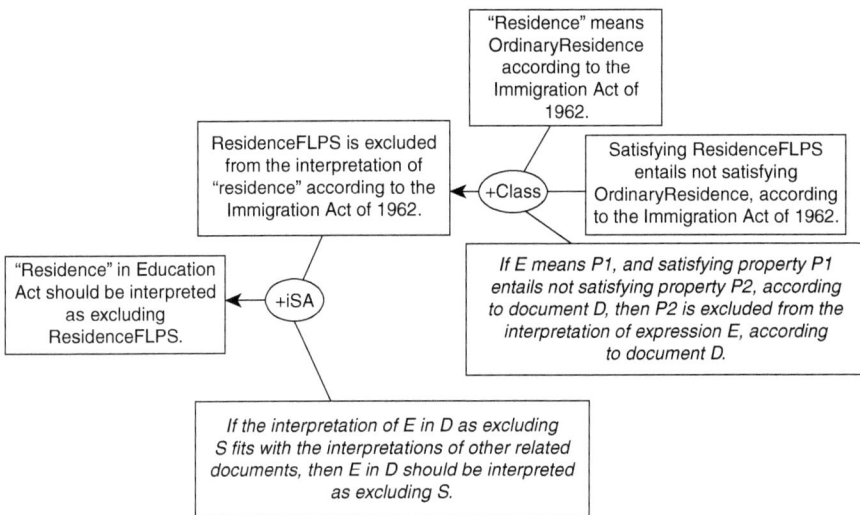

FIGURE 6.5 Respondent's premise attack in the educational grants example

depth and more implicit premises and arguments are brought out. Building an argument diagram can often raise important questions of argument interpretation and analysis that might not be initially visible to someone who is trying to deal with the argument or find out what to do with it. To illustrate some of the problems inherent in such tasks, we go back to the *Dunnachie* example.

6.3.4 *The* Dunnachie *Example: Fitting Interpretative Schemes to Cases*

Dunnachie, following the commentary of MacCormick (MacCormick, 2005, 128), offers an example of argument from contextual harmonization. The scheme for argument from contextual harmonization requires that a particular sentence in a statute should be interpreted in light of the whole statute and any set of related statutes that are available. In line with the model of interpretative schemes introduced in Section 6.2, the abductive scheme for the systematic argument (contextual harmonization) as applied to *Dunnachie* takes the following form.

Major Premise	+SA: If the interpretation of E in D as M fits the context, then E in D should be interpreted as M.
Minor Premise	The interpretation of *"loss"* in section 2 of the *Employment Rights Act* as *PecuniaryLoss* fits the context.
Conclusion	*"Loss"* in the *Employment Rights Act* should be interpreted as *PecuniaryLoss*.

The reason this interpretation fits the context is provided by the following supporting argument, which addresses the case in which the same expression occurs in different positions in the document (for simplicity's sake we do not include in the scheme the other occurrences of the expression in the same document).

Major Premise	+*Class*: If E in addition to occurring in position P_1 of document D also occurs in positions $P_2, \ldots, P_n$, where it has meaning M, then interpretation M of E in P_1 fits the context.
Minor Premise	"*Loss*" in addition to occurring in Section 2 of the *Employment Rights Act* also occurs in section 4 where it has the meaning *PecuniaryLoss*.
Conclusion	The interpretation of "*loss*" in Section 2 of the *Employment Rights Act* as *PecuniaryLoss* fits the context.

Again following the commentary of MacCormick (MacCormick, 2005, 128) on *Dunnachie*, Figure 6.6 shows how Carneades models a pro argument supporting a claim in a case where there is also a con argument attacking the same claim.

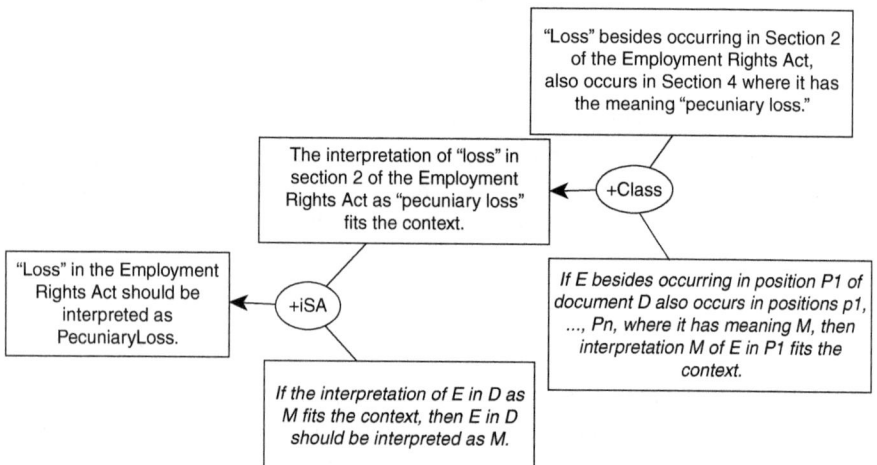

FIGURE 6.6 The use of the scheme for the systematic argument (contextual harmonization) in *Dunnachie*

The claim that "*loss*" should be interpreted as including both financial and non-pecuniary loss was partly based on a statement made in an earlier case. In that case, *Johnson v. Unisys Ltd*, Lord Hoffmann had stated that an extension of the word "loss" to emotional damage could be made. So it would appear, at least initially, that the argument drawn from the statement can be classified as an instance of a pro argument from precedent.

The reader will recall from the list of arguments provided in the Introduction and in Chapter 5 that according to the description given by MacCormick and Summers (MacCormick, 1995; MacCormick and Summers, 1991), an interpretative argument from precedent requires that if a term has a previous judicial interpretation, it should be interpreted to fit that previous interpretation (we do not distinguish here the vertical obligation to follow a decision from a higher court from the horizontal obligation to follow a decision by the same court in a previous occasion – or *stare decisis*; see Schauer, 2009, 35–36). In Chapter 5, we pointed out how this type of interpretative argument can be translated into an authoritative argument (authority of previous interpretations).

In a case previous to *Johnson*, *Norton Tool Co. v. Tewson*, it had been ruled that "*loss*" was to be interpreted as signifying exclusively financial loss. Following the lines of the analysis of the structure of interpretative schemes in Section 6.2, the scheme for the argument from the authority of previous interpretations (*PR*) can be cast in the following inclusionary and exclusionary forms.

Major Premise	+*i/ePr*: If the interpretation of E in D as excluding/including S fits precedents, then E in D should be interpreted as excluding/including S.
Minor Premise	The interpretation of "*loss*" in the *Employment Rights Act* as including/excluding *EmotionalDamage* fits precedents.
Conclusion	"*Loss*" in the *Employment Rights Act* should be interpreted as including/excluding *EmotionalDamage*.

This type of reasoning is grounded on two crucial premises, namely that *Norton* is an authority (not supported by arguments), and more importantly that it is precedent to *Dunnachie*. The similarity between *Norton* and *Dunnachie* is based on the following elements: (1) the subject matter of the dispute (in each case, the employee sought additional damages for noneconomic loss after an unfair dismissal); (2) the context (a previous act, the Industrial Relations Act 1971, whose unfair dismissal provisions were consolidated in Part X of the Employment Rights Act 1996); (3) the object of interpretation ("*loss*"). Since the court in *Norton* held that "*loss*" based on its "natural meaning" and in the context of the rule that preceded Section 123 of the Employment Rights Act 1996 "does not include injury to pride or feelings," the same interpretation should be applied in *Dunnachie*. The argument that establishes the similarity relation between the two cases can be represented as a reasoning from classification, where the relevant predicate "to be prior and similar" is attributed to *Norton* based on the following reasoning.

Major Classification Premise	+*Class*: If two cases are about the same issue, even though they concern the interpretation of different Acts, they are similar.
Minor Classification Premise	*Both Norton and Dunnachie concerns the concept of "loss" relation to noneconomic loss after an unfair dismissal, even though the first deals with the interpretation of the Industrial Relations Act (whose relevant section was consolidated in the Employment Rights Act) and Dunnachie the first deals with the interpretation of the "loss" in the Employment Rights Act.*
Conclusion	*Norton is similar to Dunnachie.*

This reasoning provides the ground for another classificatory argument, which proceeds from the similarity judgment to the classification of *Norton* as a "precedent" of *Dunnachie*.

Major Premise	+*Class*: If E in D was understood in previous and similar case P as M, then the interpretation of E in D as M fits precedents.
Minor Premise 1	*Norton* is similar to *Dunnachie*, and it is prior to it.
Minor Premise 2	"*Loss*" in the *Industrial Relations Act* was understood in *Norton* as excluding *EmotionalDamage*.
Conclusion	The interpretation of "*loss*" in the *Employment Rights Act* as excluding *EmotionalDamage* fits precedents.

This argument can be represented in Figure 6.7. For graphical reasons, we abbreviate the *Employment Rights Act* as ERA" and the *Industrial Relations Act* as "IRA."

This argument was analyzed by considering its counterargument, provided by the Employment Tribunal. The lower court used a similar argument from the authority of previous interpretations, pointing out the similarity between *Dunnachie* and a precedent case in which an inclusive interpretation was given, namely *Johnson v. Unisys Ltd* UKHL 13; IRLR 279, 2001. The argument is opposite to the previous.

Major Premise	+*iPr*: If the interpretation of E in D as including S fits precedents, then E in D should be interpreted as including S.
Minor Premise	The interpretation of "*loss*" in the *Employment Rights Act* as including *EmotionalDamage* fits precedents.
Conclusion	"*Loss*" in the *Employment Rights Act* should be interpreted as including *EmotionalDamage*.

Again, the reasoning follows from a judgment of similarity between two cases, based on the same elements: (1) the subject matter of the dispute (in each case, the employee sought additional damages for noneconomic loss after an unfair dismissal); (2) the context (the Employment Rights Act 1996); (3) the object of interpretation ("*loss*"). The reasoning can be represented as follows.

Major Classification Premise	+*Class*: If two cases are about the same issue, concerning the same law, they are similar.
Minor Classification Premise	*Johnson* concerns the concept of "*loss*" in the *Employment Rights Act* in relation to noneconomic loss after an unfair dismissal; *Dunnachie* concerns the concept of "*loss*" in the *Employment Rights Act* in relation to noneconomic loss after an unfair dismissal.
Conclusion	*Johnson* is similar to *Dunnachie*.

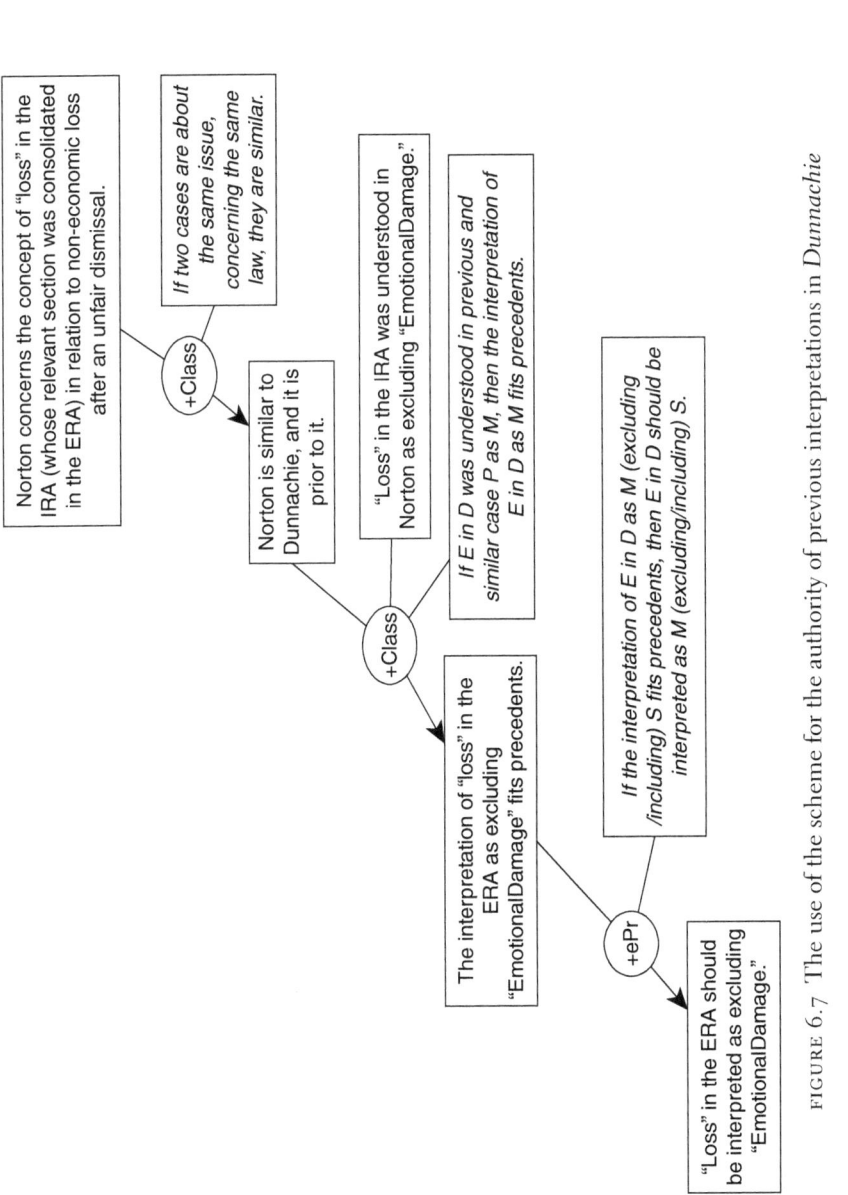

FIGURE 6.7 The use of the scheme for the authority of previous interpretations in *Dunnachie*

This reasoning provides the ground for another classificatory argument, which proceeds from the similarity judgment to the classification of *Norton* as a "precedent" of *Dunnachie*.

Major Premise	+*Class*: If *E* in *D* was understood in previous and similar case *P* as *including S*, then the interpretation of *E* in *D* as *including S* fits precedents.
Minor Premise 1	*Johnson* is similar to *Dunnachie*, and it is prior to it.
Minor Premise 2	"*Loss*" in the *Employment Rights Act* was understood in *Johnson* as including *EmotionalDamage*.
Conclusion	The interpretation of "*loss*" in the *Employment Rights Act* as including *EmotionalDamage* fits precedents.

This argument, analogous and contrary to the previous one, can be represented in Figure 6.8.

The interpretation of "*loss*" is thus supported by the same types of arguments, but they reach contradictory conclusions. This conflict can be resolved by considering the defeasibility conditions of the arguments. In this sense, the crucial dimension of this legal dispute is focused on the arguments provided by each party against the other's. The starting point is the analysis of the conflicting interpretations, which is summarized in Figure 6.9.

There are two main arguments shown in Figure 6.9. The one at the top, labeled +*ePr*, offers a pro argument from precedent giving evidence to support the conclusion that "*loss*" should be interpreted in the Employment Rights Act as excluding emotional damage. This pro argument is supported by bringing forward the case of *Norton Tool Co. v. Tewson*. But now let us look at the argument along the bottom. This con argument, an argument in favor of an inclusive interpretation, has been labelled –*ePr*/+*iPr* since its function is to attack the exclusive interpretation (which in our diagram is presented as the final conclusion included in a box with thicker lines) by arguing for inclusion (i.e., to be a con argument against exclusion). This argument offers another case claimed to be a precedent the case of *Johnson v. Unisys Ltd* (indicated as "+*Class*" as it is an argument supporting another argument, regardless of the function of the latter). So here we can see the main conflict in the sequence of argumentation in the case to this point. A pro argument from precedent is pitted against a con argument from precedent.

Can we say anything at this point about how the sequence of argumentation can be evaluated, based on which premises are accepted and which conclusions can be drawn from these premises? Can the pro and con arguments be weighed against each other, so that we can tell which is stronger than the other? In some cases of such conflicts, argumentation modeling does not yield such an outcome. The system tells you that the case is a deadlock. However, even so, the model can tell the user quite a bit about the structure of the argumentation and can serve as a basis for saying that

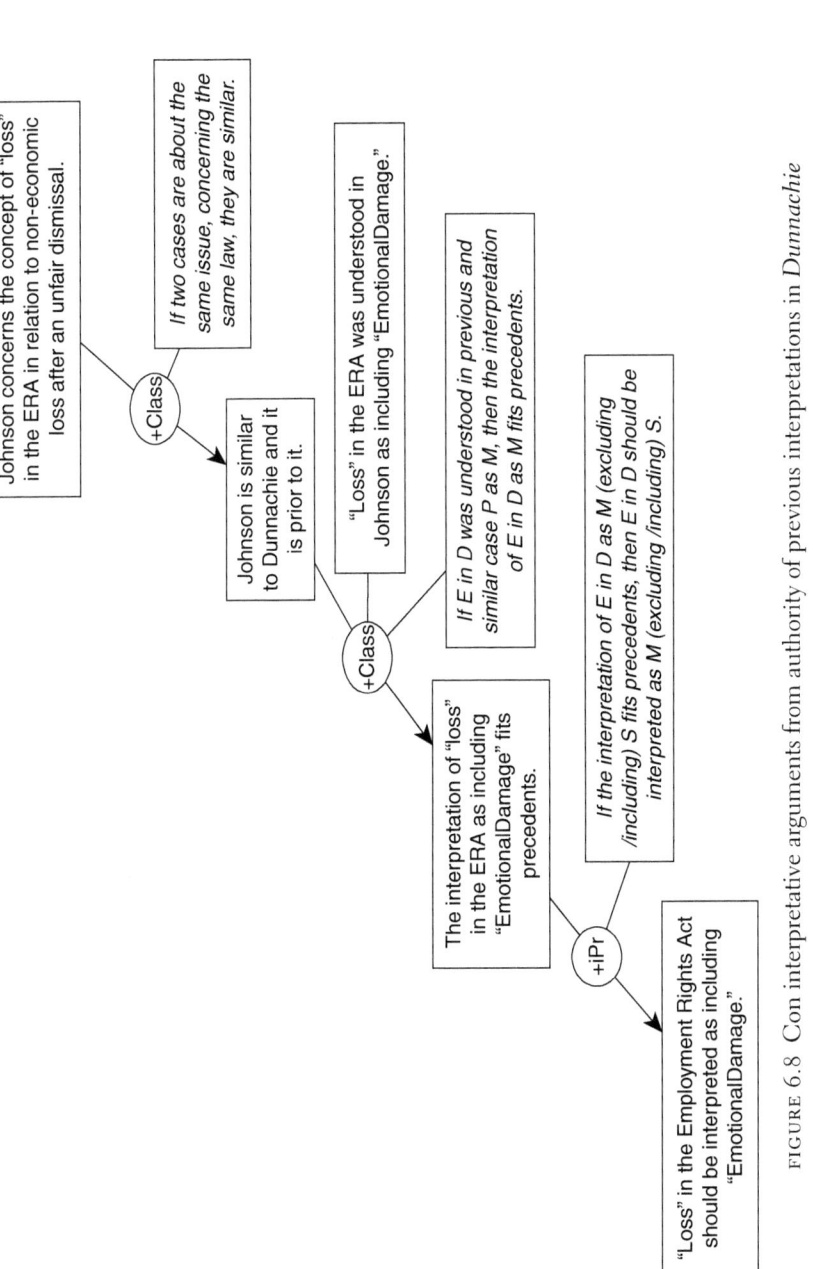

FIGURE 6.8 Con interpretative arguments from authority of previous interpretations in *Dunnachie*

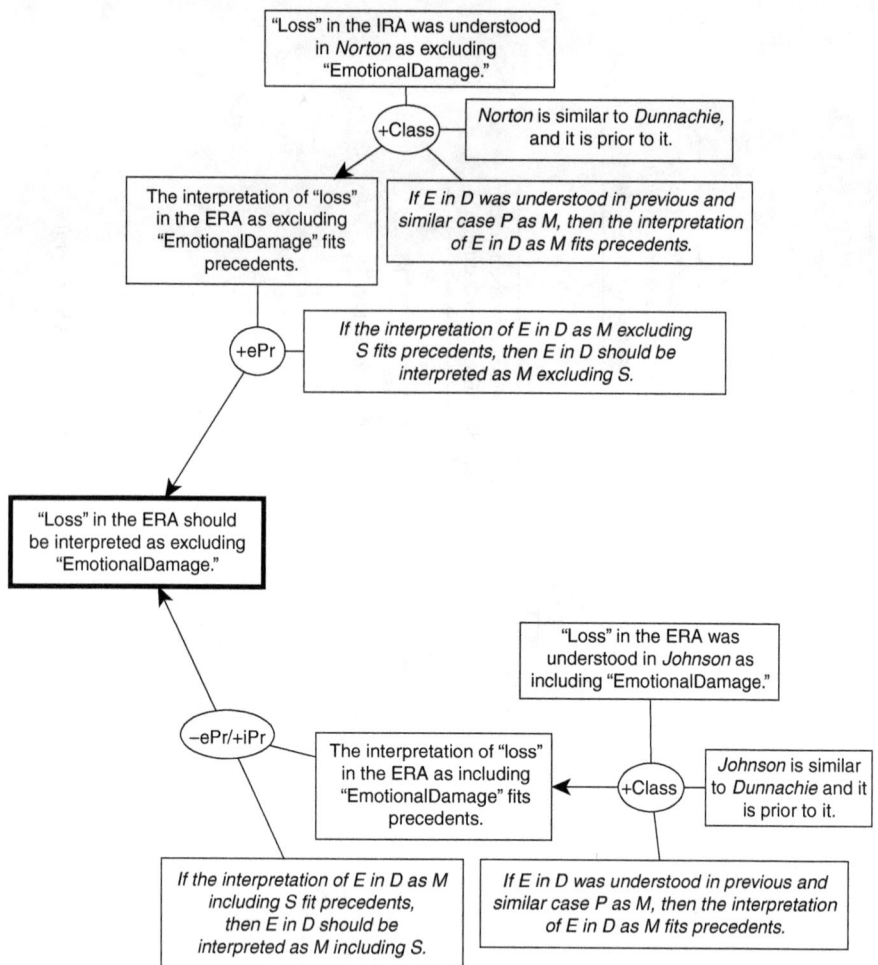

FIGURE 6.9 How interpretative arguments from authority of previous interpretations defeat each other

the one argument carries more weight than the other. In legal cases the evaluation of conflicting arguments often depends on the standard of proof in the case. For example, one such standard might be that of beyond reasonable doubt, while another standard might be the preponderance of the evidence. However, such standards are decisive on matters of fact, they do not apply on matters on interpretation. Nevertheless, not taking such factors into account here, using argumentation tools can be very helpful in elucidating the nature of the conflict.

In *Dunnachie*, the court considered the grounds of the authority of a previous interpretation, analyzing both the arguments in favor and against each one of the two conflicting precedents. In Figure 6.10, the pro arguments supporting the exclusive interpretation are represented as "+A" nodes. Each of the two arguments supporting the proposition that *Norton Tool Co.* v. *Tewson* is a precedent case has only one premise, and let's say that in both instances that premise is accepted by the audience, the judge or jury who is the argument evaluator. Let's also say that the proposition in the middle at the top left, stating that in Section 116(1) of the IRA the word "*loss*" was interpreted as excluding emotional damage, is accepted. These three propositions are shown in boxes with a light grey background.

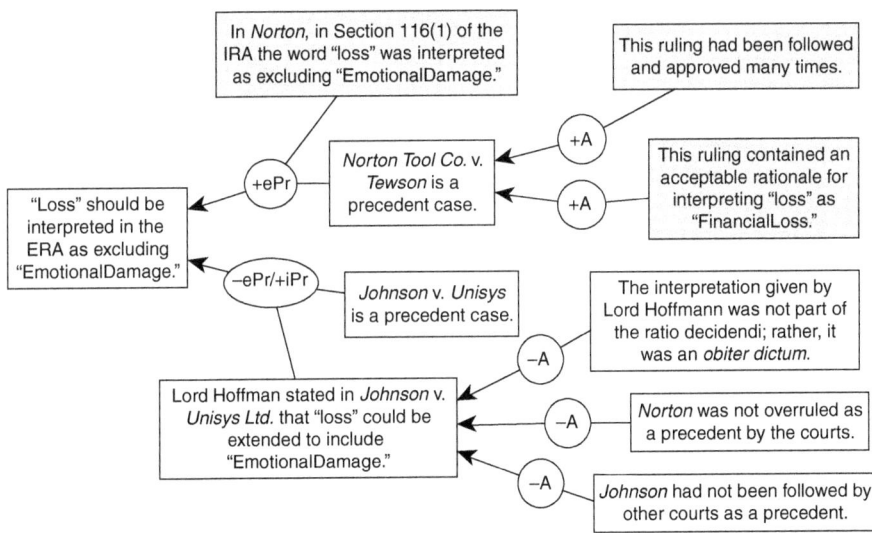

FIGURE 6.10 Step 1 in evaluating interpretative argument from authority of previous interpretations

What follows next? There are two arguments supporting the conclusion that *Norton Tool Co.* v. *Tewson* is a precedent case. One is that the ruling has been followed and approved many times. The other says that this ruling contained an acceptable rationale for interpreting "*loss*" as "financial loss." Neither of these arguments is labeled with an argumentation scheme, but they seem like reasonable arguments to use in supporting a claim made that one case can be taken as a precedent case for another. So, let us assume that both arguments would be relevant and acceptable to the audience as presenting evidence that should be taken into account.

Based on this input, Carneades automatically colors the background in the rectangle stating the proposition that *Norton Tool Co.* v. *Tewson* is a precedent case. Now that both premises of the argument labeled +ePr have been accepted by the audience, then the ultimate conclusion, the proposition that "*loss*" should be interpreted in the Employment Rights Act as excluding emotional damage, should also be accepted. So Carneades automatically shows the rectangle containing that conclusion with a light grey background. So now, overall, based on the evidence considered so far, the pro argument at the top has prevailed over the con argument shown along the bottom. This result is shown in Figure 6.11.

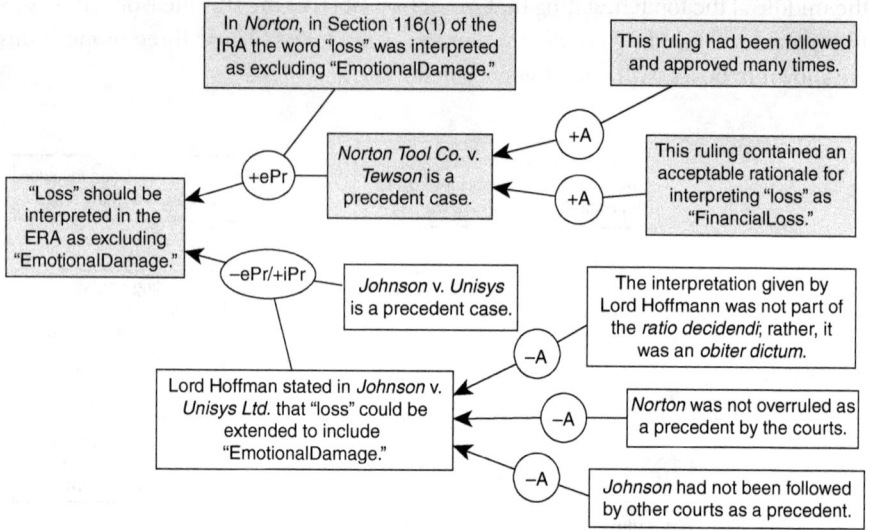

FIGURE 6.11 Step 2 in evaluating interpretative argument from authority of previous interpretations

Now we turn to Figure 6.12 to consider the con argument shown along the bottom, based on a consideration of which premises are acceptable to the audience and what conclusions follows from this. So, suppose that the two premises of the con argument *–ePr+iPr* are tentatively acceptable, subject to further questioning.

Figure 6.12 visually represents the question: What happens if the two main arguments supporting *–ePr+iPr* are seen by the court as being acceptable on a tentative basis? The answer is that since both premises of this argument have now been deemed to be acceptable, and the argument from precedent based on them fits the argumentation scheme for argument from precedent, and since *–ePr+iPr* is a con argument in this instance, the ultimate conclusion that was formerly shown in light grey (Figure 6.11) is now displayed in a rectangle with a blank background, showing it is no longer accepted. Here, in other words, what is shown is that the argument from precedent at the bottom has defeated the argument from precedent shown at the top.

This outcome might seem to be dubious because the precedent of *Norton Tool Co.* v. *Tewson* is supported by two pro arguments, each of which is based on a single premise that is accepted. Insofar as *Norton*'s precedence has more arguments in its favor, the top argument seems to be stronger. But it is not a matter of the number of premises. Even though the top argument may seem to

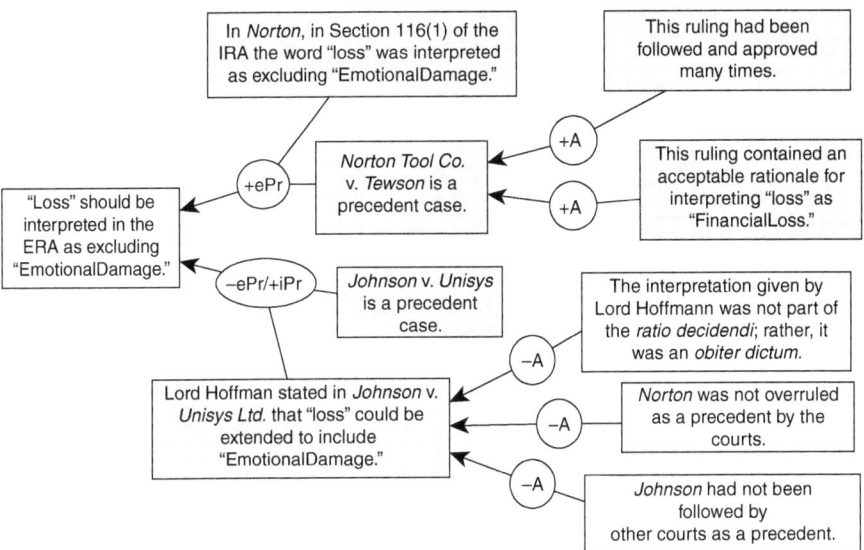

FIGURE 6.12 Step 3 in evaluating interpretative argument from authority of previous interpretations

have carried weight in supporting the ultimate conclusion based on the precedent argument offered, the con argument at the bottom may have lessened the weight accorded to the top argument enough to make that top argument fail to be strong enough to meet the burden of proof demanded by the standard of proof applicable in the case.

What the analysis of the argumentation has shown us so far, where the state of argumentation is represented by Figure 6.12, is that one argument from precedent can be used to attack another one, and even though the attacking argument may not be as strong as a supporting argument it may create enough doubt to undermine the acceptability of the supporting argument. There may be various ways that this can happen, including different kinds of argument defeats and structured argumentation systems such as Carneades. But we will not pause to take these matters into account here, because the example is being used only as an illustration of how argument evaluation generally works in such systems.

Next, let's take the further step of considering the con argument at the bottom right, the argument that has three premises and that attacks the premise of *–ePr+iPr* claiming that Lord Hoffmann stated in *Johnson v. Unisys Ltd* that "*loss*" could extended to include *EmotionalDamage*. Let us suppose, as shown in Figure 6.13, that all three of these premises are accepted by the audience.

Now let's suppose that all three premises shown at the bottom right in Figure 6.13 are accepted. Since the argument is a con argument, assuming that it either fits an

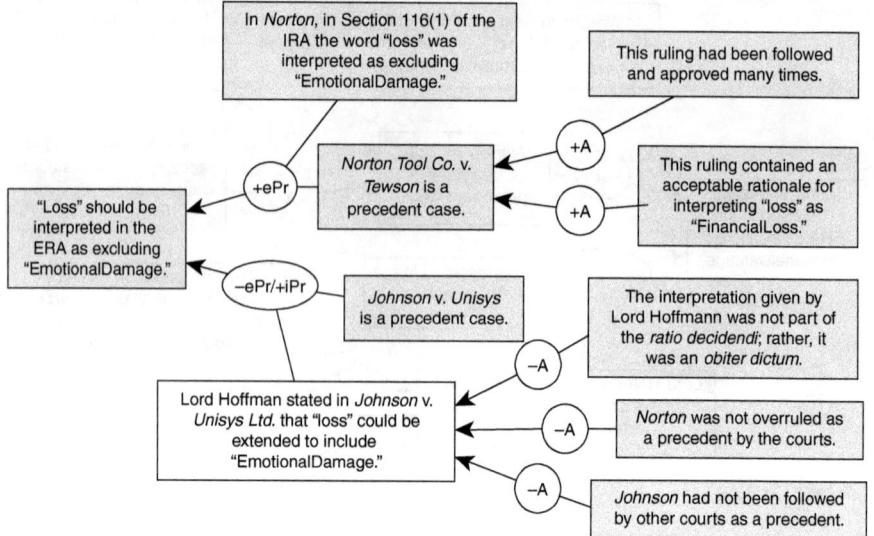

FIGURE 6.13 Step 4 in evaluating interpretative argument from authority of previous interpretations

argumentation scheme (not modeled in the analysis given in Figure 6.13) or is accepted by the audience as a reasonable argument, the conclusion of the argument (claiming that Lord Hoffmann stated in *Johnson v. Unisys Ltd* that "*loss*" could be extended to include "emotional loss") now has to be shown as neither accepted nor rejected. The white background of the rectangle containing this proposition indicates this loss of status of the conclusion. The ultimate outcome of this evaluation of the argumentation at this point is that the con argument at the bottom fails to disprove the ultimate conclusion, the proposition at issue, and by default, the argument at the top carries the day.

The last line of analysis concerns the arguments provided against the use of *Norton* as a precedent, which was the ground of the previous decision of the Court of Appeal. The inclusive interpretation was defended by attacking the acceptability of the contrary argument from the authority of the interpretation provided in *Norton*. According to this attack, on which the judgment of the Court of Appeal was based, the previous case cited in support of the inclusive interpretation (*Johnson*) contained a statement made by one of the judges, Lord Hoffmann, which could be interpreted as claiming that *Norton* was wrongly decided. For this reason, *Norton* was claimed to be not a precedent for the case, while the *ratio decidendi* provided by Lord Hoffmann in *Johnson* was used as a reason for the inclusive interpretation. This strategy can be represented in Figure 6.14.

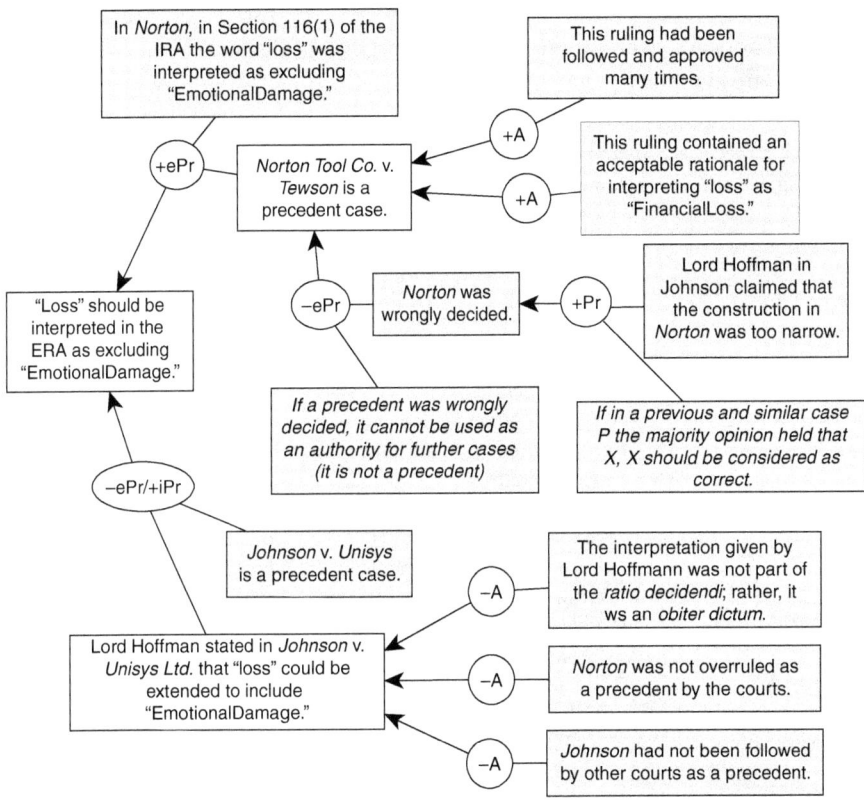

FIGURE 6.14 Analysis of the precedent used for supporting the exclusive interpretation (attacks)

The aforementioned argument used for attacking the reliability of *Norton* is based only on one premise that is accepted, namely the fact that Lord Hoffmann claimed that the construction in *Norton* was too narrow. However, the court analyzed the other premises leading to an attack to the use of *Norton* as a precedent. In particular, two reasons for not considering the opinion of Lord Hoffmann as a basis for judging the correctness of *Norton* were given (see also MacCormick, 2005, 129): (1) the correctness of the *Norton* ruling was not an issue in *Johnson* (undermining the acceptability of the argument from the authority of the precedent used to support the underminer); and (2) the statement concerning the correctness of *Norton* was not given as a part of the *ratio decidendi*, as Lord Hoffmann described it as a "comment" on a "doubtful question." The words of Lord Hoffmann are used as an abductive argument to conclude that he did not intend to ground his decision on the incorrectness of *Norton*, and for this reason this statement cannot be considered as an authority for discarding *Norton*. This complex evaluation is represented in Figure 6.15.

To make Figure 6.15 more easily readable the key list below present abbreviated versions for each proposition in the argument diagram. The two implicit premises are italicized.

LH_Lang_Excludes	Lord Hoffmann's language clearly excludes that his comment on *Norton* is part of the *ratio decidendi*.
In_Norton_116	In *Norton*, in Section 116(I) of the IRA the word "loss" was interpreted as excluding *EmotionalDamage*.
Many_Times	This ruling had been followed and approved many times.
Norton_Precedent	*Norton Tool Co. v. Tewson* is a precedent case.
Ruling_Fin _Loss	This ruling contained an acceptable rationale for interpreting "loss" as *Financial Loss*.
Norton_Wrong	*Norton* was wrongly decided.
LH_Narrow	Lord Hoffmann in *Johnson* claimed that the construction in *Norton* was too narrow.
LH_Academic	In *Johnson*, Lord Hoffmann described the correctness of Norton as "a doubtful question." He described it as "academic." Then he introduced his comments by the words "But perhaps I may be allowed a comment all the same."
Prec_Wrong	*If a precedent was wrongly decided, it cannot be used as an authority for further cases (it is not a valid precedent).*
Majority_X	*If in a previous and similar case P the majority opinion held that X, X should be considered as correct.*
Loss_ERA_Fin	"Loss" should be interpreted in the ERA as excluding *EmotionalDamage*.
Not_Disputed	The accuracy of this account of the law in action was not disputed before the House.
John_Uni_Prec	*Johnson v. Unisys* is a precedent case.
LH_Obiter	The interpretation given by Lord Hoffmann was not part of the *ratio decidendi*; rather, it was an *obiter dictum*.
Norton_Not_Overruled	*Norton* was not overruled as a precedent by the courts.
Johnson_Not_Followed	*Johnson* had not been followed by other courts as a precedent.
LH_ Inc_Emotional	Lord Hoffmann stated in *Johnson v. Unisys Ltd* that "loss" could be extended to include *EmotionalDamage*.

Since the premises concerning the nature of the words of Lord Hoffmann were accepted, the attack against *Norton's* correctness is defeated, and its function as a precedent in support of the exclusive interpretation remains in force.

Summing everything up, we notice that the pro argument from precedent at the top prevails over the con argument from precedent at the bottom, because one of the premises of the con argument is unacceptable. Only the pro argument is accepted, and so the conclusion is accepted. Hence the conflict is resolved.

This case has another interesting alternative interpretation. It might be possible to argue that even though the ruling in *Johnson* on how to interpret *"loss"* was not a binding precedent, because it was not necessary to the decision made in that case,

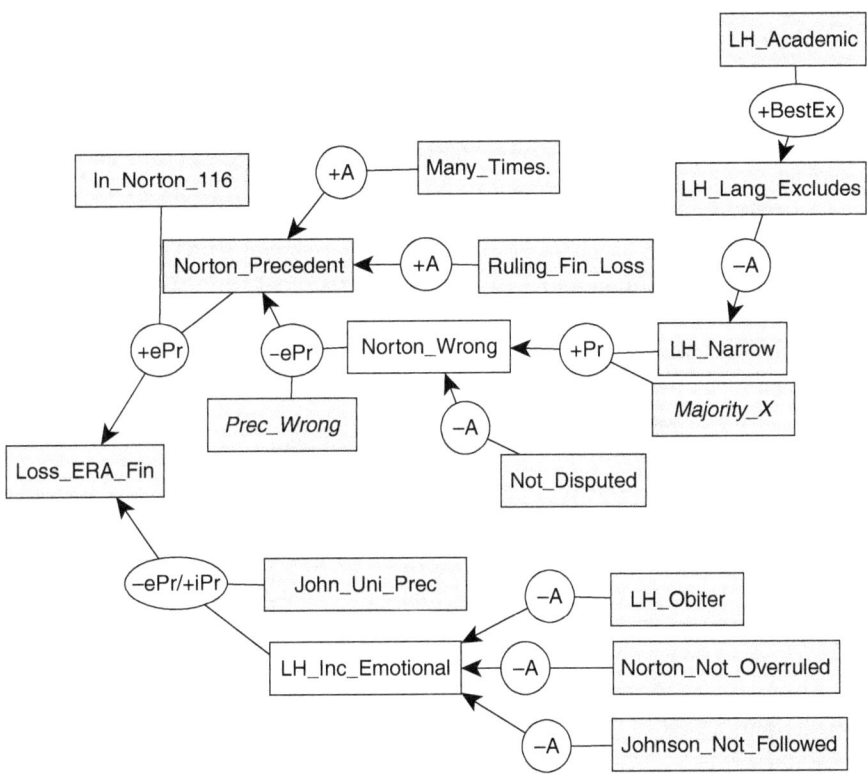

FIGURE 6.15 Analysis of the precedent used for supporting the exclusive interpretation

still it could be taken to be a weaker kind of precedent. MacCormick (MacCormick, 2005, 129) distinguishes between a binding precedent and a precedent that is persuasive but not binding. Honoring this distinction, interpretation of the word "*loss*" in *Johnson* could be taken as a weaker kind of precedent. Following this line of argument, the conflict between the two arguments from precedent no longer represents a deadlock because the stronger precedent from *Norton* would have priority over the weaker precedent from *Johnson*. Carneades and ASPIC^{+}, as well as other systems, recognize different kinds of priority orderings on rules, and so that would be another way that AI systems could model the argumentation in this case.

In Section 6.2 we proposed schemes for some of the interpretative arguments to give the reader an idea of what these schemes should ultimately look like. However, especially with some of the schemes, the descriptions of the different kinds of interpretative arguments given by MacCormick and Summers are not enough in themselves to definitively formulate the matching scheme. In particular, the scheme for argument from precedent needs more study by applying it to cases before a definitive version can be given.

6.4 THE LOGIC OF INTERPRETATIVE ARGUMENTS

In this section we shall provide a general formal structure for interpretative arguments, on the basis of the approach to interpretative arguments introduced and exemplified in the previous sections. Let us first summarize that approach.

Interpretative arguments can be distinguished along two criteria: positive versus negative and total versus partial. The first criterion concerns whether the argument addresses the adoption or the rejection of a certain interpretation. The second criterion concerns whether the argument addresses the whole interpretation of a term, or only the inclusion or exclusion of a subclass in the term's meaning. Correspondingly, partial interpretative arguments can be distinguished into exclusionary and inclusionary ones.

All interpretative arguments we shall consider are based on canons, namely, defeasible conditionals stating that if certain conditions are or are not met, a certain interpretation is or is not correct or appropriate (it should or should not be adopted).

6.4.1 *Interpretative Canons as Defeasible Rules*

In this section we shall propose appropriate formal structures for capturing interpretative arguments.

Let us start with positive and negative total interpretative arguments. Both structures have the following elements: an expression E (word, phrase, sentence, etc.) occurs in a document D (statute, regulation, contract, etc.) and interpreting this occurrence as meaning M satisfies the condition of a certain interpretative scheme (of ordinary language, technical language, purpose, etc.). Positive canons state that if all these elements are satisfied, we may derive the interpretative conclusion that M *is the best (the right) interpretation for E in D*. Negative canons state that if an interpretation I would not fit the scheme, then M *is not the best (the right) interpretation for E in D*.

In a previous paper (Sartor et al., 2014), we modeled interpretative claims as deontic claims, stating the obligation to adopt a certain interpretation. Here we follow a different approach, focusing on the relationship between an interpretation and its justification, as a metalinguistic discourse on why a meaning is the best interpretation of an expression. In this sense, we model interpretative claims as terminological assertions concerning best interpretations of contested or potentially contested expressions within a legal text (for a similar idea, see Araszkiewicz, 2013).

For reasoning about interpretation we need an argumentation system including strict rules, defeasible rules, and preference between rules, such as the system developed by Prakken and Sartor (Prakken and Sartor, 1996), the ASPIC$^+$ system

(Prakken, 2010) or the Carneades Argumentation System (Gordon and Walton, 2009a). We express defeasible rules in the form

$$r : \varphi_1 \& \ldots \& \varphi_n \Rightarrow \psi$$

where r is the rule name 1 and $\varphi_1, \ldots, \varphi_n$ and ψ are formulas in a logical language, $\varphi_1, \ldots, \varphi_n$ being the *antecedents* and ψ the *consequent* of the rule. The symbol & denotes the conjunction "and." The rule means that if all antecedents are established then the consequent can be presumably (defeasibly) inferred: given $\varphi_1, \ldots, \varphi_n$ we can derive the consequent ψ, unless there are prevailing arguments to the contrary, as we shall see in the following. Similarly, we model strict rules in the form

$$r : \varphi_1 \& \ldots \& \varphi_n \longmapsto \psi$$

The rule means that if all antecedents $\varphi_1, \ldots, \varphi_n$ are satisfied, then ψ can be conclusively inferred: given the antecedents the consequent follows necessarily. We use arrows $\rightarrow$ and $\leftrightarrow$ respectively for the material conditional and biconditional of propositional logic. We also assume that our system includes the inferences of classical logic, namely, that for any propositions of classical logic φ and ψ, if φ entails ψ, then we have a strict rule $\varphi \longmapsto \psi$.

We model all interpretative canons as defeasible rules (expressed in the form $r : \varphi_1 \& \ldots \& \varphi_n \Rightarrow \psi$). The interpretative conclusions ψ is a claim concerning a conceptual relation between a meaning M that is proposed and the outcome of the best legal interpretation of the linguistic occurrence at issue, namely, expression E in document D. Such outcome is denoted by the functional expression $BestInt(E, D)$. Conceptual relations are expressed with description logic symbols: $\equiv$ for conceptual equivalence, $\sqsubseteq$ for inclusion, $\sqsubseteq\neg$ for exclusion (inclusion in the complement), $\not\equiv$ for difference, $\not\sqsubseteq$ for noninclusion, $\not\sqsubseteq\neg$ for nonexclusion. We will also use $\sqcup$ for the union of two concepts ($A \sqcup B$ denoting the concept of A or B).

Thus, a general pattern for positive-total interpretative canons can be expressed as follows:

C: expression E occurs in document D, and
the interpretation of E in D as M *satisfies the condition of positive canon* C $\Longrightarrow$

$$M \equiv BestInt(E, D)$$

where $M \equiv BestInt(E, D)$ may be read as M is (the same concept as) the best interpretation of E in D. Here is an example:

OL: expression E occurs in document D, and
the interpretation of E in D as M fits ordinary language $\Rightarrow$

$$M \equiv BestInt(E, D)$$

where $M \equiv BestInt(E, D)$ may be read as M is (i.e., is equivalent to or is the same concept as) the best interpretation of E in D. Note that the "and" is between brackets since it is not needed in the formal language, "," stands for "and". Here is an example:

+OL: expression E occurs in document D, and
the interpretation of E in D as M fits ordinary language $\Rightarrow$

$$M \equiv BestInt(E, D)$$

As an example of a negative use of canons, consider the following example based on the nonredundancy canon (also called economical interpretation), which argues for the rejection of a redundant interpretation:

−NR: expression E occurs in document D, and
the interpretation of E in D as M is redundant $\Rightarrow$

$$M \not\equiv BestInt(E, D)$$

Let us now provide examples for canons being used for partial interpretations, such as, exclusionary *a contrario*:

+eAC: expression E occurs in document D, and
the interpretation of E in D as including S conflicts with usual meaning $\Rightarrow$

$$S \sqsubseteq \neg BestInt(E, D)$$

where $S \sqsubseteq \neg BestInt(E, D)$ is to be read as "subclass S is excluded from (i.e., included in the complement of) the best interpretation of E in D."

The following is an example of an inclusionary use of *a contrario*:

+iAC: expression E occurs in document D, and
the interpretation of E in D as excluding S conflicts with usual meaning $\Rightarrow$

$$S \sqsubseteq BestInt(E, D)$$

where $S \sqsubseteq BestInt(E, D)$ is to be read as "subclass S is included in the best interpretation of E in D."

We can also identify patterns for priority arguments between different (instances of) interpretative canons (we use $\succ$ to express priority).

P_X: according to priority criterion X, the conditions for canon C_1 to have priority over canon C_2 are satisfied, relatively to expression E in document D, $\Rightarrow$

$$C_1(E, D, M_1) \succ C_2(E, D, M_2)$$

Where $C_1(E, D, M_1)$ denotes the application of canon C_1 to E in D to obtain interpretation M_1 (and similarly for $C_2(E, D, M_2)$).

Consider, for instance, Alexy and Drier's idea that ordinary language has priority over technical language (+P_{OL}, priority for ordinary language) when the interpretation concerns a criminal provision (this being the condition that triggers the priority).

+P_{OL}: expression E in document D pertains to criminal law $\Rightarrow$

$$C_{OL}(E, D, M_1) \succ C_{TL}(E, D, M_2)$$

Given appropriate priorities, interpretative arguments can be ordered in hierarchies depending on the specific legal context.

6.4.2 *Defeat Relations: Rebutting and Undercutting*

An argument A including defeasible rules may be defeated in two ways. The first consists in successfully *rebutting* A, that is, in contradicting a subargument of A, through an argument that is not weaker than the attacked subarguments (we assume that A too is a subargument of itself). More precisely, B *rebuts* A when (1) B's conclusion is incompatible with the conclusion of a subargument A' of A and (2) A' is not stronger than B, that is, $A' \not> B$ (see Prakken, 2010). Condition (2) corresponds to the idea that if A' were stronger than B, then A' would resist B's challenge. With regard to comparative strength, we assume that the comparison between two arguments A and B is to be assessed according to two criteria:

1. Preference for strict arguments (those that contain only strict rules) over defeasible ones (those that also contain defeasible rules): if A is strict and B is defeasible, then $A > B$.
2. Preference between defeasible arguments according to the last link principle: if A is preferable to B according to the last link principle, then $A > B$.

The *last link principle* assumes a partial strict priority ordering over defeasible rules and compares arguments A and B having incompatible conclusions by considering the sets of the last defeasible rules that support such conclusions in the two arguments (see for a formal characterization, Prakken and Sartor, 1996; Prakken, 2010).

The second way of defeating an argument A consists in undercutting A, that is, in producing an argument B that concludes with the inapplicability of a defeasible rule used in A. Let us express the applicability of rule through a special predicate *appl*, so that an argument for the inapplicability of a rule r has the conclusion $\neg appl(r)$. Then we can say in general terms that argument B undercuts argument A if B has the conclusion $\neg appl(r)$ where r is the top rule of a subargument A' of A. For instance, argument

$$[a; r_1: a \Rightarrow b]$$

is undercut (defeated through undercutting) by argument

$$[c; r_2: c \Rightarrow appl(r_1)].$$

6.4.3 *An Extension-Based Argumentation Semantics*

A semantics for an argumentation system can be constructed on the basis of the idea of an *extension*, namely, a set of compatible arguments, which includes resources (arguments) that respond to all defeaters of arguments in the set. Here we adopt the approach that consists in looking for the most inclusive extensions, which are called preferred extensions (Dung, 1995). An argument is then considered to be justified if it is included in all such extensions. It is considered defensible if it is included in some (but not necessarily in all) extensions. The arguments that are defensible but not justified are included only in some preferred extensions: their status remains undecided, as their inclusion in a preferred extension depends on what other arguments are already included in the extension, different choices being possible. Consider for instance the following set of arguments:

$$\{[a], [b], [a, r_1 : a \Rightarrow c], [b, r_2 : b \Rightarrow \neg c]\}.$$

We have two preferred extensions:

$$E_1 = [a], \; [b], \; [a, r_1 : \; a \Rightarrow \quad c]\}$$

and

$$E_2 = \{[a]\{[a], [b], [b, r_2 : b \Rightarrow \neg c]\}$$

Each extension includes an argument that is defeated, but also defeats an argument in the other extension: $A_1 = [a, r_1 : a \Rightarrow c]$ for E_1 and $A_2 = [b, r_2 : b \Rightarrow \neg c]$ for E_2. So, each one of the two extensions responds to all defeaters of any argument it includes. However, A_1 and A_2 are merely defensible as they are incompatible, and we do not have, in the given set of arguments, reasons for preferring one to the other. Assume that we add preference argument $[r_3 : \Rightarrow r_1 \succ r_2]$. Then we have just one preferred extension, namely

$$\{[a], [b], [a, r_1 : a \Rightarrow c], [r_3 : \Rightarrow r_1 \succ r_2]\}$$

since according to the preference $r_3 : \Rightarrow r_1 \succ r_2$, A_1 is no longer defeated by A_2, while A_2 continues to be defeated by A_1.

Moving from arguments to conclusions, we have two possibilities for defining what conclusions are justified. One option is to view a conclusion as justified when it is established through a justified argument. The other option consists in viewing a conclusion as justified when it is supported in all preferred extensions, though possibly through different arguments. More precisely, we get the following definitions:

- *Defensibility.* Claim φ is defensible with regard to argument set $\mathcal{A}$ if there exists a preferred extension of $\mathcal{A}$ that contains an argument with conclusion φ.
- *Strong justifiability.* Claim φ is strongly justifiable with regard to argument set $\mathcal{A}$ if φ is the conclusion of an argument $\mathcal{A}$ that is contained in all preferred extensions.
- *Weak justifiability.* Claim φ is weakly justifiable with regard to argument set A if every preferred extension contains arguments having conclusion φ.

Note that the weak definition of justifiability is broader than the strong one, since it allows a conclusion to be justified through different incompatible arguments, included in different extensions. This is the notion that seems to be more appropriate to interpretative argumentation, as we shall argue in the following section.

6.5 FORMAL DIALECTICAL STRUCTURE OF INTERPRETATIVE ARGUMENTS

In this section we shall consider how interpretative arguments can be formalized by using the formal resources introduced in the previous section.

6.5.1 *The Structure of an Interpretative Argument*

An interpretative argument can be constructed by combining an interpretative canon with the corresponding interpretative conditions. For instance, an argument from ordinary language would have the following form (we abbreviate "Section 123(1) of the Employment Rights Act" with 123(1)ERA):

Argument A_1

Premise	Expression "*loss*" occurs in document 123(1)ERA
Premise	The interpretation of "*loss*" in 123(1)ERA as *PecuniaryLoss* fits ordinary language
Major premise *(Canon)*	Article I. OL: expression E occurs in document D & the interpretation of E in D as M fits ordinary language $\Rightarrow$ $M \equiv BestInt(E, D)$
Conclusion	*PecuniaryLoss* $\equiv BestInt(loss, 123(1)ERA)$

6.5.2 *The Dialectic of Interpretative Argument: Rebutting and Undercutting*

Interpretative arguments can be attacked by counterarguments. For instance, the following counterargument based on technical language successfully rebuts the above argument based on ordinary language, by providing a different incompatible interpretation (assuming that no priority can be established, and that concepts are different when denoted with a different name):

Argument A_2

Premise	Expression "loss" occurs in document 123(1)ERA
Premise	The interpretation of "*loss*" in 123(1)ERA as *PecuniaryLoss* $\sqcup$ *EmotionalDamage* fits technical language
Major premise **(Canon)**	+TL: expression E occurs in document D & the interpretation of E in D as M fits technical language $\Rightarrow$ *PecuniaryLoss* $\sqcup$ *EmotionalDamage* $\equiv BestInt(E, D)$
Conclusion	*PecuniaryLoss* $\sqcup$ *EmotionalDamage* $\equiv BestInt(loss, 123(1)ERA)$

Note that *PecuniaryLoss⊔EmotionalDamage* denotes the concept of *PecuniaryLoss or EmotionalDamage* which covers both pecuniary losses and emotional damage.

The interpretation of the term "loss" based on ordinary language could also attacked by directly denying its conclusion, for instance by a nonredundancy argument claiming that *"loss"* should not be interpreted in this way, since this would make 123(1)ERA redundant.

Argument A₃

Premise	Expression "loss" occurs in document 123(1)ERA
Premise	the interpretation of *"loss"* in 123(1)ERA as *Pecuniary Loss* makes 123(1) ERA redundant
Major premise (Canon)	–NR: expression E occurs in document D & the interpretation of E in D, as M makes D redundant ⇒ $M \not\equiv BestInt(E, D)$
Conclusion	$PecuniaryLoss \not\equiv BestInt(loss, 123(1)ERA)$

A rebutting attack can also be played by using partial (inclusionary or exclusionary interpretative) arguments.

Argument A₄

Premise	Expression "loss" occurs in document 123(1)ERA
Premise	the interpretation of *"loss"* in 123(1)ERA as including *EmotionalDamage* conflicts with usual meaning
Major premise (Canon)	+eAC: expression E occurs in document D & the interpretation of E in D as including S conflicts with usual meaning ⇒ $S \sqsubseteq \neg BestInt(E, D)$
Conclusion	$Emotional\,Damage \sqsubseteq \neg BestInt\left(loss, 123(1)ERA\right)$

Here $\neg BestInt(loss, 123(1)ERA)$ denotes the complement of $BestInt(loss, 123(1)ERA)$, i.e., it covers whatever is outside of it. Thus $EmotionalDamage \sqsubseteq \neg BestInt(loss, 123(1)ERA)$ expresses the view that emotional damage is outside of what is covered by the best interpretation of "loss."

Given that *Pecuniary⊔EmotionalLoss* includes *EmotionalDamage* we can conclude:

$$BestInt(loss, 123(1)ERA) \not\equiv PecuniaryLossOrEmotionalDamage$$

which contradicts the conclusion of the above argument A₂.

An undercutting attack against the ordinary language argument could be mounted by arguing that the expression *"loss"* in the Employment Rights Act is used in a technical context, for example in the context of the discipline of industrial relations, and so arguments from ordinary language do not apply. Thus, the ordinary language canon is inapplicable to the expression *"loss"* in 123(1)ERA.

Argument A_5

Premise	Expression "loss" occurs in Section 123(1)ERA
Premise	Section 123(1)ERA is a technical context
Major premise (Canon)	+eTC: expression E occurs in document D & D is a technical context $\Rightarrow \ \neg Appl(OL, E)$
Conclusion	$\neg Appl\left(OL, 123(1)ERA\right)$

6.5.3 *Preference Arguments over Interpretative Arguments*

We may argue for preferences over interpretative arguments. For example, in Italy the Court of Cassation revised its interpretation of the term *"loss"* (*danno*) as occurring in the Italian Civil Code using an argument from purpose (the constitutional value of health). The court thus rejected the traditional interpretation (that based on legal history) of *"loss"* as pecuniary damage, arguing that damage to health should also be included in the scope of the term (and consequently compensated), based on the purpose of implementing the rights and values of the Italian Constitutional system (we classify this as a systematic argument, SA). Here are the two competing arguments:

Argument A_1

Premise	Expression "loss" occurs in Section 123(1)ERA
Premise	The interpretation of "loss" in Art2043ICC as *PecuniaryLoss* fits legal history
Major premise (Canon)	+LH: expression E occurs in document D & the interpretation of E in D as M fits legal history $\Rightarrow \ M \equiv BestInt(E, D)$
Conclusion	*PecuniaryLoss* $\equiv BestInt(loss, Art2043ICC)$

Argument A_2

Premise	Expression "loss" occurs in Section 123(1)ERA
Premise	The interpretation of *"loss"* in Art2043ICC as *PecuniaryLoss* $\sqcup$ *DamageToHealth* fits the purposes of the law
Major premise (Canon)	+ SA: expression E occurs in document D & the interpretation of E in D as M fits system of law $\Rightarrow \ M \equiv BestInt(E, D)$
Conclusion	*PecuniaryLoss* $\sqcup$ *DamageToHealth* $\equiv BestInt(loss, Art2043ICC)$

These two arguments conflict (rebut each other), as:

$$PecuniaryLoss \neq PecuniaryLoss \sqcup DamageToHealth$$

To address the conflict, the judges argued that the second argument defeats the first, according to a principle of preference for the constitutional values (P_C): a systemic argument appealing to constitutional values overrides a traditional argument based on legal history:

Argument A_3

Premise	The systemic interpretation (SA) of expression "loss" in Art2043ICC as Pecuniary Loss ⊔ DamageToHealth according to contributes to constitutional values
Premise	The interpretation of expression "loss" in Art2043ICC as *PecuniaryLoss* fits legal history (LH)
Major premise (Canon)	If $+SA(E, D, M_1)$ is a systemic interpretation that contributes to constitutional values and $LH(E, D, M_2)$ is an interpretation that fits legal history $\Rightarrow$ P_C: $+SA(E, D, M_1) \succ LH(E, D, M_2)$
Conclusion	$SA(loss, \text{Art2043ICC}, Pecuniary\ Loss ⊔ DamageToHealth)$ $\succ LH(loss, \text{Art2043ICC}, PecuniaryLoss)$

6.6 FROM BEST INTERPRETATIONS TO INDIVIDUAL CLAIMS

We must be able to move from interpretative claims to conclusion in individual cases, namely, from conceptual assertions to individual claims. For this purpose, we can adopt general patterns for strict rules, which provide for the transition from interpretative claims to assertions concerning individuals.

1. $M \equiv BestInt(E, D) \mapsto \forall x[M \leftrightarrow E_D(x)]$
2. $M \sqsubseteq BestInt(E, D) \mapsto \forall x[M(x) \rightarrow E_D(x)]$
3. $M \sqsubseteq \neg BestInt(E, D) \mapsto \forall x[M(x) \rightarrow \neg E_D(x)]$

where x is a sequence of variables required by concept M, $M(x)$ is the predicate corresponding to concept M, and E_D is a predicate representing the occurrence of E in D. Consider for instance the above interpretative claim according to which

$$PecuniaryLoss \equiv BestInt(loss, 123\text{ERA})$$

The corresponding instance of transition rule 1 would be:

$$PecuniaryLoss \equiv BestInt(loss, 123\text{ERA})$$
$$\mapsto \forall x, y, z[PecuniaryLoss(x, y, z) \leftrightarrow Loss_{ERA}(x, y, z)]$$

This formula is to be read as follows: if concept *PecuniaryLoss* is the best interpretation of expression "*loss*" in Section 123 of the Employment Rights Act, then if and only if a person x in an event y has a pecuniary loss of amount z, that person has a corresponding loss according to Section 123 of the Employment Rights Act.

Let us assume that Sandra consequently to her unfair dismissal by Tom had a pecuniary loss of £10,000 (10 thousand), expressed as

$$PecuniaryLoss(Sandra, DismissalByTom, 10)$$

We can then build the following argument (where we list the premises and inference rules in the argument as well as the intermediate conclusions).

Argument $A_{1,a}$

Premise	Expression "loss" occurs in Section 123(1)ERA
Premise	The interpretation of "loss" in 123(1)ERA as *PecuniaryLoss* fits ordinary language
Major premise (Canon)	+OL: expression E occurs in document D, the interpretation of E in D as M fits ordinary language $\Rightarrow M \equiv BestInt(E, D)$
Conclusion	$PecuniaryLoss \equiv BestInt(loss, 123(1)ERA$

By combining the conclusion of *Argument$A_{1,a}$* with the transition pattern above we can expand $A_{1,a}$ as follows

Argument $A_{1,b}$

Previous conclusion	$PecuniaryLoss \equiv BestInt(loss, 123(1)ERA$
Transition pattern	$PecuniaryLoss \equiv BestInt(loss, 123ERA) \mapsto \forall x[PecuniaryLoss(x, y, z) \leftrightarrow Loss_{ERA}(x, y, z)]$
Conclusion	$\forall x[PecuniaryLoss(x, y, z) \leftrightarrow Loss_{ERA}(x, y, z)]$

Finally, by combining the conclusion of argument $A_{1,b}$ with the factual premise that Sandra missed gains for 10 thousand pounds, we can conclude that her missed gains qualify as a loss according to the ERA.

Argument $A_{1,c}$

Previous conclusion	$\forall x[PecuniaryLoss(x, y, z) \leftrightarrow Loss_{ERA}(x, y, z)]$
Premise	$PecuniaryLoss(Sandra, DismissalByTom, 10)$
Final conclusion	$Loss_{ERA}(Sandra, DismissalByTom, 10)$ (by classical logic)

When alternative interpretations lead to the same interpretative conclusion in a concrete case, we do not need to choose among them. For instance, assume that we know that Sandra has sustained a pecuniary loss of 10 thousand pounds as a consequence of her unfair dismissal. Since the concept of pecuniary loss is included in the concept of pecuniary or emotional loss, we can infer that she suffered a pecuniary or emotional loss. This conclusion would enable us to conclude that Sandra has suffered a loss in the sense of Section 123 ($Loss_{ERA}$(Sandra; DismissalByTom; 10), also on the basis of the interpretation of loss as *PecuniaryLoss* ⊔ *EmotionalDamage*, according to an argument *Argument* A_2 which includes this interpretation.

Argument $A_{2,a}$

Premise	Expression "loss" occurs in Section 123(1)ERA
Premise	The interpretation of "loss" in 123(1)ERA as
	PecuniaryLoss ⊔ *EmotionalDamage* fits technical language
Major premise	TL: expression E occurs in document D ∧ the interpretation of E in D as
(Canon)	M fits technical language $\Rightarrow M \equiv BestInt(E, D)$
Conclusion	$PecuniaryLoss \sqcup EmotionalDamage \equiv BestInt\left(loss, 123(1)ERA\right)$

By combining the conclusion of *Argument* $A_{2,a}$ with the transition pattern above, we can expand $A_{2,a}$ as follows

Argument $A_{2,b}$

Previous conclusion	$PecuniaryLoss \sqcup EmotionalDamage \equiv BestInt\left(loss, 123(1)ERA\right)$
Transition pattern	$PecuniaryLoss \sqcup EmotionalDamage \equiv BestInt\left(loss, 123(1)ERA\right)B$
	$\mapsto \forall x, y, z[PecuniaryLoss\ (x, y, z)$
	$\lor EmotionalDamage\ (x, y, z)] \leftrightarrow Loss_{ERA}(x, y, z)$
Conclusion	$\forall x, y, z[PecuniaryLoss\ (x, y, z)$
	$\lor EmotionalDamage\ (x, y, z)] \leftrightarrow Loss_{ERA}(x, y, z)$

Finally, by combining the conclusion of argument $A_{2,b}$ with the factual premise that there were £10 thousand of missed gains, we can conclude that the missed gains qualify as a loss according to the ERA.

Argument $A_{3,c}$

Previous conclusion	$\forall x, y, z[PecuniaryLoss(x, y, z)$
	$\lor EmotionalLoss(x, y, z)] \leftrightarrow Loss_{ERA}(x, y, z)$
Premise	$PecuniaryLoss(Sandra, DismissalByTom, 10)$
Final conclusion	$Loss_{ERA}(Sandra, DismissalByTom, 10)$ (by classical logic)

Arguments A_1 and A_2 are inconsistent, as they include incompatible interpretative conclusions (incompatible subarguments): according to A_1 the best interpretation of "*loss*" in Section 123 is *Pecuniary Loss*, while according to A_2 the best interpretation is *PecuniaryLoss or EmotionalDamage*. However, the two arguments lead to the same conclusion in the case of Sandra's dismissal: the financial detriment she suffered counts as a loss of 10 thousand pounds under Section 123 of the Employment Rights Act. Therefore, we may view this conclusion as legally justified, even though we are unable to make a choice between the two incompatible interpretations (the two competing interpretative arguments are both defeasible, and neither is justified), as the conclusion follows from both such interpretations. This view corresponds to the idea that only relevant issues (i.e., issues the decision of which influences the outcome of the case) have to be addressed in legal decision making: the issue of whether "*loss*" is limited or not to pecuniary losses is irrelevant in Sandra's case, since she has only suffered a pecuniary loss (this issue would be relevant if she had on the contrary suffered instead, or additionally, an emotional damage).

Note that in the above model, for simplicity's sake we have assumed that interpretative reasoning is defeasible, but that it leads to conceptual determinations that indefeasible. For instance, the determination that if and only if a loss is pecuniary then it is a loss according to the *ERA* is expressed through the classical logic formula, $PecuniaryLoss(x, y, z) \leftrightarrow Loss_{ERA}(x, y, z)$, meaning that all and only pecuniary losses are losses according to the *ERA*. It would be possible to model as well defeasible conceptual ascriptions, according to which, for example, if a loss is pecuniary then presumably it qualifies as a loss according to the *ERA*, and if the loss is not pecuniary then presumably it does not qualify. The specification of this extension of our formal model will be left to future research.

6.7 CONCLUSIONS

In this chapter, we have shown how interpretative schemes can be formulated in such a manner that they can be incorporated into a formal and computational argumentation system such as Carneades or ASPIC$^+$, and then applied to displaying the pro–con structure of the argumentation using argument maps applied to legal cases. To this purpose, we analyzed the most common types of statutory arguments and brought to light their common characteristics. We showed how canons of interpretation can be translated into argumentation schemes, and we distinguished two general macrostructures of positive versus negative and total versus partial uses of canons, under which various types of schemes and rebuttals can be classified. This preliminary classification was then used for modeling the interpretative arguments formally and integrating them into computational systems and argument maps.

The interpretative schemes can be applied initially when constructing an argument diagram to get an overview of the sequence of argumentation in a case of contested statutory interpretations. The schemes can be applied in order to help the argument analyst convey an evidential summary showing how the subarguments fit together in a lengthy sequence of argumentation in a case, as indicated in the main example of the educational grants case. The next step is to zoom in on parts of the argumentation sequence that pose a problem where critical questions need to be asked or refinements need to be considered. Here the critical questions can be applied in order to find further weak points in an argument by bringing out implicit premises that may have been overlooked and that could be questioned.

The function of the set of critical questions matching a scheme is to give the arguer who wants to attack the prior argument some idea of the kinds of critical questions that need to be asked in replying to it. Thus, critical questions can offer a respondent guidance as to where look for weak points that could be challenged. However, there are theoretical issues of how to structure the critical questions. If critical questions can be modeled in the argument diagrams as additional premises, ordinary premises, assumptions, or exceptions such as is done in Carneades or ASPIC⁺, they can be modeled in argument maps as undercutting or rebutting counterarguments. The problem that always arises in attempts to fit critical questions into argument diagrams in this manner is one of burden of proof. Is merely asking a critical question enough to defeat a given argument? Or should a critical question be taken to defeat the given argument only if some evidence is given to back it up? Carneades and ASPIC⁺ provide ways of dealing with this problem that have been shown to be applicable to interpretative schemes.

The danger with using such schemes to construct hypotheses about the best interpretation is one of jumping to a conclusion too quickly. This danger can be overcome by asking critical questions matching the scheme, and by considering possible objections to the arguments fitting an interpretative scheme. As we have seen in our examples, a sequence of argumentation based on the application of interpretative argumentation schemes is defeasible, and can be attacked by undercutters and rebutters in an opposed sequence of argumentation. Indeed, it is this very situation of one sequence of interpretative argumentation being used to attack another one that is characteristic of the example we studied, *Dunnachie v. Kingston-upon-Hull City Council*, a standard example of statutory interpretation.

We also provided a fresh logical formalization of reasoning with interpretative canons. Rather than modeling interpretative conclusion as deontic claims, as we did in a previous work (Sartor et al., 2014), here we modeled them as conceptual (terminological) claims concerning best interpretations.

We then considered how interpretative arguments can be framed within argumentation systems, including defeasible and strict rules. We argued that a semantics based on preferred extensions can provide an appropriate approach to the interpretative conclusions, and to distinguish between defensible and justifiable interpretative claims. With regard to justification, we argued for weak justifiability (derivation in all extensions, also through different argument) to be more appropriate to interpretative reasoning in legal contexts.

This work still is quite preliminary, but necessarily so, since AI and law research has neglected issues pertaining to statutory interpretation, and more generally, the issue of determining the correct meaning of authoritative sources of the law. Further research should include a more refined classification system for interpretative schemes. Also, the idea of merging argumentation with deontic logic (as advanced in Sartor et al., 2014; Walton, Macagno, and Sartor, 2014) needs to be reconsidered, and integrated with the different framework presented in this chapter.

REFERENCES

Alexy, Robert, and Ralf Dreier. 1991. "Statutory interpretation in the Federal Republic of Germany." In *Interpreting Statutes. A Comparative Study*, edited by Neil MacCormick and Robert Summers, 73–121. Aldershot, UK: Dartmouth.

Araszkiewicz, Michał. 2013. "Towards systematic research on statutory interpretation in AI and law." In *Proceedings of JURIX 2014: The Twenty-Seventh Annual Conference on Legal Knowledge and Information Systems*, edited by Rinke Hoekstra, 15–24. Amsterdam, Netherlands: IOS Press.

Atlas, Jay David. 2005. *Logic, Meaning, and Conversation*. Oxford, UK: Oxford University Press.

Atlas, Jay David, and Stephen Levinson. 1981. "It-clefts, informativeness and logical form: Radical pragmatics (revised standard version)." In *Radical Pragmatics*, edited by Peter Cole, 1–62. New York, NY: Academic Press.

Butler, Brian. 2016. "Law and the primacy of pragmatics." In *Pragmatics and Law: Philosophical Perspectives*, edited by Alessandro Capone and Francesca Poggi, 1–13. Cham, Switzerland: Springer.

Carston, R. 2002. *Thoughts and Utterances: The Pragmatics of Explicit Communication*. Oxford, UK: Blackwell Publishing Ltd.

Carston, Robyn. 2013. "Legal texts and canons of construction: A view from current pragmatic theory." In *Law and Language: Current Legal Issues*, edited by Michael Freeman and Fiona Smith, 8–33. Oxford, UK: Oxford University Press.

Cross, Rupert. 2005. *Statutory Interpretation*. Edited by John Bell and George Engle. Oxford, UK: Oxford University Press.

Dascal, Marcelo. 2003. *Interpretation and Understanding*. Amsterdam, Netherlands: John Benjamins Publishing Company.

Dascal, Marcelo, and Jerzy Wróblewski. 1988. "Transparency and doubt: Understanding and interpretation in pragmatics and in law." *Law and Philosophy* 7(2): 203–224. https://doi.org/10.1007/BF00144156

Gordon, Thomas. 2010. "An overview of the Carneades argumentation support system." In *Dialectics, Dialogue and Argumentation. An Examination of Douglas Walton's Theories of Reasoning and Argument*, edited by Christopher Reed and Christopher Tindale, 145–156. London, UK: College Publications.

Gordon, Thomas, and Douglas Walton. 2009a. "Legal reasoning with argumentation schemes." In *Proceedings of the 12th International Conference on Artificial Intelligence and Law*, edited by Carole D. Hafner, 137–146. New York, NY: ACM Press.

Gordon, Thomas, and Douglas Walton. 2009b. "Proof burdens and standards." In *Argumentation in Artificial Intelligence*, edited by Iyad Rahwan and Guillermo Simari, 239–258. Berlin, Germany: Springer.

Gordon, Thomas, and Douglas Walton. 2011. "A formal model of legal proof standards and burdens." In *7th Conference on Argumentation of the International Society for the Study of Argumentation (ISSA 2010)*, edited by Frans van Eemeren, Bart Garssen, Anthony Blair, and Gordon Mitchell, 644–655. Amsterdam, Netherlands: Sic Sat.

Hage, Jaap. 1996. "A theory of legal reasoning and a logic to match." *Artificial Intelligence and Law* 4(3–4): 199–273. https://doi.org/10.1007/BF00118493

Hage, Jaap. 1997. *Reasoning with Rules*. Dordrecht, Netherlands: Kluwer Academic Publishers.

Heine, Bernd, Heiko Narrog, and Kasia Jaszczolt. 2015. "Default semantics." In *The Oxford Handbook of Linguistic Analysis*, edited by Alex Barber and Robert Stainton, 193–221. Oxford, UK: Oxford University Press.

Horn, Laurence. 1995. "Vehicles of meaning: Unconventional semantics and unbearable interpretation." *Washington University Law Quarterly* 73: 1145–1152.

Jaszczolt, Kasia. 2005. "Default semantics." In *Concise Encyclopedia of Philosophy of Language and Linguistics*, edited by Alex Barber and Robert Stainton, 128–130. Oxford, UK: Oxford University Press.

Macagno, Fabrizio. 2015. "A means-end classification of argumentation schemes." In *Reflections on Theoretical Issues in Argumentation Theory*, edited by Frans van Eemeren and Bart Garssen, 183–201. Cham, Switzerland: Springer.

Macagno, Fabrizio. 2017. "Defaults and inferences in interpretation." *Journal of Pragmatics* 117: 280–290. https://doi.org/10.1016/j.pragma.2017.06.005.

Macagno, Fabrizio, and Alessandro Capone. 2016. "Interpretative disputes, explicatures, and argumentative reasoning." *Argumentation* 30(4): 399–422. https://doi.org/10.1007/s10503-015-9347-5.

Macagno, Fabrizio, and Douglas Walton. 2010. "Dichotomies and oppositions in legal argumentation." *Ratio Juris* 23(2): 229–257. https://doi.org/10.1111/j.1467–9337.2010.00452.x.

Macagno, Fabrizio, and Douglas Walton. 2011. "Reasoning from paradigms and negative evidence." *Pragmatics & Cognition* 19(1): 92–116. https://doi.org/10.1075/pc.19.1.04mac.

Macagno, Fabrizio, and Douglas Walton. 2015. "Classifying the patterns of natural arguments." *Philosophy and Rhetoric* 48(1): 26–53. https://doi.org/10.1353/par.2015.0005.

Macagno, Fabrizio, and Douglas Walton. 2017. "Arguments of statutory interpretation and argumentation schemes." *International Journal of Legal Discourse*, 2(1): 47–83.https://doi.org/10.1515/ijld-2017-0002.

Macagno, Fabrizio, Douglas Walton, and Giovanni Sartor. 2018. "Pragmatic maxims and presumptions in legal interpretation." *Law and Philosophy* 37(1): 69–115. https://doi.org/10.1007/s10982-017-9306-4.

MacCormick, Neil. 1995. "Argumentation and interpretation in law." *Argumentation* 9(3): 467–480. https://doi.org/10.1007/BF00733152.

MacCormick, Neil. 2005. *Rhetoric and the Rule of Law*. Oxford, UK: Oxford University Press.

MacCormick, Neil, and Robert Summers, eds. 1991. *Interpreting Statutes: A Comparative Study*. Aldershot, UK: Dartmouth.

Miller, Geoffrey. 1990. "Pragmatics and the maxims of interpretation." *University of Wisconsin Law*, 1179–1227.

Moreso, Josep Joan, and Samuele Chilovi. 2018. "Interpretative arguments and the application of the law." In *Handbook of Legal Reasoning and Argumentation*, edited by Giorgio Bongiovanni, Gerald Postema, Antonino Rotolo, Giovanni Sartor, Douglas Walton, and Chiara Valentini, 495–517. Dordrecht, Netherlands: Springer.

Pollock, John. 1995. *Cognitive Carpentry*. Cambridge, MA: MIT Press.

Prakken, Henry. 2010. "An abstract framework for argumentation with structured arguments." *Argument & Computation* 1(2): 93–124. https://doi.org/10.1080/19462160903564592.

Prakken, Henry, and Giovanni Sartor. 1996. "A dialectical model of assessing conflicting arguments in legal reasoning." *Artificial Intelligence and Law* 4: 331–368. https://doi.org/10.1007/BF00118496.

Reiter, Raymond. 1980. "A logic for default reasoning." *Artificial Intelligence* 13(1–2): 81–132. https://doi.org/10.1016/0004-3702(80)90014-4.

Rotolo, Antonino, Guido Governatori, and Giovanni Sartor. 2015. "Deontic defeasible reasoning in legal interpretation: Two options for modelling interpretative arguments." In

Proceedings of the 15th International Conference on Artificial Intelligence and Law, 99–108. New York, NY: ACM Press.

Sartor, Giovanni. 2018. "Defeasibility in law." In *Handbook of Legal Reasoning and Argumentation*, edited by Giorgio Bongiovanni, Gerald Postema, Antonino Rotolo, Giovanni Sartor, Chiara Valentini, and Douglas Walton, 315–364. Dordrecht, Netherlands: Springer.

Sartor, Giovanni, Douglas Walton, Fabrizio Macagno, and Antonino Rotolo. 2014. "Argumentation schemes for statutory interpretation: A logical analysis." In *Frontiers in Artificial Intelligence and Applications*, edited by Rinke Hoekstra, 271: 11–20. Amsterdam, Netherlands: IOS Press.

Schauer, Frederick. 2009. *Thinking Like a Lawyer: An Introduction to Legal Reasoning*. Cambridge, MA: Harvard University Press.

Sinclair, Michael. 1985. "Law and language: The role of pragmatics in statutory interpretation." *University of Pittsburgh Law Review* 46: 373–420.

Smolka, Jennifer, and Benedikt Pirker. 2016. "International law and pragmatics. An account of interpretation in international law." *International Journal of Language & Law* 5: 1–40. https://doi.org/10.14762/jll.2016.001

Soames, Scott. 2009. *Philosophical Essays, Volume 1: Natural Language: What It Means and How We Use It*. Princeton; NJ: Princeton University Press.

Tarello, Giovanni. 1980. *L'interpretazione della Legge*. Milano, Italy: Giuffrè.

Verheij, Bart. 2008. "About the logical relations between cases and rules." In *Legal Knowledge and Information Systems. JURIX 2008: The Twenty-First Annual Conference*, edited by Enrico Francesconi, Giovanni Sartor, and Daniela Tiscornia, 21–32. Amsterdam, Netherlands: IOS Press.

Walton, Douglas. 1990. "What is reasoning? What is an argument?" *Journal of Philosophy* 87: 399–419. https://doi.org/10.2307/2026735

Walton, Douglas. 1995. *Argumentation Schemes for Presumptive Reasoning*. Mahwah, NJ: Routledge. https://doi.org/10.4324/9780203811160.

Walton, Douglas. 2004. *Abductive Reasoning*. Tuscaloosa, AL: University of Alabama Press.

Walton, Douglas. 2015. *Goal-Based Reasoning for Argumentation*. Cambridge, MA: Cambridge University Press.

Walton, Douglas, and Thomas Gordon. 2005. "Critical questions in computational models of legal argument." In *Argumentation in Artificial Intelligence and Law, IAAIL Workshop Series*, edited by Paul Dunne and Trevor Bench-Capon, 103–111. Nijmegen, Netherlands: Wolf Legal Publishers.

Walton, Douglas, Fabrizio Macagno, and Giovanni Sartor. 2014. "Interpretative argumentation schemes." In *JURIX 2014: The Twenty-Seventh Annual Conference*, edited by Rinke Hoekstra, 21–22. New York, NY: IOS Press.

Walton, Douglas, Christopher Reed, and Fabrizio Macagno. 2008. *Argumentation Schemes*. New York, NY: Cambridge University Press.

CASES CITED

Dunnachie v. Kingston-upon-Hull City Council 2004 UKHL 36.

Johnson v. Unisys Limited 2001 UKHL 13.

Norton Tool Co. v. Tewson [1973] 1 WLR 45.

R. v. Barnet London Borough Council [2004] 1 All ER 97.

CPSIA information can be obtained
at www.ICGtesting.com
Printed in the USA
BVHW030415170822
644726BV00006B/30